Islam, Gender, and Development

Islam, Gender, and Development

Rural-Urban Migration of Women in Iran

Masoumeh Velayati

LEXINGTON BOOKS
A division of
ROWMAN & LITTLEFIELD PUBLISHERS, INC.
Lanham • Boulder • New York • Toronto • Plymouth, UK

Published by Lexington Books
A division of Rowman & Littlefield Publishers, Inc.
A wholly owned subsidiary of The Rowman & Littlefield Publishing Group, Inc.
4501 Forbes Boulevard, Suite 200, Lanham, Maryland 20706
http://www.lexingtonbooks.com

Estover Road, Plymouth PL6 7PY, United Kingdom

British Library Cataloguing in Publication Information Available

Library of Congress Cataloging-in-Publication Data

Velayati, Masoumeh, 1963-
Islam, gender, and development : rural-urban migration of women in Iran / Masoumeh Velayati.
p. cm.
Includes bibliographical references and index.
ISBN 978-0-7391-1452-0 (cloth : alk. paper)
1. Rural-urban migration—Iran. 2. Migration, Internal—Sex differences—Iran. 3. Women—Iran—Social conditions. 4. Women—Iran—Economic conditions. 5. Internal migrants—Iran—Social conditions. 6. Internal migrants—Iran—Economic conditions. I. Title.
HB2096.4.A3V45 2011
307.2'40820955—dc22

2010039529

™ The paper used in this publication meets the minimum requirements of American National Standard for Information Sciences—Permanence of Paper for Printed Library Materials, ANSI/NISO Z39.48-1992.

Printed in the United States of America

For Hossein and my four children

Contents

Foreword

This is a path-breaking book, working directly with slum dwelling women in Tabriz and reflecting and analyzing their experiences, responses and strategies in terms of opportunities and life choices open to them within the limitations of faith, culture and relocation. The work is an important step in breaking silences. For the first time their experiences in this region have been considered in great detail and they are given a voice to speak for themselves. With meticulous attention this study dismantles some of the stereotypes of disempowerment and despair often projected about the ability of women to deal with obstacles that in the first instance may appear insurmountable. The findings are both refreshing and unexpected. It is a must read for all those interested in Islam gender and development.

Professor the Baroness Afshar OBE AcSS
Department of Politics
University of York
York YO10 5DD

List of Figures

Figures

List of Tables

Preface

Many studies of female migration indicate that there is a positive and direct correlation between migration and socio-economic mobility of migrant women. Using general feminist literature on gender and work, this book assesses the relationship between female migration and development in Iran and aims to understand the implication of different socio-cultural, economic and political conditions in motivating peasants to migrate. Given that rural-urban migration in Iran is often family migration (Jamali 1985; and Bayat 1997), and there are high living costs in the cities, migrant women are more likely to be involved in income generation activities. However, the social and economic motivations of female migrants and their contribution to family income have not been investigated in existing Iranian migration literature. Thus, this book aims to look at the main factors contributing to the process of female migration in Iran, particularly in East Azarbaijan and its central city Tabriz, which is the country's fourth major host city for rural migrants. Yet there is almost no literature, particularly in English, which explores work and living conditions of the migrant population in general and migrant women in particular, in Tabriz. Some literature that I have used in this study is either related to urban planning of the city of Tabriz, or looks at the phenomena of migration and urbanization in general in this part of country.

Iranian migration literature mainly covers the pre-revolutionary era and focuses on Tehran, and is blind to gender issues and the social and economic situation of migrant women in the cities. In Iran cultural factors often prohibit married women's independent migration, and the prevalent form of migration seems to be occurring within the context of family migration.

Although the statistics indicate that women have constituted a large part of internal migration, particularly since the 1960s, their independent responses to many economic and non-economic factors have been ignored in the literature. In fact, there is a significant gap about the impact of local and global policies and the feminization of the labor market due to women's rural-urban migration in Iran.

Under-reporting of the position of women in migration literature is partly due to the role that domesticity plays in Iranian traditional culture. In Iran, like many other societies, sex segregation of roles has been traditionally viewed as necessary for preserving social structures within the family and society. The invisibility is also partly due to the construction of Iranian Family Law, even under the former Pahlavi regime[1]. According to Articles 1105, 1114, and 1117 of Iranian Family Law, men are the heads of households and also according to Articles 1106 and 1107 they are considered as the main breadwinners of the family. Responsibility for the family's welfare and maintenance is seen as a man's religious and national duty, and a wife does not have any responsibility for her own and her children's maintenance, even if she is very rich (Iranian Civil Law, 1991).

As a result of these cultural and legal factors, women have often been considered economically inactive and thus invisible in official statistical reports. This is despite the fact that, for a large proportion of women in lower sections of Iranian society, work has been a matter of necessity. However, strict definitions of what constitutes the economically active population, assumptions about housewives who are not economically active, and methods for measuring labor force participation in terms of international guidelines, such as self-employment, seasonal work, underemployment, integration of domestic production for use and exchange value, all contribute to the omission of women from census data, not only in Iran, but also in other developing countries (Boserup, 1970; and Dixon-Mueller, 1991: 226-27). Thus, home-workers, unpaid family workers and many other workers in informal sectors, largely women, are disproportionately and systematically excluded from national censuses and social studies.

Despite an extensive body of literature on Iranian women's issues (Afshar, 1985b, 1989a, and 1997; Friedle, 1981; Ghavamshahidi, 1996; Hoodfar, 1996; Kar, 2001; Moghadam, 1993; Nakanishi, 1998; Poya, 1999; Razavi, 1992; Shahshahani, 1987; Tabari, 1982; Tohidi and Bayes, 2001), only a few studies concentrate on women's work; the rest pay little attention to working-class women's employment or economic position, particularly that of migrant women. Similarly, most of the literature on Iran concentrates on Tehran, reflecting the situation of middle-class educated women who have been exposed to educational and employment opportunities in the capital. Generally literature in the 1980s and early 1990s dealt with Islamization of social norms and morality, due to the enforcement of Islamic ideology in the post-revolutionary era with particular reference to women. Most published literature considered the oppressive nature of Islamic gender ideology due to the imposition of the veil, sex segregation, the abolition of Family Protection

Law, and the adoption of an Islamic penal code that effectively reduced women's legal rights and socio-economic life (Afshar, 1982, 1985b, 1987, 1989a and 1989c; Tabari, 1980; Tabari and Yeganeh, 1982; Touba, 1980; Moghadam, 1993; and Poya, 1999). They argued that women's active participation in the 1979 revolution adversely ended in their exclusion from economic, social and political life by the gender policies of the Islamic republic. In the 1990s, gender consciousness began to develop in the post-war era[2], and Iranian women began to call for change[3]. In contesting state ideology and policies about women and denial of their rights, women, particularly Islamic reformists offered different interpretations and readings of Quranic passages and Islamic laws, which led to some reforms in women's position in terms of law, education and employment, all despite the affirmed gender ideology of the Islamic state. This trend led many secular feminists to pay attention to the centrality of women's political discourses under the internal dynamics of Islamic-oriented policies and ideologies (Najmabadi, 1991; Afshar, 1994, 1997 and 1999; Moghissi, 1994; Tohidi, 1994; Mir-Hosseini, 1995 and 1996; Hoodfar, 1996; Nakanishi, 1998; Paidar, 1996; Kar, 2001).

Tohidi differentiated Islamic women based on their opposition to the government. According to her, Islamic women are those who are in opposition to a secular government in the case of, for instance, Egypt, and Islamic reformist women are those who are active in societies like Iran where Islam has become a state ideology (Tohidi, 1994: 141). Nakanishi 1998 states that: "Islamic reformist orientation has been an important alternative in improving women's lives in Iran," and that: "Islamic reformist women can reverse the logic of the regime's denial of women's rights by defining those rights within the framework of Islam" (Nakanishi, 1998: 86 and 97). Keddie argues that "it is wrong to think that Islamists are necessarily harmful to the interests of nearly all women . . . In Iran there are women often called 'Islamic feminists' who fight for women's rights in Islamist contexts with Islamist arguments" (Keddie, 1995: 256).

In Iran, based on gender-egalitarian interpretations of Islam, the main argument of the Islamic reformist/feminists is that men and women are different, but have equal rights. They argue that based on scriptural decrees, they have been created equal and God has given men and women equal value and virtue. The Islamic system should reflect the equality of men and women in its gender policies and legislation without abandoning Islamic principles.[4] The growing opposition among Islamic women, and their discussions and questions about women's rights, led to a unity between secular women and conservative religious women as early as 1991, which contributed massively to a gender awakening movement in Iran[5]. The One Million Signatures Campaign for abolishing discriminatory laws in Iran, also known as Change for Equality, officially launched in 2006, has received wide international recognition and many awards, and is an impressive example of this unity and the women's independence movement in Iran. The campaign demands equal rights in marriage and inheritance, and stricter punishments for gender-based violence such as honor killing, and reforming of laws that promote gender discrimination. The organizers of the campaign, which demands unconditional elimination of discrimination against women, argue that their demands conform to Islamic principles and are in line with Iran's international commitments.[6] However, despite their non-violent movement towards a just society, many of the organizers and supporters of the campaign have been attacked, arrested, and sentenced to jail. As of January 2010, at least 138 female civic activists had been arrested within the eight months since the presidential election of June 2009[7].

In Iran state policies, through distinct and different gender ideologies, play important roles in determining women's economic and social position within society. In the pre-revolutionary era, emphasis was on capitalist modernization based on Western values and principles (Najmabadi, 1991; Tohidi, 1994; Paidar, 1996); during the subsequent political era, this moved to advocating "ideal" Islamic women and their primary role in the family. After the 1979 revolution, natural and biological differences between the sexes were highlighted and patriarchal relations over women strengthened by giving men the right to control women's access to every aspect of life including education, employment and travel. A gender ideology based on domesticity, strongly emphasized by the Islamic state, not only limited many women's access to the socio-economic sphere, but also had a direct and in many cases a detrimental effect on poorer women (Afshar, 1989a; Ghavamshahidi, 1996). On the other hand, despite the claims of women's emancipation, the reforms under Pahlavi did not improve the socio-economic position of women in the lower classes (Najmabadi, 1991; Hoodfar, 1993; Ghavamshahidi, 1996: 115-17).

In this book I will examine the nature of migrant women's work with two sets of questions: one related to their migration history and another to their involvement in economic activities. Questions with regard to migration look at the factors which play a crucial role in motivating migration within the chosen region. I asked my informants, to what extent women are likely to migrate independently, and how far they travel. What is the impact of women's marital status, class, and life stage so far as their migration is concerned, as dependent or independent? How did/do the migration decisions and associated negotiations occur? Do they have limited power to act independently? How do rural traditional and kinship relations affect female migration? What difficulties and obstacles do female migrants confront during the process of migration and through their involvement in economic activity? How do they find work outside the village? Given that economic variables are the most important explanatory variables for migrants in most migration literature, my aim was to uncover their survival strategy, women's contribution to the family's cash income, and how their contributions are perceived by their families. I was also interested in women's position within the nuclear family, particularly the relationship between migrant women and their husbands after migration to the city. I wanted to find out how the absence of a rural female hierarchy, based on age and status, on which their husbands relied, has reshaped their position in the new situation. Women's responses to these issues shape the structure of this book.

Chapters 1 and 2 review the main literature on migration in general and female migration in particular. The principal objective of Chapter 1 is to examine how migration occurs. It examines the theoretical and mostly economic aspects of migration and their association with the process of development, and the results of migration in urban sectors. Female migration and its differing consequences and patterns around the world, specifically female labor market participation, shape the structure of Chapter 2. It looks at the different factors which have been important in stimulating internal female migration. The structural exploration of these two chapters frames the empirical chapters of this book, to discover to what extent migrant women in Tabriz have been able to break away from their traditional roles to find new opportunities. The empirical study considers if there is any variation or correlation, positive or negative, between urban migration as an independent variable and the socio-economic development of women as a dependent variable, and if migration as a component of economic development has improved women's access to economic and social resources. Differences and similarities between younger and older women regarding migration and economic engagement help reveal intended or unintended implications of gender policies exercised by both the secular Pahlavi and the Islamic Republic's ideologies of ideal women.

Chapter 3 provides background information on the processes of migration and urbanization in Iran, focusing on structural factors with their important social, economic, political and cultural impact in terms of population redistribution from rural areas to urban ones. It also examine the process of migration in East Azarbaijan province, and the influx of rural population to its capital city, Tabriz. Chapter 4 addresses the methodological processes upon which this study is based. Since my aim was to study migrant women's experience of rural-urban migration and also study their involvement in income generating activities, I used feminist methodology. The chapter first concentrates on the theoretical and practical issues regarding the production of knowledge. Then it presents the method and practical details of my study in terms of gathering data and getting access to the informants.

Chapter 5 describes and explores the survey data, drawn from 925 questionnaires collected in the summer of 2000. This chapter provides a general overview of migrants' lives in the slum areas of Tabriz, using four different sets of information. The discussion in Chapter 6 looks at female migrants' education and literacy both in their places of origin and destination. It reviews different social, economic and ideological factors that have a positive or negative impact on female literacy among the informants in this study. By comparing migrant women in terms of factors such as age, social class, marital status during migration, marriage age, reasons for migration and so forth, I will try to show that access to knowledge and education has been a scarce resource in its availability to old, poor and particularly those women who accompanied or joined their husbands in the process of migration. I will try to show that, on the other hand, migration and urbanization led to an increased access to education for the younger generation of migrants or those who migrated in their childhood. I also look at women's fertility behavior as well as infant mortality and their correlation with the level of literacy among my informants.

Chapters of 7 and 8 will explore migrant women in different sectors of the formal and informal economy. At an empirical level, these two chapters describe women's work, education, wages, hours of work, and employment and family relations. Chapter 7 explores in detail migrant women's involvement in the largest domestic industry, carpet making, in the slum areas of Tabriz. In the analysis of women's work in this home industry, I use the concepts of housewifization, patriarchy and subsistence labor, which are relevant to the analysis of women's unpaid work at home. The analysis demonstrates women's invisibility as well as vulnerability due to the nature of this type of work. I briefly argue that there is changing attitude towards the carpet industry among young unmarried migrant women.

Chapter 8 focuses on female wage earners in different sectors of the informal and formal economy in terms of age structure, education and marital status, as well as their economic needs. Younger, unmarried and educated women in this sample are more visible in factories or small-scale units of production lines, or even in state employment depending on the level of their educational achievement. Their engagement in the labor market and their income play important roles in the socio-economic changes in migrant households and increased gender consciousness.

At a theoretical level, using feminist literature and hypothesis, this study will demonstrate that migration and employment can only play a liberating role when women enter into more visible and regulated sectors of the economy. The inadequacy of conceptual tools to define different forms of employment, particularly the more invisible and hidden forms, often done by women, paves the way for greater exploitation of women both in the households as unpaid family labor, and by employers. The inadequacy of conceptual tools also plays an important role in social relations and creates the basis for class as well as gender oppression of poor women by both the state and rich private employers, men and even women (in the case of paid domestic workers), particularly when there is no written employment contract between the worker and employer.

Within migrant families, one can find a contradiction of co-existing ideologies regarding women and work. Older illiterate married women are more restricted and confined to the private sphere and unpaid family labor by traditional norms and practices. In response to my question about whether they looked for a paid job outside their home after moving to the city, they often replied that: "it is a disgrace (*ayeb*) for a woman to work outside the home." However, their work in domestic industry, mainly as unpaid family labor, solves the conflict between traditional, cultural and patriarchal ideologies on one hand, and economic realities on the other. This reality makes women's work invisible, unrecognized and unrecorded. The pattern is very common in South and West Asia (Mies, 1982; Afshar and Agarwal 1989; Shaheed, 1989; Custers, 1997). Only economic deprivation, mainly as a result of widowhood, divorce, or having disabled husbands, compels some poor women to seek paid employment outside the home. For younger educated unmarried girls of migrant families, the ideologies of domesticity concerning women's restriction to the confines of the home are often diluted, a process internalized and accepted by many families whose older daughter(s) have been controlled by traditional ideologies regarding education and paid employment. This is despite the state's gender ideology, which puts more emphasis on women's role in the family. In this process of social change, younger educated women exercise greater autonomy within the family over decisions that affect their lives, such as work, education, marriage and fertility, and like their counterparts mainly in the Asian continent are active subjects in social change.

Notes

1. It is important to note that almost all countries with majority Muslim population follow some interpretation of Islamic *Sharia* in their laws, particularly those concerning family, marriage and women's rights. However, due to the rise of the women's rights movement around the world, the Pahlavi regime gradually reduced the centrality of religion in laws affecting women's issues, and as a result "the Family Protection Law" was passed in late 1970s, only a few years before the revolution of 1979, which gave women more rights in marriage and divorce. The new rulers of the Islamic government, due to their orthodox doctrine concerning gender roles, expanded *Sharia* law with regard to family structure to transform parameters and reduce the rights of women by giving further privileges to men.

2. Eight years of war between Iran and Iraq (1980-1988). In Iran this war is also known as Imposed War (*jang-e tahmili*), or Holy Defense (*defa-e moghaddas*), as the war was imposed on Iran less than six months after the revolution of 1979 by Saddam Hossein, who took advantage of Iran's revolutionary mayhem to solve long-term border disputes and also to prevent *Shi'a* insurgency in Iraq.

3. According to Kar (2001), during the Iran-Iraq war, the guardianship of children whose fathers were killed in the war and child payment were given to their paternal grandfathers. This raised the earliest opposition among the widows of martyrs, mostly Islamist with traditional and religious upbringing, towards the violation of their rights. As a result of their political activities and massive petitions to the Martyr Foundation (*Bonyad'e Shahid*), the authorities managed to obtain a permit

from Ayatollah Khomeini that allowed the parliament (*Majlis*) to pass a bill transferring the rights of guardianship of martyrs' children to their mothers, limiting the automatic guardianship rights of paternal grandfathers. This success gradually motivated other conservative Islamic women to challenge the Islamic government about the violation of women's rights in the realm of the family, politics, and society (Kar, 2001: 180).

4. Their platforms are and continue to be weekly and monthly women's journals, which, despite financial and political pressures, advocate women's rights, gender equality, and social justice, such as *Payam-e Hajar* (Hajar's message), *Zanan* (Women), *Zan* (Woman), and *Irandokht* (Daughter of Iran) published by Islamic feminists Azam Taleghani (daughter of Ayatollah Talegani), Shahla Sherkat, Faezeh Rafsanjani, and Fatemeh Karrobi, respectively. The difference between them is their approach to women and gender issues. *Payam-e Hajar,* for instance, advocates women's rights within the framework of Islam, questioning patriarchal interpretation of Islamic teachings of Islam, and at the same time being critical of Western discourses on women's rights. *Zanan* (Women) simultaneously criticized legal laws, examined women's experiences in Iran, and provided an egalitarian reinterpretation of Islamic teachings, while using secular feminist discourses and inviting many secular women to write articles. In early 2008, after 16 years of publishing 152 issues, *Zanan* was banned by the authorities claiming that the magazine was a "threat to the psychological security of the society, as it showed Iranian women in a black light."

5. Despite the disagreements among different groups of women, when it comes to the improvement of women's lives, feminist groups have proven that they share a sincere commitment to initiating constructive change on women's rights and gender equality by working together on common ground.

6. For detailed information, see: http://www.we-change.org/english/.

7. See Gender Equality for Iran website for detailed information: http://www.irangenderequality.com/.

Acknowledgments

I would like to offer my special thanks to my husband Hossein Godazgar. I am indebted for my educational success to him. His compassion, encouragement and support did not waiver, even when it meant personal sacrifices on his part. He has helped me to progress throughout the different stages of my further education, with his love, grace and even anger. He went through the loneliness stage of his life for the sake of my success. He is the man of my heart.

Special thanks go to my four lovely children, Mahdi, Hadi, Faezeh and Mahdieh, without whose love, emotional and practical support and understanding of my situation, I really could not have managed. They had to learn to cook and keep the house at the stage in their lives when they should be playing. They tolerated lonely weekends and late evenings when I had to stay in the university when I was working on my research. I gratefully acknowledge Hadi and Mahdi's late night escorts home, with their stress-relieving stories. I would like also to offer my special thanks to Faezeh and Mahdieh for being patient and understanding that mum had to be busy with her work. I will always remember the late night e-mails: "Mum when are you coming home? Stay as long as you want, we can come and collect you" and their warm hugs to welcome me home. I am proud of all of them.

I would like to express my love and gratitude to my father, Karim, who always encouraged me for acquisition of knowledge and to my mother, Fatemeh, who I remember with love and who was so proud of my progress.

Many thanks go to my mother-in-law, Laya, who endured the pain of separation from her grandchildren because of my study.

I would like to offer my thanks to Professor Haleh Afshar, for her intellectual guidance, patience, support, and helpful suggestions throughout the different stages of my study as well as during difficult stages of my personal life. I also indebted to Professor Nayereh Tohidi for her review of the manuscript and her intellectual comments and ideas for correction and improvements to change the dissertation format into a publishable book.

I would like to offer my gratitude to all my interviewees for their valuable help in terms of giving their time and willingly sharing their experience with me. Certainly without the co-operation of these women, completion of my research and certainly this book would have been impossible. I am equally grateful for the students as well as the staff of Faculty of Humanities and Social Sciences of University of Tabriz, who collected questionnaires from migrant women in my absence. I also would like to express my special thanks to Masoumeh Sadeghi, who accompanied me during the fieldwork.

My gratitude to Ms. Laura Mason and Ms. Laura Grzybowski for their very special support for editing and proofreading the book; Ms. Margaret Binns for doing the index; and Mr. Chris Mercer for printing the book; and Dasha Zhurauskaya for her kind support. Last but not least, I am also grateful to my many friends, especially Vahideh Bayat and Shahla Tizro, Sheelan Jamal, Maria Sossoki, and Catherine Browne, all of whom were superb in giving support, comfort and boosting my strength.

Chapter 1

Theoretical Debates on Rural-Urban Migration

"The city is the defining element of a civilization, and the transition to an urban society and the concentration of population are key elements of human progress."

- Skeldon, *Migration and Development: A Global Perspective*

Migration has been a subject of interest in several disciplines. Depending on emphasis given to key determining factors, fundamental contributions have been made to theories, models and conceptual frameworks of migration in various branches of social science (Cohen, 1996: xv). As an integral part of development, it has attracted considerable attention in the literature of this subject (Skeldon, 1997). At the macro-level, economists pay attention to labor transfer and adjustments in the labor market. The motivation, social mobility, assimilation, adaptation and individual behavior of migrants within new urban settings have attracted the attention of sociologists and anthropologists. Demographers have traditionally been interested in migration selectivity, while geographers are more interested in spatial patterns of population redistribution, and their consequences for areas of departure and destination in terms of social, economic and environmental changes.

By reviewing the literature on internal rural-urban migration, the principal objective of this chapter is to examine how migration occurs from the "structural" as well as the "individualistic" approaches[1]. The structural approach concentrates on theoretical and economic aspects of migration in the process of labor transfer under dualistic conditions. It also examines urban population growth, urban unemployment and the growth of informal economic sectors in cities as a result of migration and urbanization. An analysis of female migration is absent from almost all econometric models which assume that men and women migrate as a result of the same motivations (Thadani and Todaro, 1984: 36). Since the 1990s, however, researchers have begun to look at why and how a gender division of labor developed at the heart of the migrant labor system.

The individualistic approach to migration utilizes various economic and non-economic factors with specific focus on migrants themselves in order to explain who is more likely to migrate and why. A third approach to migration links the interaction of these two approaches to a consideration of the mutual dependency of human agency and social structures on migration (Wright, 1995: 771). Gender-related differences in the migratory process will be discussed in chapter 1 at three distinct levels: the micro-level of individual behavior/agency, the macro-level of political economy, and the household level.

The Structural Approach

The structural approach, with its econometric framework, takes into account the more theoretical and economic aspects of labor migration in less developed countries in terms of capitalist development. Out-migration, particularly from rural to urban areas as a form of labor transfer from labor-surplus origins to labor-scarce destinations, was traditionally associated with a dynamic process of employment opportunities. Therefore, it was seen as a positive and beneficial movement for development in terms of a fuller utilization of the labor force, income distribution among the population, reducing regional income disparities, and providing the required labor force in urban industrial and service sectors. In this sense, rural-urban migration represents a basic transition in "spatial dimensions" by moving from low-productivity traditional areas to high-productivity modern and capitalist areas. However, a rapid socio-spatial growth at the national level manifests itself in population growth in urban areas, and structural transformation in ecological systems due to the disappearance of agricultural lands and their transformation into industrial or residential areas. All of these are common features of most developing countries. The contribution of rural-urban migration to urban population growth differs around the world. The European population shift to urban areas was initiated by the Industrial Revolution and was followed by the growth of the service sector (Smith *et al.*, 1984: 18). Capitalist accumulation and the gradual transition of a society from a pre-capitalist situation to a "dependent capitalist position" (Amirahmadi and Kiafar, 1993: 114-130) have been the causes of rapid urban growth and uneven spatial development in most developing countries. On average, migration has caused nearly half of the growth in the urban population in developing countries, and even more in some (Todaro, 1994a).

Two-thirds or more of the adults in many large and expanding cities in developing countries are young migrants. Their high fertility, due to their youthfulness and higher birth rate, often combined with a decline in mortality as a result of improved sanitation and health care, contributes to the rapid growth of cities (Jamali, 1985).

Rural-urban migration also takes into account "socio-economic dimensions" in terms of permanent transition of skills, attitudes and behavior patterns (Mabogunje, 1970). This transition has resulted in a high percentage of young migrants engaged mostly in informal sectors of the economy (Smith *et al.*, 1984: 18). In the pre-capitalist period, production took place in rural areas and peasants were normally tied to the land; cities were a centre for the distribution of national surpluses as well as political and administrative activities. In this phase the disparity between rural and urban areas was not very profound, despite heavy taxation on rural areas. In the capitalist era, on the other hand, cities, apart from being the centre of political activity, became the centre of often state-led capitalist systems within which emerged the middle and working classes (Hemmasi, 1974 and 1976; Amirahmadi and Kiafar, 1993: 109-10; Jamali, 1985).

Prior to the 1970s, the traditional indicators of development were economic growth and the capacity of a national economy to generate and sustain an annual increase in its Gross National Product (GNP), by moving from a traditional economic structure of subsistence agriculture to a more modern diverse manufacturing and service economy. Definition of economic development was based on an alteration of production and employment structures (Todaro, 1994: 14), even though it was driven by a "leading sector"[2], or limited number of primary industries with a high growth rate in relation to the rest of the economy (Lewis, 1954; Ranis and Fei, 1961; Brigg, 1971; Brydon, 1989: 124; Hakimian, 1990: 1-2). However, the shift in the spatial dimension, as the experiences of many developing countries show, has created a disharmonious relationship between internal migration and job creation in urban areas and has caused imbalances in rural-urban structures.

An influential article by Lewis (1954) on economic development with an unlimited supply of labor, which introduced the "dual-sector model", was one of the earliest theoretical models for the economic development of less developed countries. In this model, migration was regarded as a "natural process" (Todaro, 1994: 260). He argued that an unlimited supply of labor is available at subsistence wages in over-populated economies where the "marginal productivity of labor is negligible, zero or even negative": not only in agriculture, but also in petty retail trading, domestic service and other casual jobs (Lewis, 1954: 141-42). Due to their dualistic structure, in labor-surplus economies there are two distinctive sectors that have a basic relationship with each other and are essential for economic growth. Lewis focused on various aspects of the interaction between the non-capitalist and capitalist sectors, the latter being able to use reproducible capital. For economic development and industrialization to occur, he argued that a gradual reallocation of labor should take place from a large stagnant rural subsistence economy with low productivity to a dynamic capitalist economy (either private or public), without any fall in rural output (Hunt, 1989: 63). The capitalist sector, therefore, should have access to the subsistence sector in order to hire labor for profit in both the urban industrial sector and also in plantations and mines where output is greater[3]. In terms of the adjustment mechanism, Lewis argued that the loss of under-employed people in rural areas should not result in a significant decline in the volume of agrarian output. Rather, it should result in an increase in the productive capacity of the remaining units, as some migrants might partially or wholly give up their rights to productive resources, especially to the land. The remaining villagers will be able to produce more, not only for their own consumption, but also for the increasing demands of the expanding capitalist sector for food as well as raw materials for industrial production[4].

This is particularly true in the context of closed and dual economies where "input-output relations ensure perfect complementarities in production between agriculture and industry" (Bacha, 1995: 385). However, Mabogunje's study from Nigeria (1970) indicates that isolated and self-sufficient villages are not likely to experience rural-urban migration and interaction between traditional rural subsistence and capitalist sectors. For him, a combination of different factors such as industrial development, integration of the rural economy into the national/regional economy, improved transport and communication technology, educational, health and social welfare development, as well as legislation and policies creates an environment for increased social and cultural integration of rural and urban areas, and decreased isolation of villages.

Lewis and Rostow's theories were formalized and extended by Ranis and Fei in 1961 to explore the role of the traditional agricultural sector in the process of economic development (Todaro, 1976: 21). They subdivided the process of labor transfer into two phases. Phase one was the transition of a redundant labor force, with zero marginal productivity in the agricultural sector, into the capitalist sector where labor's marginal productivity rises to a positive level and wage rates equal the marginal productivity of labor. The second phase was the transition of a surplus labor force with marginal productivity, whose earning is less than the wage in urban areas (Ranis and Fei, 1961: 537). For Lewis earning in the subsistence sector determines the wage level in the capitalist sector. But, to encourage labor migration and to cover its relevant costs such as transport and housing, he suggested that urban wages have to be at least 30 percent higher than average rural incomes (Lewis, 1954: 149-50). The greater the difference between rural and urban areas in terms of economic opportunities such as high wages, job availability, and social services, the greater the flow of migrants to urban areas.

For early economists, a crucial factor in economic development was capital accumulation within a dualistic economy where only small minorities of people, the capitalists, are able to save and reinvest. Urban wages in Lewis's model are constant and determined by earning in the subsistence sector. According to the price adjustment model of Ranis and Fei (1961), when the structural transformation of the economy takes place and disguised rural unemployed labor shifts into the industrial sector, the wage differentials between the two locations would cease as agricultural incomes increase and urban incomes decrease. As the capitalist sector expands the proportion of income represented by profits and saving is relatively higher than the national income. Therefore, Lewis argued: "the central fact of economic development is that the distribution of incomes is altered in favor of the saving classes" (Lewis, 1954: 157). By redirecting capitalist surplus to productive investment, new industries will be created or old industries in the capitalist sector will expand, and more out-migration from the rural subsistence sector will occur until the labor surplus is absorbed by the capitalist sector. Since the Lewis model concentrates on the role of both capital accumulation and structural transformation in the development process and the acceleration of economic growth, it preserves its analytic value, despite the many criticisms of the applicability of the model to less developed countries (Meier, 1995: 125).

The main criticism of structuralist theories on economic growth is the relevance of these theories to the industrially developed countries of Western Europe and North America whilst at the same time claiming universality and applicability to less economically developed countries (Hirschman: 1981, Hunt: 1989). Many migration studies indicate that the deterioration of rural social structures and the destabilization of rural employment in most developing countries are due to population pressure on limited rural resources, the sale of land, expansion of capitalist farming, and the breakdown of traditional rural economies. The combination of some of these factors on the one hand, and improvements in transport and communication technology on the other, accelerate the volume of rural-urban migration disharmoniously (Bromley and Gerry, 1979: 17). Therefore, out-migration causes and is caused by changes in the economic, social and political structures of both sending and receiving areas (Skeldon, 1997: 3).

Rapid capitalist development and uneven distribution of wealth within cities, however, intensifies urban poverty, creating a greater gap in income and benefits among different social classes. In the pre-capitalist era, despite the existence of different social groups, there was no such spatial segregation, but in the capitalist era socio-economic differences led to spatial separation of different social classes (Bayat, 1997: 24-25). Expansion of slums and squatter settlements in the main cities of contemporary developing countries, which in many cases form more than 60 percent of urban areas, is a by-product of a process of social change resulting from the combined effects of continued in-migration, urbanization and uneven development (Todaro, 1994a).

Since the most urgent need of migrants on their arrival is accommodation, heavy in-migration contributes to a shortage of housing, a rise in construction costs, and high rents in cities. Investment priorities of governments in less developed countries that favor industrialization and defense rather than social welfare (Afshar, 1985a: 58-62; Pesaran, 1985: 18-19), as well as strict regulations in urban planning policies, prevent poor people from buying or renting an officially "legal" house (Lloyd, 1979: 23; Jamali, 1985: 336). Such policies, therefore, contribute to the growth of slums and squatter settlements. As a consequence, land invasions and illegal house building without public services such as clean water, sewage systems or electricity have become a common practice in most developing countries (Todaro, 1994: 248-252). In the case of Iran, particularly Tehran, the construction standard set by the City Planning Department established in the 1940s made house building unaffordable for low-income groups. As a result marginalized settlements were set up informally and often illegally outside the city boundaries (Bayat, 1997: 25-26). By the late 1950s and 1960s, the distinction between the prosperous north and industrial south of Tehran was pronounced in terms of several quantifiable variables such as population density and average monthly income. By the mid 1970s, Tehran had around fifty overcrowded slums and squatter settlements, some of them virtually without any amenities, all of which indicated growing social, economic and cultural inequalities. By 1980, of five million people in Tehran at least one million were living in slums and 400,000 in squatter settlements (Bayat, 1997: 29). The rapidity of rural-urban migration and urbanization in most parts of Africa, Latin America and Asia intensifies slum formation. In some of the world's largest cities, more than half of the population lives in slums. For instance, in Nairobi, the capital city of Kenya, 60 percent of the population lives in slums and squatter settlements occupying only 5 percent of the land, without adequate shelter, clean water or decent sanitation (UN-HABITAT 2007).

On the other hand, the growth in urban surplus labor in less developed economies, as a result of irregular but continued large scale city-ward migration, the concentration of population in a few large cities, and the failure of productive sectors of those cities to absorb the increased numbers of migrants often reduces their marginal productivity to very low levels. In many developing economies, the reinvestment of surplus capital in labor-saving technical equipment also causes a disharmonious relationship between labor transfer, and difficulties of job creation and a shift in un/underemployment from rural to urban areas (Todaro, 1976: 23-25). If migration is the inevitable result of rural-urban wage differentials, why is it not reduced by the increasing difficulties of finding an urban job and urban poverty? Todaro provided a more realistic model that viewed labor migration as a two-stage phenomenon, and explained the decision to migrate through a number of variables, particularly the probability of finding a more permanent modern urban job (Todaro, 1969: 139; 1976). Independent variables which have been used to explain migration from a place "i" to another place "j" (M_{ij}) are wage and income levels (Y), unemployment rates (U), the degree of urbanization (Z) for the people in the areas of "i" and "j", the distance between "i" and "j" (D_{ij}) and the presence of contact in the form of friends and relatives in the destination "j" (C_{ij}) (Yap, 1975: 11). Economic variables such as the disparity between rural and urban incomes appear to be the most important explanatory factor for the decision to migrate in the countries that have been the subject of most studies. Yap (1975) stated: "when wage or per capita income differentials are included explicitly, the rate of migration increases with the size of the differential. When average wages for the two areas are included separately, migration is positively related to the wage level in destination and negatively related to the wage level in origin" (Yap: 1975: 13). The variables of distance and access to contacts at the destination, though not precisely economic variables, both have an economic component, since the existence or lack of contacts and the variation of distance reduces or increases the cost of moving (Yap, 1975: 2). Dealing with internal migration, however, some studies concentrate on the socio-economic structure of the place of origin only, and some others only on the attributes of the place of destination.

Given that migration is basically sensitive to economic conditions, and thus a rational individual decision, Todaro (1969) assumes that migration is a response to rural-urban differences in "expected" income rather than "actual" income. There is no distinction between men and women in this regard. Expected income is determined by the interaction of two variables: rural-urban real income differential, and the probability of getting an urban job that is indirectly related to urban unemployment. By formulating the probability variable Todaro explained his migration model in this way: if un/semi-skilled labor has a choice between working in the agricultural sector for annual average of 50 units, or working in the urban sector for annual average of 100 units, in terms of the traditional economic model which emphasizes the wage differential factor, the worker would choose the urban job. But, in the context of most developing economies, this analysis is not realistic. Due to urban-surplus labor, many newly arrived migrants are unable to find a highly paid job soon after their arrival in the urban labor market. As a result, for a certain period of time, most of them would remain totally unemployed or irregularly employed in the informal or "urban traditional sectors" (Todaro: 1969: 139).

The decision to migrate should, therefore, take into account the limited chance of finding an urban job upon arrival and the probability of being un/underemployed for a certain period of time, as well as the positive rural-urban income differentials. In Todaro's model, rural-urban migration continues until there is equality between the actual rural wage and the expected urban wage (Meier, 1995: 114). He argues that the actual probability of securing a higher paid job within a one-year period is one chance in five and the "expected" urban income in the first year of migration should be 20 units not 100. Thus, with a one-year period horizon and a probability of 20 percent success, it would be irrational for a migrant to seek an urban job. But if the decision to migrate were made on the basis of a "permanent income" calculation, then it would be rational, even though the expected urban income during the initial years would be lower than the real rural income.

Although the idea of the "expected" income is supported by many migration studies, the importance of the probability of employment as a significant variable in the decision to migrate has not been proven by some rural-urban studies (Yap, 1975: 14). As in Todaro's model, the actual rural and urban wage is assumed to be fixed over time, and the migrant is assumed to migrate only once. Moreover, the costs of migration, the possibility of searching an urban job from a rural base, and job turnover, all are ignored (Gallup 1997: 3-4).

Despite the possibility of finding an urban job while residing in a rural area, urban-based job searching is more efficient. For those who choose to migrate when they have secured an urban job and remained employed during the job-searching period, a rural-based search reduces the equilibrium relationship between unemployment and migration, known as the Harris-Todaro model (1970). It is also possible that those employed in the urban traditional sector can search for a better job in the urban modern sector. However, the probability of being successful would be less for them than for the unemployed.

Although spontaneous large-scale in-migration is a major factor contributing to increased urban unemployment, it is also a major contributor to the growth of the informal economic sector.[5] This sector, through its connection to the unlimited labor force from rural areas, subsidizes the formal sector by providing raw materials and cheap labor (Todaro, 1994b: 253-57; Bayat, 1997; Harris, 1999: 10). As shown, the availability of a job is a major reason in migration decisions, but the majority of newly arrived migrants are not able to find a job in the formal sector. As a result, they become involved in the traditional or informal sectors of the economy doing casual work and hoping eventually to move into the formal sector[6]. The migrants who form low-income groups or working classes in the cities are hardly financially secure or able to obtain a guaranteed job (Amirahmadi and Kiafar, 1993: 118). There is little evidence, however, to indicate that migrants disproportionately dominate the informal sector. Different studies demonstrate similar proportions of migrants and non-migrants in it, and some even reveal a predominance of non-migrants in the informal sector, depending on the type of work (Yap, 1975).

Casual work has been divided into four categories of: "short-term wage-work" contracted on a daily, weekly, or monthly basis for specific periods; "disguised wage-work" in which part of the production is performed through the piece work system by out-workers often in their own homes; "dependent work" in which the worker is dependent upon one or more larger enterprises for credit, premises or equipment, or the monopolistic supply of raw materials; and "true self-employment" in which a person is in control of the means of production, though s/he might be constrained by general economic and social conditions (Bromley and Gerry, 1979: 5-11). A substantial number of low-income groups often combine two or more of the above categories by having several jobs at the same time in order to manage their lives.

Casual workers do not enjoy job security, good working conditions, pensions or other forms of protection, and their incomes are sometimes too low to meet even their primary needs such as shelter (Todaro, 1994b: 253-57). To make their living, they have to carry the burden of risk, particularly the excluded groups such as older people, young children, or those who do not have work permits (Bromley and Gerry, 1979: 10). But some of them seem to have greater flexibility and mobility. For instance, street subsistence workers are sometimes free from the discipline and controlling relations of modern institutions (Bayat, 1997: 12-14).

Another issue raised here is the possibility that migrants might take the jobs of the lower skilled native workers. In answer to this question, Harris (1999) argues that migrants do not compete with native people for the same jobs. Rather, they do jobs which are refused by them due to poor conditions of work or low wages (Harris, 1999: 8-10). Although Harris's study covers international migration to Europe, his findings also apply to rural-urban migration too. This is due to the fact that the characteristics of migration from low-productive economies to more advanced ones are similar to rural-urban migration from traditional rural subsistence sectors to a high-productivity modern urban industrial sector as detailed by Lewis. Therefore, despite high levels of urban unemployment, migration still correlates with labor demand in destination areas (Skeldon, 1997: 82-84; Harris, 1999).

The Individualistic Approach to Migration

In detailed anthropological and sociological case studies at the micro-level, the individualistic approach concentrates on migrants themselves to explain who is more likely to migrate. They look at various non-economic factors such as social, cultural, demographic, physical, and communication variables influencing migrants' decision to migrate. However, economic variables remain the main basis for migration. One of the earliest contributors to this approach was Ravenstein (1885) [7]. His "Laws of Migration", published in

1885, is one of the most long-standing theories of migration, which introduced the pull-push hypothesis to explain why people migrate. Accordingly, economic inducement is the major reason for the "rational" behavior of most migrants responding to negative circumstances of origin, such as the lack of job opportunities or population growth on agricultural resources, and the beneficial socio-economic character of another geographical location. For some people, like children and wives who are bound to the familial residence, and therefore, followers of men in the process of migration, "the decision to migrate is never completely rational" (Yap: 1975: 13). Thus, net gain from migration would be negative for some members of the family, particularly women, because of their divergent interests and the loss of alternative means of social support in their places of origin (Gallup, 1997: 5).

In an attempt to understand backgrounds to migrational movement, Mabogunje's study (1970) identified basic interacting elements in the migration system. He identified various institutions in rural and urban areas (sub-systems) that control the flow of migration. Urban sub-systems operate mainly at residential and occupational levels, often under national laws in order to control, regulate or limit the free movement of people (Mabogunje, 1970: 48). During the colonial era in Southern Africa, urban areas were defined as "white" spaces in order to prevent permanent African urbanization and so that the colonial state benefited from subsidization of the rural economy by women. Women's mobility in Southern Africa was thereby deliberately controlled and restricted through a variety of practices and prohibitions exercised by the colonial state (Wright, 1995: 784-87). Family and rural communities are sub-systems that react differently to migration within different societies. Rural communities might impede migration where cooperative farming and marketing is prevalent, or promote it where upward social mobility is privileged through education and employment. Marital and gender status of potential migrants, the role of the sexes in agricultural activities, and the relation of family members to family land are crucial factors for rural sub-systems in determining who does, and who does not, migrate (Mabogunje, 1970: 48). In terms of the sex of migrants, men are the largely dominant group, as they have universally been regarded as the obvious source of labor. However, comparative studies of urbanization and migration in developing countries indicate variability in how the sexes predominate in different parts of the world. This variability is mostly related to a society's marriage customs and economic transition patterns as well as socio-cultural aspects (Smith *et al.*, 1984: 15).

Apart from the role of the colonial rulers in preventing female city-ward migration in Africa, rural authorities were also against female migration. Women's central role in food production, the benefit derived from both women's productive and reproductive labor, and the need to secure male migrant's links with their places of origin, thereby retaining access to some of their earnings, were important reasons for rural authorities preventing female out-migration (Wright, 1995: 784-87). As a result, in terms of rural/urban sub-systems and based on very different objectives, a curious alliance formed between colonial and rural authorities to hold back female migration to major African cities.

In terms of the role of distance in migration, researchers are divided between those who find a link between migration and distance and those who do not. The first group hypothesizes that most migrants move only a short distance, and that long distance migration to major trading and industrial centers often occurs in different stages as migrants pass through a series of places, a process called step-by-step migration or step-wise migration (Ravenstein, 1885, and 1889; Redford, 1964; Makower *et al.*, 1938, 1939 and 1940), which often occurs in three forms as rural-intra-regional, inter-regional, and intra-regional migration. Step-migration also occurs inter-generationally, when parents move from rural areas to small cities and their children move on to larger cities (Jamali, 1985: 136). Many migrants use a halfway or first quasi-permanent destination on their way to more economically and socially developed regions. This way migration becomes less expensive, migrants are able to remain in contact with their origins, and have easier access to information regarding possible job opportunities in a nearby destination. Studying labor migration in England during 1800-1850, Redford stated that "migration into any centre of attraction having a wide sphere of influence was not a simple transference of people from the circumference of a circle to its centre, but an exceedingly complex wave-like motion" (Redford, 1964: 186). Makower *et al.* (1938, 1939 and 1940) found a strong relationship between distance and mobility in their studies: an increase in distance resulted in a decrease in mobility and the redistribution of labor. They argued that labor movement between districts and industries takes time and that labor is not perfectly mobile. If it were so, workers would move into any district or industry that tended to have a higher level of affluence or general prosperity. Rothenberg (1977) introduces three different costs that often prevent long distance migration: 1) moving costs including transport and the removal of personal belongings, 2) transition costs including the costs of settling in a new environment, and 3) loss of friends and relatives.

Some studies, on the other hand, indicate that there is not necessarily a direct relation between mobility and distance (Stouffer, 1940; Lee, 1966; Hemmasi, 1974; Yap, 1975; Hakimian, 1990; Bayat, 1997; Todaro, 1976). The negative impact of distance as an intervening obstacle can be balanced by considerable income differences and economic and occupational attractions elsewhere. The distance coefficients in migration, when combined with existence of alternative opportunities in the destination, such as employment, education, technological improvements in transport, high wage levels, and availability of information about the destination itself, are very significant factors, particularly for more educated migrants who seem to rely less on friends and relatives (Yap, 1975: 22-23). In his theory of "intervening opportunities," Stouffer (1940) argues that the ratio between opportunities in the place of destination and intervening opportunities in the place of origin are important factors when considering mobility and distance: "The number of persons going to a given distance is directly proportional to the number of opportunities at that distance and inversely proportional to the number of intervening opportunities of their origin" (Stouffer, 1940: 846). However, job opportunities and their distribution in different places and between different occupational or ethnic groups very much depends on political, geographical, economic and social factors, which vary from situation to situation. Hakimian (1990) recorded the first traces of migration in Iran as early as 1855 among the peasants from the northwestern province of Azarbaijan to Russia in search of short-term seasonal employment. Given the shorter duration, the "international migration" of Azari peasants to Russia seems to support the positive link between distance and migration. What makes this more complicated is the usage of the boundaries as the "measures of distance which is mainly based on binary divisions of national and international" (Skeldon, 1997) to separate spatial units in order to define short or long distance. If in this case one ignores the boundaries, migration to Russia can be accounted as a short distance for Azari peasants when compared to the principal migrant-receiving cities of the time within Iran's national boundaries.

Intervening obstacles and personal factors are the main factors used by Lee (1966) in his analysis of the internal migration process. Most of the studies from developing countries indicate that rural migrants are not a random sample of the rural population; rather they are from two main economic groups. One group is the very poor, landless, unemployed, and unskilled who are mainly compelled to move as a result of economic necessity. The other group is those with education or wealth who are pulled into the cities by attractive opportunities in terms of both employment and consumption: to improve their education and skills, and benefit from better working and living conditions (Brigg, 1971; Todaro, 1976: 28). These in the former group tend to be "negatively" selected and the latter are "positively" selected, and able to move longer distances (Lee, 1966). There is, however, a correlation between migration, and age and education: migrants from these two economic groups tend to be younger, often between the ages of 15 and 24, and are educationally superior to rural natives in their place of origin, and in some cases to urban natives. The availability of different types of education in urban areas, particularly in less developed countries, is an explanatory variable influencing the migration of young people, particularly from wealthier sections of rural areas (Brigg, 1971; Yap, 1975: 17; Jamali, 1985; Bayat, 1997). It has been strongly argued that rural development projects are less likely to reduce the migration of the more educated for whom still more opportunities exist in urban areas (Yap, 1975: 15).

Two different views have been stated regarding the responsiveness of the young to employment opportunities in urban areas. The economic view is explained as the "human capital investment model" in which the costs and returns of migration are important indicators for individuals whose decision is made in terms of net benefits (Gallup, 1997). "Investment in migration, like other investments of the human being, is expected to pay-off in the long run if not immediately" (Jamali, 1985: 383). The possibility of early employment and a longer period of earning for young migrants increases the expected returns and the profitability of migration, in terms of a better job, education, housing and social status. This is the case particularly for skilled migrants (Brigg, 1971: 67). Thus, the older people are, the less they will be inclined to migrate because of the intensive economic costs of migration combined with a shorter period of net benefit. On the other hand, the non-economic costs of migration are less for young people. They are usually able to adjust and assimilate more easily to the social, psychological and environmental conditions of their chosen destination than older people are (Jamali, 1985: 383). At times non-economic aspects such as freedom from rural elders and social pressures, escaping from rural violence, or political instability in part of a country can encourage out-migration (Brigg, 1971). The demographic selectivity in migration, however, results in a decline of valuable human capital in rural areas, and a growth in the urban unemployment rate (Byerlee, 1974: 548).

Banerjee and Newman (1998) examined the interactions between different institutional arrangements in the dual economy and how information asymmetries in traditional and modern sectors affect credit availability and consequently the rural population's decision to migrate. Their study also supported a bipolar division of migrants. The wealthiest are able to finance themselves without a consumer loan and have much to gain in the modern sector, and the poorest, who do not have access to rural informal security mechanisms such as credit institutions and loans, have nothing to lose (Banerjee and Newman, 1998: 632).

Many studies demonstrate a positive correlation between migration and destination contact in the form of friends and relatives who provide information about the new location, and can make the social transition and adjustment of migrants to the new environment easier. In many cases, the choice of location is influenced by the existence of such contacts. In fact, the existence of previous migrants encourages new migration. The positive benefits of migration to individual migrants, at least to those who gradually establish a permanent residence in the cities, reinforce its attractiveness for potential new migrants with whom they have contact (Yap, 1975: 35). They often provide necessary information about job and other opportunities, and act as initial financial security during job finding processes by offering low-cost or even free accommodation and, of course, companionship (Brigg, 1971; Byerlee, 1974: 547; Todaro, 1976: 73). A study of poor people in Tehran reveals not only ethnically based communities with a high degree of internal cohesion and solidarity, but also occupationally based communities (Bayat, 1997:

30-31), who often construct their identity as the basis of the community in which they live.

Considering the age/education composition of migrants and urban natives, many rural-urban migration studies show that migrants tend to have lower unemployment rates and higher labor force participation rates than urban natives (Jamali, 1985: 373; Yap, 1975: 29). Young migrants tend to enter lower quality employment when their urban counterparts are either at school or not willing to take such low paid and low status jobs. Un/semi-skilled migrants, who might have been regarded as skilled in their place of origin, "can reduce the levels of urban unemployment by supplying complementary rather than competitive inputs" (Harris, 1999: 12). This applies not only to rural-urban migration, but also to international migration. Therefore, since the majority of migrants appear to be unskilled, poor and unorganized, they have a minor impact on the earnings and job opportunities of natives in terms of increasing their unemployment. They are willing to take jobs that skilled workers would not take.

Conclusion

This chapter sought to outline the literature on rural-urban migration as an integral part of societies and economies, and a dominant type of population distribution in developing countries. The literature illustrates that migration is not only a simple labor transition from rural to urban areas. Rather, it is a complex system that has a close relationship with social and economic development, caused by economic as well as non-economic variables. It can be simultaneously positive and negative for development, depending on the context and the level of analysis—individual, community, state—which is also true for international migration.

Despite the limited capacities of large cities in less developed countries to provide employment, public services and decent accommodation for migrants, all are targets for considerable in-migration. Studies show that the trend of increased rural-urban migration is due to the relatively better conditions of life in urban areas and higher labor force participation rates of migrants compared to urban natives. The existence of the informal sector, which offers ample job opportunities in construction, manufacturing and service for un/semi-skilled migrants, often through personal network channels, positively contributes to the process of migration.

The cities that have high net in-migration often have high net out-migration, often up the hierarchy either to other urban areas within national boundaries, or to more developed countries. This part of the argument, however, is not in the scope of my research. In the next two chapters, I will focus my attention on female migrants and gender relations in the migration process; and the structural causes of rapid, irregular rural-urban migration and urbanization in Iran.

Notes

1. Chapter 3 will explore the causes of migration in Iran.

2. The concept of the "leading sector" was introduced by Rostow (1960) in his stages theory, analyzing the interrelationship between the growth of different sectors, where the leading sector plays a key role during the take-off period of growth process or even subsequent periods of economic growth. For instance, the leading sector in Britain during the take-off period was the textile industry.

3. Lewis, 1954: 142-46. Comparing the dual-sector model proposed in this with Rostow's theorization of the "take-off" (1960), Diana Hunt (1989: 86-120) states that these two share a common core and are complementary to each other. She states that Lewis's theory concentrates on the expansion of the capitalist sector, whether state or private, by absorbing the unlimited supply of labor. Rostow focuses on different stages of capital accumulation as well as the social, political and institutional changes that are likely to happen during the take-off process. For further details, see: chapter 4, "The Paradigm of the Expanding Capitalist Nucleus" in her book *Economic Theories of Development: An Analysis of Competing Paradigms.*

4. To increase agricultural output and the net income of remaining villagers, through state policies, some governments play a direct role in the distribution of productive resources such as land, for the favor of some sections of rural population. Direct involvement of the governments sometimes leads to an accelerated migration from the rural areas. I will discuss later, in Iran, how state policies directed by the land reform project in 1963 resulted in heavy migration in the 1960s and afterwards. Many studies, however, indicate that migrants retain close ties with their place of origin by sending contributions in the form of cash or goods. The studies of Byerlee (1974) and Farsakh (1999) from African countries indicate that these contributions not only improve the living standard of the remaining individuals, but they also act as a system of security for retirement and return migration, when migrants' rights to the land remain intact.

5. The informal sector is the unorganized, unregistered and unregulated sector of the economy that acts as a major source of earning opportunities for many unemployed or underemployed people. It does not have a fixed definition. It is sometimes defined by the industries involved, such as construction, commerce or services; or by the size of firms which do not contribute to national social security or tax; or ones which are neither governmental nor professional organizations. In terms of Merrick's definition, self employment, autonomous subsistence activities such as street vending, hawking and many other similar activities and services constitute the informal economic sector.

6. Bromley and Gerry (1979) subdivide employment into "stable wage-work" with a considerable degree of security and stability; and "casual work" as any form of employment, either productive or unproductive, legal or illegal activities without any security of income or continuity of employment.

7. The nineteenth and early twentieth century British economist Ernst Ravenstein who examined internal migration in the British Isles during the period between the censuses of 1871 and 1881 called his study, "Laws of Migration." In 1889, he expanded his study to other areas, collecting data from twenty countries in which he found more evidence for his 1885 findings.

Chapter 2

Gender Analysis of Migration

Gender is a social construction that systematizes relations between males and females. Therefore, a gender analysis of migration is useful in distinguishing different causes, practices, and behaviors between men and women in the process of migration. Traditionally defined gender roles and expectations, social norms, customary patterns, and social networks around the world have hampered, deterred, or permitted women's independent movement and productivity in different societies and cultures (Bauer, 1984 and 1985; Brydon, 1989; Buijs, 1993; Fawcett *et al.*, 1984; Smith *et al.*, 1984; Strauch, 1984; Swaisland, 1993; Thadani and Todaro, 1984; Wright, 1995; Zhang, 1999). The aim of this chapter is, therefore, to review some gendered aspects of migration which lead to the emergence of different patterns of female migration around the world. It will also examine the gender inequalities that are shaped by social and cultural contexts, and the influence of economic and political conditions underlying women's decisions about migration. Since economic factors play an important role in stimulating not only internal, but also international female migration, concentration will be on female labor market participation along with the gender-specific patterns of urban employment and rural poverty. Women's challenges to different socio-cultural factors and the impact of migration on women either as a result of their own migration, or that of their male relatives will all be the focus of this chapter.

Female Migration

Female migration happens in either associational or autonomous forms, or a combination of both. Associational migration occurs through marriage or family migration where women accompany or join their male migrant relatives. The autonomous migration of women, which is rapidly increasing around the world, is an independent response to many economic and non-economic factors (Elmhirst, 1998a and 1998b; Davin, 1998; Zhang, 1999; Rudnick, 2000). Until the mid 1970s, most migration literature was gender indifferent or had a male bias, by describing typical migrants to most metropolitan areas of the world as young adult males usually in the 15-24 age group (Buijs, 1993: 1). When women appeared in migration literature, they were considered within the category of dependents whose traditional and associational migration was not seen as having much social or economic impact on their place of origin or destination. This view was based on the assumption that women were not economically active (Smith *et al.*, 1984: 22). More comprehensive approaches to female migration commenced in the 1980s, following the feminist analysis of women and development and women's significant absence from historical accounts of migration (Zhang, 1999: 21; Wright, 1995: 781). Feminist analysis also concentrated on the inevitable consequences of male domination in migration for women left behind in the sending areas, who remained invisible in the literature. The alteration of the demographic balance in sending and receiving areas as a result of male migration or desertion often led to important changes both in terms of the sexual division of labor and the formation of de facto female-headed households. These hardly ever brought any changes to the benefit of women in terms of, for instance, property or land rights (Davin, 1998: 55-56). In some countries, in *de facto* female-headed households, both in developing and industrialized countries, women embark on the same tasks as men or participate more in activities that traditionally were defined as male (Brouwer and Priester, 1983: 120). In other societies where women have relatively less power to act independently or are secluded, or there are cultural taboos against women's participation in specific activities, for instance, ploughing, they become more dependent on male relatives, or face greater poverty and destitution, which in some cases may lead to their migration to urban areas (Agarwal, 1989: 73-89; Chant, 1997: 15-19). In some cases, the marital relationship comes under strain, when men form another family in their destination, and send small and irregular remittances back to the family left behind (Brouwer and Priester, 1983). In other societies where there are stronger family ties and reciprocal obligations, the whole family benefits from male migration (Mascarenhas-Keys, 1990: 116-123; Davin, 1999: 125-26). Again, women have to perform greater roles in the family by providing extra emotional support for their children and carrying additional responsibilities.

The early male dominance in migration within European societies was due to the uncertainty of the first migratory movements: "when men settled, their families followed them. In this way, the number of female migrants gradually expanded or even exceeded that of males, particularly as the character of the urban economy shifted from manual to non-manual occupations" (Thadani and Todaro, 1984: 37). Some European studies trace the early and extensive migration of women back to the industrialization process, as a result of the expanding occupational opportunities for women in textiles, manufacturing and domestic services (Lesthaeghe, 1977 cited in Smith *et al.*, 1984: 16).

In the United States, at the beginning of the 19th century, the earliest workers in urban factories were generally rural women who could easily be withdrawn from agricultural labor and placed in the textile factories. In Southern Africa, during the colonial period, despite prevention of female migration by both rural authorities and the colonial rulers, there were a small but very visible number of female migrants in the African cities. Often these women were not employed (Wright, 1995). In some regions, the wives of African miners were permitted to join their husbands, but unmarried women were prevented. Employers were heavily subsidized by women's non-waged domestic work and services offered to migrant men working in the mines which gave a boost to profits, as their expulsion from urban areas would cause some miners return to home (Moroney, 1982: 261 cited in Wright, 1995: 785). In some cases policy planners, despite colonial legislative constraints upon women's mobility, promoted female migration. In early 20th century Zimbabwe, female migrants were punished by the state, but at the same time, their migration was tacitly encouraged (Wright, 1995: 785). In other cases, missionaries, who often offered refuge to runaway African women passively facilitated the liberation of many women from male control and customary laws governing gender relations (Walker, 1990: 182; Gaitskell, 1982: 342; and 1990: 253; Hughes, 1990: 209-12, all cited in Wright, 1995: 785).

Women's Association with Migration and the Feminization of the Labor Market

The patterns of female migration are "both a reflection and a cause of some of the major social and economic transformations of their societies" (Fawcett *et al.*, 1984: 5). Different factors, such as relaxation of migratory rules, independence, the gradual eradication of institutionalized economic barriers and social stratification, as well as institutional changes in the structure of urban employment in terms of gender-specific patterns of the urban labor market, became important elements in accelerating independent migration of women in the late 20th century (Boserup, 1970; Wright, 1995; Zhang, 1999). On the other hand, the undermining of women's traditional activities in agriculture or craft industries, the lack of a male breadwinner or his insufficient wage, devaluation, inflation, difficulties caused by structural adjustment policies and poverty, and rural-urban income differences demanded extra contribution to the family income, sometimes for the mere survival of households. A combination of some of the above factors, particularly considerable urban wage-earning opportunities often encourages women's migration to cities (Brydon, 1989; Amin, 1997; Safa, 1995). A study of female migration in the Anhui province of China, where women traditionally work in agriculture, shows that a surplus of labor on the land is one of the reasons for the migration of young single women to the big cities to work as domestic servants (Davin, 1999). A strong agricultural sector, little or no male out-migration, and poor development in urban areas seem to be directly related to low female migration (Walker, 1990: 190-91 cited in Wright, 1995: 785).

Gender-specific patterns of urban employment developed as a result of the rapid expansion of "transitional production." Maximizing profits and minimizing the costs of production in industrialized countries required the production process to be divided into several integrated stages. The assembly stage, which is low technology and labor-intensive, moved into developing countries where there is an abundance of cheap labor. This led to the appearance of multinational factories in Latin America, Southeast Asia and China. The traditional views held by states, employers, policy planners and families about women as supplementary wage-earners is one of the major reasons for drawing women into the labor force as cheap labor during industrialization and development (Afshar, 1989a). This led to global feminization of a labor market that targets women as a "cheap labor force" (Hancock, 1983; Safa, 1986; Bakker, 1988; Ecevit, 1991; Pearson, 1998), particularly in export-oriented factories that operate on the basis of the sexual designation of industrial tasks. This phenomenon increasingly led to the feminization of migration within many developing countries with an influx of women into factory employment, most of whom are young, unmarried or the sole breadwinners of their families. This trend has been witnessed on a massive scale in Latin America (Safa, 1986), West Africa (Brydon, 1989), Southern Africa since independence in the 1950s and 1960s (Wright, 1995), and China, following the 1980s post-Mao economic reforms, which resulted in a massive city-ward population movement (Yu and Day, 1994: 124-25; Zhang, 1999). There are variations of this sequential feminization of labor and migration in different parts of the world, both within countries and regions and across borders. The independent migration of women in many Asian or Middle Eastern countries, however, is relatively low, compared to other parts of the world, mainly due to religious and ideological restrictions.

It is not, however, easy to separate female autonomous migration from associational migration. Single women often enjoy more opportunities as a result of migrating. However, a lack of skills and educational qualifications affect many poor female migrants' access to better economic opportunities. This makes them less able to support themselves adequately or experience modest social mobility or gender equity within the family, particularly for married women (Lessinger, 1990: 129-148). In urban areas, due to the absence of extended family structures, traditional shared childcare is replaced by expensive and scarce state or private childcare, which causes difficulties for working mothers, particularly the poor, when coping both with the demands of childcare and an urban job simultaneously. Their substantial contribution to the subsistence needs of the family, as well as their traditional roles in rural societies make them better suited to work within the flexible arrangements of the informal sector, often as home-workers without job security or other benefits (Thadani and Todaro, 1984: 46-47). In some countries, leaving young children with their grandparents in natal villages where childcare is cheaper, has become a common practice for many migrant women (Chant, 1997). In China, under the household registration system, migrants are given a temporary residency, which does not give them the same rights as urban people who have permanent household registration, particularly in terms of their children's access to schools, or to free or low cost healthcare facilities in the cities. These strict regulations compel female migrants to leave behind their dependent children, particularly the school-aged ones under the guardianship of their families. Moreover, children's household registration follows that of their mother. Therefore, rural migrants who may marry men of urban origin are also compelled to return to or send their school-age children to their villages, or obtain very expensive permanent residence permits for their children (Davin, 1998: 59-60).

The ideology of space, which divides society into private and public, particularly in Asian countries, is a major factor that traditionally imposes a limitation and boundary on women's mobility and participation in the labor market (Shaheed, 1989). However, empirical country-level studies and sociological and anthropological observations from Asia suggest that the feminization of migration, particularly of single women, has become an integral and growing part of the process of economic change in some Asian countries (Smith *et al.*, 1984: 15). Some studies suggest that poverty relaxes and modifies the role of conservative norms and practices, and cultural and religious beliefs as far as women's participation in the labor market is concerned (Feldman, 1983; Amin 1997). For instance, Bangladesh is a patriarchal society where women are prevented by the cultural norms from working outside their home (Rudnick, 2000). However, increasing poverty since the 1970s as a result of economic erosion, famine and high pressure on available land has resulted in the increased participation of women, particularly young poor rural women, not only in the urban centers of Dhaka and Chittagong, but also in export-oriented factories of Malaysia (Rahman and Sen, 1994 cited in Amin, 1997: 216; Rudnick, 2000).

Responses to urban economic opportunities have different patterns and consequences among female migrants in different parts of the world. In some areas, most female migrants become engaged in domestic work; in others the majority work in the expanding export industries. In some areas the decision is made for them. In Latin America, a substantial number of young girls are sent by their relatives to work in multinational factories or in the domestic sector to send remittances back to their families in rural areas (Brydon, 1989: 126). In South-East Asia, among some poor families, young girls are forced into prostitution or are taken away from their homes by agents to support the needs of their impoverished families (Lee, 1991). In others, women are active agents in the process of decision-making and convincing their families to allow them to migrate. One survey found that many Filipina and Sri Lankan women tend to take their own decision to migrate. This is mainly because they already enjoyed considerable autonomy and decision-making power within the family, and also in regard to household finances (Oishi, 2002).

Many women, the majority of them young migrants and better educated than men, are involved in multinational industries. However, occupational segregation, sexual inequality and wage differentials based on gender are common practices. Women are employed in low-ranking unskilled occupations for a minimal wage, and men are employed in managerial, professional or supervisory positions with higher salaries (Safa, 1995: 105). This is despite the fact that women are preferred to men due to their greater productivity in detailed manual tasks because of assumed innate qualities such as discipline, submissiveness, quickness, dexterity, careful concentration, nimble fingers, and the fact that they are easy to control (Hancock, 1983; Ecevit, 1991; Safa, 1995). In the Special Economic Zones of China, employers even send their agents to the villages to recruit cheap female labor, by offering the girls dormitory accommodation in the city and helping them with transport as part of the employment agreement (Davin, 1999: 115-119). Although in export-oriented factories the wage is based on gender, in some other sectors or regions wage differentials between the sexes are related to the supply and demand equilibrium of female labor. In different parts of India, women's wages reflect the different patterns of their participation in work. In the regions with a large supply of female labor, women's wages are lower in relation to men's; whereas in regions with a small supply of female labor due to restrictive attitudes towards women's employment, customary sex wage differentials are eliminated, and men and women tend to be paid equal wages (Boserup, 1970: 73-75).

The important issue regarding women's independent migration is that the pull factors from the urban area are enhanced by social networks that are based on kinship ties (Elmhirst, 1998b: 8-14). In urban-oriented labor markets, settled migrants, besides monetary remittances, offer additional support for their natal rural communities by finding suitable jobs or securing reliable homes for younger relatives moving to the city for the first time for education or employment. Social networks offer village parents peace of mind, as young migrants, particularly women, are well supervised and controlled in the cities by them (Strauch, 1984: 67). In fact, social networks and destination contacts "enable the exertion of power and influence by certain actors over individuals without face-to-face contact" (Elmhirst, 1998b: 13), particularly as far as female migration is concerned.

Kinship groups may, and sometimes do, impose limitations on women's freedom of movement in a wider society that has a heterogeneous nature containing more unknown men, particularly in respect of women's morality under religious and traditional patriarchal beliefs (Shaheed, 1989: 20). The rules relating to women's mobility in urban areas, however, depend on women's age, class, marital status and socio-economic conditions. Older women (who maintain more traditional gender roles in terms of patriarchal norms), the divorced, widowed, and poorest have the least restriction imposed upon them and have more freedom even in respect of their resistance to male autonomy. Younger and unmarried women, however, are considered more vulnerable and in need of more supervision in terms of protecting their virginity which affects their marriageability (Bauer, 1984 and 1985; Davin, 1999).

Although rural and urban social systems are spatially separated from each other, they are often interdependent socially, economically and politically (Ross and Weisner, 1977: 360-61 cited in Strauch, 1984: 60). In the process of internal migration, people alter and re-evaluate the old and traditional social relationships in order to form new ones: "when one party moves to the city and becomes a potential link to new opportunities for others still in the village. Female mobility today results in just such a re-valuation of kin connections that traditionally lay relatively dormant" (Strauch, 1984: 61). Elmhirst's study (1998) indicates that the existence of an institutionalized social network adjusted unmarried women's factory work according to prevalent local cultural ideologies and prescriptions. In China, the traditional kinship networks took on a new role in linking rural women to emerging urban employment opportunities through information exchange about jobs (Zhang, 1999).

One of the characteristics of young unmarried women's migration is "seasonal circulation migration" as a result of which female migrants keep close ties with their villages and often return to their place of origin after many years (Davin, 1998; Elmhirst, 1998a and 1998b; Rudnick, 2000). Because of a rapid increase in female circular migration in the 1980s and 1990s within China, migrant women themselves became a vital source of continuous connection between their friends and relatives in the place of origin and employers in the place of destination. For instance, migrant women in domestic service in China are often identified by their origins. This identification, as well as the close and informal association of migrant women through the mutual aid and exchange of information about jobs, not only helps them to adjust easily to the new environment, but also provides them with a strong, collective bargaining position in relation to their urban employers (Zhang, 1999: 27-28).

In the early 1990s, when unmarried women in the North Lampung area of Indonesia began their circular migration to work in export-orientated factories, women's own informal networks consisting of friends and relatives helped them to gain parental consent for their migration, despite the strict sanctions on their movement and work practices. Parents were, however, concerned for their daughters' morality due to the loosening of parental control on them whilst they were in the city. Later, local cultural and religious figures together with a member of a prominent family from the village who had lived in the city for a long time but had retained close ties with it, institutionalized the city-village social network. This formal network "increased parental trust and smoothed the path of the migration decision-making process between parents and daughters" (Elmhirst, 1998b: 13) and enabled not only parents, but also village authorities to exert control over the practice and behavior of young migrant women in the city.

In Asia and Africa, more women have become primary wage earners in domestic and cleaning jobs, child rearing, care of the elderly, and as nurses and hospital aides (UN World Survey, 1999). In the late 1990s, one million Filipinas, 500,000 Indonesian women and 40,000 Thai women were working outside their countries, and these numbers have since grown to where they account for 60-80 percent of their labor migrants (IOM). As explained earlier, the high emigration of women in these societies has been possible because of the greater flexibility in gender roles in those societies. In Vietnam and Ethiopia, migration provides women with employment opportunities and the ability to improve their living standards at home, mostly through domestic work (ILO). In Indonesia, women displaced from agriculture have found alternative means of earning a living in urban homes, particularly as lower middle class women are moving into the labor force.

Cultivation Systems and Social Norms

Since rural-urban female migration is the concern of this study, it will also be useful to consider how different social norms, ideological belief systems and customary patterns of women's mobility and productivity exist in different cultivation systems within rural areas.

Most African, and some Southeast Asian countries, particularly the tribal people of India, have a shifting cultivation system with a high percentage of female participation in nearly all agricultural tasks. In Latin America, female farming has also been widespread among Indian and black communities. The transplantation system of agriculture in rice and tea-producing districts also demands more female participation. In the regions that have a long tradition of female wage labor in agriculture, including the northern provinces of Iran, women enjoy a degree of status and economic independence due to their active participation in agriculture (Afshar, 1989a: 48-49).

Their heavy involvement in productive activities paves the way for their participation in the urban informal sector, particularly in retail marketing and trading. In many regions, particularly in African countries, traditional trading and marketing of food is left mostly, or even entirely, to women as a main occupation or as a subsidiary occupation to agriculture (Boserup, 1970). Although, in terms of independent access to material means or legal rights, they have a relatively powerless position (Wright, 1995), they enjoy a degree of economic independence through access to markets, which enables them to generate income by selling their surplus production. In many cases, however, their restricted access to capital or the means of production for market-oriented work causes polarization between them and men, both economically and politically, and this makes the competition between the sexes more difficult (Todaro, 1994b: 257-58; Mies, 1982). In the case of creating opportunities for women to earn more from trading and marketing, men perpetuate their gender superiority over women, particularly if women do not enjoy the support of a male relative (Lessinger, 1990: 129-148).

Some agrarian regions, however, have plough cultivation systems, which employ a high percentage of hired male agricultural laborers. A social and class hierarchy due to the privatized land ownership by a minority of the population is one of the major characteristics of these regions, particularly in some parts of India. Lack of access to land increases the risk of poverty and affects the well-being of landless families, particularly women and children. The land owners, however, have greater advantages in terms of having direct and indirect access to credit from moneylenders or institutional sources in order to purchase agricultural technology and modern agricultural inputs. A common practice in these areas is male control over agriculture. There are also ritual taboos against women ploughing, the breaking of which (even when survival is threatened), may result in severe punishment for women (Boserup, 1970; Agarwal, 1989).

Apart from land privatization, limited female inheritance rights also create a gender hierarchy which bars women's independent involvement in agriculture (Agarwal, 1989: 73; Hoodfar, 1993). In India, under traditional Hindu law, women do not inherit any ancestral land or immovable property. However, among some of the matrilineal societies, women's inheritance rights to immovable property, including land, has been traditionally recognized. According to Islamic law, women can theoretically inherit ancestral land and wealth and have the right to control them after marriage, and a father is not allowed to deprive his daughter of her right. But often in practice, even if women are entitled to land, their ability to claim their legal share is circumscribed by patriarchal, traditional, social and psychological resistance (Afshar, 1985a: 68). In Tanzania, women have found themselves compelled to migrate, either for work or marriage, due to their exclusion from land inheritance (Black, 2004).

Post-marital residence in the case of village exogamous marriage automatically deprives women of their parental land in favor of their brothers, or poses practical difficulties in managing the parental land. Intimidation by male kin to prevent women from claiming land, and official colonial policies by giving the land title to men as the heads of households are important factors in contributing to women's disadvantages in these rural communities (Agarwal, 1989).

A feature of gender hierarchy in these societies is the existence of strong ideological barriers that restrict women's mobility and participation in outside activities, often through social institutions. These institutions, by exercising the ideology of space, *purdah* and seclusion, take control of female sexuality, particularly when women have some economic independence. Ideological practices, such as that of domesticity, have a close connection with families' upward social and economic mobility in sharecropping families for describing women's social status in the society as housewives or outdoor worker (Boserup, 1970; Mies, 1982). In some societies, particularly in India and Pakistan, and some parts of Iran in rich families, women's unpaid work in the fields is replaced by male laborers. Women, due to the rules of *purdah,* the domination of the domestic ideology and importance of the family's social upward mobility (Shaheed, 1989), are driven into seclusion. This, however, does not mean non-participation of secluded women in production, as they often perform domestic duties, or contribute to harvest work and to the care of domestic animals. Also the ideology of *purdah* does not apply to rural women in Iran compared to their counterparts in India and Pakistan. Only women in the lowest social groups, who are working-class laborers from the indigenous point of view, and the "African" type of women, are expected to have an outdoor job (Boserup, 1970). Since the majority of rural people are poor and women's economic and reproductive labor is essential for the family's survival, they are more likely to observe sex segregation roles, but not seclusion (Razavi, 1992; Hoodfar, 1993: 6).

In rural societies where strong ideological controls are exercised over women, household industries, often categorized as housework and subsistence work, absorb quite large numbers of women who remain "invisible" in national and international data, despite their active role in production and wealth generation for their families and communities, as well as their nations. Studying rural lace-makers in India, Mies (1982) found that this industry was introduced by early missionaries to provide work for poor converted Christian women, with an intention to fit into a superior ideological framework. Through conversion to Christianity, and by learning the lace industry, the untouchable women who were doing all kinds of agricultural labor were given the status of respectable housewives who could move away from their lowest caste by generating income within the home. With the growth of pauperization in India, she observed that more respectful rural housewives of other castes were drawn into this industry out of necessity. Faced with absolute poverty and aware that they would earn more in the fields, women were not willing to lose their social identity and secluded status as respectable housewives by working or moving outside their home. Although both they and agricultural laborers belonged to the same class of pauperized peasants, they were distinguished from each other, as one group was considered as housewives and the other as workers according to both their own perception and that of others. In practice, therefore, based on the ideology of the domestic sphere, women's whole production process becomes "invisible" and the exploitative relationship between them and their employers was reinforced economically and politically (Mies, 1982; Ghavamshahidi, 1996).

However, social norms and the strict regulation of women's mobility and economic activity are diluted by poverty, particularly when women are obliged to contribute to the household economy. Extreme poverty, deterioration of their socio-economic position, male desertion and the struggle for survival force some women to migrate, though the range of their movement might be very limited (Mies, 1982: 114). It seems that the lower class status of women, along with the existence of social networks in urban areas, gives poor women greater flexibility to some extent in social terms. As a result, the poor and those who can not rely on the protection of a male relative are more likely to move as independent agents in search of paid employment, and challenge the social, political and sexual order. In Rudnick's case study (2000) of Bangladeshi women working in Malaysian export industries, poverty and economic pressure were important reasons for the majority of women to migrate.

Costs and Benefits of Migration and Economic Involvement for Women

Various studies indicate that the burden of economic hardship at the household level falls primarily on women who have to minimize expenditure and maximize earnings not only through their non-wage domestic work, which is universally and socially considered to be women's duty, but also through their paid or un-paid labor (Afshar and Agarwal, 1989; Amin, 1997; Mies, 1982; Razavi, 1992; Safa, 1995). When their contribution to the familial economy involves spending more time on cost-saving activities or home-based production which are not measurable and do not generate cash, most women do not see their unpaid contribution to the familial economy as "work" and do not identify themselves as potential workers (Elson, 1991; Ghavamshahidi, 1996). Access to paid employment and contributing to the household economy, however, despite the inferior position of the majority of women in the labor market, are liberating experiences, which enable women to challenge traditional patriarchal patterns of authority and move beyond the physical and psychological constraint of familial control towards more egalitarian family structures (Afshar and Dennis, 1992; MacEwen, 1994; Safa, 1995; Amin, 1997; Poya, 1999). "When male bread-winning inadequacy becomes chronic and women became co-breadwinners on a permanent basis, men are no longer able to maintain their superior and authoritarian position vis-a-vis their wives" (Safa, 1995: 122), "even if women consider their husbands to be the head of household" (Safa, 1995: 111). Women, who become the main supporters of their families, often question the ideology of the dependent housewife and show a new gender awareness and self-confidence, though due to the informal nature of their work, they do not see themselves as workers. Moreover, "control over distribution is a critical economic aspect of the status and power differential between men and women. Since women usually are in a subordinate position in the traditional social hierarchy, urban migration and urban jobs may represent the promise of economic independence which is a positive differential for women compared to men" (Thadani and Todaro, 1984: 47).

Amin, however, argues that the cultural impact upon women's status is such that as women's liberty increases in one sphere, there is a decline in another. This is so particularly in societies where, due to the impact of religion and traditional patriarchal patterns, women's social role is more strictly prescribed and their seclusion and exclusion from outside work might be considered a symbol of status. She states that in such societies, apart from the inferior position of women in the male-dominated labor market, their paid job also results in a loss of status, higher spousal separation, or even lower chance for marriage for some single women (Amin, 1997: 215). Although women's inferior position in the labor market has been revealed by many studies, less work has been done on the relationship between women's status and paid employment. Most of the studies of migrant women in different parts of the world implicitly or explicitly indicate the opposite result. For instance, Elmhirst's (1998b) study of migrant women in the North Lampung area of Indonesia shows that, despite cultural and moral prescriptions and restrictive attitudes to rural women's mobility and participation in work, the unmarried women's circular migration was accepted by the rural community. Their factory work did not cause them a loss in status rather it was highly valued by their communities, their parents and themselves for three reasons: "Firstly, in terms of aesthetics and prevailing ideas about female beauty and appearance such as wearing beautiful clothes and jewellery; secondly, in terms of expanding more worldly experience, learning and developing social skills; and thirdly, in raising the value of unmarried women in the marriage market" (Elmhirst, 1998a: 14).

Non-Economic Factors Influencing Female Migration

Although economic motives are the main drivers for greater female out-migration, freedom from parental supervision, greater personal autonomy regarding marriage and fertility, and a sense of self-esteem have all been considered important motivating factors for female migrants (Davin, 1998;

Zhang, 1999; and Elmhirst, 1998a and 1998b; Rudnick, 2000). When women, mostly single and unmarried, are active agents in the process of decision-making and convincing their families the studies show that their involvement in urban paid employment is not merely related to economic reforms. Changes in the structure of urban employment and official relaxation of rural-urban migration controls, both in the case of African countries and China, also demonstrate that migrant women are actors and agents in an economic and social transformation of their communities and wider societies. They win a gradual battle against traditional values, patriarchal authority, state control and restrictions over their lives, economic opportunities and freedom of movement. Increase in women's active and autonomous migration and involvement in the labor market is a measure of women's challenge to traditionally defined gender roles and expectations, as well as to spatial and socio-economic boundaries which prevented women having their own aims and achievements (Zhang, 1999: 21-25). Most women in Elmhirst's (1998b) and Zhang's (1999) case studies were not taking urban jobs out of necessity. Rather, a large proportion of their wages were spent on clothes, jewellery or household goods bought in expectation of marriage.

Migration also offers many women an escape. Social pressures and a hard life in the village, sexual subordination in patriarchal rural households, women's traditional status, and customary sanctions against unmarried mothers, the experience of widowhood, and an unhappy and broken marriage can all reinforce women's final decision to migrate (Bryceson, 1985: 144-45; Boserup, 1970; Wright 1995: 786; Little, 1973 cited in Thadani and Todaro, 1984: 45). In many cases, African women in Kenya, Basutoland, and Zambia were escaping from unendurable male oppression or unwanted prospective or violent husbands, the quarrels of polygamy, and the stigma of childlessness (Bonner, 1990; Kimble, 1983; Nelson, 1992; Hansen, 1984, all cited in Wright, 1995: 786). Those who could not be re-absorbed into their natal kin-group were forced to migrate due to the lack of a "male guardian" as a result of widowhood or abandonment by a migrant husband. For instance, according to the 1967 Tanzanian census, the proportion of divorced women in urban areas was twice as high as in rural areas, whereas this was not the case for men in urban areas. Of the 295 women workers interviewed in Dar-es Salaam, 63 percent were single, divorced or widowed, and most of them were the heads of their households with children to support (Bryceson, 1985: 144-45).

Marriage customs, which often dictate a woman move to her husband's place of residence, also play an important role in female migration in the forms of rural-rural, rural-urban, urban-urban migration, involving either short or long-distance movements. Marriage migration usually takes place where village exogamy (marrying someone from outside natal village) and patrilocality patterns of marriage are prevalent, and where village endogamy is forbidden for example in southeastern China and in some parts of rural

India, particularly the northwest (Strauch, 1984: 62; Davin, 1998; Agarwal, 1989: 70-82). In such societies, economic factors do not seem to play an important role. In Bangladesh, a country of large internal movements, there is considerable internal female migration, but more than 56 percent of the women who migrate do so across rural areas, indicating a high prevalence of marital migration (Afsar, 2003). In Pakistan, both the Integrated Household Survey (PIHS) and the Labor Force Survey of 1998 found that more women than men were migrating internally. However, closer observation indicated that many of these movements were marriage-related or to accompany spouses (Memon, 2005).

Migration for marriage, "marital migration," has been suggested as another reason for female migration. Through marital migration, women expect to gain socio-economic status or achieve upward social mobility: such marriages are called "mobility marriages" (Thadani and Todaro, 1984: 45-46). Mobility marriage is common in West Africa, where there is an imbalance between the sexes or local marriage prospects are not good for young women. The higher the probability of mobility marriage or the higher the actual disproportion between the sexes, the greater the female out-migration rate (Thadani and Todaro, 1984: 52). This statement would be true for any sort of female migration including rural-urban migration and international migration. The emigration of many single British women from impoverished laboring and middle class families to South Africa as domestic servants during the late 19th and early 20th centuries may have been as a result of marital as well as economic concerns (Swaisland, 1993: 161-76). Women's emigration was a result of two main events in their own society. On the one hand, industrialization and urbanization in Britain had brought about socio-economic upheavals, and on the other hand, the expansion of the British colonial empire and the exodus of many young men to colonized territories had resulted in a high imbalance between the sexes. Therefore, due to poverty, distress and lack of any welfare provision, many single women emigrated to societies where their "past" was unknown in order to cross class boundaries and improve their social status and/or get married. Swaisland notes that although the outcome of marriage for middle-class servants was often not good, marriage provided upward mobility for most working-class servants who married men of a higher class who wanted British wives (Swaisland, 1993: 175-76).

Although, there is a correlation between education and migration, it seems that when women use migration as an escape, or migrate to the cities as wives or as domestic servants, their level of education is not as important a factor in their movement as it is for men or autonomous female migrants, who are mainly economic migrants (Bauer, 1984, 1985; Brydon, 1982, 1985).

Conclusion

As the gender analysis in this chapter illustrates, the migration choices and the constraints or the opportunities for female migrants show a discrepancy depending on their socio-cultural situations and the gender attributes assigned by different cultures. The more restrictive role assigned to women at their place of origin, by culture or religion, the less actual female migration takes place. Often the lowest proportions of migrant women are from the Muslim population compared with the women from other religions. But sometimes, restrictions imposed by culture or religion can have diverse effects and can force women to move, or to use marriage or work offered by recruiters to escape such situations. Although the number of migrant women is rapidly increasing in most parts of the world, single women are more visible than married women in this process. This is a reality, particularly where multinational factories prefer a single female labour force without family responsibilities who can work longer hours in sometimes harsh conditions. Like any other social change, migration can be seen as both positive and negative from different angles. Women's economic independence, autonomy and self-esteem in terms of making important decisions for themselves, weakening of family power structures and hierarchy, challenging tradition gender relations and greater freedom of mobility, balanced against their experiences and remittances and other factors indicate that female migration is a liberating experience for many migrant women. However, engagement in low-wage, low-status temporary jobs, the replacement of family authority with that of their employers, poor work conditions and other factors related to employment are negative implications of female migration. Despite this studies show that the benefits of migration and employment for female migrants exceed the costs. On the other hand, for women who are left behind in the sending areas either as a result of male or female migration, costs exceed the benefits.

Chapter 3

An Overview of Migration and Urbanization in Iran

In the first chapter, structural and individualist approaches to migration were explored in terms of how migration happens and who is more likely to migrate. The first sections in this chapter deal with structural factors from rural push and urban pull perspectives, which play effective roles in encouraging irregular internal rural-urban migration in Iran and the relocation of some rural industries. This is followed by a discussion of migration in East Azarbaijan province[1], with specific focus on the *Shahrestan-e* Tabriz[2], (Tabriz district), and the city of Tariz, the capital city of both the province and the district. There are differences within and between push and pull factors, but each has had different effects on population redistribution in Iran. Sometimes the combination of the two has simply accelerated the process of internal migration. So this chapter also looks at the socio-political and economic structure of Iranian rural society, particularly in terms of land ownership and tenancy, the influence of Western powers from the mid-19th century onwards, and subsequent chronic poverty in rural areas.

The 1960s land reform project which claimed to modernize and commercialize the agricultural sector had macro-economic and political consequences in rural areas, leading to disorganization and radical change in the socio-economic structure of rural society and further deterioration of the rural economy. Many Iranian and Western scholars who have closely observed and analyzed the Iranian land reform project, believe that state intervention in land redistribution and land relations played a major role in facilitating the push factors in rural areas, resulting in the displacement of substantial numbers of peasants from subsistence farming and their eventual exodus to the cities. From the 1920s onward, the modernization program, by neglecting the traditional sector and demanding large quantities of unskilled cheap labor for industrialization and economic development in the cities, acted as a major pull factor in stimulating rural-urban migration and contributing to a massive urbanization process in Iran. Apart from economic factors, cultural variables in the cities also acted as pull factors in mostly attracting slightly wealthier residents of the countryside, often single men, particularly at the early stages of migration.

Historical Outline of Land Tenure System and Agrarian Conditions in Iran

In Iran, ownership of land, particularly the most productive, was traditionally under the control of a landowning class. Possession of land rather than income obtained from it was the main source of privilege and socio-political power[3]. For instance, for a long time in the modern history of Iran, landlords have been strongly influential in appointments of officials, particularly local officials, and indirectly controlled the affairs of the villages. They were also heavily represented in national government to safeguard their broader interests. Their economic and political position above the peasants was reinforced from the mid-19th century onwards through the increasing political influence of Western powers in Iran, and the desire of central government to buy Western products, especially weapons (Keddie, 1981: 25-27). As a result, there were almost yearly auctions of crown lands and governorships to the highest bidders. To keep incomes high, the landlords also arbitrarily raised taxes at the expense of the masses. By the end of the 19th century, the non-cultivating and absentee owners were increasing at the expense of a declining and relatively small peasant ownership.[4] In some provinces not more than two large landlords owned 75 percent of the total land. They were sometimes from the same family or from hostile factions, whose rivalry often adversely affected the prosperity of the area and solidarity among the peasants. The lands were cultivated through sharecropping agreements or tenancy (Keddie, 2006: 26), based on annual redistribution of the share of ploughs, the rotation of water-supply or yokes of oxen (Lambton, 1953: 295-305). The sharecropping aspect was based on a traditional group farming system called *boneh*[5] in order to adapt to irrigation problems in arid and semi-arid regions. Most surpluses beyond the immediate domestic needs of peasants were taken away in the form of tributes, taxes and rents. In parts of the country the peasants who brought the land into cultivation enjoyed some customary rights, which gave them some security of occupancy but not full rights of ownership, due to periodic redistribution of means of production, particularly land.

To reduce the socio-political power of large landowners, particularly tribal leaders, from the early years of his reign Reza Shah[6] attempted to reduce the extent of their lands through policies of confiscation and tribal settlement[7]. The confiscated lands became either the private property of Reza Shah or part of crown land to be sold for the highest bids. However, some reforms introduced by Reza Shah strengthened the position of landlords within the agricultural sector and capital investment in unproductive areas, i.e. money lending, which worsened the economic status of the villagers (Keddie, 1972: 370-75). Land registration laws of 1928-29 enabled some landlords, by virtue of their wealth and power, to register lands to which peasants had titles (Keddie, 2006: 90). Lambton (1953) identified four different types of landowning classes in Iran up into the mid-20th century: 1) a class of long standing land proprietors who had almost always owned land, generation after generation, despite periodic losses; 2) tribal leaders; 3) religious *ulama*[8]; and 4) new landowners who could be sub-divided into three main groups: a) the administrators of the large landlords; b) government officials—civic or military; and c) merchants who invested their money in land to gain the status of the land holding class. However, the complete lack of statistics or accurate measurement makes it impossible to properly assess the total land holdings of large landowners in comparison with other forms of landownership (Lambton, 1953: 260-74).

Political influence of foreign powers and the policy of selling or leasing crown lands to wealthy individuals for short periods of three to five years affected both the welfare of the peasants and the productivity of land. Rushing to extract the maximum gain from the land during short contracts often led to bad farming practices, lack of care for the land, and an ever-increasing gap and mistrust between peasants and landowners, all affecting self-sufficiency in many rural areas (Lambton, 1953: 260-74). Significant measures for improving agricultural productivity, natural resource management and technical capacities required capital investment (Lambton, 1953: 359-78). However, since the peasants' labor was extremely cheap, combined with the fact that they did not have any rights protected by law, landlords preferred the old system of cultivation and considered investment in modern productive enterprises to be risky (Pesaran, 1985: 16-7). The methods used in agriculture remained extremely primitive, the land often ploughed by an ox-drawn plough, rather than tractors, weeding and harvesting done by hand, all of which affected the amount of the land to be cultivated and the small share of the peasants, which was inadequate to meet the domestic needs of an increasing rural population.

As well as a substantial decrease in production of subsistence food crops due to lack of investment in agriculture, a response to demands of foreign markets with production of cotton and opium for export, particularly in market-oriented areas, contributed to chronic rural poverty (Katouzian, 1981, 90-95; Razavi, 1992).[9] International demands for agricultural products put the Iranian export market at the mercy of world price fluctuation as well as market demands (Keddie, 2006: 26). The displacement of some villagers, the relocation of some rural industries such as the carpet industry[10], soap, and some textile, and footwear production to the cities (Katouzian, 1981: 95), or the replacement of some handicrafts by manufactured products (Keddie, 1972: 365-68), were some results of foreign influences in Iran.

The nature of early migration, however, was slow, restricted, and seasonal because of technological and institutional conditions such as poor transport, difficult access to urban areas, and feudal relations with landlords who relied on extensive use of cheap labor, thus imposing implicit rights on peasantry (Zahedi *et al,* 1367/1988). Reza Shah's urban-orientated industrialization and modernization program in the 1920s and 1930s, based on strong central bureaucracies for the development of the oil industry and foreign trade in general, as well as heavy investment in infrastructure such as roads and railways, contributed to worsening conditions of agriculture, the major sector of the economy, and the welfare of peasants in other parts of country. The intention of Reza Shah's policies was to include the rural population in state investment activities, particularly through internal migration to "absorb the periphery into a centralized bureaucratic state" (Akhavi, 1986: 204-5).

These measures became more severe after the Shah's abdication in 1941, during the Second World War. The general pattern of urbanization in Iran indicates a higher concentration of population in urban areas after 1940. A dualistic approach to the country's development planning, designed mainly by foreign companies, again neglected the agricultural sector and gave more attention to selected industries which demanded large numbers of unskilled laborers, accelerating the migratory process in Iran (Afshar, 1985a: 58; Bayat, 1997: 26). During the early 1950s, this process was briefly halted due to economic sanctions and rapid deterioration of the economy as a result of the oil nationalization crisis. But, after the post-oil-nationalism and the CIA-led coup of Dr. Mossaddeqh[11] in 1953, foreign interventions including private investment and economic aid increased, particularly from America. In 1955 another development plan was launched and again very small funds were allocated to the agricultural sector, less than those allocated industry. As a result of this plan, making a living from agriculture became increasingly difficult (Afshar, 1985a: 60-62, Mohtadi, 1986; Mohtadi, 1990; Pesaran, 1985: 18-19).

In general, lack of capital investment in agriculture, exploitation of peasants by landlords and government officials, indebtedness, rural overpopulation, and insecurity in rural employment due to periodic redistribution of tenants, all had crippling effects on the welfare of peasantry, whose "social and health conditions were among the worse in the world" (Keddie, 2006: 116).

The Land Reform Project and its Impact on Migration

As noted, important causes of backwardness in the traditional sector were absentee landlordism together with strong political power, backed by law, where landlords took the bulk of agricultural surpluses to the cities. In the modern history of Iran, calls for the abolition of feudal controls, radical land reform, and modernization of agriculture can be traced back to a period before and during the Constitutional Revolution (1906-11) [12]. There were different trends of thought in secular, communist, and modern Islamist oppositions using different ideological frameworks. As a result, by the early 1960s, land reform was considered essential for the economic development of the country (Keddie, 1972). In response to internal and external pressures a land reform project was launched in 1963 as a form of structural change to the land ownership system in Iran. The project was carried out in three stages during the years 1963-1970. The first stage redistributed possessions of large absentee landlords whose land incorporated more than one village to tenants and sharecroppers who had rights to cultivation under the old land tenure system. Under the provisions of the program, orchards and mechanized farms with hired laborers that had developed at the expense of small subsistence farms were exempted from the reform. This first phase of reform covered only one-fifth of the total land and 20 percent of peasants. Agricultural laborers, called "*khwushneshins*", who according to the 1960 survey constituted 47.5 percent of the rural population, did not benefit from the reform and once more this deprived population, at the bottom of the rural socio-economic ladder, were discriminated against by law. The landless peasants had to work as agricultural laborers for new landlords and unemployed labor was assumed to be willing to migrate to cities to strengthen the country's selected industrial and manufacturing sectors (Afshar, 1985a; Ajami, 1976; Danesh, 1987; Keddie, 1972; Pesaran, 1985; and Razavi, 1992). They had no job security, no right to loans from agricultural banks, no life insurance from the government, and were reluctant to work for their co-villagers who had newly acquired land.

The land reform project, like any other modernization program of the Pahlavi state, was a top-down program ignoring traditional structures and methods of production, capacities, and techniques, and their potential for development. The approach was not to improve the existing system but to introduce modern capitalist commercial relations incompatible with the traditional structure of Iranian rural society (Schirazi, 1993: 7-23). For instance, traditional irrigation systems were destroyed by replacing them with new wells equipped with motor pumps or the construction of dams. The artificial irrigation did little to improve yields and the construction of dams benefited the urban sector by providing drinking water and electricity (Afshar, 1985a; Pesaran, 1985; Schirazi, 1993). The oil boom of the 1970s and revenue from it made the state independent and in lesser need of income from an agricultural sector which was considered old-fashioned. Government policies and programs such as promotion of cash crops and capitalist farming, strict price control on agricultural products beneficial to urban consumers and harmful for rural producers, and imports of large quantities of animal products, grain and rice from the United States, made it impossible for the majority of small scale farmers to make a modest living from the land (Friedl, 1981: 16).

Before the reforms, most villagers were alienated from land and water, the prime means of production. They were governed by the landlord-tenant relationship and dependent on the *kadkhoda* (headman—the landlords' representatives in the village), to administer their concerns with the landlord and urban administration (Ajami, 1976: 190-91; Craig, 1978, 143-44). Although implementation of the reform was meant to improve the overall economic situation of the country through modernizing a backward subsistence agricultural sector, its main objectives were political rather than economic development. Through the reform, firstly, the power of the landed aristocracy against the Shah was being eroded, and secondly, villagers who were oppressed socially, politically and economically by the landlords would become a class which the Shah could count as an ally (Craig, 1978, 141).

As reform moved on from its first stage, it became less effective and less beneficial to the villagers. In 1965, the second phase of reform gave landlords the right to keep a reasonable proportion of their most fertile lands with proximity to the market.[13] Some villagers, who had gained land in the first stage were immediately dispossessed from land ownership during the second phase of the reforms (Afshar, 1985a: 62-3; Ajami, 1976; Pesaran, 1985: 28-31; Craig, 1978). In practice, land reform stratified the formerly homogeneous villagers into two classes of landed and the landless. The latter occupied the lowest level on the social ladder. This socio-economic change was not just a material process, but also a moral one. The impact of change was felt not only through alterations in income and production, but also through the restructuring of identity and power relations. "Absentee landlordism" which was supposed to be abolished, was recreated in a new form by the land reform project. Moreover, instead of creating an ally in the peasantry class for the Shah, the project created a situation in which landless peasants felt hostility toward both the landed peasants and central government (Craig, 1978, 146).

Implementation of 1960s land reforms and decline of the landowners' power led to social stratification in villages, deterioration of the socio-economic situation of *khwushneshins*, and the destruction of traditional management system of soil and water and the participatory method of the cultivation that had developed under the various *boneh* systems with their inherent structures and functions of group formation, organizational leadership, division of labor, and individual members' duties and privileges[14]. Those who received land from the state were obliged to pay annual installments to government agents to legalize their ownership. Thus, because of the rapid fragmentation of land ownership and disintegration of the *boneh* systems, most villages lost self-sufficiency in traditional agricultural production and became importers of goods[15]. In some regions new landholders had to transfer their lands to the farm co-operative in order to modernize agricultural production. They could either sell their land to state-run co-operatives,[16] or became shareholders employed by the co-operative as agricultural laborers, receiving a proportion of the products, or simply migrate to the cities (Ajami, 1976: 200-3). Many case studies from different provinces as well as national agricultural censuses found a positive correlation between landlessness and migration. According to a calculation from the agricultural census of 1960-1974, Danesh (1987) shows that in 1960, 63 percent of rural residents held less than five hectares of land or were completely landless, occupying 19 percent of the land with an average of 2.60 hectares of land per household. In the same year, 79 percent of the land belonged to 37 percent of landowners. By 1974, the percentage of those who owned less than five hectares of land or remained landless had increased to 70.5 percent, occupying 15 percent of the total land with an average of 2.53 hectares per household. However the number of large landowners decreased from 36.9 percent to 29.5 percent, but their share of land increased to 85 percent.[17]

Land reforms and related policies and institutions led to increased social and income inequalities, marginalization of the peasantry, rural unemployment and underemployment. Therefore, the reform played a major role in motivating both landless and landed peasants, who found it difficult to cope with high costs and low profit levels from agriculture activities, to move to the edges of large cities. The early internal migrants were mostly men who migrated permanently or seasonally, leaving their families behind to take over the work previously performed by them. Men's rural-urban migration exacerbated gender disparity in rural areas and adversely affected the socio-economic status of rural women (Beck, 1978; Tabari, 1980; Afshar, 1985b; Hoodfar, 1993). During her research in a region near Esfahan, Touba (1980: 58-59) visited villages that were almost completely without young adult males and studies in northern Iran illustrated that the migration of men resulted in greater participation of women in non-traditional aspects of agriculture (Safai, 1978 cited in Touba, 1980: 59).

Apart from land reform related city-ward migration, overpopulation in rural areas, due mainly to the general improvements in health and hygiene within the country, which led to a reduction in the death rate without any change in the birth rate, was another push factor in rural areas. The amount of land under cultivation did not increase, but the surplus population did. As a result, a large proportion of this increasingly surplus population was left with the same amount, or even less land for production[18]. After 1970, the size of farming employment was reduced to the size of farming employment in 1956, despite the population growth[19].

Economic Opportunities in the Urban Areas and its Impact on Migration

Political and economic contexts in Iran were of crucial importance in underpinning "pull-push factors" in migration by creating economic distress in the socio-economic structure of rural sectors and economic opportunities in the rapidly growing urban economy, and thus the hope of better living conditions in the cities (Bayat, 1997: 24-29). Despite the rapid rate of economic growth in the country, disparity between rural and urban incomes was increasing (Afshar, 1985a: 59-68). As a result, most migration studies in Iran indicate that a person's decision to migrate is a response to employment opportunities both in the place of origin and the destination. However, in the case of Iran, like most developing countries, the push factors carry more weight.

Unequal income distribution not only resulted in socio-economic imbalances between rural and urban areas, but also created a severe regional disparity in income, health care services, and educational facilities which attracted migrants to the fast-growing and overcrowded cities with other occupational and entertainment opportunities (Hemmasi, 1974; Hossein-Zadeh-e Dalir, 1982; Jamali, 1985). In 1973 half of the country's doctors were located in Tehran, while in the rest of the country there was one doctor for every 5,011 people, and even fewer in remote provinces. In the same year, the literacy rate for Tehran was 76 percent, while that for the rest of the country was 38 percent, and less for remote areas (Pesaran, 1985:26). This also affected the changes in the composition of jobs in favor of higher paying professional occupations as the urban economy grew, requiring more training and education which increased the numbers of professional and technical jobs, particularly by 1976 (Ramin, 1988: 27-28). As a result, the annual number of rural-urban migrants increased by 78 percent during 1966-76 compared with the period 1956-66, and the urban population rose very sharply from 31.4 percent of the total in 1956 to 46.6 percent in 1976 (Pesaran, 1985:29). Three out of twenty-one provinces attracted nearly 90 percent of the total inter-province migrants in the two decades between 1956 and 1976 (Jamali, 1985). Moreover, in terms of the number of the net in-migrants, there were massive differences between these three provinces. The Central province, in which Tehran is located, attracted migrants from all over the country: more than 50 percent of the total in-migrants settled in Tehran, and the other cities of the Central province acted as temporary residencies for a large number of step-to-step migrants. By the mid-1970s, Tehran had some fifty slum and squatter communities and Tabriz had the highest ratio of slums and squatters in the country (Bayat, 1997: 26).

The primary pattern of migration in Iran was mostly male-dominated oscillating (circular) migration, usually temporary or seasonal laborers, who maintained their relationship with their origins by sending a portion of their wages to families left behind (Hoodfar, 1993: 10-13). Although this form of migration is still prominent in Southern Africa, South Asia and Latin America (Brydon, 1989:130), in Iran this pattern is prevalent among single migrants who tend to migrate further afield, whereas shorter distance migration is usually a "family migration" (Jamali, 1985).

Like elsewhere, migration in Iran has been a selective process dominated by the 20-24 age groups, who have had the highest percentage of migrants in all national censuses. Although on the whole the percentage of male migrants has been higher than female, the difference has not been great. For instance, in 1966, 13.6 percent of the male population and 12 percent of the female population were reported as migrants. In 1976, the number of male migrants increased by 2.1 percent, and female migrants by 1.4 percent. In 1976, within the age groups of 20-24 and 25-29, female migrants outnumbered male migrants in inter-*shahrestan*[20] (district) migration (Jamali, 1985: 103). However, men dominated inter-province migration.

Post-Revolutionary Migration

Extensive rural-urban migration continued after the 1979 revolution. From its early days, the Islamic Republic showed a strong commitment to rural development and structural change in the national economy by giving a pivotal position to agriculture in its first five-year development plan, aiming to reach self-sufficiency in agriculture by the year 1992, and reduce dependency on revenues from oil. Land reform became the main focus of the political agenda for the Provisional Revolutionary Government, and a series of land reform bills were introduced to parliament during 1981-82. However, the Council of Guardians rejected the bills on Islamic grounds and the land question remained unresolved[21]. This was mainly due to the friction between the Islamic Left with radical social views, who supported a type of Islamic socialism with state control over the economy, and conservative clerics who constituted the majority in the Guardian Council and were supportive of private property ownership[22]. The absence of radical land reform, one of the most important points in agriculture, therefore meant less land was distributed among the peasantry (Keddie, 2006: 256).

An early development in 1979 was the mobilization of urban-based volunteers to help farmers during the harvest season. This revolutionary action known as *Jahad-e Sazandegi,* the holy struggle for construction, soon took a broader and more official role as one of the revolutionary institutions[23] to improve rural conditions, providing not only economic incentives for the rural population to stay on the land, but also other aspects of the development. With the help of local people[24], many rural development projects such as road construction, telecommunications, building of schools and health clinics, providing clean drinking water and electricity supplies, irrigation projects, and small-scale mechanization of agriculture (which in some places led to diversification of crops and their sale in urban markets), were carried out. *Jahad* also provided hygiene and medical care[25], technical training, and services for diversification of rural occupational structure all of which improved the living conditions of the rural population[26]. Another important strategy was decentralization to give local administrations and community associations authority in policy and decision-making processes through active popular participation[27]. The initial purpose of taking advantage of the potential and capacities of local human resources was reduced to limited participation of the rural population in different stages of design, management, and maintenance of rural development policies and projects, which made the rural development projects less relevant to the needs and realities of rural people[28]. Overall, a multitude of developmental disparities left behind from the pre-revolutionary era in addition to fluctuations in the international oil market[29], Iraq's attack on Iran[30], population growth, economic sanctions against Iran, and most importantly the contradictory nature of the Islamic Republic's policies due to its failure in an indisputable land distribution, all had negative impacts on post-revolutionary development policies in general, and agricultural policies in particular. Although the Islamic Republic made successful steps in increasing agricultural outputs, these have been achieved through labor-intensive methods of production and a heavy budgetary increase for the agricultural sector, without technical changes and the development of productive methods in agriculture. Therefore, the agricultural sector in the post-revolutionary era experienced growth rather than development (Haghayeghi, 1990).

All these factors led to failure of the government's unrealistic goals for achieving self-sufficiency in agriculture and reversing or at least slowing the tide of city-ward migration. In parallel with changes in rural areas, villages were losing more population. In some cases, the migratory process accelerated as communications improved. Increased exchange between the countryside and cities as a result of rural development projects combined with insufficient production from the land led to more of a rural exodus. Between 1976 and 1986 the urban population increased by about 72 percent, with an annual growth rate of 5.5 percent. Between 1981 and 1984 migration was at its highest level, and Tehran received 1,500 newcomers each day. Other big cities, such as Mashhad, Isfahan, and Tabriz, had similar experiences (Bayat, 1997).

The early post-revolutionary migrants came to the big cities hoping to get free housing[31], jobs and other fruits of the revolution. Later on migrants were forced out of their places of origin by economic pressures (Bayat, 1997: 81-83, 136). A survey conducted by *Jahad-e Sazandegi* in 1984 indicated that over 85 percent of the peasants in the provinces of Isfahan and Hamadan left their birth places due to low income, an inadequate water supply, or unproductive land (cited in Bayat, 1997).

Migration in East Azarbaijan

According to the statistics and limited literature available, migration has been widespread in East-Azarbaijan. In 1956, of the total population of the province, 50 percent were involved in agriculture and 19 percent in manufacturing (Hemassi, 1974: 89-90). Almost three-quarters of the population were living in rural areas and one-quarter in urban ones. In 1971 the province's population was still mostly concentrated in rural areas and the agricultural sector. In the 1996 census, however, 60 percent were living in urban areas.

The city of Tabriz, the fourth largest city in the country, due to its strategic position as a political, economic, administrative, educational, industrial and trading centre, has been a destination for massive in-migration. Figures 3.1 and 3.2, showing the population of Tabriz over five decades indicate a rapid growth in the urbanization process. In 2006, the city had 5.5 times more people than it had in 1956, and the most growth was between 1976 and 1986 with a 62 percent increase.

Figure 3.1. Population of Tabriz between 1956-2006

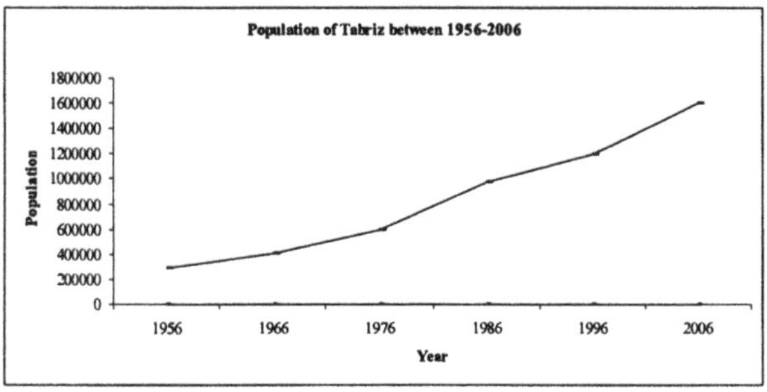

Sources: Hemmassi (1974); Jamali (1985);National Censuses of Population and Housing, the Whole Country (1991; 1996; 2007)[32].

Figure 3.2. Percentage of Population Growth of Tabriz between 1956-2006

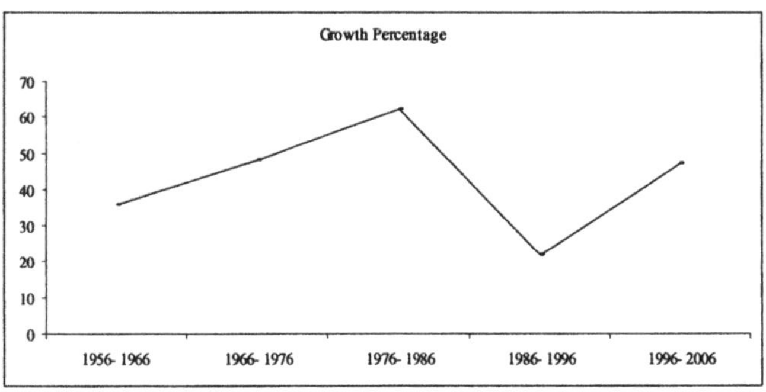

In 1984 illegal night time construction in the squatter settlements of Tabriz was seen by the city authorities as a major threat that had to be stopped (Bayat, 1997). In the period between 1986-1996, that had lowest growth in terms of migration, 161,395 people migrated to the *Shahrestan* of Tabriz or moved within it, of whom 61 percent were male and 39 percent female. Migration was highest amongst the group aged 20 to 29 years. The most commonly available source of information about internal migration is the Population and Housing Census data, which is carried out by the Statistical Centre of Iran (SCI) every ten years[33]. However, there is no separate data for the city of Tabriz, and no data available on the intra-*shahrestan* level, to show the volume of the rural-urban migration within the *shahrestan* and the city of Tabriz. Instead, data has been provided on the inter-*shahrestan* level. Information has been collected based on the place of residence before the census, and the age tables are designed separately for rural and urban areas and for men and women. During the fieldwork, efforts to obtain access to existing local data and information, published or unpublished, in order to estimate female rural migrants in the city level were fruitless, as such data does not exist. However, according to the 1996 census, 90 percent of the urban population of the *Shahrestan* were living in Tabriz, and it can be deduced that most of the migrants' destination is the city of Tabriz.

The comparison between previous place of residence and current one during census collection shows that 24.2 percent had migrated from rural areas to urban ones; 63.7 percent had gone from urban to urban ones, often to more important centres; 1.94 percent went from rural to rural areas; and interestingly, 9.07 percent made a city to village migration during the 10 years before the 1996 census[34]. This village directed migration might be explained by relative improvements in some rural areas resulting from the rural development projects after the revolution[35]. Distribution of migrants in terms of residency in the Tabriz district also shows that the greatest number (14.83 percent) had entered the S*hahrestan* or moved within it one year before the census, and the lowest number (3 percent), had moved nine years before the census, which indicated the continuation of population movement to or within the S*hahrestan*. However, the most interesting point is that 18.27 percent of migrants had migrated to rural areas in less than a year before the collection of the national census[36].

According to 1996 Population and Housing Census data, the population of S*hahrestan-e* Tabriz was 1,486,509, constituting 44.7 percent of the population of East Azarbaijan. Table 3.1 and Figure 3.3 indicate the population of this province and its distribution in rural and urban areas, and in the *Shahrestan-e* Tabriz and the city of Tabriz[37].

Table 3.1. Population of East Azarbaijan and its distribution in rural and urban areas (1996 census)

Population	n.	% of the province population
Population of the Province	3,325,540	100%
Resident in urban areas	2,004,484	60%
Resident in rural areas	1,320,788	40%
Resident in *Shahrestan*-e Tabriz	1,486,509	45%
Resident in Tabriz city	1,191,043	36%

Source: National Census of Population and Housing: Detailed Findings of the Whole Country and Shahrestan-e Tabriz: 1385 (1996).

Figure 3.3. Population of East Azarbaijan and its distribution in rural and urban areas (1996 census)

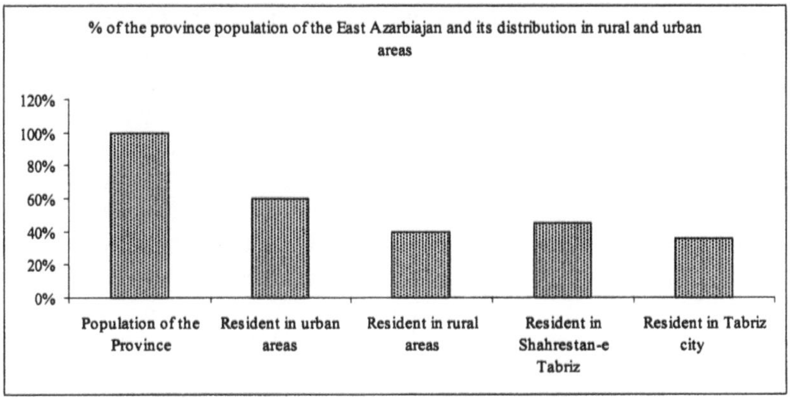

Table 3.2 and Figure 3.4 show the population of the *Shahrestan-e* Tabriz and its distribution in rural and urban areas, and the city of Tabriz, according to the Iranian National Census (1996).

Table 3.2. The Population of the *Shahrestan*-e Tabriz and its distribution in rural and urban areas (1996 census)

Population	n.	%
Population of *Shahrestan-e* Tabriz	1,486,509	100%
Resident in urban areas of the *Shahrestan*	1,304,584	88%
Resident in rural areas of the *Shahrestan*	181,925	12%
Resident in the city of Tabriz	1,191,043	80%

Source: National Census of Population and Housing: Detailed Findings of the whole Country and Sharestan-e Tabriz: 1385 (1996).

Figure 3.4. The Population of the *Shahrestan*-e Tabriz and its distribution in rural and urban areas (1996 census)

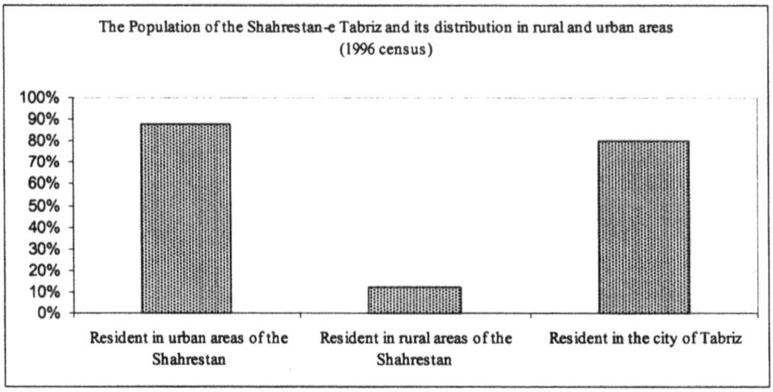

Table 3.2 shows that of the residential population in the *Shahrestan*, 80 percent live in Tabriz. The remaining 20 percent of the urban population is distributed between the other eight cities of the *Shahrestan*. The low percentage of rural population in this region may be attributed to two factors. One is that some rural areas were re-classified as urban ones in the latest administrative divisions of the province due to their demographic growth; the other is the migration of peasants to cities, particularly to Tabriz. Given the population of Tabriz[38] the second seems more likely, particularly when bearing in mind that more than 90 percent of the urban population in the *Shahrestan* was living in Tabriz alone.

Investigations of early migration to Tabriz reveal that the negative impact of the 1963 land reform on landless peasants resulted in heavy out-migration (Hossain Zadeh-e Dalir, 1982 and Jamali, 1985). East Azarbaijan was the first province to which the project was applied. This caused several economic and social problems for those who did not benefit from the project but also lost access to rural employment[39]. Disparity between urban and rural areas in services and facilities was huge. For instance, the 1976 National Census of the East Azarbaijan indicates that 63 percent and 81 percent of residential units in the urban areas had piped water and electricity, while this percentage for rural areas was only 4 percent and 9 percent respectively. Rapid industrialization and increased building construction in the domestic sector of Tabriz, on the other hand, created demand for unskilled laborers which stimulated a large-scale movement of the rural population to the city in search of work and a better standard of living than that available in their place of origin.

To estimate net female rural-urban migration in 1996, access to two successive censuses (1986 and 1996) was needed to be able to use the Census Survival Ratio (CSR) formula[40]. The formula was applied by Jamali (1985) to estimate net rural-urban migration in East Azarbaijan. However, since the geographical boundary of the *Shahrestan* changed between the two successive censuses of 1986 and 1996, this estimation was not possible[41].

Densely Populated Slum Areas in Tabriz

As discussed in the review chapter, migrants often live in slums and shanty towns, and migrants to Tabriz are no exception. Slums and squatter settlements in Tabriz are located in the northern (mountainous region) and southern fringes of the city, and have different geographical characteristics. They are located on undesirable land, and in terms of infrastructure, urban services, and quality of houses do not enjoy good urban standards[42]. Although an exact figure for the number of slum dwellers is not available, according to the latest statements of the city authorities in 2000 the population of the northern and southern fringes was about 400,000 people, approximately one-third of the city's population, representing 70,000 to 75,000 households with an average family size of 5.8 persons. This can be compared with 1995, when the slum population was about 310,000 people, with around 45,000 households and an average family size of 6.5 persons, forming about 20 to 25 percent of the city's population. Further back, in 1982, this percentage was about 7.5 percent of the city's population[43].

Although there are some scattered slums in different parts of the city, there are 5 major densely populated squatter areas in Tabriz. As shown in Table 3.3, the northern fringe is divided into four locations: *Daraeichi, Gorbani, Selab, Hydarabad-Dadashabad,* and in the southern fringe there is one location, *Yanuog.*

Table 3.3. Squatter areas of Tabriz with estimated population and household number, 1995[44]

Location	Population	Households
Daraeichi	61,587	8,714
Gorbani	93,395	13,516
Selab	42,625	6,436
Hydarabad-Dadashabad	46,458	7,225
Yanuog	65,516	9,119

Source: Tables 5-11 of Tabriz University Research, conducted in 1995.

The northern settlements are mostly occupied by migrants from the rural areas of Ahar *Shahrestan*, a mountainous area where socio-economic conditions are the worst in East Azarbaijan. Environmental, physical and ecological factors such as water shortages, soil infertility, and harsh climate all adversely affect agricultural production and undermine the subsistence economy. The remoteness of the villages from prosperous centers, and lack of public, educational and social facilities as a consequence of uneven distribution have also reinforced out-migration in this region (Jamali, 1985). Seventy-nine percent of the northern fringe dwellers in Hossain Zadeh's study (1982) were rural migrants who lived in densely populated slums and squatter areas. More than half of them had migrated to the city during the post-land reform and pre-revolutionary decade of 1963-1973. For the majority, the lack of effective social services and other means of supporting themselves, such as access to land, were the main reasons for migration. Only a small number were concerned about the pull factors of the city (Hossain Zadeh-e Dalir, 1982, Table 14). The southern fringe, close to the industrial zone of the city, has attracted rural as well as urban migrants from the southern districts of East Azarbaijan province (Jamali, 1985).

In the 1980s, the Iran-Iraq war was instrumental in accelerating migration to Tabriz. Information about female migrants in Tabriz is almost non-existent, except in some research into the squatter settlements of Tabriz, in which Hossain Zadeh-e Dalir (1982) allocated a small amount of space to women. Two tables in his work (57 and 59) indicate that migrant women were engaged in carpet weaving, but other lines of enquiry did not offer any indications for motivations of women, their role in the process of decision-making for migration, or in other forms of economic activity. The main focus of Hossain Zadeh's and subsequent research by Jamali, 1985 concentrated on household as unites and male motivation, units was equated with the concept of the household. Jamali's study particularly concentrated on inter-province migration in Iran with specific reference to East-Azarbaijan Province.

Notes

1. Eastern Azarbaijan is one of the four Turkic speaking provinces of Iran. North west Iran comprises three provinces: Eastern Azarbaijan, with its capital in Tabriz; Western Azarbaijan, with its capital in Uromiyeh; and Ardabil, whose capital is also called Ardabil. A fourth Iranian province, Zanjan, with a capital city of the same name, also has a dominant Azari population. Azarbaijanis/Azaris in Iran are the largest ethnic minority group, constituting up to 25 percent of the population, between 16 and 20 million people. They are mainly *Shi'a* Muslim, well integrated into Iranian society, and well represented at all levels of political, military, intellectual, as well as religious hierarchies. Azarbaijanis are the largest non-Persian ethnic group, comprising about a quarter of the total population, with close economic and cultural ties with Persian speakers. Those who are scattered throughout many other parts of the country

often form a strong middle class. For further information see The Hutchinson Softback Encyclopedia (1996), CIA World Factbook, and Encyclopedia of Iranica.

2. The *shahrestan* of Tabriz is one of the fourteen administrative districts of East Azarbaijan, located in the west of the province. Tabriz district is divided into three sections, each having three cities. The city of Tabriz is not only the largest and most important city in the province, but also in Iran. Tabriz district, therefore, includes nine cities, fourteen rural neighborhoods, and one hundred and sixty habitable villages.

3. Landlordism in Iran has been always different from landed aristocracy in Europe in the sense that land is transmitted in its entirety from one generation to the next. This is partially due to the political and dynastical changes in the country so that often many former landowners lost their lands and new ones were created with every new ruling dynasty; and partially due to Islamic inheritance law according to which land is inevitably subdivided. For detailed analysis of this process in Iran from Islamic times down to the mid-20th century, see Part I of A. K. S. *Lambton's Landlord and Peasant in Persia: A Study of Land Tenure and Land Revenue Administration* (London, New York: Oxford University Press, 1953).

4. The peasant proprietors were often restricted to the less fertile land and more remote parts of the country, where crop failures were more common. The living from these lands was often inadequate and families needed supplementary income from men's casual labor in towns, women's weaving or other activities, or as loans from money lenders, which in some cases led to the loss of the land (Lambton, 1953: 275-280).

5. For detailed information, see Amir Ismail Ajami: The *Boneh* System In Iran's Rural Society. *Iran Nameh* (Vol. 13, Issue 4: Special Issues on Civil Society in Iran, 1995) published by the Foundation for Iranian Studies.

6. The founder of the Pahlavi dynasty (1925-1979) in Iran.

7. In Iran, there have been several important tribes with very strong and influential leaders in different parts of the country, who mostly live in a semi-nomadic way. Reza Shah regarded the pastoralist societies as an anachronism. To reduce the political power of tribal leaders as well as to serve his modernization program, he introduced the settlement/tribal policy to convert the tribesmen into agriculturalists. He used forced prevention of annual migration of the tribes and cruel suppression of tribal uprising, and the exile of tribal leaders. However, the policy was not successful: it had an adverse impact on the economy of the country due to heavy losses of livestock. The policy also was not able to integrate the tribal system into the sociopolitical structure of the country for the benefit of semi-nomadic people, leading to their poverty and hostility between them and settled people. For detailed information, see "Chapter XV: Tribal Areas" of A. K. S. Lambton's *Landlord and Peasant in Persia:* A *Study of Land Tenure and Land Revenue Administration* (1953: 283- 294).

8. *Ulama* are often referred to as the higher ranks of scholars of Islam and *Sharia* who have been trained in different fields of Islamic studies for several years. The power of *Shia* religious leaders increased from the beginning of the Safavid dynasty (1502-1736) which established the greatest Iranian empire and made *Shia* Islam the official religion throughout Iran. Their power, which was often exercised independently of the government, was challenged and weakened by Reza Shah (1925-1941) and his secular modernization program.

9. The main export-oriented part of Iran in the 19th century was southern Iran where the merchants, landlords and officials found trade with British India more profitable than local commerce. At the opening of the Suez Canal in 1869, merchants and landlords had enough economic power to extend control over the bulk of agricultural land in the region, transforming the agricultural economy from one based on staple crops to one based largely on cash crops, particularly opium. Opium cultivation made the situation of the villagers and urban poor deteriorate so that by 1880, neither the villagers not central government could put any restrictions on its production. For a detailed study, see Roger T. Olson (1981: 173-189): "Persian Gulf Trade and the Agricultural Economy of Southern Iran in the Nineteenth Century," in *Modern Iran: The Dialectics of Continuity and Change*, edited by Michael Bonine and Nikkie R. Keddie. New York: State University of New York Press.

10. Since ancient times, the carpet industry has always made up the bulk of Iranian manufacturing exports.

11. The Iranian Prime minister, who in 1951 nationalized the Anglo-Iranian oil company, the forerunner of BP, which had a monopoly on Iranian oil.

12. For detailed information on opinions and thinking on the question of land and agriculture in Iran, see Schirazi, (1993: 34-64), *Islamic Development Policy: The Agrarian Question in Iran*. Translated by P. J. Ziess-Lawrence. Boulder & London: Lynne Reinner Publishers.

13. During the second phase of the reform, many landlords found legal ways to keep their lands by transferring their ownership to their family, relatives and dependants.

14. Through an examination of case studies of various types of *boneh*, Ajami (1995) argues that the absence of landowners and/or their agents generally played a significant role in development, management and control of the *boneh* system. The implementation of land reform and rapid fragmentation led to the disintegration of the *boneh* and a drastic decline of managerial control in village communities.

15. Despite a relatively low level of productivity, most Iranian villages prior to land reform were self-sufficient and generated around 36 percent of the country's GNP, providing employment for more than 75 percent of the economically active population. During period the 1956-1976, the contribution of the agricultural sector to GNP declined to 15 percent, and to 9.6 percent by 1978. For detailed information, see Danesh (1987: 72-81): *Rural Exodus and Squatter Settlements in the Third World: Case of Iran.* Lanham: University of Press of America.

16. The state-run cooperatives penetrated the market economy into rural areas, benefiting agribusiness enterprises and large landlords by providing interest-free loans. During the fifth development plan, only 10-15 percent of peasants received small loans, which were used to bring their living conditions close to subsistence level. The ratio of unequal distribution of state sponsored funds was about 400:1. For detailed information see Part I: "The Agrarian Question Prior to the 1979 Revolution" of Schirazi, 1993; Danesh, 1987: 72-81.

17. Danesh, 1987, Table 4.3: patterns of land distribution among lower and upper rural classes based on households and land size in Iran, 1960-1974. The table has been adopted and calculated based on the 1960-1974 Agricultural censuses.

18. See Ajami, 2005 for a per capita decrease in arable land, which covers a period up to 1996. Based on calculation from data on the rural population provided in

the 1956 and 1996 censuses and on the arable land area reported in the First National Census of Agriculture, 1961, and 1993 Agricultural Census, Ajami shows an overall per capita arable land decline of an estimated 24 percent.

19. A comparison between National censuses of 1956 and 1996 shows that the percentage of the population age 10 and older engaged in agriculture has declined from 76.6 percent to 49 percent (Danesh, 1987: 17).

20. In Iran each *shahrestan* is a smaller administrative division of a Province, which in turn is divided into many sections, cities, rural areas, and villages.

21. For detailed information on Reform of the Land Tenure, Land Reform in Islamic Law, see Haghayeghi (1990), and for Problems of Agricultural Management after the revolution, see Schirazi, 1993: 169-259.

22. The conservative clerics, some of whom were land owners themselves, were also opponents of the Shah's land reform project in the 1960s. For detailed information on different positions of various Islamic groups on the land question and its redistribution including that of Ayatollah Khomeini, see Haghayeghi, 1990: 38-44; Schirazi, 1993: 45-64.

23. One of the negative consequences of the establishment of revolutionary institutes such as *Jahad-e Sazandegi* in parallel with other Ministries was the dualistic administration, having the same or similar tasks in different areas, particularly in agriculture. In 1991, *Jahad-e Sazandegi* was awarded ministerial status, and as a result, this new ministry overtook some duties of the Ministry of Agriculture. However, in December 2000, the two Ministries *Jahad-e Sazandegi* and Agriculture combined together to form the Ministry of *Jahad-e* Agriculture to avoid deficiencies incurred by this dualism. For detailed information, see Schirazi, 1993: 147-161, and the Ministry of *Jahad-e* Agriculture's website: www.maj.ir/english/Main/Default.asp

24. Participatory methods became one of the highest priorities in rural development policies to empower rural people and take advantage of their knowledge, potentialities, and capacities. To encourage active participation of rural people, different structures of governance such as Rural Islamic Councils, Co-help Houses, Construction Groups, Rural Youth Club, and Cooperatives for Natural Resources were created to decentralize rural development to the people themselves. For detailed information on the roles and duties of these different governance bodies, see Aligholi Heidary's paper presented in the Seminar on Rural Life Improvement for Community Development, held by the Asian Productivity Organization in Japan, 22-26 April 2002.

25. In *Modern Iran: Roots and Results of Revolution*, Keddie states that: improved primary health care even in remote rural areas led to decline in infant mortality "from among the highest in the Middle East to among the lower" (Keddie, 2006: 288).

26. By 2000, over 70,000 of rural roads were built compared to 8,000 before the revolution; over 28,000 of villages had access to electricity; and 34,000 access to safe drinking water, compared to 4,327 and 12,000 villages in 1979 respectively. Over 75 percent of rural areas had, by 2000, access to health services. For further information on rural improvement, see Moosavi Ghahderijani, 2003: 99-102. For transformation in rural life in the past few decades, in terms of social, political, and economic foundations, see Ajami 2005.

27. Rural Islamic Councils were set up to replace the traditional rural management institutions that were weakened and mostly broken after the 1960s land reform project.

28. Moosavi Ghahderijani argues that: "the Ministry of *Jahad* in a tendency towards using scientific methods, statistics, estimations and predictions lost touch with what made it so successful in the first stages. People's participation became limited to financial contributions and manual labor. Projects were implemented at a fast rate, but with less and less consideration for the living conditions of rural people" (Moosavi Ghahderijani, 2003: 101).

29. Oil has been Iran's primary export product. However, in a period between 1977 through to 1988, Iranian oil exports and income show a persistent fall from $23.6 billion in 1977 to only $5.9bn in 1986 and $9bn in 1988. For detailed information see table 3.2: Iranian Oil Exports and Revenues, 1976-1988, adopted from Iran's Statistical Yearbook, in Schirazi, 1993: 77.

30. The costs of the imposed eight year war were enormous. According to an official reconstruction plan, 750 villages were destroyed, 3 cites completely destroyed and at least another 3 cities were badly damaged. Damage to the large oil refinery was estimated to be around $9bn. Schirazi, 1993 has extracted some financial figures from Iranian periodical newspapers and UN reports. For further details see: Schirazi, 1993: 80-82.

31. Excessive and arbitrary land seizure of large estates, national forests and pastures by peasants, landlords, and tribal leaders immediately after the revolution, mostly through peaceful mass actions and occasionally through violent mass quarrel was not confined to rural areas. In the major cities, particularly in Tehran, empty buildings whose owners had escaped from Iran during the revolution were also occupied by poor, deprived people, mostly migrants. For further details on land confiscation and Islamic government's policies in dealing with the issue, see: Schirazi, 1993: 169-232; Haghayeghi, 1990: 36-45. On housing issues in urban areas, particularly Tehran, see Bayat's *Street Politics, Poor People's Movements in Iran* (1997).

32. Statistical information in this book is mainly based on the National Census of Population and Housing, and Country's Statistical Yearbook. Most of the information for the City of Tabriz has been extracted from the Country's Statistical Yearbook, and the statistics for the *Shahrestan* level come from the Detailed Finding of the East Azarbaijan Province, *Shahrestan'e* Tabriz of the National Censuses.

33. Since, during my fieldwork in 2001 I only had access to the 1996 national census, the statistical information does not include subsequent years, unless otherwise indicated according to smaller surveys.

34. Information has been extracted from National Census of Population and Housing 1375 (1996), (*Shahrestan*-e Tabriz Summary): Table 5: Migrants entered in the last 10 years according to previous residential place and age.

35. According to some informants for this book, whose villages were close to the city of Tabriz and enjoyed from educational and health services, migration from those villages has not only decreased, but they also were aware of some counter-migration back to their villages. See analysis chapters.

36. 89 percent of migration to or within *Shahrestan* includes people resident in urban areas compared to 11 percent in rural areas. However, the interesting point is that according to the 1996 Census, in the last three years before collection of the census, there was steady and continuous increase among migrants to rural areas year after year: 12.54 percent (3 years before the 1996 census collection); 13.74 percent (2 years before), 15.67 percent (1 year before), and 18.27 percent (less than a year).

These percentages were greater for both the migrants who entered or moved within the *Shahrestan*, and the migrants residing in urban areas. Percentages for the whole district were 11.51 percent, 12.37 percent, 14.83 percent, and 13.32 percent respectively; and for urban areas 11.39 percent, 12.20 percent, 14.73 percent, and 12.70 percent. This comparison shows that if the living conditions are suitable for the countryside population or if the rural development projects have a people-oriented focus and participatory approach, peasants can be encouraged to stay or even to return to their place of origin.

37. The statistical information in this book is based on surveys carried out every ten years by the Statistical Centre of Iran (SCI), recognized as the country's most reliable source of statistics. SCI is part of the Planning and Budget Organization (PBO).

38. Apart from the role of migration, natural population growth due to a fall in the mortality rate and a relatively high fertility rate, particularly among migrants, is another factor in the population growth in Tabriz.

39. Ajami (2005) argues that the land reform program of the 1960s and the 1979 revolution represent primary turning points in rural transformation. The former, through intense state intervention, significantly destroyed the traditional sharecropping system. Peasant uprisings and the forcible occupation of large estates during revolutionary upheavals in 1977-1979 and after the revolution, and the agrarian policies of the post-revolutionary state led to the demise of the urban agricultural bourgeoisie and empowerment of the peasants. For socioeconomic and political transformations of Iranian agriculture and rural society, see Ajami, 2005. He traced the patterns of socio-economic change of one village over a 35-year period, providing a longitudinal study within the general conceptual framework of agrarian transition theory.

40. The technique was used for the first time by the United Nations, 1970, in the Methods of Measuring Internal Migration.

41. According to the 1986 census, the *Shahrestan-e* Tabriz was divided into 6 sections, encompassing greater geographical areas. However, in the later administrative changes, three sections were separated from the *Shahrestan*. Therefore, any comparison between two censuses in terms of population movement within or to the *Shahrestan* would have provided incorrect data.

42. Residential units in these areas have been built on weak soil, steep hills or even rocks. The inappropriateness of the land, in addition to low quality building materials, often without legal housing permission, and therefore without professional and technical supervision, makes these houses vulnerable, particularly to natural disasters such as earthquakes and gales.

43. University of Tabriz Report: 1995: 222.

44. I did not have access to detailed breakdowns of population and number of households for the 400,000 migrants which the city authorities claimed were residents in 2000.

Chapter 4

Methodology

As the main aim of this study was to understand women's experience of migration and their economic activity, it was logical to use feminist methodology. Thus, this chapter first describes the theoretical and practical issues regarding the production of knowledge and how research should be conducted from the feminist perspective which informed the study. After this, the method and practical details of gathering data and accessing informants is presented.

The Feminist Critique of Epistemological Issues

Questions about the production of knowledge from a feminist perspective and the analysis of a sex/gender system described in terms of "patriarchy," "misogyny," "sex-roles," "subordination of and discrimination against women" led feminists to argue that there is a distinctive feminist method of conducting social research (Oakley, 1974; Elshtain, 1981; Harding, 1983). This perspective, however, developed historically through continuous criticism of traditional social science methods and the original feminist orthodoxy became a complex area of methodology and epistemology (Maynard, 1994: 10). Changes in feminist personal and social consciousness emerged from the interaction of academic and activist approaches to the situations and problems of women during the women's liberation movement in the early 1970s (Millman and Kanter, 1987: 30). Friedan's *Feminist Mystique* (1963) and Millet's *Sexual Politics* (1971) played important roles in unveiling "the ideological nature of the 'values,' 'norms,' and 'beliefs' concerning women's role and the relations between the sexes which was taken for granted" (Smith, 1979; 136). This ideological unveiling made some early scholars critical of male-oriented concepts, methods and theories in mainstream studies. In almost all disciplines women had been silenced, marginalized and misrepresented, but sociology was the focus of attack for its empiricist-driven epistemology (Oakley, 1974; Smith, 1987 and 1979; Harding, 1983: 314-17). Early feminist critiques primarily addressed methodological issues and the way sociological theories were applied to women as a social group, which made them invisible either by omitting or distorting their experiences. Epistemological issues were also considered important. The main argument was that pre-defined and "taken for granted" assumptions in sociology do not provide an objective, reliable and universal ground for knowledge. Rather, they produce gendered and biased knowledge by fitting women's experiences into pre-existing sociological categories leading to over-generalization or misinterpretation (Oakley, 1974, 1981; Graham, 1983; Jayaratne and Stewart, 1991). Therefore, the external validity of accepted methodologies and theories in social sciences that underlined the importance of the researcher's gender in terms of access to knowledge were questioned by female social scientists. This phenomenon is particularly important in sex-segregated societies, where due to exclusion of men from women's world, access to knowledge is more limited (Altorki and El-Solh, 1988: 4-5). The existence of male dominance or the "sex/gender system," like race and class based variables, was seen as an "organic social variable" penetrating into all social institutions and structuring every aspect of social relations, actions and thoughts in both domestic and public arenas of life (Smith, 1979, 1987; Harding, 1983: 311-14). It was argued therefore that women's experience should be understood and interpreted from the perspective of feminism (Smith, 1979, 1987) or what Harding calls "the feminist standpoint" (Harding, 1986: 26-27; Harding 1987b: 184-86).

It was also argued that sociology has a socio-spatial dimension due to focus on public, official and visible spheres of social life, rather than the private, unofficial and invisible spheres, which are largely populated by women (Millman and Kanter, 1987: 32-33; Oakley, 1974; Graham, 1983). Focus on the public sphere produces distorted pictures of women's lives and experiences in sociology. For instance, excluding the private sphere from both the sociology of the family and the sociology of work led to the omission of an analysis of housework (Oakley, 1974). The two worlds of public and private, and thus the basis of men's and women's knowledge and experience, were not considered equally. The public world, which is constituted by men, remains authoritative over the women's world, which stands in a dependent and subordinate relationship (Smith, 1979; 1987: 86).

Sexual and spatial dimensions of disciplines were seen to have their equivalent within language in terms of "dominant" and "muted" modes of expression (Graham, 1983: 135). Since the experiences or actions of the muted group remain unexplained or un-verbalized, significant aspects of their experiences remain not only unspoken but also unspeakable due to the lack of a conceptual framework (Graham, 1983: 135). Thus, feminists sought a research approach to maximize the ability of the researcher to explore the experiences of women's lives: "the world that emerges through the words of women is a world fundamentally different from the world prescribed by the 'pervasive' male discourse"(Mernissi, 1984: 4). Feminists emphasized the importance of listening to the language of silence, and an open-ended exploration of women's own descriptions and accounts of their experiences in order to see how they are subordinated, how their world is organized and to what extent their world is different from that of men (Graham, 1983: 143). This means the legitimization of the subjectivity, body and emotions associated with femininity as an empirical and theoretical source of knowledge (Maynard, 1994: 21).

In this perspective, quantitative research methods, enumerative measurements, were seen as a male type of knowledge, though they acknowledged that quantitative analysis significantly contributed to the feminist understanding of gender issues such as violence against women, the feminization of poverty and women's lack of progress in achieving equality with men in paid work (Maynard, 1994: 13). The solution for these methodological and epistemological problems was suggested to be a "feminist empiricism" (Harding, 1986; 1987a), which by removing a sexist bias, and adding feminist values to the research process, could produce value-free and unbiased knowledge regardless of the social identity of the researcher (Harding, 1986: 24-26; Harding 1987b: 182-84). However, some feminists argued that objectivity, which in the social sciences was considered necessary for avoiding subjective bias in the researcher, could, in its impersonal approach to subject matter, lead to an exploitative relationship between the researchers and researched (Smith, 1987: 88; Oakley, 1981).

The survey method, one of the dominant research methods in social science, particularly in family and household studies, was criticized as an unsatisfactory source of data. This is especially so when the aims of a study are sociological understanding of women's experiences, because this method deals with individuals in terms of equivalence and rationality, while women often have different and unequal positions (Graham, 1983: 132-41). The family, in household surveys, is considered as the unit of social stratification, an autonomous and self-functioning entity, in which the members are attached to men, and not made up of individuals with different gender and generational characteristics. Differences are, therefore, highlighted between families rather than within them, and as a result, inequalities in the distribution of resources and responsibilities between members of the family are neglected (Oakley, 1974; Graham, 1983: 139).

By doing feminist research *with*, *by* and *for* women in the 1970s, one of the hallmarks of feminism was to add women to sociological analysis in order to universalize their experiences and validate their subjective situation in society. Their research used qualitative methods with which they could generate useful knowledge about women through their experiences, "though the qualitative methods are all an integral part of social science research, not specific to or created by feminism" (Maynard, 1994: 14). Feminist criticism was based on the premise that there is no one reality in the world, there are different experientially based world views and that these multiple constructions may all be equally valid (Smith, 1987: 93; Glucksmann, 1994: 159), but they do not necessarily reflect those of society in general (Altorki and El-Solh, 1988: 4). The social identity of the researcher, knowing a socially constructed reality from within its own context and not from a privileged location, was also seen as an important factor in the creation of knowledge (Kelly *et al.* 1994). Although sociological research necessarily requires social relations, sociology recovers only one part of these relations: it views knowledge as if it "stood all by itself and of itself" and does not provide a place for the presence and the experience of the researcher as knower and discoverer of other's experience (Smith, 1987: 92).

Thus, as a result of the theoretical division between the public and private domains and the methodological division between "quantitative" and "qualitative" methods, an in-depth face to face interview and a more personal approach involving direct contact with women was considered by feminists as the best method to acquire knowledge about women (Oakley, 1974 and 1981). This also reduces power relations to some extent, when the interviewer can slip out of the role of researcher and share information about herself and her experiences (Oakley, 1981; El-Solh, 1988). The interview method in classical methodological textbooks was criticized for using a masculine imagery of "mechanical and psychoanalytic" paradigms in which objectivity, detachment and hierarchy were highly valued. It was seen as a one-way process without personal meaning in terms of social interaction in which both parties in an interview are "depersonalized participants in the research process whose role is merely data-producing and data-collecting particularly when the interviewer is not the researcher" (Oakley, 1981: 35-37). Feminists were also critical of the hierarchal relation within the interview process which creates a dominant and subordinate position insofar as "the interviewer utilizes non-directive comments to encourage the respondent to reveal whatever truth the research has been set up to uncover particularly when the interviewer is the researcher" (Oakley, 1981: 37).

Rethinking Feminist Methodology

Attempts to establish a non-hierarchal relationship between interviewers and interviewees became a feminist research strategy. Respondents were encouraged to consider the researcher as a friend and to understand the goals of the research project (Oakley, 1981). Although this approach was "so useful in their early work when women were more invisible in research topics, it gradually developed into a concrete principle against which all feminist research should be judged" (Maynard, 1994: 12). It became "a form of political practice in feminist research method which if it is achieved successfully, it would count as being or acting feminist" (Glucksmann, 1994: 150-51). Another problem with feminist research was its continuous and intentional ignorance of "women's differences" and emphasis on their socially constructed oppression "in order to create an illusion of solidarity and sisterhood." (Kelly *et al.* 1994: 31) Thus, "the category of women in feminist writing appeared to be all white, middle-class, First World women only whose oppression was treated to be single, determined and universal" (Stanley and Wise, 1990: 21-22).

Classical feminist research concentrated its focus on "feminist research practice," "the position from which distinctively feminist research questions might be asked, and the political and ethical issues involved in the research process" (Maynard, 1994: 14). Since the mid-1980s, however, major developments have emerged in epistemological and methodological areas of the feminist discipline. These developments are indebted to the accessibility of conceptual language as a result of widely disseminated writings of feminist scholars, as well as post-structuralist, deconstructionist and post-modernist theoretical writings (Stanley and Wise, 1990: 25; De Groot and Maynard, 1993: 2). Three interwoven aspects of research in both traditional social science and feminist approaches to research are: "method," techniques of data collecting; "methodology," a theoretical framework of how to conduct research and how to apply the general structure of theories to the research process in order to produce an undistorted knowledge; and "epistemology," theory of knowledge. A lack of clarity in these three aspects has been problematic in terms of feminist methodology and epistemology, as they tend to be confused methodologically (Harding, 1987a: 2-3). The focus of the feminist debate on methods and dynamics of the traditional research process led them to reconsider many aspects of their epistemology, which came to be known as the "feminist critique" of the social sciences. But feminist methodology is still identified with the ethical questions and feminist values posed by early feminists, which were leading to "a feminist methodology without any particular feminist methods" (Jayaratne and Stewart, 1991: 92).

Although concentrating on women or including them in feminist research was the main feature of feminists' academic research, "which women" became a fundamental feminist question in the mid 1980s, both in terms of the researcher and the researched (Kelly *et al.* 1994: 28-29). "Diversity" among women, was seen to have two corollaries of *differentiation* and *variation* (De Groot and Maynard, 1993: 150-51). *Differentiation* refers to the fact that women's lives are not always structured in the same way; rather there are dissimilarities as well as similarities in their lives, both of which need to be taken into account. Women do not all share the same problems and difficulties. *Variation,* on the other hand, refers to different experiences of women which are structured in similar ways; or to women's similar responsibilities such as motherhood, but with different social attributes such as class, race, religion, nationality, physical ability, culture (De Groot and Maynard, 1993: 150-52). Influenced by post-modernism, the discovery of diversity led feminists, particularly feminists of color, to be critical of the legitimacy of many universalized and generalized theories and concepts of classical feminists which were based on the idea of homogeneity of womanhood (Harding, 1986). Patriarchy, the sexual division of labor, women, experience, truth were some of these generalized theories and concepts of culture (De Groot and Maynard, 1993: 155-56).

In addition to neglecting the diversities between women and their experiences, feminist writings were also criticized from another perspective. Based on feminist theories, two kinds of women often appeared in feminist research: women who contributed to public life, i.e, to the "men's world," and women who were the victims of male dominance either individually in the domestic sphere through male violence, or collectively in the public sphere through economic exploitation and political discrimination. Female researchers, who were supposed to produce objective knowledge, also produced a partial analysis of women's lives. In the case of women's public activities, they ignored the *meaning* of the public activities for different *women*, and in the case of women's victimization, women were only victimized people who could never successfully defend themselves or resist male domination (Harding, 1986: 26-27; 1987a: 4-5). The recognition that there is no "universal woman" means that there is no universal women's experience too. Experiences appeared to be problematic, as they are shaped according to race, class, culture and so forth, all of which differ across cultural categories (Harding, 1987a: 6-8, 188; Kelly *et al.* 1994: 28-29). Post-structuralist thinkers believe that people's experiences of their lives are not "raw" experiences. They are not only culturally structured, but are also a mixture of facts colored by people's own interpretation (Maynard, 1994: 23). This growing awareness that knowledge is historically, culturally and socially conditioned illustrates that the production of knowledge and its validity is closely associated with the social identity of the producer (Altorki and El-Solh, 1988: 3-5). The fundamental questions and rethinking about the production and validity of knowledge, and the fragmentation not only of experiences, but also individuals in terms of their personal and social identity, led feminists to reject the idea that a single appropriate research method existed. Instead they focused on multiple research methods (Maynard, 1994: 19).

As a result, many feminists adopted a combination of different research methods in a complementary rather than a competitive relationship, and promoted the value of both qualitative and quantitative methods with a framework of feminist values and ideology (Jayaratne and Stewart, 1991: 90-91). Many feminist scholars claimed that the polarization of qualitative versus quantitative methods reduces the validity of research. Therefore, "feminist researchers must be critical of both quantitative and qualitative research which is used against women and must be able to marshal the richest and most persuasive evidence in the service of women" (Jayaratne and Stewart, 1991: 100). For instance, for Kelly and her co-researchers' study of sexual abuse, the use of questionnaires produced more reliable information about distressing and sensitive experiences than interviews (Kelly *et al.* 1994).

The participation of the researcher in the construction of knowledge, and the relationship between the researcher and researched which was criticized by early feminists, were also reassessed. Glucksmann (1994) argues that the power hierarchy between the researcher and researched is unavoidable, even if an ethical behavior is adopted. The researcher and the subject of the research have different attitudes to the production of knowledge, as the primary aim of the researcher is to produce knowledge. It is the researcher who is in control of data and decides what material needs to be collected during the interview. It is the researcher who decides how the different accounts of past experiences should be analyzed, explained and interpreted in the light of other secondary data to which the researcher has easier access. An interpretive analysis will not be produced if the study is confined to repeating and describing women's accounts (Glucksmann, 1994: 154-56). In her study of female assembly line workers, Glucksmann argued that she did not rely entirely on women's own understanding of their situation, even though her aim was to give priority to women's subordinate position at work. This was because they had a partial and fragmented knowledge of the assembly line procedure due to their position, where they tend to have an inferior position as operators, compared to men who were further up the hierarchy and in charge of machinery, or in supervisory and management roles (Glucksmann, 1994: 157-58).

Another development in feminism was the inclusion of men in feminist research. The discovery of sex/gender systems in terms of division and inequality, and the emergence of theoretical perspectives such as patriarchy, created a number of intended and unintended exclusions of men from feminist studies, but any concern with gender necessarily requires a close focus upon men and masculinity (Stanley and Wise, 1993). To understand women's experience of oppression, and to know how their experience is structured in a male world, men and male institutions, the individual and collective dominance of masculinity should also be included in feminist research (Glucksmann, 1994; Kelly *et al.* 1994: 33).

The Methods Used in This Study

Reviewing feminist debates on qualitative and quantitative methods of research led to a decision to employ a combination of methods, as the appropriate use of both types have been considered satisfactory in promoting feminist theory and goals (Harding, 1987a). The data for this study includes a survey of 925 migrant women in Tabriz, using questionnaires from a random sample of women residing in slum areas of the city. The survey then was followed by more than 120 focused and semi-structured informal interviews. Over 90 female migrants fully participated in the interview process and responded to all interview questions; about ten men participated in the interviews either out of interest or to control, influence or dominate the interview process. Those who participated in the whole process of interview out of interest were sons, brothers, and colleagues of my informants. Two male employers and two husbands who hung around during the interview process tried to control the interviews and sometimes were dominant in answering the questions, even those that were directed at the women. As the interviews often happened in groups, there were other women who partially participated in the research and responded to some of the questions, often in approval of the main interviewees' accounts, or sometimes in rejecting them, by talking about their own experiences. The combination of research methods was important for taking advantage of their potential for bridging a significant gap in the existing literature, relating to the impact of local and global policies and feminization of the labor market in determining women's city-ward migration in East Azarbaijan or their involvement in the labor force.

Interviews helped extensively. They revealed women's work and their contribution to their families' well-being. As discussed later in the analysis chapters, most of my informants were working in the informal economy or as unpaid family workers, whose contribution to the welfare of their families was considered part of their domestic life, rather than economic activity. All women interviewed were involved in income-generating activities. However, only ten of them were registered as workers, four of whom would have been automatically sacked from their jobs as soon as they married.

By and large my respondents had similar social attributes in terms of religion, language, class, and ethnicity. However, there were differences in patterns of their work, education, and marital status, particularly between the younger and older women, which will also be discussed fully in the following chapters.

The Data

The initial data, upon which this study draws, were collected from 925 questionnaires from migrant women in 31 locations in the five main densely populated slums and squatter areas in the northern and southern fringes of Tabriz during summer 2000. According to the studies conducted by the University of Tabriz in 1995, the population of the city's slum and squatter settlements was about 310,000 people, 20 to 25 percent of the city's population, constituting about 45,000 households with an average family size of 6.5 persons (Tabriz University Report, 1995: 222). Therefore, my statistical sample of 925 respondents constituted about 0.3 percent of the city's slum and squatter settlements' population. During the second stage of field work in 2001, however, the latest announcements of the city's authorities showed that this population had increased to 400,000 people, about one-third of the city's population, constituting about 70,000 to 75,000 households with average family size of 5.8 persons. In this case, my statistical sample would be 0.23 percent of the city's slum and squatter settlements' population.

I had planned to employ local researchers with prepared questionnaires to collect data from 1000 slum dwelling migrant women. Questionnaires were composed at the University of York, translated into Persian and sent to the Faculty of Humanity and Social Science of Tabriz University to be administrated by female students who had applied to conduct the survey. Via e-mail and telephone, the questionnaire was discussed with two lecturers in the Faculty who had worked in the relevant areas of Tabriz (although not with migrant women). This consultation aimed at ensuring the data would be collected according to the social and geographical situations of migrants. At the initial stage some minor changes were suggested to some questions with a few additional sub-questions, particularly to those about the materials used in the buildings and the kind of ownership the interviewees had over their houses. It was argued that these questions would distinguish the social groups of the informants. In one of the questions, the lecturers suggested replacing "economic activities," *faaliyyatha-ye Egtesadi,*[1] with "job," *Shogl.*[2] I rejected this suggestion and explained that the informants might work at home and not be paid for their work, which is not accounted as a formal job, *Shogl*, and as such they would not answer to this question. One division for the type of work, which was "working outside the home as a self-employed," did not seem to them to be standard in terms of the job divisions in sociological textbooks in Iran. This slight change was accepted, dividing "work" into three parts: working outside the home for an employer; as an independent laborer; and as an unpaid apprentice. After this process, female students were recruited from the Faculty to collect data from female migrants living in the slum and squatter settlements of Tabriz. Thirteen students, the majority of whom were in the final year of their studies[3], were selected from twenty one students who had applied. One student was also given the responsibility of staying in the office to collect completed questionnaires, and to be available if help was needed. The selected students were all from the same ethnicity as the rural-urban migrants in Tabriz, and all spoke the local language (Azari Turki) fluently as both ethnicity and language are essential in establishing trust and support between researchers and those who are being studied (Jamali, 1985).

Before going into the field, one of the lecturers went through the questionnaire with the students, in case something was not clear. For some students and even for some of the lecturers of the University, some questions about migration and economic activities of migrant women were difficult to absorb, due to public perception of traditional culture of rural areas and complete female dependence on their male relatives there. Questions which were confusing for them were for instance, "Did you want to leave your village?" and "Did you come to the city alone?" with yes/no answers. The students and lecturers' perception of the rural norms and traditions was that, in rural areas, women are not allowed to leave their places alone or do not contribute in the decision making process about something important like migration. Thus their desire for migration, or the lack of it, could not have any impact on the process of migration. Another question was: "Who helped you in your migration?" Two of the options for this question were "Future employer" and "Potential employer." This question was ridiculed, as if I did not know anything about Iranian culture and how an unknown person could have access to a rural woman as a potential employee. They asked: "where were their fathers and brothers to allow the potential employer to help their women in the process of migration?" I explained that my supervisor, an Iranian woman who has experienced the period of land reform in Iran, had added these two options. I also explained that by "future or potential employer" I did not mean any business or firm. Rather, according to my supervisor's own experience, in many cases rural girls or women were accommodated as domestic workers in the houses of the landlords or wealthy families in the cities, though in most cases the decision might had been made for them by their parents or employers, particularly in the case of maids. But women who had to fend for themselves and their families, due to widowhood or divorce, might have an active role in the decision-making process.

The data were collected over three weeks from the slums areas of Tabriz. The choice of these geographical areas for statistical study was due to the fact that most migrants live in slums and shantytowns. These locations were divided equally between the 13 questionnaire distributors to collect data from all migrant settlements. In the biggest locations the data was collected in a cluster method. The female students were also divided into four groups in order to go together into the field. To give self-confidence and security (at least psychologically), the most experienced student who was familiar with the area either by doing research or being close to the area was selected as the head of the team.

There were two main concerns before and during the process of data collection. One of them was about gaining research permits from the local authorities, which often makes the process longer as, in Iran, social science research, particularly that undertaken by Western academic institutions, is always the subject of political suspicion (Razavi, 1992; Godazgar, 2008). I established some form of co-operation with the Social Science Department of Tabriz University to avoid potential problems with the authorities regarding the study. I also assumed that since the research would involve the study of migrant women, the majority of whom belong to the lower strata of society and lived in slums, the nature of the work might not be considered explicitly political, giving fewer potential problems with the authorities during the research. I assumed that the authorities were not aware that feminist research, because of its emphasis on "research *for* women," is something political, even though feminism has a political aspect due to a commitment to challenge patriarchal social structures, so as to change women's lives (Smith, 1979; Elshtain, 1981: 201-98; Harding, 1986: 24; Stanley and Wise, 1990: 21; Glucksman, 1994: 149). Feminists are also committed to raising gender consciousness, not only for women, but also for the authorities that are in a key position to make changes in the wider society[4]. If feminist research is not directly linked to policy transformation, it is often associated with a drive for political empowerment by providing knowledge and authority for women in order to increase their ability to change their conditions (Maynard, 1994: 17). Thus the process of research can lead to awareness on the part of the women who could exercise choices.

The students were advised not to declare in the streets that they were researching, but just to knock on doors and ask one of the female members of the household to answer the questions. They were given an official letter from the head of the Social Science Department, and the interviews were carried out under the authority of Tabriz University. Although the letter did not guarantee the protection of the researchers either from the police or the revolutionary guards, data was collected without any real problem or confrontation with authorities.

The questions were asked in the Turkic language, and were explained whenever necessary. The students filled in the questionnaires in the presence of the respondents even if they were literate. In a few cases where the questionnaires were not filled in completely the students were sent back to the field to complete them. In general, there was good co-operation between the students and the respondents. On the first day, a few students offended some women because they asked them if they were villagers (*Katdi*), an offensive word for migrants. The students asked for advice and they were told that they should ask that question indirectly; for instance they should first ask the respondents where they came from if they named a city, ask them if they are from the city itself or from its rural areas, in this way discerning their respondents' origins.

The completed questionnaires were coded and recorded in SPSS by two MA research students. This process took between two and three weeks. The whole process from sending the translated questionnaire until the information was completely recorded in the computer took three months.

I conducted an initial analysis of questionnaires on migrant women's social and economic characteristics and the factors associated with their migratory movement, which will be dealt with in detail in chapter 5. The main purpose of the primary data was to help me to identify individuals for in-depth interviews. Although the majority of women had stated nine different reasons for not working in the city, their responses to two other questions indicated that most of them had been involved in income generating activities either by working in or outside the home.

The Interview Process

The second stage of the study was conducted by myself in Tabriz in summer 2001. Learning from the experience of the first stage, a research permit to confirm the work was attained in advance. Moreover, being a native Iranian woman helped my entry to the field[5]. My marital status also played a positive role in encouraging my respondents, most of whom were married, to express freely their beliefs, their womanly experiences and problems at home and in the wider society.

I interviewed more than 120 migrant women in their homes or workplaces, including 5 women in the city's prison. Having started with the expectation of interviewing some of the informants from the first stage of study, a decision was made to choose my interviewees randomly, in order to integrate more migrant women in the study, particularly those who had paid jobs and were working outside the home. This was mainly because the majority of women who had participated in the survey had home-based, often unpaid jobs. At the first stage, the data were collected in slum areas; migrant women working outside the home were mostly excluded at that stage. Therefore, to make a balance, at the interview process I concentrated mostly on women who had paid jobs[6]. Interestingly, the "factual information" about the demographic, social, and economic features of the participants in the second stage of the study, were more or less similar to that of the information in the first stage. Most of the interviews took place at home, and those who had a paid job outside the home were interviewed at their workplace, with the exception of domestic workers. Most of the interviews took place in groups. Sometimes the group was made up of mother and daughter(s), with, in two cases sons; mother-in-law and daughter-in-law; neighbors; wife and husband; in the workplace, as co-workers, and employees and employer. The interviewees were selected from each stratum of pre- and post-revolutionary migrants, which crossed generations of young and older women who were engaged in income-generating activities regardless of whether they received a wage for their work, based on their willingness to participate in the interview process.

To obtain a fuller picture of the motivations and experiences of female migrants, a less structured interview with open questions followed. Five areas were covered: 1) background information and family, education and literacy levels at the points of departure and destination; 2) background information about migration and factors contributing to their mobility such as living circumstances in their villages and destination; 3) employment and socio-economic features of their occupational and their economic situations, the reason for being involved in that activity, skill, income; 4) what their work and earning meant to them and their families; and 5) family relations and kinship ties in the city, the spatial and physical constraints placed on them as a result of their migration by the family and society and most importantly their relationship with their husbands after migration, if they were married. The factual questions were useful in terms of processing data, particularly in terms of categorizing the respondents.

The personal interviews were most useful, as they provided details of personal experiences, attitudes, opinions, and reactions of the women in the "context of the social and economic structures within which they live" (Franks, 2001: 114). They also gave opportunity to observe the emotions and nonverbal behavior of the interviewees (Frankfort-Nachmias and Nachmias, 1996). Since the focus of the study was upon women, in order to "give them an opportunity to provide a spoken account of their existence" (Elshtain, 1981: 304), I tried to adopt an egalitarian, reciprocal and non-hierarchal relationship with my respondents. Interviews commenced with an informal introduction about the research and why I needed to interview them and how important they and their information were to the work.

The first hesitation that the majority of women expressed was a sense of inadequacy by saying that they were illiterate and would not know what to say. I explained that my research was on migrant women's work and that I was interested in listening to their stories and that questions would only be related to their households, children, and the work they did. Then they took an active role. During the interview, I noticed that the women were pleased and felt important by being research subjects and asked questions about the details of their work and their contribution to the welfare of their family, particularly if they were interviewed in the presence of their husbands. This was mainly because women's work, particularly when it is unpaid family labor, is often undermined even by women themselves. I also noticed that apart from some degree of confidence that women might have gained from the interviews, men found it interesting to see that for the first time their women, not they, were being asked for information about the reasons behind their migration or about work.

I asked permission to record the interview or take pictures, and reassured them that their information and personal details would be treated confidentially and I would be the only one to listen to the tapes. I taped some of the interviews and when they preferred not to be taped, interviews were recorded in writing. Most women were afraid that their interviews, if taped, would be exposed to the public on TV or radio, the most used media among the migrants. Franks (2001) also experienced the same feeling from her British interviewees, more than half of whom had university education. In the field, I preferred to tape the interviews as it made the process more like a conversation, carried out without any pause, allowing me to be a more active participant during the interview and have a proper exchange of emotions of sadness, fear, anger, or laughter and joy and happiness as appropriate. In some cases I cried with them when I saw their problems in dealing with poverty combined with other misfortunes of life such as having disabled children, or a violent relationship. Writing the interviews made me more distant, as I was more of a note-taker and kept interrupting the informants to repeat what they said already or to stop them in order to write their words before I forgot them. I was also more conscious about time and found that writing the answers down made the process slower and disorientated. In some cases I was not able to write down everything that was said, particularly in the case of group interviews when women kept interrupting each other. In these situations, I tried to remember the conversations and note down the key points. But in all cases, I followed the respondents' wishes about the use of tape. However, during the transcription of the tapes, I found some of the taped interviews difficult to handle, as background noises were sometimes disruptive, sometimes because of the very quiet voice of the respondent, or because of many people speaking at the same time. In one case, a child was crying continuously whilst the mother was talking to me. I also lost two or three of my valuable interviews by unconsciously taping other interviews over them.

Probing, an important instrument in this sort of interview, was also used to encourage the respondents to clarify the answer or to explain further, particularly when their accounts, opinions and attitudes seemed to vary during the course of the interview. This was important, because for many women, the interview was like telling their life histories/stories. Some even mentioned that their stories would make a good film. However, some respondents required constant prompting, and some said the most interesting things after the tape recorder has been switched off and during informal conversation. Respondents were also encouraged to say more about issues that were important and interesting to them but had not been covered by the interview.

During the interview, I talked with my informants about our common experiences and similarities such as motherhood, child rearing, housework, all of which were strategies that have been employed by many other feminists (Oakley 1981; El-Solh, 1988). Although there was an implicit power relationship between interviewees and myself in terms of, for instance, knowing the questions and their order, controlling the flow of the interview, I found that shared experiences and having common language and ethnicity and a real interest in the women and their lives could create an intimate relationship for producing a new level of self-knowledge for my informants. This knowledge was sometimes very useful for establishing trust between us. Often it was not just me interviewing my informants. They were also interviewing me by asking questions about my family life, where I came from, how many children I had, where I lived, what was my husband's job, did he help me at home. In some cases, when I criticized them for having so many children,[7] they threw similar critical questions back to me by saying that: "Why do you have four children? We were illiterate and unaware of our surroundings, what about you? You are literate and you should have had fewer children." The questions that my informants were asking from me, I think, were useful for them in producing a degree of unwritten and unrecorded knowledge and in making comparisons between themselves and middle class women. They found my life interesting because they rarely have the opportunity of probing into the lives of educated urban women such as primary teachers, nurses and doctors, with whom they have either very limited contact or social relations which are mainly constructed in terms of power relationships.

Access to the Informants

Before going to the field, I thought that to get access to the women and obtain their trust, as well as to avoid creating suspicion towards myself and the research, I would use my personal contacts through an informal network of relatives and friends or through local communities such as schools, mosques or female religious ceremonies as safe channels. In the field, however, I soon realized that I did not need any intermediary in order to get access to most of my informants. In fact, some of the "safe channels" that I had planned to employ in the field turned out to be a major obstacle between the women whom I wanted to interview and myself. For instance, I learnt that I could get access to some women with migrant backgrounds in schools such as teachers, cleaners and even pupils or their close female relatives who were involved in income-generating activities. I was informed that in two high schools, some pupils came from nearby villages and commuted everyday. But because the schools in Iran are under tight state control, getting access to schools, even to the private ones, was not actually possible without getting a written letter from the top educational authorities of the city. My support letter from the Social Science Department of Tabriz University proved to be worthless. In one of the high schools my request for an interview was rejected immediately. In another school, two of the teachers showed interest in being interviewed, but because the head teacher was not in, her assistant said that she needed to get permission from the Governmental Office (*edareh*, educational authorities), and she was advised that I would not be allowed to interview anybody unless I personally applied for permission from the Office. However, I did not want to get involved with educational authorities, as I knew that it would be a long process and, at the end, my request might be refused and jeopardize my research. I only managed to get access to one primary school through one of my informal channels. Fortunately my uncle's wife was the deputy to head teacher of the school. I interviewed her in front of her colleagues, and she asked them to participate in the interview and cooperate with me. Two of the teachers were interviewed, both of whom were urban-urban migrants from small cities up the hierarchy with rural-urban migrant husbands.

Access to women who were interviewed in their own homes was easy. In most cases, I received a warm welcome from my informants and was touched by their hospitality and generosity. In some cases, when my informants were older, I was treated as a member of the family and was invited to eat with them, particularly when it was around lunchtime. In one of the poorest areas, the people had a good experience with a woman MP who had brought water and electricity to their area. Therefore, they perceived me as a state agent and, in addition to the interview, they discussed the problems of their area such as sewage, etc., which needed to be improved by the council. In that area, I felt that I was seen as a savior. I found this perception unpleasant as I felt that I extracted information from them without being useful to them. In contrast with the poorer women, women in better-off families were more hesitant to let me enter their houses. However, their initial suspicion did not affect subsequent willingness to give information about their work experience or talk about their daily life and problems. Sometimes, for more than an hour, I had to sit or stand on my feet in alleyways while I was writing the interviews, and meanwhile had to explain about the research to other women who came to see what was going on. However, as soon as suspicion and fear were removed from their minds they became more relaxed and invited me into their homes where we carried out the rest of the interview.

The Presence of Men and its Effect on the Interviews

The focus of the interviews was on migrant women, but a few men were partially interviewed, mainly when they were present during the interview and felt obliged to talk when the questions were on the issue of migration or paid jobs. They were more eager to talk about political, economic, and social as well as climatic factors that had played important roles in their decision to leave their villages. In a few cases, male employers stayed during the whole period of the interview. In one factory, the manager stayed with us while I interviewed four of the employees. In one case, the employer stayed for a while and interrupted and answered the questions that were related to such things as wages, insurance, and benefits, and explained about the difficulties of running and continuing his business. However, once he was sure I was not a state agent and that I was more interested in women's work and experience, rather than in his business, he left us alone. In another case (in the University kitchen), the manager became aware of my presence among his workers and came to see who I was and what I was doing there. I explained I was from the University and was carrying out research on migrant women. The women laughed and said that "they want to deport the villagers from the city," and again after awhile we were left alone. In fact the presence of the employers did not have any profound effect on the process of the research, as far as the questions were related to women's life experiences.

Various studies indicate that the presence of husbands during interviews is problematic for the research process, directly or indirectly; sometimes they do not let their wives participate in research, or they take over or stay in the room. Though they may keep silent this still has a definite impact upon the interviewer and interviewee, insofar as women do not reveal the truth in front of their husbands, or women may defer to them and let them answer the questions (Shaaban, 1988; Razavi, 1992; Glucksmann, 1994; Ghavamshahidi, 1996). Some researchers have stated that in many cases their informants wished to be interviewed whilst not in the presence of their husbands.

In my work although the presence of the husband disturbed the process of the interview, it produced a different picture of women's views and their relations with their husbands. In most of the interviews that took place at home, the husbands/men were either not at home, or in a few cases, when they were in, did not get involved and left us alone. The norm in Iran is that the husband leaves the room or even the house when an unfamiliar woman enters so that the women feel comfortable in their socializing. In one of the interviews, however, the husband stayed with us until the end of the interview, because of his mistrust towards his wife, and to a lesser extent, because of his curiosity to know what I was doing. It was obvious that his lack of trust in his wife was because of the greater education that she had had, which he perceived as a threat to his superiority and tried, directly or indirectly, to control his wife. Unlike cases when women only talked freely when their husbands got bored and left the room, in this case, the husband's presence did not stop the woman from telling me everything that she wanted to say. In fact, in some cases, he was surprised by his wife's answers to my questions and interrupted the interview to express his unawareness about the issue, particularly about her teaching the Quran in one of the mosques the previous summer. She talked freely in front of her husband of her preference to study rather than marry, but because her father had died, her mother wanted to marry her off. She also said how her husband had broken his promise after their engagement regarding her continuing with her education, and about him preventing her from getting involved in social activities outside the home. When I asked about her job, she explained that she was invited by mosques to teach the Quran to young children during the summer holidays, an activity which her husband prevented her from doing. She did not look at her job from an economic point of view and mentioned that she had not used the money that came from teaching the Quran for herself or her family, as the maintenance of the family's welfare is her husband's responsibility. Rather, she had used her wages in a charitable way, most of the time helping a poor, old widow in the neighborhood, as she believed that teaching the Quran is her religious responsibility and one which gave her an opportunity to get involved in social activities which generate money to benefit her charitable interests. She had progressive ideas about gender relations and Islamic womanhood according to which she believed she had a right to education, social and economic activity, and freedom of movement. She actively resisted her husband's traditional notion of Islamic gender relationships between husband and wife, and was fighting for her Islamic rights, particularly in terms of having freedom to get involved in social activities and continuing her education.

What I found interesting was that it was not only the presence of the husband that affected the process of the interview, but sometimes the presence of another woman could be as distracting as the presence of a man. In one case, I asked a widow who had retired from carpet weaving about her engagement in income-generating activities in front of her daughter-in-law and my assistant. She replied to me with pride that "I have not worked at all. I have been a *khanoum* (lady) and have only eaten and slept." When I probed her: "but you have worked on carpets, don't you consider it as a work?" she found it very offensive and replied "so what, you are working too, aren't you? The only difference is that you are working outside the home." However, when her daughter-in-law left the room and my assistant went out to make a call, she admitted that she could not speak in their presence. Then she began to talk about her sufferings and the hardships she faced in bringing up her young children for many years after the death of her husband, with only her income from weaving carpets and some contribution from a local religious mission. She explained how some nights she could not go to sleep for fear of what would happen to her family, how she would cope with such a life and many similar questions.

In one of the group interviews, with seven women, one of the interviewees' daughter's interrupted the interview whenever her mother was talking about her husband, particularly about his violent behavior or negative attitudes towards her. In such cases, her daughter found those claims offensive, and tried to protect her father. I asked her to not interrupt her mother, as her mother's truth about her husband was reflecting her personal experience with the man with whom her daughter had a different fatherly-daughterly relationship. He might construct his relationship with his wife based on marital gender relations from a dominant position, but at the same time, his relationship with his daughter might be constructed based on affection, care and love in filial relations. However, at the end, the interview remained unfinished as the mother said: "I have too many things to say, but I can't." This was the only case that the conflict of interest between a mother and daughter affected the process of the interview. In contrast, there were cases in which daughters-in-law were talking about their unequal relationships with their husbands, and their mothers-in-law did not find it offensive. Sometimes they showed sympathy and assured them that their husbands' behavior would get better with the passage of the time.

In one case, I found the daughter of one of my informants very supportive of the process of the interview. By chance, she was an undergraduate student at the Social Science Department of Tabriz University, who constantly reminded her mother about the importance of the research and the co-operation of respondents, according to her knowledge from her studies. In some cases she even corrected her mother and explained to her that she should not underestimate the interview.

The Advantage of my Gender and Native Status in This Study

The importance of gender in the production of undistorted and unbiased knowledge about women's lives from a feminist perspective and standpoint has already been discussed in this paper. Apart from these arguments, gender has a great significance, in terms of access to the research community and to specific information, particularly where segregation leads to the separation of men and women's social and cultural knowledge, but even in less sex-segregated societies, it is influential (Altorki and El-Solh, 1988: 2). In sex-segregated societies, female researchers might have access to the world of men due to the role of other factors apart from gender, mainly education and class, but their male counterparts are excluded from the world of women regardless of education and class. Therefore, exclusion of men from the female world increases the possibility of neglecting important differentiations in gender roles in different "situational contexts" (Clark, 1983; Altorki and El-Solh, 1988: 4). The importance of gender roles increases when studying one's own society, particularly when that society has a high degree of sex-segregation, rigid definition of gender roles and expected behavior (Schwartz and Schwartz, 1955; Altorki and El-Solh, 1988: 11). This is why it is important that local women become more engaged in the accumulation of knowledge about women in their own societies. They can then produce more complete and less distorted knowledge than that produced by men (El Guindi, 1981; Mernissi, 1984, 1985; Altorki and El-Solh, 1988; Abu-Lughod, 1988, 1993; El-Solh, 1988; Shaaban, 1988).

I believe that my gender and native status facilitated my entry to the field and the world of migrant women making the research easier than it would be for a female outsider or a male insider researcher. Male kin would rarely permit the women to talk freely with a male researcher in their home, particularly without them being present. Migrant women fulfill expectations and display more of the behavior expected from them by their community during contact with the outside world, especially with men in an urban society where there are "more unfamiliar and strange men around" (Bauer, 1984, 1985). Women themselves also might not be willing to be interviewed by a male researcher, particularly talking about their intimate marital relationships[8]. In migrant communities, women often observe a greater degree of sex segregation. On the other hand, my freedom of mobility and interaction with men were not restricted by my gender role, mainly because of other critical variables such as my age, marital status, class, education, and the topic of research. Like other researchers who have studied their own sex-segregated society, I was able to manipulate traditional social barriers which exist between men and women among migrant families.

Studying my own society also had other advantages. Having the same nationality, ethnicity or language as my informants not only avoided problems but also defined my native status, a definition that often gives the researcher a safe passport into the world of the informants with whom s/he shares a similar body of knowledge. Being a native researcher had a profound impact on the process of both stages of my fieldwork. The initial stage was facilitated by my contacts in Tabriz University, who managed to complete the data collection process without my physical presence. My continuous communication with the lecturer in charge of data-collection compensated for my absence during that stage. Sharing similar culture, language and ethnicity were important factors in securing my access to communities for research and structuring my relationship with my informants. But at the same time, I had to remain aware of the possibility of being confronted with local authorities who were suspicious of social science research, particularly that being undertaken by Western academic institutions. From another perspective, having a native status, which in one sense implies being an insider, enabled me to understand easily the social realities and meanings of cultural patterns. Knowing my respondents' customs, beliefs and cultural norms was an invaluable asset both in establishing trust and support, and in making interpretation of the research much faster than would be possible for a non-native researcher who is unfamiliar with the culture of the wider society (Razavi, 1992).

In the research process, having a shared language is not only a tool for communication, but also a symbol of closeness (Pelto and Pelto 1973; Altorki and El-Solh, 1988: 7). In his study of Tabriz squatter settlements, Jamali (1985) and his team found that being from Tabriz and familiar with the study area and fluent in the local language, Azari Turki, allowed them to easily obtain the confidence of their informants (Jamali, 1985: 350). Moreover, speaking the same language makes differences between passive and active understanding (Schuetz, 1944; Altorki and El-Solh, 1988: 7). For a non-native researcher employing a native speaking assistant, there is always the possibility of summarizing, simplifying or leaving out some parts of the study that seems to the interpreter to be irrelevant. I personally experienced how an assistant could affect the quality of data, particularly in the case of interview recording. All of my interviews were conducted in the Azari-Turkish language, the native and only spoken language, while the writing was in the Farsi language, which meant I had to conduct three processes of listening, translating, and writing at the same time. I found these simultaneous tasks very difficult particularly at the beginning, since I had not practiced Persian writing for many years and could not write as fast as the informants talked. At times, a student who was one of the data-collectors from the first stage of the study and familiar with the field accompanied me. On the first day she asked me to let her write down the interview. Later on that day, I noticed that she had not recorded most of the interviews and had written only the parts that she recognized or considered to be important for the study.

In the next four chapters, we will hear the voice of women through their own experiences and accounts.

Notes

1 . *faaliyyatha-ye Egtesadi* is any form of activity that generates income.

2. The term "*Shogl*" is a formal definition that is used to refer to paid employment undertaken outside the home.

3. University courses in Iran are 4 years.

4. De Groot and Maynard: 1993; Kelly *et al.* 1994.

5. The status of the researcher as insider/outsider or indigenous/non-indigenous seems to be one of the important elements to the construction of sociological knowledge. Although there is not an agreed criterion for the definition of an insider, it indicates that the researchers belong to a cultural group that mainly covers language, religion, and ethnicity. This status gives the researcher more confidence in terms of familiarity with the culture of the society under study. For an outsider, there is no belonging to a specific sub-culture under study or sharing a similar body of knowledge with the informants. However, whilst a researcher in the field can be an insider because of the shared cultural similarities, s/he can be an outsider or a "partial insider" due to the differences such as class, education, gender, etc. It is worth mentioning that despite the advantages that being an insider give to the researcher, it does sometimes put limitations on him/her that an outsider does not have. For detailed information on conducting research on your own society, see: Altorki and El-Solh, 1988; Abu-Lughod, 1988.

6. Only two of the interviewed women participated in both stages of the study.

7. See chapter 6 about the fertility behavior of my informants.

8. Hossain Zadeh-e Dalir, a male researcher who conducted research in slum areas of Tabriz in 1982, did not have access to the women's world.

Chapter 5

Survey Analysis of Migration in Tabriz

"I wanted to become a khanoum[1]*, now look at my hands!"*
"I had heard that women in the city are khanoum and I wanted be one of them!"
(Interviews with two migrant women)

Migration is considered in most of the relevant literature as one of the structural characteristics of capitalist development, undertaken mainly by younger people who supply low-wage workers to labor-deficient economies within and across national boundaries. Informants in this study, the majority of whom came from the poorest rural areas of East Azarbaijan, mentioned economic factors as one of the main reasons for their migration. The study also shows that migration to Tabriz is mostly influenced by inequalities in income, resources and services between rural and urban areas, which affect various age groups differently. However, examining individual motivations, with particular emphasis on differences in gender, age and marital status provides a richer account, showing that migrants are not moving uniformly, but wider socio-economic factors motivate individuals in different ways. For instance, those who migrated with their family, particularly in their childhood, did not play an important role in the decision; as a result migration was not a rational decision for them, though for many it had positive impact. This was more or less the same for women who migrated to start their married life. However, married women with children were more involved in such decisions as they could significantly improve the family economy and provide better health and educational opportunities for their children.

This chapter describes the preliminary data drawn from a structured survey based on 925 questionnaires collected from migrant women in summer 2000 during the first phase of the research. The questionnaires also gathered some information about family members such as husbands (840 men), and children as well as some members of extended families. The chapter analyzes four sets of questions to describe the social and economic characteristics of the informants.

There are different criteria for identifying migrants (Skeldon, 1997), and in Tabriz, there are several types of migrants. Within these, policy makers, researchers and migrants themselves may use different classifications. Those who migrated permanently a long time ago, or in their childhood, might not consider themselves to be migrants and may put greater emphasis on their integration into urban society. In this study, however, migrants are defined as those who have moved from rural areas to the city of Tabriz, regardless of their economic activities, marital status, age and the period of their settlement in the city. Using this definition, the questionnaires were collected from migrant women with rural origins.

Factual Information about the Informants

Age

The ages of the respondents were within a range of 71 years and had an interquartile range of 17. The age of two of the women was missing. About 95 percent of the sample was between the ages of 19 and 60. However, the exact age given by many may not be very reliable, especially when given by older women. This can be explained by three factors: the fallible memories of older women; the fact that in the case of infant mortality, birth certificates were passed on from the dead child to the newborn baby, and in rural areas, particularly among older generations, dates of birth are/were not usually used except on special occasions such as marriage. Moreover, as the data records, more than two-thirds of the respondents were illiterate, contributing to the fact that some women did not know their precise age.

Table 5.1. The age frequencies of respondents

Mean	37	Minimum age	12
Median	35	Maximum age	83
Mode	30	Range	71
St. Deviation	11.96	Inter-quartile	17 (45-28)
Variance	143	No. of respondents	923*

* Two women did not know their ages.

Marital status

Ninety-one percent of the women in the sample were married, 5.9 percent widowed, 2.7 percent unmarried, and less than 1 percent were either divorced or deserted by their husbands. Table 5.2 indicates the marital status of the respondents and their ages.

Table 5.2. The frequency distribution of respondents in terms of marital status and ages

Marital status (MS)	n.	%	Ages
Single (unmarried)[2]	25	*2.7*	(12-33)
Married	840	*90.8*	(16-80)
Widowed	54	*15.9*	(30-83)
Divorced	3	*0.3*	(24-25)
Deserted	3	*0.3*	(32-80)
Total	925	*100*	(12-83)

The ages of single women ranged from 12 to 33 with the mean, median, mode and standard deviation at 20.60, 20, 20, and 4.22 respectively. The ages of married women ranged from 16 to 80, with the mean of 36.33, median of 35, mode of 30 and standard deviation of 10.66. Married women's ages had a range of 64 years and an inter-quartile range of 14 (42-28). The widows varied in age from 30 to 83 years old with the mean, median, mode and standard deviation of 55.81, 55.50, 60, and 12.07 respectively. Their ages also had a range of 53 and an inter-quartile range of 19 (65-46).

86 percent of the informants (796 women) lived in nuclear households, and a small percentage (14 percent, 129 women) in extended families. Figure 5.1 illustrates this distribution.

Figure 5.1. The percentage distribution of nuclear and extended families among the sample

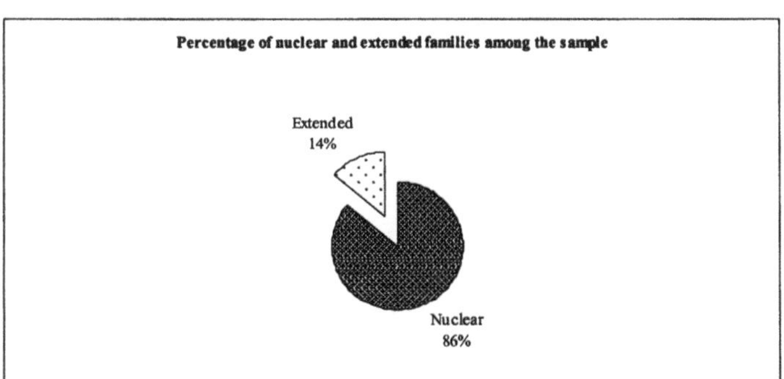

Of 840 married women, 105 of them (12.5 percent) lived in extended families; the most common pattern is for younger women to live with their in-laws rather than with their own families, and that for older women to live with their sons (and their wives) rather than with their daughters (and their husbands), unless often they do not have any son or their son has migrated (often up the hierarchy in terms of cities, usually to Tehran), and they preferred to stay in Tabriz mainly because of social and cultural factors. According to the 1996 National Census, 7 percent of households were headed by women. The highest proportion of female heads of households (49 percent) was among those aged 60 years and over and most of them (81 percent) were the head of small families with one or two members. For the majority of female-headed households the main reasons were widowhood and the spread of nuclear families, but in migrant families this percentage seemed to be lower, particularly according to information gathered in the next stage of research. However, in the questionnaire we had not allocated any questions about the status of female-headed households among the informants.

Of 54 widows, two-thirds (36) lived in nuclear families with their children; and 7 lived alone. The other 18 widowed women lived within extended families, with their sons and daughters-in-law, except one who lived with her daughter and son-in-law. Tables 5.3 and 5.4 demonstrate the distribution of extended family members among the households of married and widowed women.

Table 5.3. Distribution of other members of extended families among households in which the married women lived (n=105)

Family members	n.
Father-in-law	27
Mother-in-law	62
Father	2
Mother	5
Brother-in-law	13
Sister-in-law	17
Brother	9
Sister	8
Daughter-in-law	31
Son-in-law	1

Table 5.4. Distribution of extended family members among the households of widows (n=18)

Family members	n.	%
Son and daughter-in-law	15	*82*
Daughter and son-in-law	1	*6*
Parent and siblings	1	*6*
Brother's family	1	*6*
Total	18	*100*

The majority of single women were living within nuclear families, except four who had no father and resided in extended families with their brothers and their families. Three divorced women lived with their parents and siblings, and the deserted women with their children.

The demographic pattern and duration of migration

Table 5.5 gives the numerical and percentage distribution of the research sample by age group (their current age and their age on arrival). The demographic pattern of migrants in the table indicates age selectivity for migration. The percentages are highest for those who left their villages between the ages of 10 and 30 or in their childhood (85 percent altogether), and lowest among all other age-groups. This pattern, the association of migration with age regardless of gender, has been shown in many studies of migration. The informants who were between the ages of 15 and 22 at the time of migration and comprised 42 percent of all migrants had the highest propensity to migrate.

Table 5.5. Age-group of migrant women at the time of data-collection, and on their arrival in the city

Age Group	At the time of data collection		On arrival to the city	
	n.	%	n.	%
1-9	0	*0.0*	182	*19.7*
10-19	12	*1.3*	364	*39.4*
20-29	259	*28.1*	240	*25.9*
30-39	315	*34.1*	77	*8.3*
40-49	190	*20.5*	39	*4.2*
50-59	88	*9.5*	12	*1.3*
60-69	43	*4.6*	2	*0.2*
70-79	12	*1.3*	0	*0.0*
80-83	4	*0.4*	0	*0.0*
Unknown	2	*0.2*	9	*1.0*
Total	925	*100*	925	*100*

Figures 5.2 and 5.3 illustrate the age of the respondents at the time of migration and their ages at the time of data collection.

Figure 5.2. Age of women on their migration

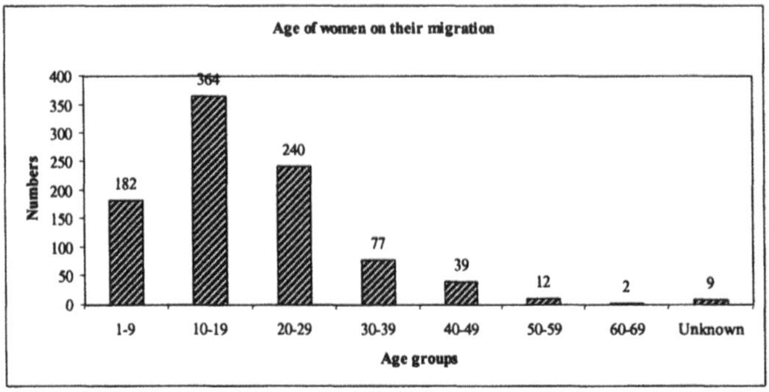

Figure 5.3. Age of migrant women at the time of data-collection

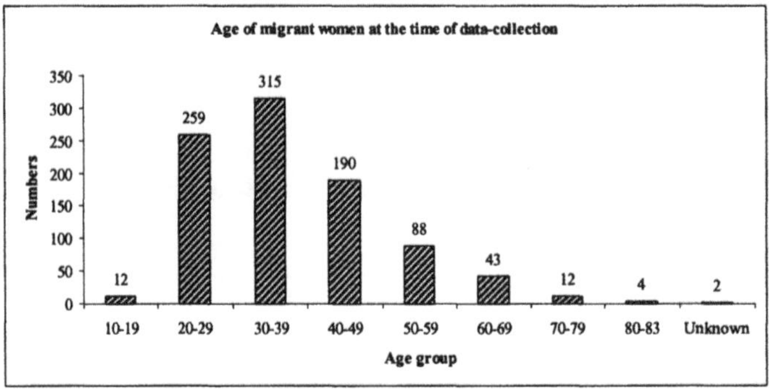

Since 85 percent of the respondents (786) migrated in their childhood or between the ages of 10 and 30, table 5.6 shows the duration of residency in the city which can be found by comparing these three age groups on arrival in the city and at the time of data-collection.

Table 5.6. Comparing the age of migrants at the time of data collection and their arrival to the city (n= 786)

Age Group	At the time of migration			
	<10	10-19	20-29	Total
10-19	8	4	0	12
20-29	76	127	56	259
30-39	62	139	99	300
40-49	26	62	60	148
50-59	7	21	16	44
60-69	3	7	8	18
70-79	0	0	1	1
80-83	0	2	0	2
Unknown	0	2	0	2
Total	182	364	240	786

Figure 5.4 shows duration of migration in chart form. Those whose age was over 70 or who did not know their age (a small proportion, 5 women) have been excluded from the figure.

Figure 5.4. Duration of migration by comparing the age of migrant women on arrival to the city (n= 781)

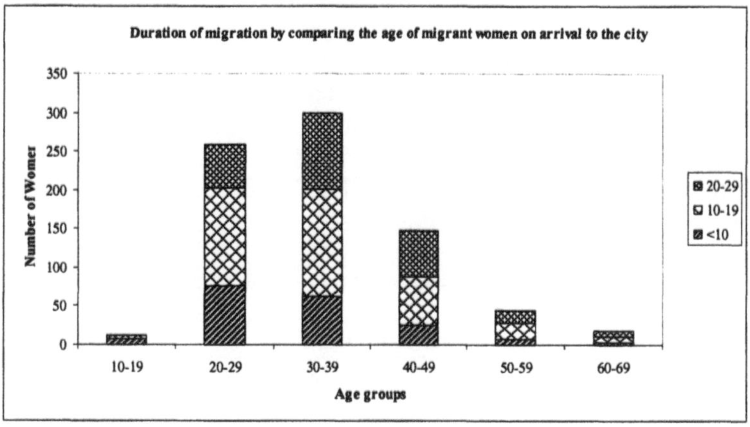

For a small number of women, the proportion of life spent as a migrant is a long period, five to six decades. For the majority, however, it is between less than a decade to two decades, which indicates that in this sample, the majority migrated during or after the revolution, particularly those with higher propensity to migrate among younger age group.

Marital status at the time of migration

Regarding marital status of women at the time of migration, the data initially indicated that the majority, about 67 percent, were married, followed by unmarried, widowed and divorced women respectively, as figure 5.5 illustrates.

Figure 5.5. Marital status of migrant women on their arrival to Tabriz

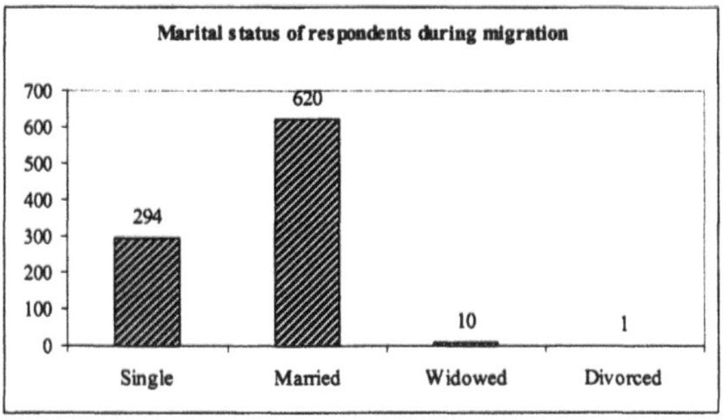

However, in analyzing other questions and comparing them with marital status at the time of migration, and also during the interview process, I noticed that women who categorized themselves as single (unmarried) or married, in practice could be divided into four categories: single, migrating with parents or immediate relatives; single, migrating autonomously for education or work; single, migrating for marriage to start their married life in Tabriz; and married women, migrating with their husbands and children or joining their already migrant husbands in the city. Only three women of the sample migrated for educational purposes, all of whom were married by the time of the survey. Of the six divorced and deserted women, three migrated with their parents, two as married women, and one for marriage. Only one woman out of 925 had migrated as a divorced woman. Table 5.7 illustrates marital status of the sample population during migration in more detail.

Table 5.7. The marital status of respondents at the time of migration

	Marital status at the time of migration						
MS during survey	SWPs.[a]	SFM.[b]	SFJ/S[c]	M.[d]	W.[e]	D.[f]	Total
Single	25	0	0	0	0	0	**25**
Married	250	124	3	461	1	1	840
Widowed	6	4	0	35	9	0	54
Divorced or deserted	3	1	0	2	0	0	6
Total	284	129	3	498	10	1	925
%	*30.7*	*13.9*	*0.3*	*53.8*	*1.1*	*0.1*	*100*

[a] Single women migrating with their parents
[b] Single women migrating for marriage
[c] Single migrating for the purpose of studying or searching a job
[d] Married women
[e] Widowed women, and
[f] Divorced woman.

Children

Apart from 25 single women in the sample, another 25 women had no children; of these 21 were married, 1 widowed, and 3 divorced. Although the ages of these women ranged from 17 to 60 years old, 65 percent of them were of child-bearing age.

Of the women who had children, the number of offspring was varied widely, ranging from 1 to 14. Of these women, however, 96 percent had between 1 and 8 children (mean 4.2, median 4, and mode 2). A few women had 10 children or more (2.2 percent). Table 5.8 and figure 5.6 illustrate the distribution of children among 900 respondents, according to which about 70 percent of women had between 3 and 6 children.

Table 5.8. Children's distribution among mothers in the sample (n= 900)

Number of children	Number of mothers	%
0	25	*2.8*
1	102	*11.3*
2	151	*16.8*
3	113	*12.6*
4	134	*14.9*
5	121	*13.4*
6	101	*11.2*
7	84	*9.3*
8	36	*4.0*
9	14	*1.6*
10	16	*1.8*
11	1	*0.1*
12	1	*0.1*
14	1	*0.1*
Total	900	*100*

Note: Single women are excluded from this table.

Figure 5.6. Children's distribution among mothers in the sample (n= 900)

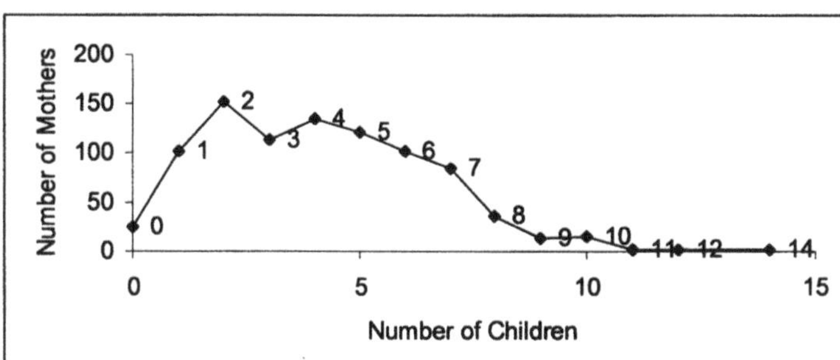

Education

Education, or "human capital formation" (Blumberg, 1995: 7), is a basic need for human development and the expansion of people's capacities. Economists, sociologists and development scholars have highlighted the integral role of education in the social and economic development of individuals and society (Todaro, 1994; World Development Report, 1990).

In this survey, I allocated certain questions relating to education not only to my informants, but also to immediate family members such as husbands and children. The data indicated that 603 informants (65 percent) in the sample were illiterate[3], of whom only 1 was single. The illiterate women ranged from 12 to 83 years old; however, 50 percent of them were between 39 and 83 years old, a group for whom the educational opportunities were very limited. 322 women (35 percent) were literate, of whom 4 were studying at the time of data collection. Table 5.9 and figure 5.7 illustrate respondents' educational levels.

Table 5.9. The educational level of respondents

Level of Education	Number of respondents	%
Illiterate	603	*65*
Basic reading skills	59	*6*
Primary	194	*21*
Secondary	43	*5*
High School	7	*1*
Diploma and more	19	*2*
Total	925	*100*

Figure 5.7. The educational percentage of respondents

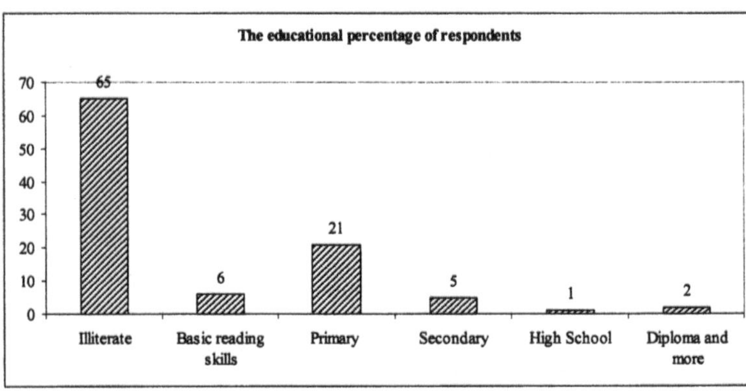

Education is an important variable especially when correlated positively or negatively between the level of education and number of children the women bore. By examining the educational level of the sample, the variation in the number of children can be related to variations in the women's level of literacy. The next chapter looks at this important factor in detail, by separately examining the women's age and marital status at time of migration as well as current age and marital status, and the numbers of children at different educational levels, showing a negative correlation between illiteracy or low level of education and higher reproductive behavior.

Information on the educational levels of husbands and other family members

The mean age of the married women in the sample was 37 and that of their husbands was 41. Comparing husbands' educational levels with that of the female respondents shows that men were more educated than women in this sample. Thirty-six percent of the husbands were illiterate against 65 percent of the women[4], a 29 percent gap. The gender gap in the literacy rate in this sample supports one also apparent at the national level. The majority of men, however, had primary education. Table 5.10 and figure 5.8 illustrate the educational levels of the 840 husbands in the sample.

Table 5.10. The educational level of respondents' husbands: (n= 840)

Level of Education	Number of respondents	%
Illiterate	304	*36*
Primary	391	*47*
Secondary	130	*15*
High School	11	*1*
Religious education	4	*1*
Total	840	*100*

Figure 5.8. The educational percentage of respondents' husbands

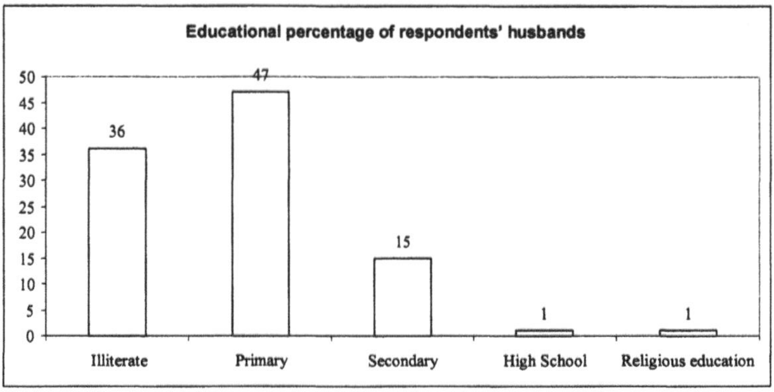

The high rate of illiteracy among the respondents compared to their husbands can be explained in terms of their poor economic conditions, particularly in rural areas, which prevented access to educational resources. I also grouped respondents' family members into four groups of husband, children, parents and siblings, including daughters or sons-in-law who lived in the same household as the respondents. Thus, any married children of the respondents living away are not included in this sample.

Table 5.11. Cross-tabulation count of family members' educational level

Level of Education	Husband	Parents	Siblings, daughters/ sons-in-law	Children	Total
Illiterate	304	132	23	65	523
Primary	391	14	74	984	1461
Under-diploma	130	0	97	1207	1433
Diploma	11	1	11	55	77
Religious Education	4	0	0	0	4
Total	840	147	205	2311	3498

Comparing the educational levels of different generations indicates that younger ones tend to have better education than the older, reflecting increased access of the population to education, particularly at the primary and middle levels of schooling in recent decades. Illiterate children are mainly those who have not reached school age.

Table 5.12. The economic activities of respondents' husbands (n= 840)

Activity	n.	%	Activity	n.	%
Construction laborer	312	*37*	Private sector worker	103	*12.3*
Carpet-weaver	92	*10.9*	Barber	2	*0.2*
Clergyman	4	*0.5*	Builder/ Painter	59	*7.1*
Driver	58	*7*	Shop-keeper	31	*3.7*
Shoe-maker	10	*1.2*	Tailor	2	*0.2*
State employee	90	*10.7*	Army officer	3	*0.4*
Un/under employment	64	*7.6*	No Answer	10	*1.2*

Some of the women mentioned that their husbands did several jobs. Categorizing these activities into state-employment, the informal sector (either as self-employment or waged-earning activities), and un-or under-employed, the data indicates informal sector absorbs the majority of the male migrants in Tabriz. In the sample, most, 44 percent, were working in the construction sector as wage-earners, and 45 percent were involved in other activities. The share of state-employment, at 11 percent, was lower than that of the informal sector[5]. About 8 percent of respondents stated that their husbands were un- or under-employed. If this is compared with the prolonged unemployment rate in the country, which has been in two digits for at least three decades, it supports the argument raised in chapter 1, that the unemployment rate among male migrants is often lower than that among their non-migrant counterparts (Yap, 1975; Jamali, 1985: 373; Harris, 1999). This is mainly due to the fact that male migrants often have lower income aspirations and enter lower quality employment. As a result, they have higher labor force participation rates compared to urban natives.

According to different sources from official surveys, unemployment rates in Iran have ranged between 13.5 percent to 16 percent, a daunting challenge for the Iranian government over several decades[6]. In 2002, for instance, Iran's workforce was 19 million, out of which, according to official sources, 16 percent were unemployed. In other words, some 17.7 million people had to earn the livelihood of 63 million, a ratio of 1 to 3.6, a high dependency ratio between the out-of-work population and the employed[7]. Unemployment is especially high among 15-24 year olds who officially constitute more than 25 percent of the labor force[8].

Some migrants had retained their rural attachments, particularly in terms of keeping their cultivatable land, even though they might have no intention of returning to their villages. Interestingly, the interviews also revealed that some male migrants had maintained their land in the villages and had dual participation in urban and agrarian activities, or had withdrawn from agriculture only after securing good occupational opportunities in the city in either the informal or formal sectors. They were often better off compared to those who did not hold any land (either due to their landless position in the village social hierarchy, sale of the land, or further fragmentation of the parental lands due to inheritance). Moreover, male migrants who left their families in the villages to take care of land or animals and migrated alone were able to consolidate their position in the city through obtaining urban occupations, or buying houses or land for building before their rural families joined them. They were also better off economically and socially than those who left the village together with their families without securing any home or job in the city. The latter group did not retain any links with or interest in their villages, whereas some of the former group did benefit from a partial involvement in farming. They could compensate for the higher living cost of the city by receiving produce from farming. Some even commercialized surplus produce in local markets or among their urban neighbors. Nonetheless, this practice was not very widespread.

Economic Activities of Respondents

The availability of urban jobs to female migrants, and migrant women's access to and attitude to work outside the home is a major focus of this study, and specific questions were allocated to this. One question in this context was whether my respondents looked for an urban job after migrating to the city. As table 5.13 indicates 88 percent were uninterested in having a job; only about 10 percent of women in the sample looked for a paid job in the city, and 2 percent of respondents did not reply to this question at all.

Table 5.13. Numerical and percentage distribution of migrant women in terms of their determination to find a paid job (n= 925)

	n	%
Looked for a job	91	*10*
Did not look for a job	815	*88*
No reply	19	*2*
Total	925	*100*

The next question was whether they were successful in finding an urban job. Only 99, 11 percent of respondents answered the question: of these 48 women were successful in finding a job and 51 were not (table 5.14).

Table 5.14. Numerical and percentage distribution of migrant women in terms of being successful in finding a job (n= 99)

	n	%
Successful	48	48.5
Not successful	51	51.5
Total	99	100

Another question asked about the reasons behind lack of motivation in looking for an urban job, or the lack of success among those who searched for one but were not successful. Forty respondents, those who were successful in finding a job did not answer the question. The total number of respondents who answered this question was 686 (74 percent). Nine different reasons were given in response. Table 5.15 shows the different reasons for lack of motivation or lack of success.

Table 5.15. Reasons for not being successful in having an urban job or for not being motivated find a job (n= 686)

Reasons	n	%
Illiteracy	206	30
Burden of motherhood and housework	156	23
Lack of husband's permission	124	18
Lack of skill	83	12
Illness	46	7
Lack of interest	37	5
Lack of work	14	2
Lack of information	8	1
Others	12	2
Total	686	100

Figure 5.9. Factors preventing migrant women's motivation for finding an urban job

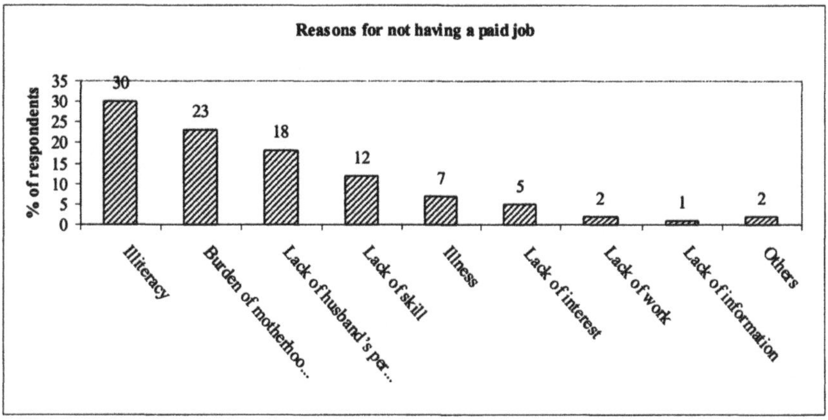

Twelve respondents gave specific reasons such as not being in need or feeling a stranger in the city; those responses were mostly from married women. However, for others being in full-time education or preparing for "*konkour*," the university entrance exam, were given as reasons, despite their interest or motivation.

The respondents were also asked two other questions about the type of activities they did after migration to the city as well as their current job. These two questions revealed that most of the women contributed to family incomes. Despite the fact that a small number of women looked for and found an urban job, in answer to the question about what type of work they did after migration to the city, the majority stated that they did unpaid work (45 percent) and paid labour (8 percent) at home, the main job being carpet weaving or relevant activities. Since the majority of informants were working at home, they looked after their children themselves, and some were able to share childcare with their older daughters or other female relatives in the home. In answer to the question: "what type of activity were you involved in after migrating to the city," 55 percent stated that they were involved in income generation activities (IGAs).

Table 5.16. Number of women involved in IGAs (n= 925)

	n	%
Involved in IGAs	505	*54.6*
No response to the question	420	*45.4*

Figure 5.10. Percentage of women involved in income generating activities after migration

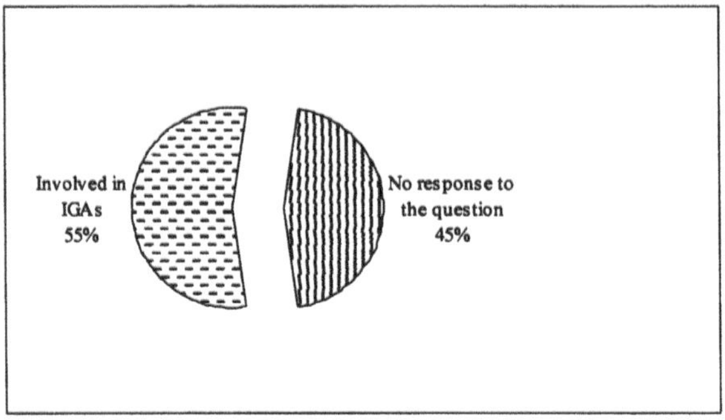

Of 505 women who were involved in some sort of income generating activities 82 percent were unpaid family workers; 14 percent were doing paid work at their own homes, as wage-earners; and 4 percent worked outside their home.

Table 5.17. Types of economic activity after migration (n= 505)

Kind of activity	n	%
Unpaid worker at home	416	*82.4*
Paid worker at their own home	69	*13.7*
Work outside the home as employer	4	*0.8*
Work outside the home as self-employed	4	*0.8*
Work outside the home at others' homes	3	*0.6*
State employee	7	*1.4*
Unpaid apprenticeship	2	*0.4*
Total	505	*100*

Figure 5.11. Distribution of working women in terms of being paid or unpaid working inside or outside home (n= 505)

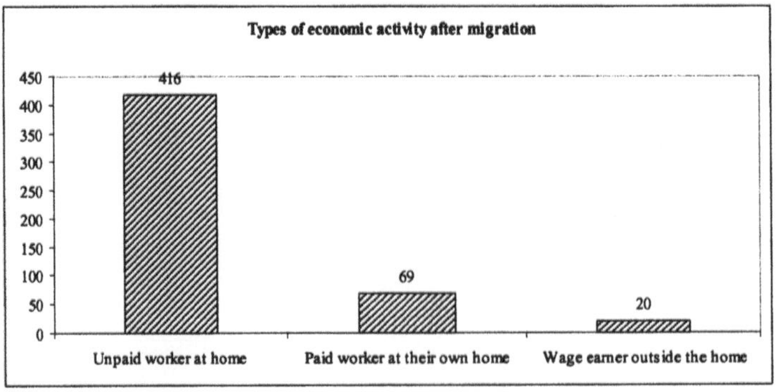

Of 505 respondents who stated that they had some sort of employment after migration, only 284 of them named their jobs, majority of which were in the carpet industry.

Household Information

House ownership[9]

At the time of data collection, 740 of the respondents (80 percent) were living in privately owned houses[10] and 104 (about 11 percent) in rented houses (91 percent altogether). Nine percent of the remaining respondents, however, had different relationships to their housing: 68 were living in their parents' or in-laws' house free of charge, a practice which is called *Belaavas*. This is different from living in an extended family. In this, the newly wed children of the family live separately, eat separately and their budget is separate from that of their parents or in-laws with whom they only share their residence[11]. Eleven of the respondents had leased (*rahn*[12]) their houses, and two remaining respondents were living in state-provided houses for a subsidized rent.

Table 5.18. House ownership situation of the sample (n= 925)

Ownership of the House	n	%
Privately owned	740	*80*
Rented	104	*11.2*
Living in parents' or in-laws' house without paying rent *(Belaavas)*	68	*7.8*
Leased *(Rahni)*	11	*1.2*
State-provided accommodation	2	*0.2*
Total	925	*100*

The majority of the respondents (510) had two rooms in their houses; 207 of the respondents stated that they had one room; and 126 said that they had three rooms (91 percent altogether). Of the remaining 9 percent, 52 had four rooms; 11 stated they had five; another 5 stated that they had six or more rooms in their houses; and 14 (1.5 percent) respondents did not give any information on the number of rooms in their houses.

About 5 percent of the total (10 respondents) who stated that they had one room were living within extended families, 5 of them with their mothers-in-law. The other 5 were living either with more than one in-law or with their daughters-in-law. It seems that they either had misunderstood the question and meant the number of the rooms in the household that specifically belonged to them, as it seems odd for married women to live with their in-laws in one room, unless they were extremely poor[13]. According to my own observations during the interview process, the extended families had often more than one room. About 53 percent of extended families in this sample had two rooms. Tables 5.19 and 5.20 indicate the number of rooms stated by respondents as well as the numerical and percentage distribution of extended family in each case. Four extended families (2.3 percent) were among those who did not say how many rooms they had in their houses.

Table 5.19. Number of rooms stated by respondents (n= 925)

No. of rooms	n	%
1	207	22
2	510	55
3	126	14
4	52	6
5	11	1
6^+	5	0.5
Not mentioned	14	1.5
Total	925	100

Table 5.20. Number and percentage of rooms in extended families (n= 129)

No. of rooms	n	%
1	10	8
2	68	53
3	29	22
4	16	12
5	2	2
Not mentioned	4	3
Total	129	100

Five different reasons were given in the questionnaire for choosing the area of their residency after moving to the city, and the respondents were asked to rank them in terms of importance to them. Table 5.21 shows these factors and their importance for the respondents.

Table 5.21. Respondents' ranking of factors vital for choosing to settle

Priorities	Factors
1	Cheapness of the land to build a house on
2	Closeness to migrant's relatives
3	Closeness to friends and village-mates
4	Other
5	Closeness to their village

The majority of the respondents, 682 women (74 percent) chose the low cost of the land on which they built their house, and closeness to their relatives as their first and second priorities. Closeness to friends and village-mates received the third highest rank.

Type of buildings in terms of construction materials

To find out about the informants' living conditions, data-collectors were asked to write down the kind of materials used in the buildings in which respondents were resident[14]. In terms of strength of the building and their resistance to natural disasters such as earthquake and flooding, the houses are divided into three sorts of buildings: strong; partially strong; and weak. However, this division does not indicate the housing material used in the construction of the buildings. In this sample, the material most commonly used in the buildings were "brick and wood[15]" of which 46 percent of the respondents' houses were made[16]. "Concrete and iron[17]," the second most common construction materials were used for 41 percent of the houses. A very small percentage of the respondents' buildings had facades. Table 5.22 shows the different kinds of buildings that the respondents lived in.

Table 5.22. Different kinds of buildings inhabited by the sample (n= 925)

Kind of building	*N*	%
Sun-dried brick and wood	17	2
Brick and wood	425	46
Concrete and wood	32	3.5
Concrete and steel/iron	389	42
Pre-assembled building	3	0.5
Reinforced concrete	21	2
Brick or stone façade	41	4
Total	925	100

Facilities

To understand the availability of urban services in slums and access migrants had to these, as well as their utilization, the respondents were asked three sets of questions. One of them was about their degree of satisfaction in terms of access to social services, such as schools, workplaces, health centers, pharmacies, shopping areas, mosques, and public transport. The second set was on the availability of public facilities and services often provided by the city council, such as piped clean water, electricity, telephone lines, gas, sewage, and to what extent they were able to utilize these in terms of, for instance, both having a bath and a separate kitchen in their house. The third set asked migrants to tick against the electrical appliances and furniture they had in their own houses.

Table 5.23 indicates respondents' satisfaction in terms of access to health, educational, economic and religious centers/mosques. The number of women responding to this question differed according to their own or their family's specific needs/interests. The last column from the right shows the numbers of respondents who answered this question.

Table 5.23. Respondents' level of satisfaction in terms of access to services

Access/ proximity	No. who responded	Level of satisfaction of respondents (%)				
		Very Low	Low	Fair	High	Very High
Schools	776	13	13	32	28	14
Workplace	169	17	15	18	17	33
Health center	905	15	16	20	26	23
Doctor	915	22	24	19	20	15
Pharmacy	892	24	22	17	21	16
Transport	918	9	8	15	30	38
Main road	919	7	8	14	32	39
Mosque	906	11	8	16	28	37
Shopping Center	923	14	12	28	20	26

As the table shows, a small number of the informants expressed satisfaction regarding being close to their workplace, which indicates the low involvement of the informants in the labor market. In terms of access or closeness to doctors and pharmacies, their satisfaction is much lower than for other services, even for health centers. This might be interpreted as showing that closeness to health centers does not necessarily facilitate their access to free or affordable health services, particularly when illnesses are serious. This is because those who work in the informal sector, and do not pay insurance, are not covered by the subsidized health care system. Table 5.12 showed that the majority of informants' husbands were concentrated in the informal sector, mostly in self-employment and the construction sector. Some employers pay health insurance for their employees, but this does not cover their dependents.

The level of satisfaction of respondents relating to some urban amenities such as better access to schools, health centers and public transport indicates the commitment of policy makers in terms of facilitating slum dwellers' access to important facilities/services close to their geographical locations. Table 5.24 shows the informants' access to different services in their houses.

Table 5.24. The percentage of informants who have access to different services in their houses (n= 925)

	Piped water	Electricity	Telephone line	Gas main	Sewage system
Access	88	91	52	42	14
No access	12	9	48	58	86

Electricity and piped water were the most common facilities: 91 percent and 88 percent of my respondents respectively had access to these in their houses. Sewage was the least common facility, with only 14 percent of the respondents' houses connected. In fact, in one of the poorest slum areas of the city, which is situated on a very uneven piece of land, one of the major problems for the residents was the lack of a sewage system. As I observed during the interview process, and also according to my informants, in both the hot and rainy seasons of the year, the conditions become very unpleasant and hazardous for the health of the residents. However, in this area, the residents had a water supply and electricity, as well as telephone lines in their homes, though many of them found the bills an extra burden to the household's limited income. Therefore, the destructive behavior of the urban poor and clandestine use of urban amenities, as recorded by researchers as daily practices in many urban centers of developing countries (Abdel Taher, 1987; Soto, 1989; Bienen, 1984, 1985; Leeds and Leeds, 1976; Leiva *et al.* 1994; Stiefel and Wolfe, 1994; Bayat, 1997) was not observed in this study.

To examine living conditions in the households or the poverty level of the respondents, I looked at the percentage of respondents who did not have the most common facilities in their houses, such as kitchen, sanitation facilities such as baths and clean piped water supplies, and compared this with other amenities that they did have access to.

About 30 percent (275) of the respondents stated that they did not have a separate kitchen in their house and that they cooked in their living rooms, which also function as a bedroom, and for some, even workshop. Table 5.25 shows these households' access to other facilities.

Table 5.25. Access to other amenities for houses without kitchen (n= 275)

Access to other amenities	n	%
Bath	82	30
Piped Water	201	73
Electricity	224	81
Telephone line	84	31
Gas main	42	15
Sewage	28	10

As the table shows, apart from access to running water and electricity, the majority of households that do not have a separate kitchen are among the poorest, also mostly deprived of access to other facilities, and often forced to use public facilities outside the home. Table 5.26 compares the percentage of houses without a kitchen that are also deprived of other facilities, with the overall sample.

Table 5.26. Percentage comparison of houses without kitchen and other amenities with the whole sample (n= 925)

Lack of access to	% Among households without a kitchen	% Among all sample
Bath	70	35
Piped Water	27	12
Electricity	19	9
Telephone line	69	48
Gas main	85	58
Sewage	90	86

About 35 percent (319) of the households in the sample did not have a bathroom in their house and used public baths. Table 5.27 shows their access to other facilities.

Table 5.27. Access to other amenities for houses without a bathroom (n= 319)

Access to other amenities	n	%
Kitchen	126	39
Piped Water	225	71
Electricity	257	81
Telephone line	87	27
Gas main	47	15
Sewage	34	11

Table 5.28 compares the percentage of houses without bath/shower that also lack other facilities with the overall sample.

Table 5.28. Percentage comparison of houses without bathroom and other amenities with the whole sample

Lack of access to	% Among households without a bathroom	% Among all sample
Kitchen	61	30
Piped Water	29	12
Electricity	19	9
Telephone line	73	48
Gas main	85	58
Sewage	89	86

About 12 percent (107) of the households in the sample did not have piped water in their houses. Table 5.29 shows their access to other amenities.

Table 5.29. Access to other amenities for houses without piped water (n= 107)

Access to other amenities	n	%
Kitchen	33	31
Bath	13	12
Electricity	56	52
Telephone line	12	11
Gas main	6	6
Sewage	7	7

Table 5.30 compares the percentage of houses without running water that also lack access to other facilities discussed here with the overall sample. This table also highlights the poverty of households without access to running water compared to the sample.

Table 5.30. Percentage comparison of houses without bathroom and other amenities with the whole sample

Lack of access to:	% Among households without piped water	% Among the sample
Kitchen	69	30
Bathroom	88	35
Electricity	48	9
Telephone line	89	48
Gas main	94	58
Sewage	93	86

As Tables 5.26, 5.28, and 5.30 illustrated, the percentage of respondents who did not have essential facilities such as kitchen, bath, or running water in their houses, were in most cases almost twice as likely to lack access to other amenities, compared to others in the sample, and in some cases even more so, indicating a chronic level of poverty and destitution.

Informants were also asked about the electronic household appliances and other luxury items that they owned. Table 5.31 shows that gas cookers, fridges, carpets/*kelims*, TVs, heaters, sewing machines and radios were the most common items to be found in the migrants' houses. More luxurious items were rarely owned or used by the informants.

Table 5.31. The percentage of access to different appliances in respondents' houses (n= 925)

Accessory	With (%)	Without (%)	Accessory	With (%)	Without (%)
Gas cooker	90	10	Sewing machine	64	36
Fridge	92	8	Knitting machine	1	99
Freezer	4	96	Heater	73	27
Fan	33	67	Washing machine	19	81
Sofa	3	97	Vacuum cleaner	28	72
Rug	81	19	Video-recorder	6	94
TV	86	14	Satellite TV	0.1	99.9
Radio	72	28	Computer	0.5	99.5

Questions Relating to Migration

When asked if they wanted to leave their villages, the data showed that the majority of respondents were willing to do so; 712 women (77 percent) of the total gave a positive answer in the questionnaire. Of the remaining 23 percent, 145 (16 percent) did not want to go, and 68 women (7 percent) had no concept of migrating. The latter group was mainly those who migrated with their parents in their early childhood.

Figure 5.12. Women's willingness to leave their native rural areas (n= 925)

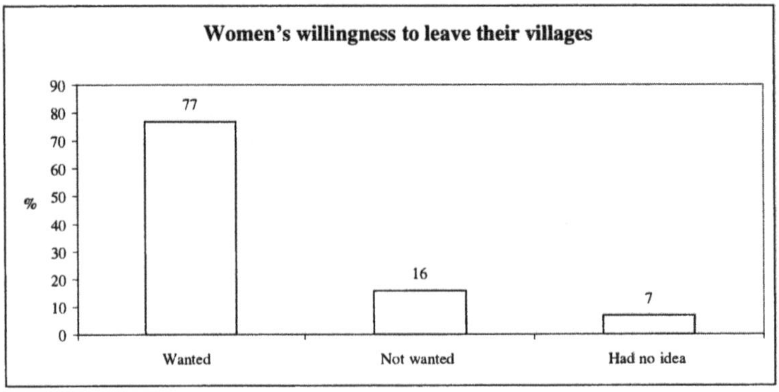

To examine reasons which motivated female migration, the respondents were asked to rank 12 factors in the questionnaire according to their own priorities. The majority chose between four to five factors in terms of importance to them. These are listed in Table 5.32 together with their ranking by the respondents.

Table 5.33 illustrates the numerical and percentage distribution of these priorities among the 925 women in the sample when ranked 1-5 by respondents. The total column, however, shows the number of informants who chose the factor, regardless of how they marked it.

As is clear from tables 5.32 and 5.33, women usually migrated for one of several reasons. "Access to better employment and higher income" is an economic pull factor, indicating the response of migrants to employment opportunities in their destination. In Tabriz, expansion of industries, mainly the construction sector, and investment in infrastructure provided employment for many un/semi-skilled laborers. This factor, which mainly applies to male migrants, was chosen by 42 percent of the respondents, mostly as their first, second or third priority. As discussed earlier, in the case of the informants' husband's literacy rates and employment, 83 percent were either illiterate or had primary education which meant their main chance of employment was in the lowest sectors of the informal economy.

Table 5.12 showed that more than half of the husbands were employed in the construction sector as either unskilled, semi, or sometimes skilled laborers. This economic pull factor was followed by other important push factors existing in rural areas, particularly "the lack of agricultural land and facilities" or "unfavorable agricultural land," mostly as first and second priorities. These economic pull and push factors mentioned by the respondents are strongly supported by other Iranian migratory literature in general and those with specific interest in the city of Tabriz in particular (Afshar, 1985a; Ajami, 1976; Akhavi, 1986; Bayat, 1997; Hoodfar, 1993; Hossein Zadeh-e Dalir, 1982; Jamali, 1985; Keddie, 1972; Pesaran, 1985; Razavi, 1992).

Table 5.32. Reasons for migration in terms of their importance for respondents (n= 925)

Priorities	Factors
1	Access to better employment and higher income in the city
2	Accompanying the family
3	Lack of health services in the village
4	Lack of agricultural land and facilities in the village
5	Lack of educational facilities in the village
6	Marriage
7	Unfavorable land for agriculture in the village
8	Other
9	Escape from social and class conflicts
10	Lack of employment possibility for women in the village
11	Escape from family authority and rural hegemony
12	Loss of family breadwinner

Table 5.33. Factors stimulating female migration and the degree of their importance to migrant women (n= 925)

Reasons	1st Priority	2nd Priority	3rd Priority	4th Priority	5th Priority	Total
Access to better employment/higher income	144	133	66	37	11	391
	37%	*34%*	*17%*	9%	3%	42%
Accompanying the family	274	33	32	15	7	361
	76%	9%	9%	*4%*	*2%*	*39%*
Lack of health services	28	107	110	61	16	322
	9%	*33%*	*34%*	*19%*	*5%*	*35%*
Lack of agricultural land and facilities	99	123	36	14	7	279
	35%	*44%*	*13%*	*5%*	*3%*	*30%*
Lack of educational facilities	26	48	82	52	21	230
	11%	*21%*	*36%*	*23%*	*9%*	*25%*
Marriage	172	20	3	4	1	200
	86%	*10%*	*1.5 %*	*2%*	*0.5 %*	*22%*
Unfavorable land for agriculture	68	47	25	10	1	151
	45%	*31%*	*17%*	*7%*	*0.7 %*	*16%*
Others	44	25	8	3	1	81
	54%	*31%*	*10%*	*4%*	*1%*	*9%*
Escape from social and class conflicts	23	31	7	9	8	78
	30%	*40%*	*9%*	*11%*	*10%*	*8%*
Lack of employment for women	7	16	19	14	12	68
	10%	*23%*	*28 %*	*21%*	*18%*	*7%*
Escape from family authority and rural hegemony	9	11	7	10	2	39
	23%	*28%*	*18%*	*26%*	*5%*	*4%*
Loss of family breadwinner	18	6	1	0	1	26
	69%	*23%*	*4%*	*0%*	*4%*	*3%*

Other factors which are relevant specifically to women such as "lack of employment opportunities for women in the village" and "loss of family breadwinner" were chosen by a small percentage, 7 percent and 3 percent respectively. At this stage, it can be argued that pull-push factors, particularly "access to better economic opportunities" because of unfavorable conditions at their origin or better ones in the city, show the reasons for migration of families as an economic unit, particularly motivation of the breadwinners of the family, such as husbands, or fathers in the case of children. After economic factors, social ones such as the lack of health and educational services and facilities are important and were chosen mostly as second, third and fourth priorities. Marriage was another important factor for 22 percent of my informants. Other factors seem to have had less importance to women in my sample.

Looking at women's marital status and their age groups at the time of migration, however, helps to gain a better understanding of variations in priorities among different categories of women.

As table 5.7 indicated, with the exception of eleven women (ten widowed and one divorced, 1 percent of all respondents), other migrants were, at the time of migration, either single accompanying their parents; single who mainly came to start their married life in the city; single who came to study or work in Tabriz; and married women who came with their families or joined their migrant husbands. Tables 5.34, 5.36, 5.39 and 5.41 divide each marital group of women at the time of migration into age groups. Tables 5.35, 5.37, 5.38, 5.40 and 5.42 illustrate the factors which were important in stimulating each marital and age group separately and cumulatively. However, since the fifth priority chosen by my sample comprised a small percentage of respondents, in the tables the concentration will mostly be on the first four priorities in terms of their significance to the respondents.

Single women who migrated with parents

Table 5.7 illustrated about 31 percent (284) of respondents migrated with their parents; Table 5.34 looks at their age groups during migration.

Table 5.34. Age-group of migrant women who accompanied their parents at the time of migration (n= 284)

Age-group	1-9	10-19	20-29	Total
n	180	95	9	284
%	63	34	3	100

As the above table highlights most of my sample who migrated with their parents (63 percent) were too young at the time of migration (less than ten years old) to reflect on the conditions that led their families to migrate. Therefore, as table 5.35 indicates, accompanying the family was the first priority for 79 percent of them (142 out of 180), as they could not stay behind on their own. Overall, for 75 percent of those women who migrated with their parents, accompanying the family was the first priority.

Only 17 percent of the first age group (1-9) identified "access to better employment" as their first or second priority. "The loss of the family breadwinner" was chosen by only 5 of them (3 percent) as their first priority and "the lack of employment possibilities for women" was chosen by 6 (4 percent), as their second or third priority. It seems that these factors might have been relevant to female relatives such as their mothers but not to themselves, as none of them either started a job in the city at the time of their arrival or even looked for job. Class conflict was chosen by 8 of them as second priority, but it is not clear if this was related to the land reform period. There is little evidence that this group of the respondents played any role in decision-making. However, the other two age groups had better ideas of factors behind migration and their family's decision to migrate, though it is not clear how involved they were in this.

Table 5.35. Factors influencing single female migrants who accompanied their parents at the time of migration (n= 284)

	Age-group of women accompanying their parents						
		1-9		10-19		20-29	Total*
		180		95		9	284
Accompanying the		142		50		3	213
family	*F.*	*79 %*	*F.*	*53%*	*F.*	*33%*	*75%*
Better employ-		30		25		6	97
ment/higher income	*S. & F.*	*17 %*	*S. & Th.*	*26%*	*F. & S.*	*67%*	*34%*
Lack of health services		28		31		1	89
	S. & Th.	*16%*	*S. & Th.*	*33%*	*Th.*	*11%*	*31%*
Lack of educational		23		22		2	70
facilities	*Th. & S.*	*13%*	*Th. & S.*	*23%*	*For.*	*22%*	*25%*
Lack of agricultural		18		23		3	61
land and facilities	*S.*	*10%*	*S. & F.*	*23%*	*S.*	*33%*	*21%*
Unfavourable land for		7		16		2	39
agriculture	*S.*	*4%*	*F. & S.*	*17%*	*F. & Th.*	*2%*	*14%*
Escape from social and		8		7		1	30
class conflicts	*S.*	*4%*	*F. & S.*	*7%*	*Th.*	*11%*	*11%*
Lack of employment		6		5		1	23
possibility for women	*S. & Th.*	*3%*	*S. & F.*	*6%*	*F.*	*11%*	*8%*
Loss of family bread-		5		6		1	13
winner	*F.*	*3%*	*F. & S.*	*6%*	*F.*	*11%*	*5%*
Others		5		4		0	13
	S.	*3%*	*F.*	*4%*			*5%*

Note: *F.*: First Priority
S.: Second Priority

Th.: Third Priority
For.: Fourth Priority
F. & S.: First & Second Priority (respectively)
F. & Th.: First & Third Priority (respectively)
S. & F.: Second & First Priority (respectively)
S. & Th.: Second & Third Priority (respectively)
Th. & S.: Third & Second Priority (respectively)

* The total column for each of the factors includes number of women who identified that factor as a reason for migration. However, since some rankings were lower than four, comprising a small number of respondents, these have not been included in the table. Thus, the total for each row cumulatively is more than the numbers of women included in the table.

In the second age group of 10-19, the first priority for 53 percent was to accompany their families in the migratory flow. Economic factors were scored as first or second priorities for the majority of women in this age group. Unfavourable economic conditions in their village such as "lack of agricultural facilities" and "unfavourable land for agriculture" were chosen mainly as first or second priority by 40 percent of women in this age-group. "Access to better employment and a higher income" was chosen by 26 percent of the respondents as their second or third priority. "Loss of the family breadwinner" and "lack of employment opportunities for women" was chosen by 11 women (12 percent), as their first or second priority. As the data indicate, two of them, who were 15 years old at the time of migration, searched for a job and only one found a job, with the state four years after her migration. Although both of them wanted to leave their villages, it is not clear what role they played in the decision making aspect of migration and to what extent they managed to influence their family. Social factors such as "lack of educational and health services" were chosen by an average of 56 percent of the respondents as second or third priority. These factors might have been important for their families in their decision to migrate to the city, for providing better health and educational opportunities for their children.

In the third age group, 20-29, there were nine women. For all of them, the pull-push economic factors in their home villages and in the city played an important role in migration. Six women chose "access to better employment" as their first or second priority. Although all of them wanted to leave their villages, they did not try to find a job in the city, for reasons such as illiteracy, or the barriers which married life in the city brought them, including lack of permission from their husband to work or go outside the home, and the burdens of housework and motherhood. For this age group, the social and cultural factors were less important.

Marriage-based migration

One hundred and twenty nine women migrated to the city to start a married life. They often married male migrants from their own villages who had gone to the city in search of employment and maintained links with their origins. However, when the family migrates as a whole, the young male's connection with their home village is cut off and the marriage pattern changes. The interviews at the second stage of the study provided more scope for exploring the pattern of marriage among migrants. In most cases, as informants mentioned about their children's marriages, male migrants or the younger generation of migrants normally find their partners in their neighbourhood in the city, often migrants from the same or other rural areas, yet sometimes migrants marry girls from their own village. It seems that those who find their wives from their own villages usually marry their own close relatives, whereas, those who marry girls from other villages are usually socially and economically deprived, and the women they choose have approximately the same or worse socio-economic conditions. Although this pattern cannot be generalised, the stories of nine women who I interviewed and who had migrated for marriage, and those of other interviewees' children's marriages to some extent reflects this argument[18]. The Advisor to the President on "Women's Affairs," at the time of my second stage of research, also stated that the number of unmarried rural women is increasing because of increased migration of rural males to the cities and a change in their ways of spouse selection[19]. Table 5.36 illustrates the age group of single women who migrated mainly for marriage.

Table 5.36. Age-group of single women (for marriage) at the time of migration (n=129)

Age-group	1-9	10-19	20-29	30^+	Total
n	1	102	24	2	129
%	1	79	18.5	1.5	100

As table 5.36 indicates the majority of women who migrated for marriage were in the age group of 10-19 followed by those aged 20-29. One woman migrated at the age of 8 and two others in their thirties, and for all three, marriage was the first priority and accompanying the family (more possibly their new family) their second priority. Table 5.37 highlights the rankings of factors which were chosen by two age groups of women, (10-19, 20-29), who migrated for marriage or to start a married life.

As is clear from the table, for 99 percent of women in this category, marriage was the main reason for migration, followed by, for 21 percent, economic opportunities in the city, mainly for their husbands. Other factors did not play an important role in their migration. "The loss of the family breadwinner" and "escape from social and class conflict" were not chosen at all. Only one woman in her twenties chose "escape from family authority and rural hegemony" as her fourth reason; and only two women chose the "other" factor. During the interview, some women from this category mentioned that they were not willing to leave their villages. Those who faced domestic violence in their marital relationships were not happy in the city mainly because of being away from their family and social support.

Table 5.37. Factors influencing women to migrate for marriage (n= 129)

	Age-group of single women at marriage				
		10-19 (102)		20-29 (24)	Total * (126)
Marriage		101		24	128
	F. & S.	*99%*	*F.*	*96%*	*99 %*
		14		5	27
Access to better employment and higher income	*S. & Th.*	*14%*	*Th. & S.*	*21%*	*21%*
The lack of agricultural		14		4	22
facilities	*S. & Th.*	*14%*	*S. & Th.*	*17%*	*17%*
Lack of health services		9		5	21
	S. & Th.	*9%*	*S. & For.*	*21%*	*16%*
Accompanying the family		5		2	11
	F. & S.	*5%*	*S.*	*8%*	*9%*
Lack of educational facili-		3		2	8
ties	*S.*	*3%*	*For.*	8%	*6%*
Unfavourable land for agri-		4		1	7
culture	*S.*	*4%*	*Th.*	*4%*	*5%*

* As was explained in the note to table 5.35, the total column for each of the factors includes the sum of the number of women who identified that factor as one of their reasons for migration. Therefore the total for each row cumulatively is more than the numbers of women included in the table.

Reasons for independent migration of single women

Three women migrated mainly to work and study, and as table 5.38 illustrates, they gave only one reason for their migration.

Table 5.38. Age and the priorities of single women who migrated to work/ study (n= 3)

Age at arrival	**Only one reason**
15	The lack of educational opportunities in the village
21	Access to better employment and higher income in the city
25	The lack of employment opportunities for women in the village

Reasons for migration of married women, at the time of migration

Married women have been subdivided into six groups on the basis of their age, and as Table 5.39 illustrates there was a concentration of respondents in the first and second age groups.

Table 5.39. Age-groups of married women at the time of migration (n= 498)

Age-group	n	%
10-19	166	33
20-29	203	41
30-39	74	15
40-49	35	7
50-69	11	2
Age unknown	9	2
Total	498	100

Compared to single women with parents, or those who mainly migrated to start married life in the city (for the majority of whom the major reason was to accompany the family or marry), married women had diverse reasons for migrating, among which economic factors were the most obvious. The prevalence of these is in evidence in all the subdivisions of married women by age group. Economic pull-push factors, however, differ between age groups. As table 5.40 indicates, the pull factors of the city were chosen as first or second priority by a high percentage of the respondents, with the exception of age groups of 40-49 and 50-59. As age increased among my informants married at the time of migration, push factors and unfavourable conditions in the rural areas, particularly adverse agricultural conditions and lack of health services were more important than potential economic opportunities/gains in the city.

Table 5.40. Factors stimulating married female migrants at the time of migration (n= 498)

	Age-group of married women						
	10-19 (166)	20-29 (203)	30-39 (74)	40-49 (35)	50-69 (11)	Age unknown (9)	Total
Access to better employment and income	77	102	40	8	4	6	270
	46%	*50%*	*54%*	*23%*	*36%*	*67%*	*54%*
Lack of health services	53	81	22	9	5	1	216
	32%	*40%*	*30%*	*26%*	*45%*	*11%*	*43%*
Lack of land/agricultural facilities	47	68	33	15	4	2	193
	28%	*33%*	*45%*	*43%*	*36%*	*22%*	*39%*
Lack of educational facilities	25	55	17	7	2	1	151
	15%	*27%*	*23%*	*20%*	*18%*	*11%*	*30%*
Accompanying the family	41	37	17	8	2	2	140
	25%	*18%*	*23%*	*23%*	*18%*	*22%*	*28%*
Unfavourable land for agriculture	25	35	13	10	0	2	104
	15%	*17%*	*18%*	*29%*		*22%*	*21%*
Marriage	33	26	2	0	0	1	72
	20%	*13%*	*3%*			*11%*	*14%*
Others	19	22	6	3	2	1	66
	11%	*11%*	*8%*	*9%*	*18%*	*11%*	*13%*
Escape from social and class contact	11	8	10	2	1	2	50
	7%	*4%*	*14%*	*6%*	*9%*	*22%*	*10%*
Lack of employment for women	6	11	2	2	1	0	42
	4%	*5%*	*3%*	*6%*	*9%*		*8%*
Escape from family and rural hegemony	9	10	2	2	0	0	33
	5%	*5%*	*3%*	*6%*			*7%*
Loss of family breadwinner	0	1	0	2	1	1	6
		0.5 %		*6%*	*9%*	*11%*	*1%*

Although the majority of married women (81 percent) stated that they were willing to leave their villages, only a small number (9 percent) looked for an urban job, and less than half (47 percent) were successful in finding a job within two years. More than half of the married women (52 percent) mentioned three main reasons for not looking for, or finding an urban job. These were illiteracy, the burden of motherhood and housework, and the lack of husband's permission for 23 percent, 20 percent and 9 percent of respondents respectively. However, as the age of married women increased, their husbands' reluctance to give them permission to work declined. So that, of the 109 women between the ages of 30 to 49, no one mentioned their husband's permission. For them, illiteracy, the burden of motherhood and housework, and illness were given as the main reasons for not looking for an urban job.

Although four women aged between 40 and 60 years old left their village due to the loss of the family breadwinner or the lack of employment opportunities for women in the village, none of them looked for a job. Surprisingly, during the interview some women mentioned that they were willing to leave the village because of women's workload in rural areas. "I wanted to become a *khanum* (lady)," was an immediate response by some women as soon as I asked them why they migrated to the city. In rural areas, women contribute substantially to the production process in animal husbandry, agriculture and industry, as paid (mainly in kind) or unpaid family labor[20]. Animal husbandry is an important economic function for rural families in which women play an important role and as a result can gain more influence over family affairs, even if they do not receive direct remuneration for their efforts (Touba, 1980: 55; Razavi, 1992). The hard labor performed by rural women in the fields or rural industry, in addition to their daily domestic work and care of children, offers them very limited, if any, social and economic privileges.

Although the social factors of health and educational services were mentioned as second or third priority, the lack of health services seems to have played a more important role than the lack of educational services. During the interviews, fewer women talked about the lack of educational services for their children in their villages or better access to educational opportunities in the city as an important factor causing family migration. This was mentioned mainly by women who came from relatively better off villages with better economic indicators. More importantly, when education became a factor encouraging migration, it was usually children, most often male children, that were sent to the city on their own. The majority of women talked about illnesses and the sudden death of family members, children, or their animals, which affected the family emotionally or economically, and their ultimate decision to leave their villages. Most women remarked how the lack of primary health care in the villages, such as vaccinations, doctors, medicine, clean water, and difficulties of emergency access to health services in the city, due to poor transport, financial, and other problems, turned simple and curable illnesses into fatal ones. For instance, one of the interviewees explained how the sudden death of her young brother a day before his wedding brought great shock, grief, and misery to the family: at the age of 13, as the oldest child of the family, she had to take responsibilities of the family. For mothers, the memory of sudden death of adolescent children was very painful, even after a passage of many years or decades. They also talked about how the death of their animals affected the family economically. For instance one of the women said that:

> In those days, in our regions, there were only a few people who could diagnose animal diseases and they were not in the village all the time. In the middle of the summer, suddenly some of the animals became ill and if we had no access to those experts, we immediately had to kill the animal for our own food consumption. There was one sort of disease called "madness"; in that case we had to leave the animal in the countryside to be eaten by predators. There was a kind of cow from which you could get between 15 to 20 kilos of milk each day. Whenever one of those cows became ill, they were immediately killed. But nowadays there are vets in the cities and nearby towns who can save the village animals. This is because of the paved road to the villages, the regular visits of the vets, and the villagers' access to transport, either their own transport or public transport.

Reasons for migration of widowed and divorced women, at the time of migration

Of 925 women, there were 10 (1 percent) women who were widowed at the time of migration. As table 5.42 illustrates for 70 percent of these, "loss of family breadwinner" was mentioned as one of the main reason for leaving their villages. "Access to better employment and higher income" was the second most important priority for 4 of them. Table 5.41 shows the age groups of widowed women at the time of their migration.

Table 5.41. Age-group of migrant women who were widows at the time of migration (n= 10)

Age-group	10-19	20-29	30-39	40-49	50-59	Total
n	1	1	3	2	3	10
%	10	10	30	20	30	100

Table 5.42. Factors stimulating widow migrants at the time of migration (n= 10)

	Age-group of widows					
	10-19 (1)	20-29 (1)	30-39 (3)	40-49 (2)	50-59 (3)	Total
Loss of family breadwinner	1 *F.*	1 *S.*	3 *F.& S.*	2 *F.*	0	7 70%
Access to better employment and higher income	1 *S.*	0	0	1 *S.*	2 *F.*	4 40%
Lack of educational facilities	0	1 *For.*	0	0	1 *F.*	3 30%
Lack of health services	0	0	0	0	1 *S.*	2 20%
Lack of agricultural facilities	0	0	2 *F.&Th.*	0	0	2 20%
Unfavourable land for agriculture	0	1 *Th.*	0	0	0	1 10%
Lack of employment possibility for women	0	0	0	0	1 *Th.*	1 10%
Escape from family authority and rural hegemony	0	1 *F.*	0	0	0	1 10%

The first and second priorities for the 15-year-old widow in the first group were respectively loss of the family breadwinner and access to better employment; however, she did unpaid work at home after migration. For the woman in the second age group, escape from family authority and rural hegemony was ranked as the first priority, though loss of her family breadwinner did not automatically lead her into having a paid job, due to lack of any skill.

None of the other eight widows, who left their villages, mainly because of the loss of the breadwinner and economic factors, had any urban job mostly because of illness and the burden of motherhood and housework. Most of them, however, did unpaid work at home as carpet-weavers and one of them as a shopkeeper.

As already mentioned, there was only one woman who was divorced at the time of migration. Her reason for migration was only unfavourable land for agriculture. At the time of migration, she was 24 years old and divorced;

at the time of data collection she was 72 years old and married with children.

With whom did the women in the sample migrate?

Of 925 women, 877 (95 percent) migrated to the city accompanied by either their husbands and children or by their parents and siblings. Of the other 48 women, two migrated with only their children, and 46 women said they migrated alone, but when I looked at their answers, I noticed that the majority misunderstood the question. For instance, for 73 percent of them, the first priority was marriage; three of them chose to accompany their families as a first priority; and two other respondents were 2 and 5 years old and obviously must have come to the city with their parents. Only three of the 48 women came to study and work, and all of them were successful in their attempt. Therefore, with the exception of a few women, the majority had family-based migration.

Tabriz the first destination for the majority of the respondents

The majority of respondents (94 percent) left their villages and came straight to Tabriz. Only 6 percent went to Tabriz on their second wave of migration; most of them had left their villages to go to a small city, and then moved from there to Tabriz. According to this sample, it can be argued that the main pattern of migration direct to Tabriz's slum and squatter settlements is rural-urban migration. In chapter 3, I explained that according to the studies, the northern squatter settlements of Tabriz are mostly occupied by migrants from the rural areas of Ahar *Shahrestan*, for whom the socio-economic conditions are the worst in the East Azarbaijan province. Geographically, Ahar *Shahrestan* is a mountainous region with very harsh winters and land unsuitable for agriculture. In this sample the largest group of respondents came from the rural areas of Ahar S*hahrestan* (34 percent); the second largest was migrants from three neighbouring districts of Ahar *Shahrestan* (21 percent); and *Bostan-abad* with 16 percent, was the third highest migrant-sending *Shahrestan* to the city of Tabiz. One hundred and ten respondents (12 percent) came from different villages of Tabriz S*hahrestan*. A small number of the respondents migrated from other S*hahrestans* of the province, and a very small number from other provinces. Therefore, as the other studies indicate, most migration to Tabriz was inter-*Shahrestan*, 96 percent of migrants undertaking intra-province migration, and only 3 percent inter-province migration. Table 5.43 shows the entry point of the migrants to Tabriz based on intra- or inter-province migration.

Table 5.43. Number and percentage of migrants to the city of Tabriz, in terms of intra- or inter-province (n= 925)

Name of Province	N	%
East-Azarbaijan	885	95.7
Ardabil	16	1.7
West Azarbaijan	10	1.1
Gilan	2	0.2
Not stated	12	1.3

Income and Expenditure of the Family

In terms of income and expenditure, the respondents were asked general questions about the level of the family income as a basic unit; the level of family expenditure; who contributes to the family income; how much each contributes; and if their income was enough to meet their basic needs. It is difficult to assess the average income and expenditure of the families in the sample, as the information given in relation to some of the questions did not match with the information given to other questions, and it seems that the majority of the respondents gave arbitrary answers to questions on income and expenditure of the family. In most cases the income and expenditure given was the same, or the expenditure was higher than the income. For these reasons, I did not construct a table for these two variables. However, according to the data, more than half of the respondents were low-income earners and the majority of the informants stated that their income was not enough to meet their basic needs and could be classified as poor. Forty-four and forty-nine of the respondents did not answer the income and expenditure questions respectively.

Of the 246 women who stated that they had jobs, only 38 percent (93 women) stated that they contributed to family income. One hundred twenty two women said two people contributed to the family income; and 4 of them did not name anyone as a contributor to their family income. The majority of women, who worked in household enterprises related to carpet making and contributed significantly to the family income[21], regarded their economic engagement as part of their housework that they did in their spare time.

Of the whole sample, 242 women mentioned only one contributor to the family income, and the earnings of that contributor were the same as the total family income. Only 27 percent of the informants named a second contributor. One of the striking issues arising from the data is that the majority of the informants had unpaid home-based jobs, they did not consider themselves as income generators for the family and did not perceive themselves as economically active. As other studies on women and work show, the upaid family labor of women means that they are not considered an economically active part of the population, and are often neglected in the process of data collection for Censuses or other studies at national, regional and local levels. The unpaid home-based engagement of women in the production process also often adversely affects their status in the family. Women's work that does not generate cash remains immeasurable, invisible and home-based, despite their economic contribution to a household's income.

Many studies claim that unpaid family labor of women and children in Iran was promoted as a result of the penetration of capital into rural areas, particularly after the land reform project (Beck, 1978; Touba, 1980; Tabari, 1982; Afshar, 1985b; Razavi, 1992). Before land reform, in the agricultural sector for instance, where the plough cultivation system was a dominant form of cultivation, men and women were in a similar position of social isolation, and both were working for landlords and receiving their earnings mostly in kind. Women received their remuneration separately from their husbands regardless of their class position, i.e., whether they belonged to sharecropping or casual labor families (Razavi, 1992, 1993). In the carpet industry too, the looms were property of a single loom owner, and women, even those who were weaving in their own homes, received a direct wage for their labor (Touba, 1980: 55). The abolition of the feudal system and the spread of "dependent capitalism" (Beck, 1978; Tabari and Yeganeh, 1982: 144) through money and market relations created a socio-economic crisis in rural areas and led to deterioration in rural women's socio-economic status. The distribution of land and looms among individual families enabled men to utilize their family's labor free of charge, particularly that of women, which intensified women's traditionally degraded status. Men took charge of the means of production and sold the final products in nearby cities. Their contact with the outside world got better through increased employment opportunities in construction and industry. All these resulted in the development of family-based agriculture and industry, which aggravated the exploitation of women (Touba, 1980: 55-59; Afshar, 1985b). The proportion of unpaid labor carried out by the rural female population increased from 31 percent in 1966 to 57 percent in 1976, not only in agriculture but also in rural industry[22]. Women's situations were different in highly industrialized regions with mechanized farms using hired labor[23], where the proletarianization of many peasants as a result of capitalist relations compelled many women to work as wage laborers for large landowners. Women's involvement in paid employment, mainly due to men's lack of access to means of production and inability to provide sufficient means of subsistence, resulted in social and cultural changes and women's better status in the family (Touba, 1980; Tabari and Yeganeh, 1982: 146; Afshar, 1989a). The growth of an urban home-market due to prosperity in urban areas, as well as traditional export markets for Iranian carpets, increased women's opportunities to contribute to the family income throughout the year (Tabari, 1982: 7). A daughter became an asset to the family and their marriage age as well as their value in the marriage market increased without any improvement in their social conditions. Despite the fact that a carpet was a cash product, sold for a profit, women remained unpaid family laborers and were excluded from money relations. They were not able to own the means of production or to sell their product, partly due to the lack of access to the market, and partly because the market was a male-oriented place (Afshar, 1985b).

My own study, particularly the interview process, discussed in the following chapters, indicates that the majority of the women were actively contributing to the income of their families. A comparison between women's answers to structured questions in the form of questionnaires with their answers to open-ended questions in the interviews highlights the importance of qualitative research method and also complementarity of combined research methods. Although questionnaires are one of the several ways of collecting information, they are not always very reliable, and they can easily omit or distort the valuable experiences of the informants.

Problems of migrant women in the city

The respondents were also asked to talk about the problems that they faced in the city. About 52 percent of the respondents answered this question. Women's lack of interest to this question also highlights the limitations of quantitative data in terms of getting more tangible answers to questions such as women's problems. More than half of these who answered this question mentioned economic problems and poverty, strengthening the previous claim that more than half of the respondents were living on an extremely low income, particularly if this is considered in the context of the housing problems and poor living facilities, highlighted above. Bayat's study from migrants living in Tehran also shows that the majority of migrants in slums are not satisfied with their new situation, but preferred it to the one they left behind, where they struggled against poverty and destitution[24].

Table 5.44. Problems of migrant women in the city (n= 486)

Problems	n	%
Economic problems	255	*52.5*
Housing problems and the lack of living facilities	150	*31.0*
Being away from home	37	*8.0*
Cultural problems and stress in the city	29	*6.0*
Having many children	9	*2.0*
Health, because of the workload	4	*1.0*
Violence by men	2	*0.5*
Total	486	

Hardly any women were keen to talk about social and cultural issues that affected their status in the family or their relationship with their partners. However, as I will discuss in detail in following chapters, during the interview women were more willing to share their problems and issues with me and to talk in detail about relationships with their partners, including domestic violence.

Notes

1. *Khanoum* literally means a lady who does not often do household or other chores.

2. Throughout the book, the unmarried women will be called single women.

3. The multiple answers to this question were set according to the conventional answers in Iranian sociological textbooks, rather than according to changes that have happened in Iran in late 1990s in terms of adult literacy and more extended schooling. Therefore, the multiple answers included: illiterate *(bisavad)*; basic reading and writing skills (*savad-e khandan va neveshtan,* which includes few years of schooling); primary education (*ebtedaei*, five years of schooling); secondary education (*rahnamaei,* which includes three years of secondary schooling), higher-school education (*dabirestan*, which includes another four years); diploma and higher. I should have included adult literacy *nehzat* or *nehzat-e savad amouzi*, as another option. If I had added this option, the total of illiterate women might have been fewer. For detailed information on women's education, particularly adult literacy, see the next chapter.

Most of the women with whom I conducted a semi-structured interview participated in *nehzat* classes. According to the 1996 census, the literacy rate for the population aged six years and over in the city of Tabriz was 82 percent: (87 percent for men and 76 percent for women). The corresponding figure for urban areas of the *shahrestan-e Tabriz* was similar to Tabriz city's literacy rate. For rural areas it was 78 percent of the male population and 64 percent of the female. However, my data indicates 65 percent illiteracy among the sample. This can be explained from two perspectives, one of which might be related to the options given in the answers, which did not include adult literacy; the second mainly due to the fact that data was mostly collected from senior women in the households who compared, to younger ones, were less exposed to educational opportunities.

At the *Shahrestan* level, particularly among the 50+ age group, the percentage of literate women was much lower than the percentage of literate men. For instance, for the age group of 50-54 the percentage was 30 percent compared to 60 percent and for 55-59, it was 20 percent compared to 57 percent. This gap was even greater between rural areas and urban areas from age 45+. Moreover, previous studies from Tabriz slums also showed a positive correlation between the level of education and the age of the population. Migrant women were excluded from these studies. Hossain Zadeh-e Dalir, 1982; Dallalpur, 1991 cited in Tabriz University Report (1995).

4. This question also did not include the option of *nehzat* among the multi-choice answers.

5. A study from slum areas of Tabriz in 1990 also shows a similar occupational pattern among male slum settlers. According to this study, the majority of the heads of household in slum and squatter areas were engaged in the informal sector of the economy. Construction laborers comprised 58 percent; self-employment, particularly in the carpet industry was about 17 percent; about 5 percent were in state employment; and a section of population close to 20 percent was fluctuating between underemployment and unemployment. Dallalpur (1991) cited in Tabriz University Report (1995).

6. These figures not only differ from one official source to another, but they also greatly differ from those from UN and other international organizations, according to Jahangir Amuzgar, often with a 10 percent margin of difference. For detailed information, see: Amuzgar, 2004: "Iran's Unemployment Crises." In *Middle East Economic Survey*. Vol. XXVII, No. 41.

7. See "Unemployment in Iran: An emerging social crisis?" written by Tytti Nahi for *Iran-Mania* in 2002. Tuesday 09 July 2002

8. In 2004, Iran's Planning and Management Organization reported an unemployment rate of 34 percent among 15-24 year olds: 22 percent for men and 41 percent for women. The report predicted that if the unemployment rate stayed the same, within two years the jobless rate would reach 52 percent among the 15-29 age group, more than 10 percent of whom are college graduates and 30 percent high school diploma holders.

9. The Planning and Budget Organization of East Azarbaijan Province analyzed the quantitative indicators of housing construction of the Province in the two censuses of 1976-1986. The comparison indicates improvements in housing construction in the province, but with considerable differences in rural and urban areas. The city of Tabriz, with an 81 percent growth rate in housing construction, had the highest growth rate, compared to the situation in the province and the *Shahrestan-e* Tabriz. Table 3.2 in this book showed a population growth of 62 percent in the city during 1976-1986. Improvements in housing construction after the Islamic revolution can be explained by reduction in land prices and the support provided by the state for low-income families. This analysis also shows a drop in population density in residential units. However, this drop in the city of Tabriz was slower compared to drop in population density in the *Shahrestan-e* Tabriz and the province (Planning and Budget Organization of East Azarbaijan: 1986).

10. In Iran the ownership of a residential house is one of the important indicators of social status, regardless of the quality of the house. However, comparison between 1976 and 1986 censuses shows that the percentage of families owning their own houses dropped from 77 percent in 1976 to 66 percent in 1986. The number of families living in rented houses or other housing arrangements, particularly in state-owned houses, increased (Planning and Budget Organization of East Azarbaijan: 1986).

11. These arrangements often respect the autonomy of young married couples and are ways of helping them to save their earnings to buy their own houses.

12. In a leased house, the tenant pays the house-owner a relatively large sum of money in advance for a contract of one or more years, without paying monthly rent. At the end of the contract, either the contract is extended for a new deal, or the

house-owner pays the same money back to the tenant. This process works due to the high inflation rate in the country.

13. The Planning and Budget Organization of East Azarbaijan Province analysis of population density in each room in the city of Tabriz in the two censuses of 1976-1986 indicates a drop from 1.8 to 1.6. This drop in population density in poorer neighborhoods of the city was from 2.3 to 1.96. (Planning and Budget Organization of East Azarbaijan: 1986).

14. According to Tabriz University's report (1995), the latest data and previous studies of slum areas of Tabriz show that only 48 percent of households build with a legal permission that follows standard construction requirements. Thirty three percent of residents did not have any legal and registered ownership documents for their residential houses.

15. Houses made of brick and wood, particularly mud-brick are very vulnerable to environmental disasters, particularly earthquake, and are indicators of the residents' long-term poverty. These kinds of houses are normally built by the migrants themselves, often without legal permission from the city council. During the interview, the residents of this type of house did not use the word of "building," the process which is done by the skilled builder, plumber, electrician etc. using proper and standard building materials. They often stated that: "we have patched the house together ourselves," sometimes with the help of a builder or even without. Women were also involved in the process of "patching" as laborers for the men who were doing the "building job."

16. A comparison in kind of the houses in the city of Tabriz between 1976 and 1986 shows an increase in the percentage of strong houses (a 38 percent improvement in 1986 against 1976) and a decrease in the percentage of the weak ones. But the percentage of the partially strong and weak houses in the slum areas and among the survey sample is still quite high. Tabriz University Report (1995) has detailed information in this respect.

17. Buildings made of concrete and iron are strong houses, with proper building construction and legal procedures.

18. Michael Fisher's anthropological study of women's position in Iran also claimed that the general rate of endogamous marriages, a practice in most parts of Iran, was decreasing. For details, see: Fisher, 1978. "On Changing the Concept and Position of Persian Women." In L. Beck and N. R. Keddie (eds.) *Women in the Muslim World.*

19. In an interview with *Ettelaat International*, on 20th September 2001, Zahra Shojaie, adviser to Mohammad Khatami, the President of Iran claimed that the number of unmarried rural women had increased. She added that: "the statistic indicates that in the current year (1380/2001) the percentage of unmarried rural women was 41 percent against 21 percent in the previous year (1379/2000)." The minimum age of marriage on the basis of which the number of unmarried rural women had been calculated, however, was not given.

20. The amount of women's participation in agriculture, as discussed in chapter 2, depends on the nature of the agricultural system as well as to the degree of religiosity in the region, which influences ideological belief systems, and social and cultural norms on women's mobility. However, different studies from different regions in Iran show weeding, fruit picking and harvesting as typical of female activities. For

detailed information see: Beck, 1978; Touba, 1980; Tabari and Yeganeh, 1982; Afshar, 1989a; Razavi, 1992; Hoodfar, 1993.

21. For further details see chapter 7.

22. Data collected by the Statistical Centre of Iran for National Census of Population and Housing, 1966, 1976.

23. As stated in chapter 3, orchards and mechanized farms with hired laborers were exempted from the land reform. These highly mechanized farms were in the north of Iran, particularly rice and tea plantations that relied heavily on female labor.

24. For detailed information see Bayat's *Street Politics: Poor People's Movements in Iran*. New York: Columbia University, 1997.

Chapter 6

Examining Practical Obstacles toward Educational Level/Success among Female Migrants

Due to its central role in women's socio-economic status within the family and wider society, female literacy has attracted the attention of researchers and scholars studying women, gender, and development (Moghadam, 1998: 27-48). In migration literature, education as an independent variable, and its correlation with migration, has an important place. However, the correlation between education and migration among women who migrate as dependents, mainly as wives, is not as important as that of men or autonomous female migrants who migrate mainly for economic purposes (Bauer, 1984, 1985; Brydon, 1989). Although the majority in my sample did not cite access to education as a main reason for their migration, interviews with migrant women confirmed that access to education was important to younger ones. The accessibility of schools in most villages, strong commitment from the government, revolutionary institutions, endorsement of girls' education by religious leaders after the revolution, and availability of female teachers and single-sex classrooms or schools has made it easier for girls to attend primary and even secondary schools in rural areas. In this chapter, I discuss the accessibility of education for women in rural and urban areas, and the different socio-economic and ideological factors that affected female literacy among the informants of this study. My analysis is based on 925 questionnaires and more than 120 interviews conducted with migrant women in Tabriz. First data from questionnaires is examined and then, in explaining factors that deprived many rural or migrant women from access to knowledge in their places of origin or destination, data from personal interviews. The latter highlight women's access (or lack of it) to educational opportunities and services, both in terms of availability, and of the traditional ideologies and practices that are used to control women and their social mobility.

I also look at other aspects of women's lives that often have some correlation with their level of literacy. These are marriage, fertility behavior, the number of children that they bear, and infant mortality. The interviews suggest that variation in levels of women's literacy plays an important role in shaping their lives. Although increasing economic difficulties in Iran have attributed to a rise in the age of women at marriage and fewer children, a rise in the level of female education, as shown by the interviews, has an important role in rise of age at marriage and stronger initiatives by women in family planning. For educated women, marriage has become a matter of negotiation between parents and children, and this change was very noticeable in my sample. Educated girls are more aware of their rights and sensitive to the loss of them. However, before analysing the data, I provide an introduction to female literacy in modern Iran.

The New Educational System in Iran With Particular Focus on Female Literacy fom the Start Until the Late 1970s

Growing contact with the West during the ninteenth century and detoriation of Iranian society in general during the Qajar period (1779-1925) led to growing awareness among several Iranian reformists of the country's backwardness compared to Western powers, particularly in military and technological areas. This awareness called for a change and imitation of the West in facing the challenges of the time, a call which was often rejected mostly by *ulama* who wanted to safeguard Islamic and traditional values[1]. Around the mid-nineteenth century, education was seen as a major factor in the political and socio-economic progress of the West, not only by Iranian intellectuals, but also by their Middle Eastern counterparts. Towards the end of the ninteenth century, a modern education from western universities gradually became desirable for young people from elite families, for whom it was initially ancestry, not competence, that determined social status and certain high political and administrative positions. Gradually, education and its interconnection with constitutionalism and people's awareness of rights became an important political discourse among Iranian intellectuals, and the new educated classes played an important role in advocating reforms, liberal social movements, and in publishing newspapers, all of which led to the Constitutional Revolution of 1906, which weakened the Qajar regime[2].

For the first time, the Constitutional Revolution provided an opportunity for Iranian women to participate in social movements. The period 1919-1932 was a time of rising interest in women's rights movements in Iran. Literate and intellectual women, mainly from upper classes and inspired by the revolution, formed their own organizations and periodicals, where they questioned Iranian women's inferior position in society and gave more priority to female education. The first private school for girls was opened in 1897[3].

The Qajar dynasty, with domestic instability and national socio-economic deterioration, worsened by World War I and the British and Russian alliance dividing Iran into zones under their control, and incapability of central government in dealing with this was ended by the Constitutional Revolution. The situation paved the way for a radical change and coup in 1921 through cooperation between an army commander, Reza Khan, and a politician, who later parted from each other; Reza Khan became dominant, concentrated all power in his hands and declared his Pahlavi dynasty in 1925[4]. As Reza Shah (1925-41) he had three broader goals: nationalism, secularization, and westernization. Unlike other intellectuals of the time, he was illiterate, but perceived educational reform as vital for meeting his goals. In his attempt to modernize, Westernize and secularize Iranian society, he replaced traditional schools with centralized Western-style ones in major urban areas. The reform increased women's access to education, mostly for the upper middle classes. Girls' schools developed much slower than those for boys, mainly due to societal resistance towards female education and ideological beliefs and practices among the majority which gave priority to that for boys (Paidar, 1997: 108; Sanasarian, 1982: 61-62). Initially girls' schools were often set up privately in major cities, particularly in Tehran. Despite support and protection from the secular state, these were attacked by those opposed to women's education (Sanasarian, 1982: 32-49), mainly religious authorities who had been exclusively in charge of education in Iran for centuries[5]. For decades, education, particularly female education, was a major ideological discourse between the Pahlavi state (1925-1975) and its religious opposers, the *ulama* who viewed the modern educational system as a hub of cultural dependency and immorality, leading to alienation of Muslim youth from Islamic traditions by importing western ideas (Nafisi, 1992: 163-64). Girls' non-religious schooling was regarded as an act against Islam which would pose a threat to society. Despite this opposition, the size of educational systems rapidly increased in urban areas during decades, and social attitudes started to change in favour of women's education. Until the late 1960s, however, literacy was practically non-existent amoung rural women (Touba, 1980)[6]. In 1971, according to UNESCO, 92 percent of rural women were illiterate compared to 52 percent of urban ones (Moghissi, 1996: 46-47). "I didn't go to school, there was no school in our village" was a statement often made by the oldest informants in my study.

The establishment of the Rural Literacy Corps in 1962/63[7], to some extent slowly improved access of rural people to education in the 1970s, but still the ideological norms played a preventative role in female literacy. For instance, the existence of male teachers in village schools often had negative impacts on girl's school attendance and education. Many of my informants were proud of sending their sons to Tabriz to continue their education at secondary and higher levels, while their daughters were prevented from studying in their own village, despite availability of primary schools. Wherever unmarried female high school graduates were part of the Literacy Campaign in rural areas, girl's attendance at rural schools improved relatively (Paidar, 1997: 158)[8]. Despite this, the literacy rate of rural women, who comprised more than half the female population, was only 17 percent in 1976, most of whom had only a few years of primary education (Mirani, 1983: 72). Despite the Pahlavi state's intention to enhance women's participation in social, economic and educational arenas, there was a continuation of social inequalities both between rural and urban areas[9], and also between different social classes of urban settlers.

Women's education, particularly in lower class families, was mainly affected by social inequality and ideology. Due to the crucial role of social class in allocation of educational resources, female migrants—normally coming from the poorest sections of peasantry and belonging to the lowest urban social strata—were more affected by social inequalities. However, interviews with my informants indicate that ideological factors, which supported traditional norms and beliefs regarding gender inequality, played a more crucial role in depriving women in traditional, religious as well as working class families from access to limited educational opportunities. Men's limited access to education in migrant families, however, was mainly affected by social inequalities rather than ideological factors.

Female Literacy, Particularly Rural Female Literacy, since 1979 Revolution

Since the early days of its establishment, the Islamic state has attempted to de-secularize the educational system and convey a new ideological framework through education[10]. However, the de-secularization of general education was not as intense because of the Islamization of higher education in April of 1980 for the purpose of "Cultural Revolution" which closed down universities for about three years[11]. Following this the Educational Services expanded in both formal education and adult literacy in urban and rural areas, and were assigned the task of transformation of secular values to Islamic ones. Article 30 of the post-revolutionary Constitution of Iran obliged the government to provide free education up to secondary level for all citizens.

During the transitional period after the revolution, illiterate adults were also encouraged to participate in literacy classes. In 1981, "*Nehzat-e savad amouzi*[12]," which literally means "Literacy Campaign" was established mainly for promoting basic literacy and eradicating illiteracy among deprived adults in rural and urban areas. A comparison of women's literacy over the period of 1976 to 1986 in different provinces of Iran with different degrees of economic development, as well as linguistic and ethnic factors, indicated that "women in less developed, more ethnic and rural regions of the country had greater access to at least elementary education in 1986 than they had in 1976" (Higgins and Shoar-Ghaffari, 1994: 27). For instance in East Azarbaijan, the female proportion of literates[13] increased by 7.5 percent between 1976 to 1986, while the increase for the whole country for the same period was 4.8 percent[14]. According to statistical yearbooks, in terms of adult literacy, women outnumber men both as the learners, "*Savad amouzan*," and as teachers, "*Amouzesh yaran.*" In most provinces of the country, the rural *Nehzat* classes and participants outnumber the urban ones. In the latest phases of the adult literacy promotion, however, the learners of *Nehzat* in urban areas outnumber rural learners at the national level (Iran Statistical Yearbook, 1996: 537-38). These facts hold true in the case of East Azarbaijan as well as Tabriz district, *Shahrestan-e Tabriz*. Mehran (2003), in her paper prepared for the UNESCO Education for All Global Monitoring Report 2003/4, using a variety of educational indicators between 1990-2000, shows considerable progress towards gender equality in education over the last decade, particularly at primary and secondary levels. According to the Islamic Republic's Planning and Budget Organization (PBO) and UN, Iran moved up from low to medium standing on the gender-related human development index (GDI) value from 0.454 in 1988 to 0.579 in 1997 (PBO and UN, 1999: 146). Adult literacy rates in Iran (age 15 and over) show an increase from 63.2 percent (72.2 male and 54 female) in 1990 to 76 percent (83 male and 68.9 female) in 2000, pointing to significant progress in female literacy over the last decade. Taking into account the literacy rates of Iranian youth (age 15 to 24), there was an increase from 86.3 percent (91.7 male and 80.8 female) to 93.8 percent (96.2 male and 91.3 female) during the 1990-2000 period (UNESCO, 2002: 218), showing further gender equality.

In rural areas, however, despite the increase in the female literacy rate from 17 percent in 1976 to 36 percent and 62 percent in 1986 and 1996 respectively, the gender gap in higher levels of schooling did not decline as it did in elementary education (Aghajanian, 1994: 45-49)[15]. Lack of access to higher levels of schooling in rural areas in general has not had the same effect for boys as it has for girls, in the case of scarcity of educational resources until recent decades. Rural sub-systems have reacted differently toward the migration of different sexes[16]. While young males, socially and culturally, have more freedom to migrate, female mobility, particularly for education, has been deliberately controlled and restricted through various deep-rooted traditional and patriarchal practices and norms. Yet migration of young rural males does not necessarily mean that they all move for educational reasons. More often, migrants in search of education are from the wealthiest section of the peasantry who can meet the associated costs. Harsh socio-economic conditions of the rural poor are often crucial factors in preventing access to educational resources in the cities for male migrants.

Gender inequality and the discriminatory attitude particularly of poor rural families towards female education originate from the fact that girls' education is costly for the family with no payoff, preventing any investment by families in this. A girl's unpaid labor around the home or farm, which needs no investment, is more valuable for poor families. R.M. who had elementary education from her village, told me that:

> I only have primary education. In our village, there weren't many educational facilities, and most importantly we were poor and my father was unaware of the value of education. Thus, I worked on carpets.

Although for R.M. access to education was limited in her village, the family's poverty was important in preventing her access to education. For her father, her involvement in the family industry of carpet-related activity, adding income to the family's budget, was more valuable than attendance in free education. In fact, in any society, any social change in women's status or any social consciousness against gender discrimination, particularly in terms of their access to social resources, needs a certain degree of socio-economic development in families. When people live in absolute poverty, female education is too much of a luxury to afford.

In addition to poverty, marriage is another factor in the discriminatory attitude of rural families towards female education. The fact that girls move to their husbands' homes after marriage contributes to their low literacy rate compared to that of boys. Thus, in rural areas, cultural norms and practices regarding education, and/or migration for education are applied more to women. Geographical distance from major urban areas is another significant obstacle to female migration for education. The greater the distance of rural areas or their isolation from the main cities, the greater the extent of poverty, which reinforces discriminatory practices and attitudes for rural women. In terms of female migration for education, an informant from a remote village stated the attitudes of rural families towards female migration for education in this way: "...in my time, it was disgraceful to send girls to the city for education."

In remote villages from Tabriz rural girls have been less likely to migrate for educational purposes, but in recent decades two important factors have encouraged it. One is the development in transport, increasing the possibility of daily commuting between villages and cities. The second is emphasis by the Islamic state on women's modesty in the society in terms of dressing, sex segregation, and male-female interactions in daily life. The regulation by moral codes, among which the practice of veiling is socially and culturally accepted, is ideologically important, giving a sense of security for families, and has had a positive impact, in increasing women's mobility. An informant who had only elementary education in her village said that:

> In our village the boys were mostly sent to the city to study. But now things are changing, there is daily transport between our village and other cities and recently some girls are going to Varzghanto study[17]. They travel every day by going to the city in the mornings and returning back to the village after school.

Since girls were not covered by the study it is unclear to which social group they belonged to, if development in transport alone caused the change of attitude by rural families, or if compatibility of new gender policies with their cultural, traditional and religious norms, brought social changes in status for these rural girls[18]. However, I interviewed five women who had migrated to Tabriz mainly for education and five others who had migrated for work. Most were from the environs of Tabriz and, as they stated, enjoyed some rural prosperity compared to remote villages. The villagers had close contact with Tabriz as the main city in the region, were more aware of the position of women in urban society and their women observed less strict cultural and traditional practices in their mobility:

> In our area many young people migrate to the city because of education. My mother stayed in the village to look after our orchard and animals and my sister and I moved to the city with our father.

From this, it is clear that discriminatory attitudes towards female migration for education have weakened, at least in the villages close to Tabriz or where there are transport facilities for daily commutes for women from better off families. In some cases, single girls had migrated independently and were living without being accompanied by their families, but in the company of female siblings, friends, or relatives. This practice is not common, but its occurrence is more observable among young literate single women. Mehran (1992) attibutes changes in female literacy to two major factors: the role of families in supporting girls' education, and the role of the Islamic Republic of Iran in introducing a "New Muslim Women" with a dual role in family and society.

One woman, who was a primary teacher and had step migration before coming to Tabriz, before the revolution, to attend a Teacher Training College said:

> After primary school, I went to Mahabad to continue my education with my other siblings[19]. My father was a religious man and against girls' education, particularly the unveiling practice in city schools. Two of my older sisters are illiterate, but my mother was behind our education and resisted against my father. She acted indirectly and more diplomatically by involving her father to persuade our father. She gave birth to 12 children, 7 of them girls. I am the fifth daughter of my mother. One of my sisters who was the fourth daughter,

> was accepted for a two-year course in Tabriz, it was 1971-72 academic year. Those times two of my mother's brothers were living in Tabriz, whatever they insisted to persuade my father, they failed. Eventually my grandfather intermediated; since my father respected him greatly, he could not say no. My sister with two other women rented a room in Tabriz, and that opened the door for rest of the sisters: three of us are now teachers. But deep down, he was not happy. He was a wealthy man, but whenever, we asked him to pay for our books, he refused and referred us to my mother, as he kept saying: "she has sent you to school, go and ask her." For years, I was sharing my pens and pencils and notebooks with one of my sisters.

Mrs. A. was a school teacher whose background included family migration from Ahar to Tabriz. For her and her husband this was the second migration, this time for children's education. She said:

> In Ahar, both my husband and I were school teachers, had a relatively good life. But I wanted better education for my children and that was not possible in a small town. Before, my oldest daughter started her high-school, I started to convince my husband that we should move to Tabriz. He initially was not fond of the idea, as we were settled and happy with our life and job. But I insisted and he eventually accepted to move. We had to sell our house, transfer our job to Tabriz, get an accommodation in a reasonably good location, register the children in school. We had to do all these within one month with lots of difficulty.

Increased presence of women in social, economic, intellectual, cultural, literary, and artistic fields has provided an alternative image to the traditional, dominant model of womanhood as one of wife and mother, encouraging families to seek education for their daughters. On the other hand, the Islamic Republic of Iran, by promoting a dominant religio-political ideology has been able to assign a dual role to the New Muslim Women. This duality between the forces of tradition and revolution is reflected in the education of females (Mehran, 1992: 15). Looking at the gross enrollment ratio in early childhood care and education for children age 3 and above, there is a shift from a gender parity index (GPI) of 0.95 in 1990-1991, a disparity in favor of boys, to a GPI of 1.06 in 1999-2000, indicating a disparity in favor of girls. As a result, attitudes towards female education have generally improved nationally and more girls are attending university courses. In 2003, about 66 percent of university students were female and nearly all university subjects were open to women (Keddie, 2006: 286)[20]. Although female graduates face high levels of unemployment, except in teaching where the salaries are comparatively lower, an increasing proportion of female teachers is a measure of gender equality for two main reasons. Training and recruiting female teachers is an attempt to improve women's participation in social and economic sectors, and a key strategy to facilitate girls' access to and retention in school (Mehran, 2003: 6). However, like most countries, there is a gender disparity in favor of men among math and science teachers (Ministry of Education, 2001, cited in Mehran, 2003: 6).

The Level of Education among Migrant Women

Of the 925 women who responded to the questionnaire in the first stage of the study, 322 (35 percent) were literate[21]. Although interviews indicate an increase in female literacy among the younger generation of migrants, as the level of education increases the number of children among literate women drops. Of the literate respondents in this sample, 21 percent had attended higher levels of schooling such as secondary or high school and 18 received a certificate at Diploma or higher level. Low attendance in levels above the elementary is not confined to this sample. At national level, too, school enrolment shows a decline for both males and females at both secondary and high school level (Aghajanian, 1994: 48).

One hundred and forty two (44 percent) of the literate women in my sample had started their education in their villages, the remaining 180 (56 percent) in the city. Although many studies indicate greater availability of education in rural areas when compared to the pre-revolutionary period, both as formal schooling or Adult Literacy Education, it seems that migrant women compared to their rural counterparts have more spare time and show more interest in this necessity of modern life. For the majority of women interviewed, whether they themselves were educated or not, education was often perceived as the best way for success and upward mobility.

Table 6.1. Educational level of literate respondents and the starting place of their schooling (n= 322)

Level of Education	Started in the village		Started in the city		Total
	n	%	n	%	
Basic reading skills	15	*25*	44	*75*	59
Primary	94	*48*	100	*52*	194
Secondary	20	*46*	24	*54*	44
High School	4	*57*	3	*43*	7
Diploma and more	8	*44*	10	*56*	18
Total	141	*44*	181	*56*	322

In terms of starting place of schooling, according to table 6.1, more than half the women began in the city. Of those who have only basic reading skills, a skill more probably obtained from *Nehzat* classes, there was a 50 percent gap in terms of where they began their education. The acceptability of *Nehzat*, among women in both rural and urban areas, might be attributed to its flexibility towards women's domestic responsibilities as well as its compatibility with ideological norms and practices. These classes are normally set up in proximity to women's houses, the teachers are female and women are allowed to take their infants to the class. In some cases, when I knocked on women's doors and asked women to interview, I was immediately asked if I was a *Nehzat* teacher and wanted to enroll them in *Nehzat* classes. Women's participation in Adult Literacy classes rarely faced any interference from their families, particularly male relatives. S.B., a 34 year-old widow, was the only woman to say otherwise:

> In the village my parents didn't send me to school and in the city when I wanted to go to *Nehzat*, my husband told me that: "if you want to go to *Nehzat*, you have to take your birth certificate with you and go to your father's house straight away." He didn't like me to study. After his death, my co-wife went to *Nehzat*; now she can read and write. She also went to the Quranic class and is able to read Koran as well. Now I am left with four children to fend for ourselves and I do not have time for *Nehzat*.

In Muslim societies gender inequalities are influenced by gender norms, values, and practices. Ideologies around sexuality and female virginity and chastity are used to control women and put unnecessary restrictions on their social mobility, leading to poverty and marginalization. It seems that for women ideological restrictions are exacerbated by poverty. The main reason that S.B. was prevented from schooling by her parents was not because the village lacked a school, but due to ideological practices and beliefs around morality designed to protect her sexual purity[22]. She was interviewed in a group of women, including her mother, her aunt, a neighbor, and her two teenage daughters. Three of S.B.'s brothers were university graduates and her mother was very proud of them. Her husband's hostility to her interest in learning was more likely due to her being his second, subordinate, wife and he wanted to limit her interactions with other women who might provoke her to be rebellious against him[23].

Although many women interviewed had attended *Nehzat* classes, most of them found it difficult to continue after the initial elementary phase (*moghaddamati*); fewer managed to do the second supplementary phase (*takmili*), and none mentioned that they had managed to pass these two stages and move to higher levels. Some interviewees, particularly the aged and poor, did not even find a chance to try the classes. Some of the informants were in dreadful plights and were struggling with absolute poverty for daily survival. The difficulty of trying out or the continuation of literacy classes for many women was mainly due to conflict with their motherly and wifely responsibilities, preoccupations with (often) large families, informal economic involvement, mental pre-occupations about their daily problems, and general poverty. Language barriers also play an important role in women's learning ability. The spoken language in the region is Azari Turki and the language of education is Farsi (Persian), so the process of learning becomes much more difficult for Turkish speaking women compared to their Farsi speaking counterparts. Thus, literacy education was not just a process of learning to read and write, but also one of learning a completely different language. It is much easier for children and younger people to pick up the Farsi language due to the availability of mass media in the houses, particularly television. These are some quotations about why the women did not take advantage of literacy classes available to them in the city:

> I was very busy with my children as well as my work as domestic servant. Then my husband became very ill and I had to look after him for more than three years. Now I have other sorts of problems. I never have had an opportunity to go to *Nehzat* (F.Z.).

> I am illiterate and have not even gone to *Nehzat*. How can a poor person get education? I have been working to raise my children (B.M.).

> I am illiterate. I didn't even go to *Nehzat*. The anxieties and worries of life do not leave any room in my mind for study (Kh.G.).

> How could I go to *Nehzat* with nine children? On top of that I have to look after my mother-in law and my deaf-and-dumb father as well as my ill husband[24]. We are very poor (S.D.).

> I have seven children with not much gap between them. My family was in the village and I did not receive any help towards raising my children in the city. I didn't take a rest, even after my births. Housework and child rearing didn't give me any opportunity to do anything else (Z.P.).

Women who found an opportunity to take part in literacy classes faced either similar problems with their maternal obligations or had others that prevented them continuing with their studies. One of the informants, who was interviewed along with her mother, said:

> I went to *Nehzat* for one year because my son's school insisted that I should go to literacy classes. I passed the first year exam, but couldn't continue after that. I always suffer from neurasthenia as badly as ever. I have too much to think about; therefore, I cannot stand things that affect my nerves (L.L.).

Her mother revealed the source of her anxiety by interrupting my informant and saying that:

> Her husband is foolish. That's why she thinks too much. She was doing well in *Nehzat*, but she didn't continue (F.Z.).

When I was interviewing L.L., her husband was a street vendor selling haircolors. He had suffered a loss in his business, and lost his shop and their family home. The family had to move to L.L. mother's house to live in one room and she was very worried about her children's future. She explained that her husband was a bad-tempered man and not only did not consult her, he did not even tell her the details of his business affairs. When she asked about the losses, her husband's answer was simple and short: "in business there are gains and losses."

Another informant who had migrated to the city for marriage and was living with her in-laws had also gone to *Nehzat,* but was not able to concentrate on her studies. She said that:

> ...my mother in-law registered me to *Nehzat,* but I couldn't study (M.L.).

She had also problems with her husband and did not know his earnings. She had a young daughter and was expecting another child. She was not cared for by her husband and was economically very dependent on her in-laws[25]. For these two interviewees, worries about marital and financial difficulties proved too distracting for continuation with any literacy training, regardless of accessibility and flexibility towards women's family responsibilities. For other women, domestic responsibilities were too heavy, which affected their learning ability. When I asked one of the informants about *Nezat* classes, her daughter laughingly replied that:

> When she (her mother) was going to *Nehzat*, we were doing her homework. She rarely did it herself.

This woman had six children, one disabled. She was also involved in spinning and carpet weaving and did not have time to practice what she was taught. In fact, for her and many like her, *Nehzat* classes provide time for getting away from domestic responsibilities for a short while, rather than one for learning a skill useful for the future. "I could not continue studying in *Nehzat"* was a statement expressed by many of the informants who had participated in *Nehzat* classes.

As a primary essential, literacy classes are a good way to increase the number of literate adults. They play direct or indirect roles in women's socialization, giving them self-esteem and knowledge about family planning, social identification, and time for themselves. Women's accounts, however, show that most of them did not achieve functional literacy and those who had studied in *Nehzat* for one or two years easily forgot learning skills and lost much of what they learnt. This is partially because of the work that the majority of migrant women are involved in, which does not require reading and writing, and partially due to the lack of usage of Persian in their daily life. In fact, they become functionally illiterate after a while, and it is no wonder that they categorized themselves as illiterate until they were asked directly about participation in *Nehzat* classes. Some women categorized themselves as illiterate, but still stated their participation in literacy classes. In this study, these have been categorized among those who have basic reading skills. Only one employed woman, who could use her learnt ability in her workplace or daily life, stated that she was literate and able to read and write because of *Nehzat* classes.

The Degree of Access to Educational Opportunities for Different Categories of Migrant Women: Questionnaire Data

Informants who migrated with their parents had more chance to receive formal education in Tabriz compared to married, divorced and widowed women, or even those who had mainly migrated for marriage. Information from interviews is quoted after data from the questionnaires. The tables below present quantitative data from the questionnaires (n=925), beginning with marital status of the respondents and their age on arrival in the city (Table 6.2).

Table 6.2. The marital status of the respondents and their age on arrival in the city (n=925)

Marital status (MS)	n	%	Ages
SWPs.[a]	284	*30.8*	(1-34)
SFM.[b]	129	*13.9*	(10-41)
SFW/E.[c]	3	*0.3*	(15-25)
M.[d]	498	*53.7*	(10-69)
W.[e]	10	*1.1*	(15-56)
D.[f]	1	*0.1*	(24)
Total	925	*100*	

Notes:
[a] Single women who migrated with their parents: 90 percent were 1-15 years old
[b] Single women migrating for marriage: 92 percent 10-20 years old
[c] Single women migrating for work or education
[d] Married Women
[e] Widowed women
[f] Divorced women

As table 6.2 and figure 6.1 illustrate the majority of migrants were married, followed by those who were single migrating with parents, and then by single women who migrated to start married life in the city. The other three categories formed less than 2 percent of the sample.

Figure 6.1. Marital Status of respondents on arrival (n= 925)

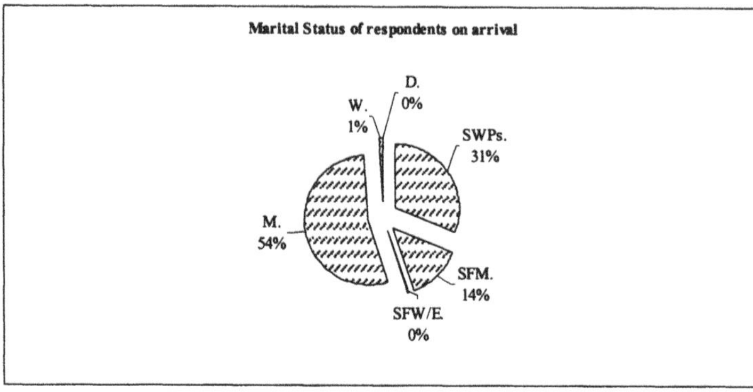

To show the gap in literacy, table 6.3 and figure 6.2 show the educational level of different categories of women in terms of marital status on their arrival.

Table 6.3. Educational level of the respondents in terms of their marital status on arrival (n= 925)

MS	Illiterate	Basic reading	Primary	Secondary	High-school	Diploma and more	Total
SWPs.	137	23	81	25	6	12	284
SFM.	65	10	46	8	0	0	129
SFW/E.	1	0	0	1	0	1	3
M.	389	26	67	9	1	6	498
W.	10	0	0	0	0	0	10
D.	1	0	0	0	0	0	1
Total	603	59	194	43	7	19	925
%	65	6	21	5	1	2	100

Figure 6.2. Educational level and marital status on arrival (n=925)

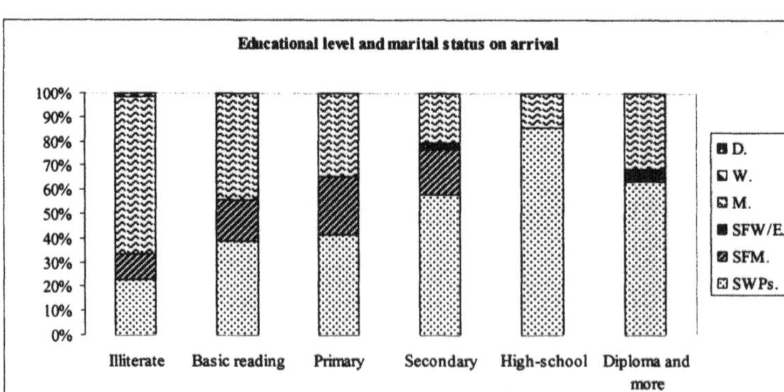

Tables 6.4 and 6.5 show separately the marital status of illiterate and literate respondents plus their ages on arrival in the city.

Table 6.4. Marital status of illiterate respondents and their age on arrival (n=603)

MS	n	%	Ages
SWPs.[a]	137	*22.7*	(1-34)
SFM.[b]	65	*10.8*	(10-41)
SFW/E.	1	*0.2*	(25)
M.[c]	389	*64.5*	(10-69)
W.	10	*1.7*	(15-56)
D.	1	*0.2*	(24)
Total	603	*100*	

Notes: [a] 87 percent ranged between 1 and 15 on their arrival, but at the time of survey, the ages of 78 percent in this category were between 30 and 69
[b] 75 percent were 15^+ on arrival
[c] 93 persent of married women were 15^+ on their arrival; at the time of survey 88 persent were 30^+.

Figure 6.3. Marital status of illiterate respondents on arrival (n=603)

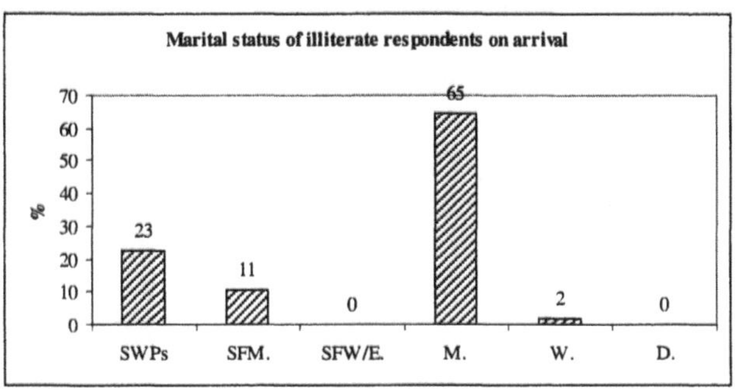

Table 6.5. Marital status of literate respondents and their age on arrival (n=322)

MS	n	%	Ages
SWPs.[a]	147	*45.5*	(1-25)
SFM.[b]	64	*19.9*	(11-22)
SFW/E.	2	*0.6*	(15 and 21)
M.[c]	109	*33.8*	(10-45)
Total	322	*100*	

[a] On their arrival, 93 percent ranged between 1 and 15. At the time of survey 65 persent were aged between 12 and 30
[b] On arrival, 80 percent ranged between 11 and 18
[c] On arrival, 94 percent of the married women in the sample were 15^+; at the time of survey, 55 percent were 30^+.

Figure 6.4. Marital status of literate respondents on arrival (n= 322)

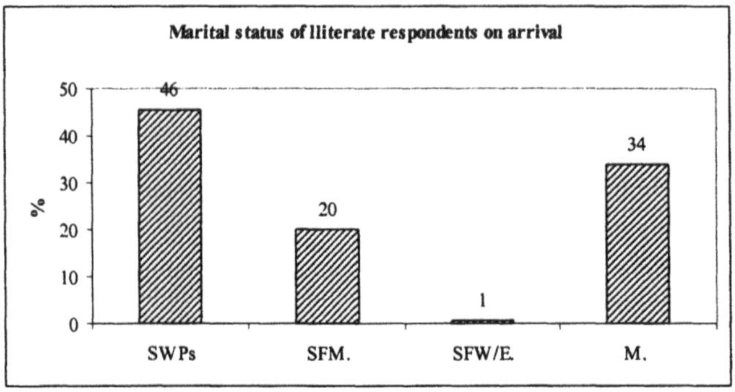

As the above tables and figures demonstrate, the highest illiteracy rate (65 percent) was for women who were married at the time of migration, and the highest literacy rate (46 percent) was for those who migrated with their parents, mainly in childhood. Attention to the notes given in the three tables above also indicates that illiterate women in the sample were older compared to their literate counterparts in each group, and were less exposed to educational opportunities either in places of origin or at destination. For instance, 78 percent of illiterate single women who migrated with their parents were between 30 to 69 years old at the time of the survey, while 65 percent of literate women from the same category (i.e., single with parents), were aged between 12 and 30 when the data were collected. It means that literate women who migrated with their parents were much younger than illiterate women within the same category, and the latter more probably married and soon after migration took adult responsibilities, as stated by some women in this category during interviews.

Of women who were married at the time of migration, 88 percent of illiterate ones were 30 years old and over at the time of data-collection, while 55 percent of the literate women were 30 years old or over. Again, literate women in the category of married (at the time of migration) are younger than their illiterate counterparts.

Migrant women who came to the city as pre-school ages accompanying parents had more opportunities than those who were teenagers or older at the time of migration. Comparison of these women in better off and poorer households during interviews also indicated that those who have better off families, who can pay their educational expenses or were not desperate for their labor, enjoyed more educational opportunities than those in poorer households where their often unpaid labor was more essential for the family's survival than their education, irrespective of their ages. Table 6.6 below indicates the literacy level of single respondents who migrated with their families.

Table 6.6. The educational level of single women who migrated with their families (n=284)

Level of Education	n	%	Ages
Illiterate[a]	137	*48.2*	(1-34)
Basic reading skills[b]	23	*8.1*	(1-17)
Primary [c]	81	*28.5*	(1-25)
Secondary[d]	25	*8.8*	(1-24)
High School[e]	6	*2.1*	(2-15)
Diploma and more[f]	12	*4.2*	(1-16)
Total	284	*100*	

Notes: [a] 87 percent were between 1and 15 years on arrival, but at the time of survey, the age of 78 percent of respondents in this category lay between 30 and 69.
[b] On arrival, 92 percent ranged between 1and 12, and the ages of all women in this category at the time of survey lay between 20and 49.
[c] On arrival, 84 percent were 1-12 years old. At the time of survey, the age of 50 percent of respondents in this category lay between 17 and 27.
[d] 92 percent were between 1-9 on arrival, and 50% of this category at the time of survey were less than 24 years old.
[e] 83 percent were between 2 and 12 on arrival, but at the time of survey, the ages of 83 percent of respondents in this category were 23 years old or less.
[f] All were aged between 1 and 16 on arrival, and 58 percent at the time of survey were 24 years old or less.

Figure 6.5. Educational level of SWPS (n=284)

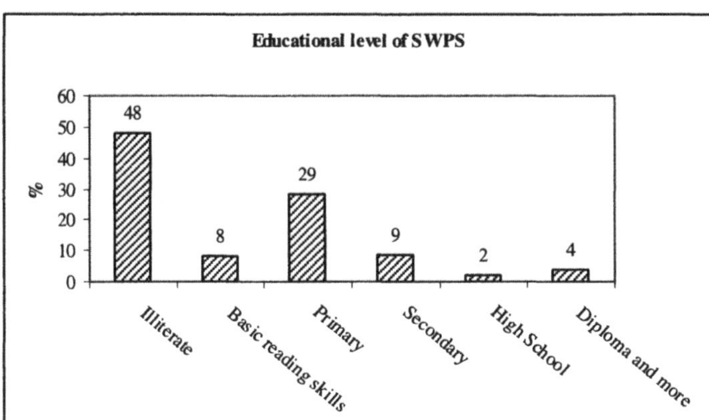

Although the gap between illiterate and literate respondents who migrated with their families is not large, their arrival age and their age at the time of survey indicate the promotion of female education for younger women, even in rural areas, and the scarcity of educational opportunities for older rural or migrant women. Notes on ages also show that the younger the informants, the better chance of receiving some education, however little. Of respondents who migrated with their parents, 25 were single at the time of data collection. All except one were educated to some extent or were at school. As table 6.7 shows for the illiterate single woman, the gap between her arrival age and age at time of survey was shorter than that for other single women.

Table 6.7. Educational level of single respondents who migrated with their families (n= 25)

Level of Education	n	%	Arrival age	Ages
Illiterate	1	*4*	19	20
Basic reading skills	1	*4*	17	25
Primary	10	*40*	(1-19)	(17-24)
Secondary	5	*20*	(1-14)	(12-20)
High School	2	*8*	(2 and 8)	(15-16)
Diploma and more	6	*24*	(2-16)	(20-28)
Total	25	*100*		

Note: it was more likely that girls with secondary and high-school education were still in education at the time of data collection, as their ages indicate.

Figure 6.6. Educational level of single respondents who migrated with their families (n= 25)

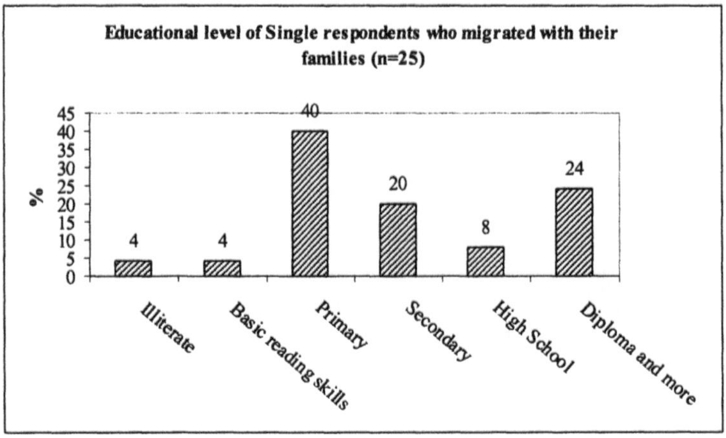

The gap in literacy is more pronounced when comparing the category of single (with parents) to other categories of migrant women. Altogether 65 percent of the respondents in this sample were illiterate, but only 23 percent of the illiterates were single (with parents) during migration; the remaining 77 percent belonged to other categories. Again, the trend is more pronounced for middle aged or older women: the older the respondents, the more illiterate they were. Table 6.8 illustrates the literacy level of different categories of migrant respondents, except of single women who came with their parents.

Table 6.8. Educational level of other categories of respondents (n= 641)

Level of Education	n	%	Arrival ages
Illiterate[a]	466	72.7	(10-69)
Basic reading skills[b]	36	*5.6*	(13-36)
Primary[c]	113	*17.6*	(10-45)
Secondary[d]	18	*2.8*	(14-27)
High School[e]	1	*0.2*	(17)
Diploma and more[f]	7	*1.1*	(20-30)
Total	641	*100*	

Notes:
[a] On arrival, 90 percent aged 15-69, and at time of survey, the ages of 80 percent lay between 30 and 83.
[b] On arrival, 80 percent were aged 15 and above, and at time of survey, the ages of 85 percent lay between 23 and 48.
[c] On arrival, 80 percent aged 15 and above, and at time of survey, the ages of 85 percent lay between 23 and 60.
[d] On arrival, 63 persent were between 14 and 18, and at time of survey, the ages of 84 percent lay between 21 and 38.
[e] 43 years old at time of data collection.
[f] All were aged between 20 and 30 on arrival; 83 percent were between 21 and 36 years at time of survey.

Figure 6.7. Educational level of other categories of respondents (n= 641)

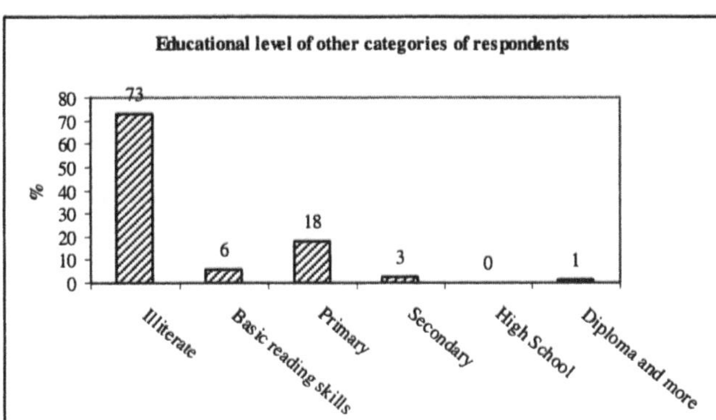

The Degree of Access to Educational Opportunities for Different Categories of Migrant Women: Interview Data

The gap in literacy among randomly selected interviewees was not as high as that among the women who took part in the survey. Table 6.9 and figure 6.8 show the marital status of the interviewees (n=126) at the time of migration.

Table 6.9. Marital status of interviewed respondents on their arrival (n=126)

MS	n	%
SWPs.	59	*47*
SFM.	9	*7*
SFW/E.	9	*7*
M.	45	*36*
W.	4	*3*
Total	126	*100*

Notes: During the interview, not all women were asked about their arrival age at the time of migration, which makes age comparison impossible. The most important part of this stage was to listen to women's accounts.

Figure 6.8. Marital status of interviewed respondents on their arrival (n= 126)

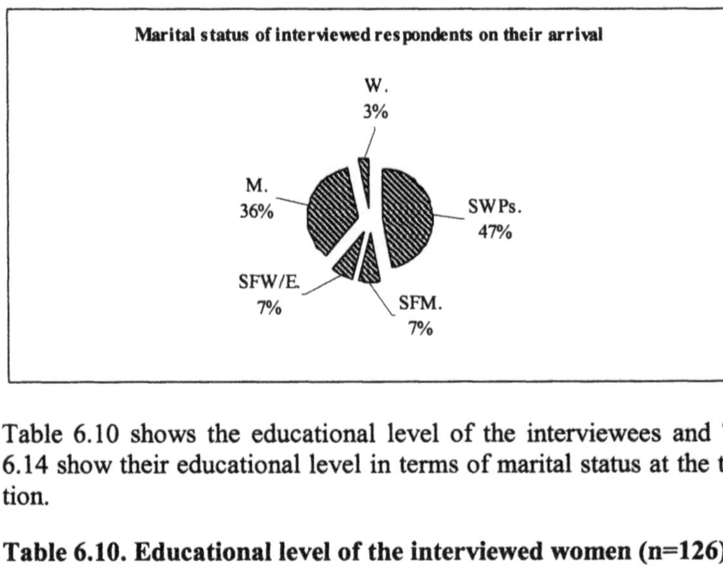

Table 6.10 shows the educational level of the interviewees and Tables 6.12 – 6.14 show their educational level in terms of marital status at the time of migration.

Table 6.10. Educational level of the interviewed women (n=126)

Level of Education	n	%
Illiterate	52	*41*
Basic reading skills/*Nehzat*	19	*15*
Primary	20	*16*
Secondary or less than Diploma	12	*10*
Diploma and more	18	*14*
In education	5	*4*
Total	126	*100*

Figure 6.9. Educational level of the interviewed women (n=126)

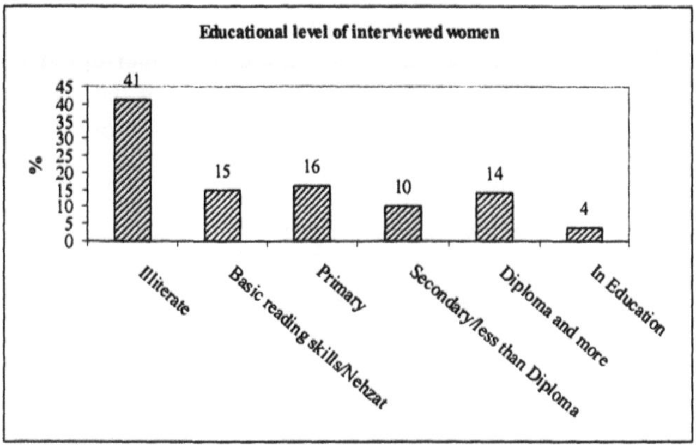

Table 6.11. Educational level of single women who migrated with their parents (n=59)

Level of Education	n	%	Age during the interview	Average age
Illiterate	8	*14*	(24-47)	34
Basic reading skills/*Nehzat*	12	*20*	(19-55)	34
Primary	11	*19*	(14-44)	27
Secondary or less than Diploma	12	*20*	(16-46)	27
Diploma	12	*20*	(`19-44)	26
B.A.	1	*2*	38	38
In education	3	*5*	(15-20)	18
Total	59	*100*		

Figure 6.10. Educational level of SWPS (n=59)

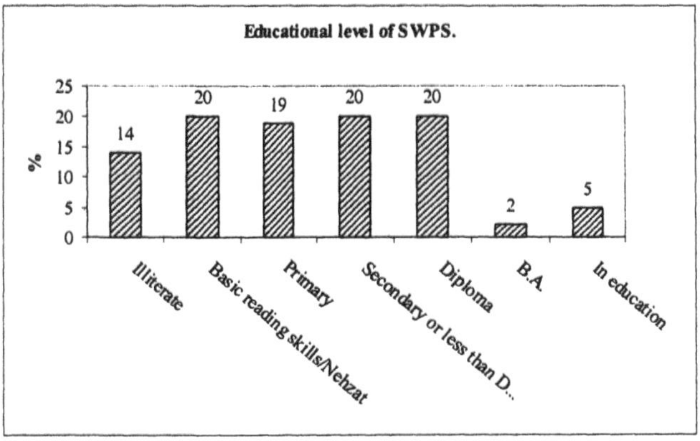

Forty-one percent of the interviewed women in the sample were illiterate. Fifteen percent were single and accompanied their parents at the time of migration; those who had basic reading and writing skills had mostly taken *Nehzat* classes. Most women with primary education stated that their education was interrupted by their family after the fifth grade. Of those who were in education at the time of interview, one was a university student, and two others had high ambitions both in terms of education and career.

Table 6.12. Educational level of women who came to study or work (n=9)

Level of Education	n	%	Age during the interview	Average age
Primary	2	*22*	(34 and 39)	36
Diploma	5	*56*	(23-30)	25
In education	2	*22*	(14 and 16)	15
Total	9	*100*		

Table 6.13. Educational level of single women who migrated for marriage (n= 9)

Level of Education	n	%	Age during the interview	Average age
Illiterate	4	*44*	(26-40)	34
Basic reading skills/*Nehzat*	1	*12*	50	50
Primary	4	*44*	(24-36)	30
Total	9	*100*		

Of the 52 illiterate women (41 percent of the total), 12 were single at the time of migration. They accompanied parents or migrated to start married life in the city (10 percent of the total, or 16 percent of those who were single at the time of migration).

Table 6.14. Educational level of women who were married before migration (n= 45)

Level of Education	n	%	Age during the interview	Average age
Illiterate	36	*80*	(25-17)	47
Basic reading skills/*Nehzat*	6	*13*	(28-56)	43
Primary	3	*7*	(23-34)	29
Total	45	*100*		

As table 6.14 shows, a high percentage of women in this category were illiterate and older compared to single women from other categories. All four women who were widowed before migration were illiterate; their ages during the interview ranged between 55 and 100, with an average age of 68.

Table 6.15. Educational level of respondents in terms of marital status on arrival in Tabriz (n=126)

MS	Illiterate	Basic reading	Primary	Secondary	Diploma	In education	Total
SWPs.	8	12	11	12	13	3	59
SFM.	4	1	4	0	0	0	9
SFW/E.	0	0	2	0	5	2	9
M.	36	6	3	0	0	0	45
W.	4	0	0	0	0	0	4
Total	52	19	20	12	18	5	126
%	*41*	*15*	*16*	*10*	*14*	*4*	*100*

Note: I could not get permission from the educational authorities in Tabriz to conduct my research in schools. Therefore, those who were still in education were those who were interviewed in their homes.

Table 6.16. Marital status of illiterate respondents at the time of migration (n= 52)

MS	n	%
SWPs.	8	*15*
SFM.	4	*8*
M.	36	*69*
W.	4	*8*
Total	52	*100*

Table 6.17. Marital status of literate respondents at their arrival (n= 74)

MS	N	%
SWPs.	51	*15*
SFM.	5	*8*
SFW/E.	9	*69*
M.	9	*8*
Total	74	*100*

It is clear from both survey and interview data that single women, particularly those who had migrated with parents, or those who migrated to continue education or find a job, had better educational levels or a better chance of obtaining education compared to other categories in both stages of the study. The majority of illiterate women in both samples were married, divorced, or widowed at the time of migration. Among the 925 women who answered questionnaires in the first stage, 78 percent of the illiterate ones were or had been married at this point. Among the women interviewed, 69 percent of women married at the time of migration were also illiterate. All divorcees and widows in both samples were also illiterate. Low female literacy and educational attainment, early age of marriage, high fertility rates, low female participation in the formal labor force and high engagement in the informal sector of traditional carpet weaving and related industries are common features of the lives of women who mainly accompanied or joined migrant husbands, or migrated after the breakup of marriage, or after the death of their partners.

Almost all the illiterate women were unhappy with their lack of education, particularly those who managed to find a job outside the home in low status positions and faced exploitation and discrimination. One woman who had almost finished a sentence in Tabriz prison said:

> I am illiterate. Illiteracy is the root of all my misfortunes. I have been working since I was a young girl. My first husband died of an illness and I was almost forced to marry my second husband, as my brothers told me who will look after me when my parents die. My second husband was not a good man. He mistreated me a lot. He involved me in a murder and got 11 confessions from me with my fingerprint, without my knowing what they were.

Although the government promotes free adult literacy classes, through schools with an inter-generational approach to education in that a literate home environment might be useful in consolidating children's motivation for learning, time is scarce for most married women, often because they have many young children. Joining a literacy class requires dedication and investment of time and energy. Most women interviewed rejected the idea of joining classes due to family responsibilities, many children to look after, poverty, and engagement in income generating activities. Linguistic differences also make the process of learning harder. High expectations make sustaining motivation even harder. It is difficult to measure effectiveness of adult literacy programs, due to the lack of access to people who drop out of classes in the middle of term, those who fail to complete the program successfully, and those who manage to complete but lose their skills due to a lack of follow up, a problem which would justify study in itself.

Constraints on the Educational Progress of Young Female Migrants

Despite the importance of education and better opportunities in the city for the majority of single women who migrated with parents, they still face obstacles that limit access to this. Poverty, marriage and honor were discussed by informants as major hindrances to their educational progress as young migrants, especially young girls both in elementary and higher levels of schooling.

Poverty

Poverty is a major factor in intensifying the discriminatory attitude of parents towards education, particularly that of girls. Although many women believed in the importance of education for both sexes, the scarcity of financial resources led them to put more importance on education of sons than of daughters. Women had different attitudes towards female education, mainly based on their own experiences of marriage and involvement in income generating activities in or outside the home. Women who were working outside the home and earning money had more control over allocation of resources and a more egalitarian attitude towards their children's education. Those working in the lowest sectors of the economy, particularly the widows were more careful to meet their daughter's needs for upward social mobility through education or vocational training. They did not want daughters to experience the same difficulties that they had been through. One of these women was very concerned about education for her daughter who was in year 4 and not keen on her studies. The mother had committed herself to her daughter's education and was doing her best to keep her interested, to raise her chance of gaining better skills and prevent her from undergoing the same experiences as herself in the future. She described the lack of education as equal to blindness, saying that:

> I encourage her very much. I go to school and talk to her teacher to know what I should do to keep her interested in her studies. I even once bought her jewelry and passed it to her teacher to give it to her in front of her classmates as a prize for her achievements[26]. If she manages to finish her secondary level successfully, then I can get her to be trained in a skill that she is interested in. Illiteracy is a great pain. I have few years of primary schooling and am like a blind person; I don't want her to be the same.

However, withdrawing children from school or not sending them at all is a common practice among the very poor. There are two main reasons for this, directly related to poverty: the need for their labor, and lack of financial ability to provide the necessities of education, particularly when a family has many school-aged children. Poorer families cannot cope with high expenditure on schooling. Whilst the post-revolutionary Constitution of Iran states that education must be free for all Iranian citizens, in practice the pupils' parents must pay towards the public schools' expenses as a "voluntary contribution." They must also provide necessities of schooling such as textbooks, stationery, uniforms for girls, and so forth. The number of children in the poorer households is an important factor in allocation of money for the education of different sexes. During an interview the daughter of my informant asked for some money that the school had asked for, and the mother, who was obviously annoyed by this, but tried to keep calm in front of me, said:

> This school asks for too much money we have to give money to the school frequently for different reasons. For us the education of boys and girls is the same. We like them to be educated. But we suffer from shortage of money and in my daughters' school they keep asking for money. My husband wants to take out the children from school due to our severe financial situation. He says in that case, at least they can weave carpets. But my oldest son has threatened us that he will kill himself, if we don't let him to study. But he doesn't study well. He is in year four and has failed once; we can't afford to pay for each year twice.

Many women from the same background connected their lack of education to the severe economic conditions their parents endured, and poor women also stated that they had withdrawn children, boys or girls, from school as a result of poverty, although they tried to keep some in school to finish at least their primary education. Almost all were involved in home-based activities, mainly carpet weaving and related activities to generate income for the family. A woman from a poorer background said that:

> I was single when we moved to the city. We were very poor and I was not sent to school. We all were weaving carpets at home . . . After marriage I also found it difficult to go to *Nehzat,* because of working on carpets, doing housework and looking after my young children (S.Y.).

Children in these households suffer interrupted education for different reasons depending on their gender. Girl's education is often interrupted as the families are concerned about the cost of schooling. For instance, according to two very poor women, the girls' uniform is an extra expenditure in the family budget. Unlike boys, who are not required to wear a uniform at any stage of education, girls have to wear it from the start at the age of six. One informant who had eight children, four of whom were school-aged, said:

> We have lots of financial problems. With the exception of three of my children, the others have been dismissed from school. These three will also be dropped out soon, because we cannot mange to provide their books, clothes, and etc. By working on carpets, they can contribute to the family income.

Boys' education is also interrupted due to economic pressure, as they are able to meet the immediate family needs for money by doing any sort of casual work. An informant's son had also been taken out of school because of family poverty. She said that:

> My husband was a plodder. The arduous jobs made him very ill, his foot was badly hurt. He was not fit for drudging or carrying weight any more. The poor man became a street vendor. He used to sit in a corner to sell cigarettes. Later on his condition became very critical. He was falling down when he was coming home. My sons, with difficulty, could take him to the street or bring him back home. In that time, one of them was in year 10, we thought what's the

> point of his studying. He could work and the poor man could stay at home. Then, we stopped the poor boy from his education to work as a construction laborer.

Another woman had two children, one boy and one girl. Her son was also removed from school while her daughter carried on her studies. Regarding her children's education she said that:

> This year, we didn't let my son go to school, because we couldn't manage to pay the rent. My husband is a street vendor and his earnings are not sufficient to cover our expenses. Therefore, we pulled my son from school to support us with his earnings.

Another woman's two sons had to terminate university education due to the death of their father in a car crash eight months before the interview; he had also been bankrupt a couple of years before his death. She said:

> My children were doing very well in their studies, but bankruptcy, poverty and now the death of my husband has changed the fate of my children, particularly my sons who had have to stop their study and earn a living for the family. My daughters carry on their studies and one of them is preparing for the university entrance exam. I don't think we can afford her studies, particularly if she is not accepted by a state university.

Meeting immediate needs for money through children working, however, cannot only be generalized to male children. M.D. was a very deprived migrant with ten children, of which the only one who could meet the family's immediate need for money was her 14 year-old daughter. She was working in a carpet workshop for daily wages. Due to severe poverty they were unable to own the means of production themselves, buy the raw materials, or even get a loom and raw materials through putting-out systems, as the girl was not skilled enough to work on her own initiative, and more importantly, they needed a daily income to spend on food. Another poor illiterate woman who had worked in a carpet workshop also said that:

> We were very poor. There were carpet workshops in our area. Therefore, on our arrival to the city, I started to work on carpets and earned money.

Despite the fact that the majority of female carpet weavers worked in their own homes, there were cases in which young girls worked in neighboring workshops when their mothers were not involved in weaving. This illustrates the discussion in some studies about the effect of poverty on the dilution of cultural norms and practices concerning women's paid jobs outside the home (Amin, 1997; Rudnick, 2000).

Another 14 year-old girl, the daughter of very poor migrant parents, had also worked in a carpet workshop from the age of seven. She was also withdrawn from school to look after her 2 year-old brother because her deaf-and-dumb father's income from casual laboring did not meet daily necessities and her mother had to take a job as a domestic servant. She had completed four years of school but was interrupted in year five. Regarding her education and work she said:

> I was working and studying simultaneously since I was seven years old. In the summer of year 1, I started to work in a carpet workshop in our neighborhood. Then I carried on during school times: in the mornings, I was at school; in the afternoons, working in the carpet workshop; and at nights, trying to do my homework. When I was in year four, I went to *Nehzat* to give my mother a chance to work in people's houses. When my brother was born, my efforts to get education lasted only a few months. *Nehzat* classes were normally set in the afternoons, but during the Ramadan it was changed to the mornings, a time which interrupted my education and I could not get any chance to go back to study[27]. If I went to school my mother would not be able to work. We desperately needed her work and money, but there was nobody to look after my little brother and do our housework. Therefore, sadly I gave up my studies.

Another girl from a poor family managed to study up to high school level, but had to stop her education because her family needed her income. One of her relatives found her a job in a hospital crèche. For some families, the death of the male head of the family intensified poverty. In my sample, some women moved to the city after the death of their fathers or husbands. Although women are active participants in agriculture, particularly weeding and harvesting, men play the primary role such as cultivation and trade. When the head of family dies, women, particularly those with few or no sons, cannot act as independent farmers cultivating land on their own. The plantation is given up or the land is leased out. Thus, the pressure of poverty and inability to contribute to agricultural work, as a result not gaining from their land, became a principal reason for migration. Once in the city, these deprived women have no chance to study and are unable to have paid jobs, even doing domestic service, because of illiteracy and their unfamiliarity with the urban environment. Therefore, they carry out traditional weaving or spinning activities at home. The following are some of the quotations about this:

> I am illiterate and have had no opportunity for study either in the village or in the city. I was one year old when my father died. My brothers were too young to cultivate father's land. Therefore, other people were cultivating for us taking two-thirds of the yields for themselves and leaving one third for us.
>
> We were hard pressed for living and could not manage our life without animal husbandry and *Kanareh* weaving. When my brothers grew up, they moved to the city to work and my mother and I came with them[28]. I did not go to school nor look for a job, as I was illiterate. I just continued carpet weaving at home (G.D.).

The father of one of the women died when she was young and her mother remarried and moved to the city with new husband, leaving her children in the village. She said that:

> I am illiterate, because I was like an orphan. I was not allowed to study and was forced to weave carpets.

T.Kh. was a 25 year-old woman who married 3 years before the interview. She had also lost her father when she was young. About her lack of education, she said:

> I am illiterate . . . It is six or seven years since we moved to the city because we were hard pressed for living, as my father had died and we were poor. In the village we were weaving carpets and my brothers were working in the city. Therefore, we came to live with them.

I interviewed two sisters in a sweatshop that produced men's trousers. Their education was mainly reading and writing. They migrated to the city after the death of their father and were taken out of school age seven and nine, despite their own desires. One of the sisters, who was 19 years old, who had been working in the workshop for the last 5 years, said:

> My mother gave birth to 11 children, three of whom died in their childhood. When my father died, she had 8 children. After his death, we came to the city, and my oldest brothers could not mange to support the family and provide our schooling expenditure. I would have liked to continue my schooling, but it was not possible for me and my two other sisters.

Some widows are lucky to have the economic or emotional support of their parents or brothers. But in the case of this rare economic support they are embarrassed at being a burden to their families. Thus, they try to rely on themselves by all means possible, even withdrawing their children from school. This is because most of the time the parents themselves suffer from economic hardship and the brothers either have their own families or need to begin their own married life. Despite the limited economic means of her family, M.'s mother who became a widow at the age of 30 with four children aged from 11 to 17 (three girls and one boy, the youngest child) preferred to have the emotional and psychological, rather than economic support of her family. About her family's support for her children's education, she said that:

> My husband died four years ago in an accident. One year, I did not let my daughters go to school and we worked on carpet making. This year with the help of my parents and my brothers, I managed to send the girls to school. Half a day they were in school, and half a day, they worked with me on the

> carpet. They are doing very well in school. Last year my oldest daughter passed her exams with high marks. My brother is engaged and will start his own family soon. I have told my daughter, if we can't manage, I will stop their studies. I have to buy them school uniforms as well as other clothes. I feel embarrassed to tell my father about our needs. If for example, he buys clothes for one of my daughters, I have to buy for another one myself. Each year, we only can manage to weave one fine carpet and what we earn from it, is spent throughout the year. When the girls go to school and I am working alone I cannot produce much work (S.B.).

And her seventeen year-old daughter, inattentive to her mother's statements, said that:

> I would like to study either "Experimental Science" or "Mathematics-Physics" courses[29]. I love science and I am good at it. But the educational advisor of the school is aware of our condition and says that if I choose one of those courses, I have to do further education to get a job. But if I choose the vocational course, I will get a job after I have obtained my diploma. She knows we could not afford university costs, even if I am accepted by the state university. I would not like to give up my education, but my mother can't cope. We have to weave carpets in order to live (M.).

They were very poor and moved in to live with their grandparents, who were also poor. But because they were losing free accommodation in the grandparents' house upon the marriage of her mother's brother, it seems unlikely that S.B.'s daughter would continue to study either in her area of interest or even in what the educational advisor had recommended. Moving to a rented house means extra economic pressure on the family and the urgent need for girls' labor on carpets. Therefore, what S.B.'s parents could offer her and her children was free accommodation that was going to be taken away, as her brother was given priority. Obviously if S.B.'s brother had the financial ability to help her, he could rent a house and let them have the free accommodation. Here is another illustration of how boys are often given priority over girls, particularly in more traditional and poor families, when resources are scarce. This is almost acceptable due to gender roles and expectations of parents about their children. For instance boys are expected to look after their parents in their old age, not girls. Therefore, parents invest for their old age by supporting male children when they have to choose between sons and daughters.

For another girl, whose father had died, access to education was also interrupted by her mother as she could not pay the school's expenses. She was two months old when her father died. Her mother said that:

> I was 25 years old with two children of four years and two months old, when my husband died. My brothers didn't let me stay with my in-laws, because I

> had an unmarried brother in-law and I was so young. I moved to my mother's house for eight years. When I was sending my kids to school, my mother ridiculed me. She even taunted me by saying that she is taking care of my orphan children. I managed to send my daughter to school for nine years, but school was demanding too much money. Therefore, I didn't let her continue.

The death of a father, and being brought up in female headed households, brings immense poverty to the family and has a negative effect on girls' lives. Informants who lost their fathers in childhood thought their lives would had been better if their fathers were alive. For some, the lack of a mother, mainly in the case of divorce, also had a negative effect on their lives. However, their attitude towards a lost mother was completely different compared to those who had lost their father[30]. Being deprived of her children in addition to emotional and psychological wounds of divorce for them are crucial reasons for many women preferring to stay in violent relationships than to get divorced. An interviewee's husband had remarried without her knowledge, even though the permission of the first wife is supposedly a condition for a man's remarriage. She said:

> My son was burnt and he was in hospital for 20 years [being looked after by this interviewee] so that my husband got his second wife. She was our neighbor. I left the house, complained to the court. But he told me, I will keep both of you.

Her mother, who also was with us during the interview, said:

> I was more concerned with her three young daughters. I did not want them to be left with a stepmother. I told her it is better for her to suffer than her daughters. Only God, me and herself know what she went through.

Those who had lived with a stepmother and experienced further discriminatory behavior were often angry with their mother for not being there for them. I interviewed some women whose mothers had been divorced. I also met one of them while I interviewed her stepmother. They were either not sent to school, particularly in the poorer households, or their studies were interrupted, not necessarily due to poverty. R.B.'s mother was divorced by his father, when she was very young. She and her two siblings lived with her father and his wife. She was one whose education was interrupted, even though her father could afford the expenses. She said that:

> I have studied for only eight years. Sometimes I cry and ask my father why he didn't let us continue our education as his brother's children had. He then lays blame on my mother and says that: "what could I do, your mother shouldn't listen to her friends. She had to tolerate any hardship and stayed in to look after you and your sibling." He says this, even though he confesses that he mistreated my mother by leaving her behind in the village with his family and ignoring her needs and rights while he was working in Tehran. I am so angry

> with my mother and I've never wanted to see her when I've had the chance (R.B.).

She and her brother and sister suffered emotionally, physically and psychologically through the misbehavior of their stepmother. They attributed their misfortunes and suffering to their own mother, despite being aware of her unhappy married life and her experience of domestic violence. In such circumstances, a great gulf is created between father and the children and in practice the children also suffer the loss of their father.

Overcrowded rooms in tiny houses, which are usually a result of poverty, cause poor academic performance, which most of the time results in terminating education. M.L. had left school at secondary level for this reason. She stated that:

> There were three rooms in our house and a family in each room and the rooms all opened to one corridor. We had one room for a family of six with a disabled brother. In each of the other rooms, there was a family of four. All together there were eight children in one house. I could not concentrate on my studies in such an overcrowded noisy house. When I saw there is no hope in such circumstances, I left the school (M.L.).

M.Gh. lived in similar conditions. Although she had left school, her sister managed to continue by staying with relatives at exam times. I interviewed M.Gh. in the exam season when her sister was not at home.

> In this house three families are living in three rooms: my grandparents (father's parents); my uncle's family of five; and our family of seven. In our family, there is no different attitude towards girls' and boys' educational success. One of my sisters is doing her final year. She has gone to my brother's house to prepare for her final exams because our house is small and too crowded. Last year she went to my aunt's house for eighteen days and came back home when she finished her exams (M.Gh.).

In the Iranian educational system each pupil has to pass the final exam of the year in all subjects to qualify for the next level. Some children have difficulty coping with the mainstream curriculum. This is partially because parents, often illiterate and poor, are unable to help their children or spend extra money on revision books and materials. If they fail any of the subjects they have a chance to re-sit at the end of summer. Sometimes they become disqualified for the next level because of their poor performance in even one subject. Difficulty with the curriculum leads to the loss of interest in education. Many respondents reported similar experiences:

> I have studied up to high school, but because I was not bright and interested I gave it up (M.Gh.).

> I studied for only five years. I was always struggling with my study and didn't

> like it. So I left the school (Z.E.).

> I have studied for five years. Then, because I was not clever enough, I could not study any more and gave up (M.S.).

Family needs for children's labor intensifies disapproval when a child has to re-sit an exam. A woman from a poor and extended household said that:

> My oldest daughter studied up to year seven. She failed two years and left the school. My other children are going to school. My son should be in year 5, but he had failed one year and is in year four.

In a discussion between one informant and her son about the children's education, the son told me that:

> My parents did not allow me to study. They put their problems on me.

The mother became offended and interrupted her son by saying that:

> He is lying, he sat exams twice each year. That's why we didn't let him go.

Then the son jokingly answered his mother back:

> I wanted my knowledge to be multiplied.

Most times, the disapproval of the family ends the children's education. But as soon as the children realize the importance of education in better upward social and economic opportunities, they put the blame on parents. F.M. explained her feeling in this manner:

> As soon as we arrived to the city, we sent the children to a carpet workshop, instead of school. Now my children taunt me for not having sent them to school. I feel ashamed towards my children. I cannot raise my head to look at their face when they complain about it. I think I haven't done my motherly obligation towards my children. But I didn't have a choice. Poverty is an evil (F.M.).

Families that are economically and intellectually better off provide better opportunities for either formal education or vocational training of daughters. They show less discrimination towards female education and are under less pressure from traditional practices and norms regarding female education.

I interviewed two single girls in their house who had come to the city for education and had a circular migration. One was studying in high school and the other in secondary school. Their father had bought a two floor house in one of the slums and all the children, including a married brother with his wife and son, were living there while their parents stayed in their village. One of the sisters said:

> We have come to the city because of education. We spend summers in the village and during school times we come back to the city. Our parents are living in the village. We prefer the city and believe that migration is good for youth, because they become educated and easily make decisions about their future. We want to find a good job when we finish our education.

Mrs. Kh. was a head teacher in a primary school in a slum squatter area and had a bachelor degree in primary education. Concerning her education, she said that:

> I was five years old when we migrated. Migration has had lots of positive influences on my educational, social, and economic situation. The environment in which we live affects our lives. Of course, family also has its own strong role to play. My uncle wanted his daughter to weave carpets, but my father said he would work to let his children to study. I am a head teacher and my cousin is a carpet-weaver. If my parents stayed in the village, I would have remained illiterate too, because there was no school for girls in our village. I would have married at an early age and had lots of children (Mrs. Kh.).

The majority of those who go to school and perform well see education as a liberalizing tool and want to go to university or get a paid job when they graduate. Many mothers also consider education as a tool that presents opportunities for personal development in terms of employment and social mobility.[31] Thus, mothers do support and encourage daughters to keep up with their education, even at university level. One mother said that:

> My daughters' education is very important for us. My oldest children are girls, while my son is in year four. We do not pay as much attention to his study as we do to our daughters'.

However, the high expenses of university affect both boys and girls' continuation of study even if they have passed the entrance exam successfully. In Iran there are two types of university: state and private. Education in state universities is free without tuition fees and entry is very challenging. In private universities, such as the Open Islamic University (*Daneshghah-e Azad-e Eslami*), one of the more popular ones, the tuition fee is very expensive and entrance is much easier compared to the state universities. One of the women said that:

> My daughter has been accepted by the Open University twice. But because of the lack of finance, we could not manage to send her to the university. She has a Diploma. We are not against her working. We have supported her both in her attempts to study and to find a job. She has applied for a job and next week will have an interview. I pray for her success.

Another mother also said that:

> In our village there was only primary education. We sent two of my sons to my sister's house to continue their education. All of my three sons have gone to private university. One of them was accepted in the Open University, but he gave up in the middle of his study as it was too expensive and he started to work in a company. For my second son, the tuition fee was about sixty-four thousand *Tomans* per term. Last term, my third son's tuition fee was one hundred and four thousand *Tomans*, very expensive.

In another case the son of one of my informants had been accepted in a state university in another city. Even though they did not have to pay tuition fees, his accommodation, travel and other expenses were too high for the family to afford and he stopped his university education after one year.

Honor and its impact on female education

Although increasing access of women to education is an important indicator of social change among the migrant households, traditional values concerning women's morality were strongly stated by some informants. Apart from the profound effects of poverty on young migrants' education, the concept of honor also plays an important role in interrupting women's progress to higher levels of education. In Iran, as in many other Muslim societies, the notion of honor is generally linked to women's sexuality. The strength of the concept differs from one society to another, from sector to sector, and from one social class to another. However, the ideology of honor is stronger in traditional and lower sections of any society (Al-Khayyat, 1990: 21-25), including rural people and particularly migrants who find the city a strange place (Bauer, 1985). Different terms are used for honor. *Aib*, translated as immodest or shameful, is more related to a behavioral concept. How to talk, walk and behave are regulated in this manner. *Ghirat*, *sharaf* and *namous* are more connected to the sexual concept of honor, which has a direct relationship to family reputation. If a woman breaks the rules of morality by sexual misconduct, she brings shame and dishonor to her family and damages its moral reputation. This damage is often irreparable (Al-Khayyat, 1990: 21-26). Since women are guardians of family honor, their behavior and sexual conduct are controlled both by family and other social controls such as gossip and accusations of acting shamefully and dishonorably. The idea of moral reputation and its relation to women's morality, particularly that of young unmarried women, was more pronounced during the interviews. Some families believe their daughter's education might not be compatible with chastity. Thus, they do not encourage education for daughters and place informal restrictions on women's mobility. Some families, particularly poorer households, believe that it would be enough for their daughter to have only an elementary level of education, enough to allow them to read and write. Different families, however, use different excuses for interrupting their daughter's education. Although restrictions on women are defended by concerns for their security, they limit women's chances in education and paid employment.

K. had only five years of formal education, because her father did not allow her to continue. She said that:

> I could not manage to finish year five. Until half way through the year my mother and I concealed my schooling from my father. But as soon as he understood our secret, he did not allow me to go to school anymore (K.).

One of the informants also stated that:

> My daughters have only studied five years. My husband didn't allow them to continue, even though they were very interested in education.

F. was 21 years old, a single woman who studied up to secondary level in *Nehzat* classes. When I asked why she did not continue her education, she replied that:

> My family: father, mother and brother did not allow me to do so because *Nehzat* classes were held in late afternoons and there were not any classes nearby for the secondary level. On top of that my parents would not let me have a paid job, even if I managed to continue my study. Then what is the point of my studying? (F.).

Obviously she was aware that she would have faced family disapproval if she had found a paid job, which adversely affected her desire to continue studying. She was a professional carpet weaver who was working with her brother on finely woven carpets. Her brother stayed with us during the interview, and in response to her comments, said that:

> You don't study to get a job. You should study for life. Tomorrow when you will have children, you can bring them up well, if you are educated (F.'s brother).

The notion of educated mothers who play a crucial role as the first nurturers and educators of the nation in rearing children emerged in reformist critical literature in Iran after the mid-nineteenth century. By the early twentieth century the idea that women deserve the blessings of education entered into Iran's political culture (Najmabadi, 1998: 94). Although the nature of early nationalism changed from a secular one to a cultural one after the mid-twentieth century, in the political arena, women were seen as the mothers of the nation, to be educated for bringing up the children of the nation. The idea was strongly accepted by many families, particularly by men who do not view women's education simply in terms of future employment. But for F.'s mother honor was more important:

> In the village you live in peace and security. But in the city if my daughter goes out, boys would start following her, harassing her and causing inconvenience. Therefore, I have no choice other than keeping her at home. If your child is abducted, you will lose both your honor and your child, won't you (F.'s mother).

The fear of abduction, particularly for girls, was also mentioned by other women. One woman, who had three young daughters when she moved to the city, said that:

> When I came to the city, I had no one to help me. I looked after them myself. When I was working on a carpet, I used to hold the youngest one in my back and the other two used to play at the room. I was afraid to let them play in the street. They were all girls and I was frightened that if they were abducted, we would lose our reputation.

An interview with two unmarried sisters, who had gone to *Nehzat* in the city for two years, revealed that their father did not let them study anymore for the same reason: perceived threat of loss of honor or reputation. At the time of the interview, one of the girls was attending a *Quranic* class in a local mosque once or twice a week. The younger, fifteen years old, felt deep anger and spoke bitterly when talking about the interruption to her education. She said that:

> My father does not let us go to school. He is a respected and well-known man in the community. He believes that the city is in a bad state and if we go to school and something unpleasant happens to us, it would result in the disgrace of him and the family. Before coming to Tabriz, I was thinking that in the city we would have more freedom and fewer relatives around to spy on us. But here is like my village; most of our relatives who have migrated live in the same street as ours and keep a close eye on our actions (M.T.).

When I asked her if she likes to study, she shook her head and said with deep regret that:

> Yes indeed. When I was in the village, my teacher told my father that: "if you let your daughter study, she will be able to work up to a doctorate". Now my Qurarnic teacher is also very astonished with my progress (M.T.).

In my view, the fear of losing honor is mostly not due to the lack of trust that parents have towards their unmarried daughters. Rather they do not trust the host society and are afraid that daughters will be at the risk from unknown threats, or be deceived through their simplicity or carelessness. At the time of the interviews, however, many of the younger girls in migrant families were studying in the higher levels of school without parents having much anxiety about loss of honor simply because of education. By comparing the women whose education was interrupted with their younger sisters, I noticed that as duration of residency in the city increases, unacknowledged fear or lack of trust in the new environment decreases. This may partially signify the importance of socio-psychological factors in the experience of marginality and insecurity of early years of migration.

It can also be argued that the imposition of *hejab* (veiling) on women by the Islamic state and Islamization policies with respect to women, such as emphasizing their modesty, chastity and dignity, demonstrates conformity to traditional norms and practices for migrant families (Mir-Hosseini, 1996). In that case, conformity could decrease education's perceived negative implications morally and politically among traditional and lower class families. K.Kh., who has been quoted already, talked about her father's reasons for interfering in her education in this manner:

> Although my father interrupted my education, my other sisters are studying and aiming to gain their diplomas. Whenever I complain about his interference in my study, he says that at that time *Mullahs* (clergies) were saying that girls should not go to school (K.Kh.).

Mrs. Kh., the head teacher also said that:

> During the revolution, I was at secondary level. One summer before the revolution, I wanted to go to a Quranic class in our neighborhood, but the cleric who was teaching Quran did not accept me, as he believed that the Quran should not be taught to girls who attend the school (Mrs. Kh.)[32].

One the informants, who was a teacher said:

> In the high-school we were not allowed to wear trousers, we had to wear skirts. I used to hide my trousers beneath my socks. I was from a religious family, and used to wear a scarf in the teacher training college, my classmates used to pull off my scarf and told me that if I was bald I could wear it. There were humiliations towards those who wanted to comply with their religious beliefs.

Such quotations show that during the monarchy, there was a prevailing negative attitude towards modern education and educated women, particularly among the lower classes who were more influenced by clerics. If it is correct that imposition of *hejab* and gender policies, particularly sex-segregation, conform with traditional norms and practices, then this could be regarded as an emancipatory tool, which has increased mobility for younger women and their access to higher levels of education in traditional families.

The introduction of compulsory *hejab* and dress code changed the definition of the public sphere from a "corrupt" environment to an acceptable one for many traditional and working class families (Mir-Hosseini, 1996: 149)[33]. In a study exploring the contradictory and complex meanings and messages of *hejab* including its compulsory imposition on women, the author of this book argued that when *hejab* is imposed into a context where it is already an important part of the culture, its practical application by women themselves is very important (Velayati, 1998). Women from traditional and religious families utilize Islamic ideology and practice of *hejab* as an accepted tool for families and society to release themselves from patriarchal domination, and at the same time struggle for emancipation and access to the public spheres and social and economic participation, "an alternative entry to modernity" (Sullivan, 1998: 226). Getting access to higher levels of education, employment and social presence for women from traditional and religious families can be regarded as taking advantage of Islamic ideology, particularly the removal of discriminatory practices against veiled women in society (Hoodfar, 1993; Mir-Hosseini, 1995; Velayati, 1998: 57).

The anxiety about honor might surface again when daughters want to further their education in universities in other cities, as they would have to leave home. Only one of the informants said that:

> My father is against my education in the university; he does not approve me going to another city. I stayed at home a year after getting my diploma. I was clever, I told myself that it is better if I can get my *"pish daneshgahi*[34]*,"* in case the possibility of education would be available later. I like to study very much. Although there was a year gap between my diploma and *"pish daneshgahi"* and I was doing a hairdressing course and studying simultaneously, I managed to pass the exam successfully (R.).

However, among my informants some single women had migrated alone to Tabriz either to study or to work in a factory. In many cases, girls negotiated with their parents, won the case and played active roles in the process of social change. Often their demands were not contrary to the basic foundation of traditional beliefs and notions.

The impact of marriage on female education

Girls' marriage is also an important factor, which interrupts their study not only during higher levels of education, but for some even the early years of schooling. In Iran as in many other Muslim countries, the institution of marriage is an essential part of a woman's life and a natural step towards womanhood. Although marriage is strongly valued by all families, it is more highly regarded among traditional social classes. F.T. married at the age of 13 and, regarding her education and marriage, said that:

> I studied three years only. I married at the age of 13. My husband's family and mine were related. One day my parents asked me: "Do you wish to go to Tabriz?" I, who didn't realize why I was being asked, said yes. Here (in Tabriz) they took me to a marriage notary office and asked me if I wanted to marry my husband and I had no choice but to nod. There, I realized that they wanted to marry me off. In those days we were embarrassed to talk about marriage with

our parents. (F.T.).

Whilst there were restrictions on female migration for education, this did not necessarily apply to other things, and for between 10 to 14 percent of informants in both stages of the study, the reason for migration was "getting married." Almost half of the women in this category were illiterate. For the majority of these, the engagement took place in their village and the wedding in the city where their migrant husbands lived and worked, as they explained in their interviews[35].

Early marriage, a practice that appears to be a norm in a number of villages where the migrants originated, seems to be an important factor in low female literacy. The early marriage of a girl, even before puberty is a matter of cultural norms about parental obligations to settle their children in marriage. It also relieves some of the parents' responsibilities for their daughters' moral conduct (Jeffery and Jeffery, 1996).

For most parents, particularly rural as well as working class, a girl's marriage is more important than her education, mainly because of poverty and the dominance of notions such as honor, dignity and modesty. According to the Iran Fertility Survey of 1986, more than 50 percent of Iranian women married before the age of 17 and the rest were mostly married by the age of 20.[36] There was/is, however, an obvious difference between rural and urban areas in terms of marriage age. Some informants talked about their marriage in terms of its destructive impact on female literacy, especially at an early age. Many women, particularly the older and aged ones, stated that they were engaged or married at the age of 12 and 13 or even 9 or 10. Most of them, however, stayed in their parental home for a couple of years where they could get training about adult duties and domestic responsibilities that are traditionally viewed "as necessary for maintaining social organization within the family and society" (Touba, 1980: 51-52). One of the illiterate women, who was married at a very young age, said that:

> I was nine or ten years old when I got married. In those times parents or the elder people of the family decided when and to whom they married off a girl. My oldest brother made the decision, as my father had died. Once I understood that I was taken to my husband's house (F.).

One of the illiterate informants did not even remember how old she was when she got married. Smiling in response to my question, she answered that:

> I swear to God if I say I don't know, you wouldn't believe me.

Another woman also did not remember her marriage age. She laughed and said that:

> I was a child when I got married. Don't ask about it, but I remember our engagement lasted eight to nine years. In those days, girls didn't have a say in

> their marriage. The parents decided everything. Nowadays, the girls want to like someone before they get married to him which I think is better.

S.B., who was also illiterate, accompanied her husband in migration and had an early marriage, as well as early widowhood at the age of 30 with four children aged between 11 and 17. Regarding her marriage, she said that:

> I married when I was 14. My mother thought that there would be a scarcity of husbands. Therefore, she married me off as early as she could.

The impact of marriage on education is not confined to rural girls. It also affects migrant girls who often live in the city according to their existing traditional norms. L.Y., who had migrated mainly because of education, was unhappy about her educational situation following her marriage. About her education and marriage, she said that:

> I have been educated upon *"piash daneshgahi."* I was fond of education and didn't want to marry, but because my father had died my mother married me off straight from school. My husband promised me that he will let me continue my education, but after the marriage he prevented me.

L.Y. was not the only woman to experience the breaking of such promises. It occurs to many women who want to refuse marriage because of education. In her case, her husband had less education than her and she was successful and more confident, which he saw as a threat to marital life or his authority, as became clear during the interview. L.Y. teaches Quran in a local mosque without her husband's consent or even his knowledge[37], and regarding her interest in education said that:

> because I had a good voice in reciting the Quran (*tavashih*), my teachers were encouraging me so much. I was doing the Quran and other recitations in school assemblies. I managed to gain second place in a semi-final national competition on Quranic recitation. I have been invited to teach Quranic recitation in many parts of Tabriz. However, he prevents me. If I find any chance to study, I would like to continue my education in religious studies, as I am very interested in theology.

The practice of early marriage has been carried out in many migrant households in the city. However, marriage age is gradually rising among the youngest generation of migrants, despite the lowering of the legal age of marriage to nine years after the revolution of 1979. In many migrant families the older daughters had married at an early age, but their younger sisters did not have the same experience. A girl's marriage in the city is seen as a potential cost because of the provision of trousseau[38], *Jahaz*, which leads to an increased anxiety on the part of the parents, particularly in poorer migrant households. Although in Iranian culture dowry is part of marriage customs, in rural practice the quantity and quality of a dowry is not very important, whereas in the city, all that matters. Thus, the higher demand or expectation about dowry in the city compared to villages is a significant factor in the increase in girls' marriage age in migrant households. For women who had many daughters, the main concern was their daughters' dowry. F.M. was a 60 year old widow whose two youngest children were girls. One of them was engaged to be married and another one was single. About this she said that:

> One of my daughters is engaged. Another one has some suitors, but I cannot afford to give dowry for two girls. I refused my youngest daughter's suitors.

Another woman from a very poor household had six daughters, four of them married and two unmarried. About her major problems in the city as a migrant, she said that:

> Our major problem in the city is the issue of dowry. Four of my daughters are married and we managed to give a dowry for one of them, but this caused problems for my other daughters. Their husbands have threatened to divorce them if they don't get any dowries. We cannot afford our expenses. How can I give dowries for my already married daughters? On top of that I have two more unmarried daughters.

Another widowed woman had a problem with her own daughter who was engaged and was demanding a dowry. She said:

> I feel so ashamed for my daughter, not being able to give her a dowry. If we had stayed in the village, our situation might have been better. Here most of our earning is spent on rent. How can I afford to give her a dowry that would please her?

Studying in the higher stages of secondary or high school is itself another important reason for the increase in the age of marriage. Early marriage not only is an obstacle preventing girls from taking up educational opportunities, but also it results in a high birth rate as well as high infant mortality among women who have married at an early age, as discussed in the following section.

Positive Correlation between Early Marriage and High Fertility Rate

Data from the first stage of the study showed that the birth rate was very high among illiterate women. On the whole they tended to have early marriages. Of the 925 women who participated in the survey, 25 were single. Of the remaining 900 respondents, 25 had no children of whom 21 (84 percent) were married, 1 was widowed and 3 were divorced. Although the ages of these women ranged from 17 to 60 years, 65 percent of them were between 17 to 26 years old, which due to their youth and marital status makes them more likely to have children.

The women who had children had between 1 to 14 children: 55 percent had between 2 to 5 children, and 61.5 percent between 4 to 7. A few women had 10 or more children. It is worth noting that in this stage, women only mentioned their existing children. In the interviews, however, women also mentioned deceased children, but did not include them in the number of their children. When the deceased children were included, the fertility rate dramatically increased among many illiterate women.

Of 126 women whom I interviewed, 29 were single at the time of the study. Of the remaining 97, 10 did not have any children; of these 7 were married, 1 widowed, 1 divorced, and 1 was deserted by her husband. The divorced woman was infertile, so she willingly gave permission for her husband to remarry in order to have children, but soon after she asked for a divorce, as she could not tolerate living with her co-wife and witnessing her pregnancy. About this she stated that:

> My husband did not want to divorce me, but I knew that I could not stand to see another woman bear my husband children. Then I decided to get a divorce before he has any children.

The ages of the women who did not have children ranged from 22 to 55; those of childless married women were 22 to 38 (3 of them between 22 and 27 years old, and thus more likely to have children). Of women who had children, the number varied widely, from 1 to 10. Ten women had step-children, numbers ranging from 1 to 7, whom they had to look after and 27 women had had children who had died in infancy. Six women, who were interviewed in the first day, were not asked whether any of their children had died.

The discussion below looks firstly at the distribution of children among questionnaire respondents and then among the 126 interviewed women, excluding single unmarried women.

Figure 6.11. Distribution of children among mothers in the survey sample (n= 900)*

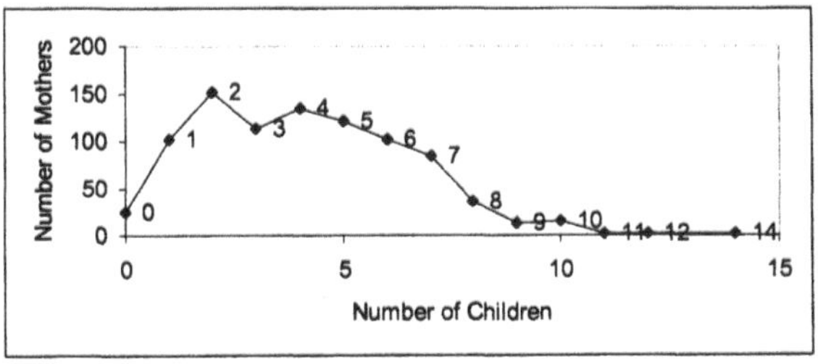

See table 5.8 in chapter 5. Table excludes single unmarried women.

In tables 6.18 to 6.36 I examine women's age and marital status at their time of migration, plus their current age, marital status and number of children against different educational levels, to see if there is any correlation between these factors and the distribution of children among women. Excluding single women, as we will see, the higher the education of the woman the fewer the number of children in the family. Those who have more children tend to be those who are illiterate or have less education.

Number of Children among illiterate women

Tables 6.18–6.21 concentrate on illiterate women among the sample, 603 in total representing 65 percent of the respondents (note: in these tables, one single unmarried woman is excluded, taking the number of women to 602).

Table 6.18. Age and marital status of 602 illiterate women in the sample at the time of migration

	MS							
Age-group	**SWPs**	**SFM**	**SFW/E**	**M.**	**D.**	**W.**	**Total**	**%**
1-9	72	0	0	1	0	0	73	*12.1*
10-19	58	50	0	112	0	1	221	*36.7*
20-29	5	13	1	157	1	1	178	*29.6*
30-39	1	0	0	66	0	3	70	*11.6*
40-49	0	2	0	34	0	2	38	*6.3*
50-59	0	0	0	9	0	3	12	*2.0*
60-69	0	0	0	2	0	0	2	*0.3*
Not known	0	0	0	8	0	0	8	*1.3*
Total	136	65	1	389	1	10	602	*100*

Table 6.19. Marital status of 602 illiterate women and the number of their children

	MS					
No. of children	**M.**	**W.**	**D.**	**Deserted**	**Total**	**%**
0	9	1	1	0	11	*1.8*
1	27	1	0	0	28	*4.7*
2	58	4	0	0	62	*10.3*
3	64	1	0	0	65	*10.8*
4	96	5	0	1	102	*16.9*
5	95	7	0	2	104	*17.2*
6	80	8	0	0	88	*14.6*
7	64	13	0	0	77	*12.8*
8	30	3	0	0	33	*5.5*
9	8	6	0	0	14	*2.3*
10	14	1	0	0	15	*2.5*
11	1	0	0	0	1	*0.2*
12	1	0	0	0	1	*0.2*
14	1	0	0	0	1	*0.2*
Total	548	50	1	3	602	*100*

Among illiterate women, the number of children was varied widely, from 0 to 14. The majority (62 percent), had 4 to 7 children. The average number of children in this category was 4.8. The total numbers of children in this category were 2,919, as table 6.20 and figure 6.12 illustrate.

Table 6.20. Number of boys and girls among 602 illiterate mothers

Number of children per woman	Boys	Girls	Total
0	0	0	0
1	15	13	28
2	61	63	124
3	106	89	195
4	200	208	408
5	273	247	520
6	283	245	528
7	252	287	539
8	136	128	264
9	68	58	126
10	76	74	150
11	4	7	11
12	5	7	12
14	9	5	14
Total	1488	1431	2919

Figure 6.12. Distribution of children among 602 mothers in the survey sample

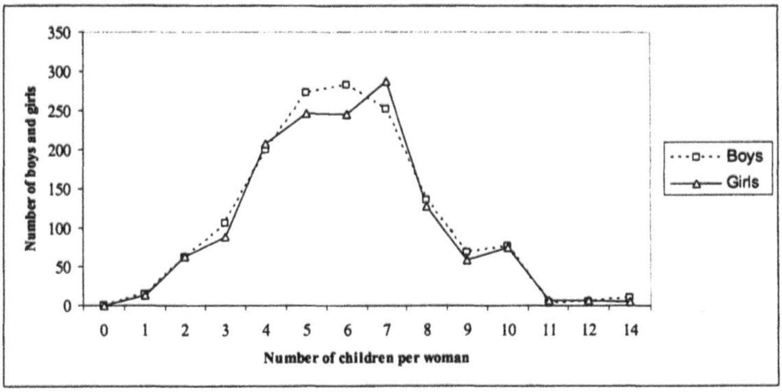

Of the 11 illiterate women who had no children, one was a 25 year old divorced woman, one a 60 year old widow, and the 9 remaining women were all married: 3 in their 20's, 1 in her late 30's, 3 in their 40's, and other 2 were 55 and 60 years old.

Twenty-eight women each had one child. All of them were married, except one 60 year-old widow. Of the married women, 18 were between 19 and 28, 3 between 30 and 37, 3 between 40 and 44, and 3 of them were more than 60 years old.

Of 62 women who each had two children, 58 women were married and four were widowed. The widows were 60 years old and older. Of the married women, one was 16 years old, 38 were between 21 and 29, 13 between 30 and 38, 4 between 40 and 46, 1 was 50 and another1 was 72 years old.

Sixty-five of the illiterate women each had three children; all, with the exception of one 38 year old widow, were married. Seventeen of them were between 22 and 29, forty were 40 between 30 and 38, and the remaining seven were between 40 and 45.

One hundred and two women, each had four children. Five of them were widows aged between 34 and 80; one was a deserted woman 41 years old. Ninety-six were married: 13 of them were between 21 and 29 years old, 59 between 30 and 39, 17 between 40 and 45, and 8 women were more than 50 years old.

One hundred and four women had five children. Seven of them were widows aged between 43 and 66, 2 deserted/separated aged 32 and 80, and 95 were married. Of the married women, 4 were between 28 and 29, 49 between 30 and 39, 25 between 40 and 48, and 18 women were more than 50 years old.

Of 88 women who each had six children, 8 were widows aged between 40 and 83, and were married. Of married women, 32 were between 30 and 39, 28 between 40 and 48, and 21 were more than 50 years old.

Of 77 illiterate women who had seven children, 13 were widows aged between 35 and 65, and 64 were married. Of married women, 1 was 28 years old, 9 were between 30 and 39, 27 between 40 and 49, and another 27 were more than 50 years old.

Of 33 women who had eight children, 3 were widows aged between 43 and 70, and 30 women were married. Of married women, 2 were between 35 and 39, 14 between 40 and 48, and 13 were more than 50 years old.

Of 14 illiterate women who had nine children, 6 were widows aged between 47 and 75, and 8 were married. Of married women, 1 was 38 years old, 5 were between 40 and 48, and 2 of them were 52 and 80 years old.

Of 15 women who each had 10 children, one was a 65 years old widow, and 9 were married women. Of them, 7 were between 40 and 46, and another 7 were more than 53 years old.

Three illiterate married women, who had 11, 12 and 14 children, were 50, 37 and 49 years old respectively.

The ages of women in different categories indicate that illiterate women were more likely to bear a high number of children until they are naturally unable to get pregnant. To what extent the current attempts of birth control exercised by the state might affect illiterate women's tendency to become pregnant is an issue which I will discuss in the section relating to in depth interviews.

Number of children among women with basic reading skills

Fifty-nine women who had basic reading skills (6 percent of respondents) had between 0 to 7 children. Tables 6.21–6.23 illustrate their marital status and their age group at the time of migration, and number of children (boys and girls). One woman, unmarried at the time of survey, has been excluded from the tables (n= 58).

Table 6.21. Age and marital status at the time of migration of women with basic reading skills (n=58)

			MS		
Age-group	**SWPs**	**SFM**	**M.**	**Total**	**%**
1-9	14	0	0	14	*24*
10-19	9	7	10	26	*45*
20-29	0	3	10	13	*22*
30-39	0	0	4	4	*7*
Not known	0	0	1	1	*2*
Total	23	10	25	58	*100*

Table 6.22. Marital status of 58 women with basic reading skills and the number of their children

		MS		
No. of children	**M.**	**W.**	**Total**	**%**
0	3	0	3	*5*
1	11	1	12	*21*
2	13	0	13	*22*
3	6	0	6	*10*
4	9	1	10	*17*
5	5	0	5	*9*
6	7	0	7	*12*
7	2	0	2	*3*
Total	76	2	58	*100*

The average number of children in this category was 3.1. The majority (71 percent), however, had one to four children. The total numbers of children were 177 (89 boys and 88 girls).

Table 6.23. Number of children including the number of boys and girls, among 58 women with basic reading skills

	Boys	Girls	Total
Number of children per woman			
0	0	0	0
1	10	2	12
2	14	12	26
3	10	8	18
4	14	26	40
5	12	13	25
6	21	21	42
7	8	6	14
Total	89	88	177

Figure 6.13. Children among 58 mothers in the survey sample

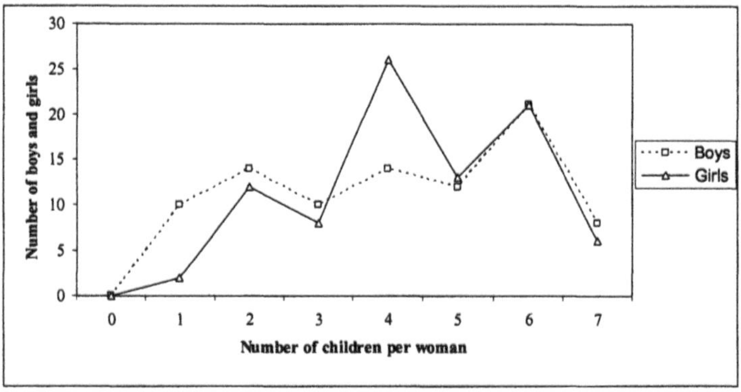

The women's ages during the survey were as follows. The three married women who had no children were aged between 25 and 29 years old. Twelve women each had one child. One of them was a 30 year-old widow, and the rest were aged between 20 and 29. Thirteen women had two children; seven were between 22 and 29, five between 30 and 39; and one was 45 years old.

Of the six women who had three children, four were between 27 and 37, and the other two were 42 and 48 years old. Of ten women who had four children, one was a 43 year-old widow; six were between 32 and 39, and three were between 40 and 46. Of five women who had five children each, three were between 33 and 37, and two were 43 and 45 years old. The seven women who had six children were all aged between 36 and 46. Two women had seven children; both were 27 years old.

Although the number of children among women who had basic reading skills is much lower than that among illiterate women, compared to the latter, they are much younger. For instance, none had reached their fifties and we cannot judge whether their small amount of education had any impact on a lower number of children as some might go on to have more.

Number of children among women with primary education

The one hundred and ninety-four women who had primary education represented 21 percent of respondents. Among them the number of children was diverse, ranging from 0 to 10. The majority, however, had one to three children. Tables 6.24–6.26 illustrate their marital status and their age group at the time of migration, and the number of children including the number of boys and girls. Ten of these women were unmarried during the survey, and have been excluded from the tables.

Table 6.24. Age and marital status of women with primary education, at the time of migration (n= 184)

			MS		
Age-group	SWPs	SFM	M.	Total	%
1-9	50	0	0	50	*27*
10-19	17	40	37	94	*51*
20-29	3	6	29	38	*21*
30-39	0	0	1	1	*1*
40-49	0	0	1	1	*1*
Total	70	46	68	184	*100*

Table 6.25. Marital status of 184 women with primary education and the number of their children

			MS		
No. of children	M.	W.	D.	Total	%
0	6	0	1	7	*4*
1	37	0	0	37	*20*
2	62	0	0	62	*34*
3	33	1	0	34	*18*
4	20	0	0	20	*11*
5	9	1	0	10	*5*
6	6	0	0	6	*3*
7	5	0	0	5	*3*
8	2	0	0	2	*1*
10	1	0	0	1	*1*
Total	181	2	1	184	*100*

The average number of children per women with primary education was 2.7. The total number of children was 490 (235 boys and 255 girls).

Table 6.26. Number of boys and girls among 184 women with primary education

Number of children per woman	Boys	Girls	Total
0	0	0	0
1	19	18	37
2	61	63	124
3	51	51	102
4	42	38	80
5	28	22	50
6	12	24	36
7	12	23	35
8	7	9	16
10	3	7	10
Total	235	255	490

Figure 6.14. Distribution of children among 184 mothers with primary education

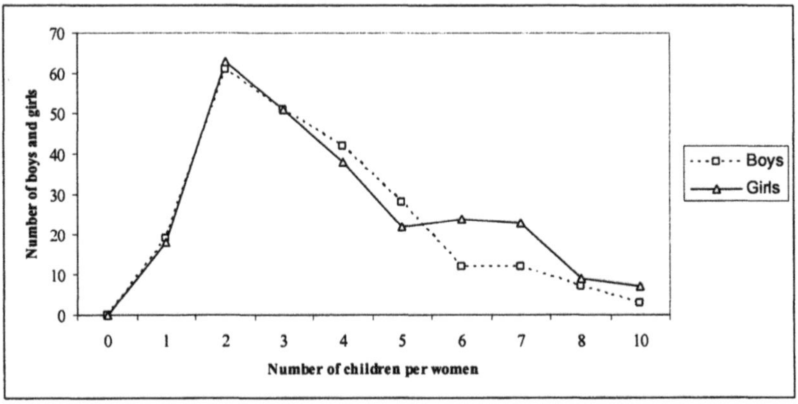

Of 7 women who had no children, one was a 24 year old divorced woman; the 6 married women were aged between 18 to 33. Thirty-seven women in the sample had one child each; all were aged between 20 and 32. Of 62 women who had two children, 37 were in their 20's, and 25 were between 30 and 41 years old. None fell in the widowed, divorced or deserted category. Of 34 women who had had three children, one was a 45 year old widow and the rest were married. Twenty-eight were between 26 and 36, and the other five between 38 and 45. 10 women had four children each; 5 were between 27 and 37 years old 1 was a 42 year-old widow, the rest were married and all were between 35 and 45. Of 6 married women in this category who had six children each, 5 were between 32 and 37 years old, and 1 was 46 years old. Of 5 women who had seven children, 4 were between 40 and 49; the other was 60 years old. Of the reminder, 2 women had eight children. One was 37, and the other 45 years old. The woman who had 10 children was 50 years.

Among these primary educated women, only three were more than 46 years old. However, a trend towards fewer children seems apparent with an increase in women's educational level.

Number of children among women with secondary or high-school education

Of 51 (5.5 percent of the respondents) women with secondary or high school levels of education (less than the national diploma), 7 were single. For the remaining 44 women, the number of children varied from 0 to 8. The majority (71 percent), however, had 1 or 2 children. The average number of children per women was 1.9.

Table 6.27. Age and marital status at the time of migration of women who had secondary or high-school level of education (less than diploma) (n= 44)

	MS					
Age-group	SWPs	SFM	SFW/E	M.	Total	%
1-9	22	0	0	0	22	*50*
10-19	0	6	1	7	14	*32*
20-29	1	2	0	5	8	*18*
Total	23	8	1	12	44	*100*

Table 6.28. Marital status of 44 women with secondary and high-school certificate and the number of their children

	MS		
No. of children	M.	Total	%
0	2	2	*5*
1	21	21	*48*
2	10	10	*23*
3	6	6	*14*
4	2	2	*5*
5	2	2	*5*
8	1	1	*2*
Total	44	44	*100*

The total numbers of children were 85 (46 boys and 39 girls).

Table 6.29. Number of children among 44 women with secondary and high-school certificate including the number of boys and girls

	Boys	Girls	Total
Number of children per women			
0	0	0	0
1	12	9	21
2	13	7	20
3	8	10	18
4	5	3	8
5	5	5	10
8	3	5	8
Total	46	39	85

Figure 6.15. Distribution of children among 44 mothers with secondary or high-school education

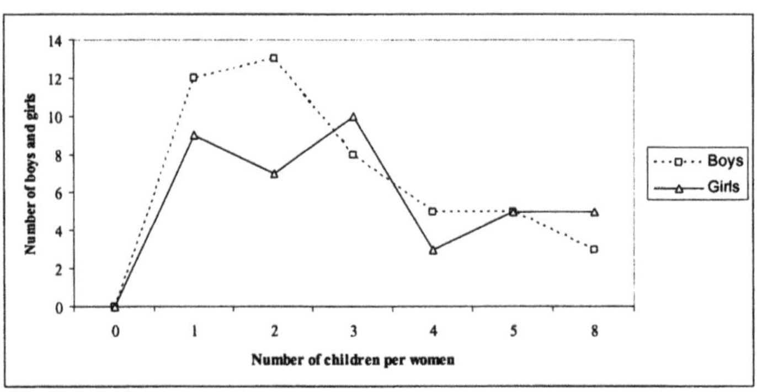

Of the two women who had no children, one was 21 years old, and the other was 26. Of twenty-one women who had one child, all were aged between 20 and 36. Of the ten who had two children each, all were aged between 22 and 36. Three women, who had three children, were all between 27 and 34 years old. Two women had four children. One was 38 years old, and the other was 45. Two women who had five children each were 34 and 43 years old. The woman with eight children was 49 years old. Although the majority of women in this category are much younger than those in previous categories, the number of children is shown to be considerably reduced against an increase in women's educational level.

Number of children among women with national Diploma certificate or more

Only 2 percent of the respondents of this sample (18 women) had certification at diploma level or higher level. Six were single aged between 20 and 28 and are excluded from the following tables.

Table 6.30. Age and marital status at the time of migration of women who had Diploma certification or more (n= 12)

	MS				
Age-group	**SWPs**	**SFW/E**	**M.**	**Total**	**%**
1-9	5	0	0	5	*42*
10-19	1	1	0	2	*17*
20-29	1	0	4	5	*42*
Total	7	1	4	12	*100*
%	*58*	*8*	*33*		

Table 6.31. Marital status of 12 women who had Diploma certification or more and the number of their children

	MS			
No. of children	**M.**	**D.**	**Total**	**%**
0	1	1	2	*17*
1	4	0	4	*33*
2	4	0	4	*33*
3	2	0	2	*17*
Total	11	1	12	*100*

Of those who had no children, one was a 21 year-old married woman and another was 24 years old and divorced. Four, who had one child were aged between 22 and 27. The four who had two children were between 29 and 40. Two women who had three children each were 40 and 41 years old. The total number of children was thirteen boys and seven girls. The average number of children in this category was 1.5.

Table 6.32. Number of children among 12 women who had Diploma certification or more and the number of their children including the number of boys and girls

	Boys	Girls	Total
Number of children per women			
0	0	0	0
1	2	2	4
2	6	2	8
3	3	3	6
Total	11	7	18

Figure 6.16. Distribution of children among 12 mothers with Diploma certificate or more

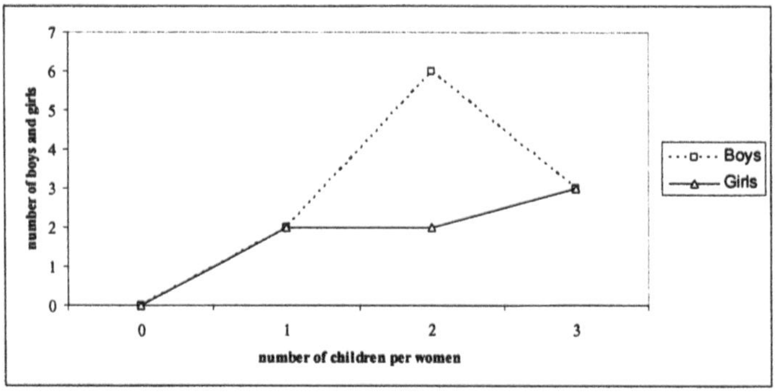

Comparison of women's marital status, age and number of children indicated that the majority of older women were illiterate and had more children, and an increase in women's educational level correlated with a rise in marriage age and a decline in the number of children they had.

In total, women in this sample had 3,689 children. When these were divided into illiterate and literate categories, 79 percent of the children (2,919) belonged to illiterate women, but they constituted 65 percent of the sample. The literate women had 21 percent of the total (770). The average number of children was 4.8 among the illiterate women, and 2.6 among the literate ones. Single, unmarried women have been excluded from these calculations.

Table 6.33. Total and average number of children among illiterate or literate women (excluding single women)

Level of literacy	Number of Women	Number of Children	Average No. of Children
Illiterate	602	2919	4.8
Literate	298	770	2.6
Total	900	3689	4

Figure 6.17. Cross tabulation count of the number of children among illiterate and literate mothers

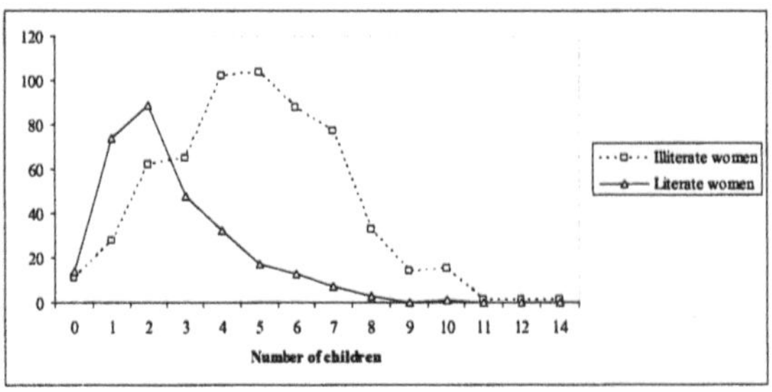

Table 6.34. Cross tabulation count of the number of children in a household in terms of illiterate and literate status of their mothers

	Literacy		
Number of children	Illiterate women	Literate women	Total of women
0	11	14	25
1	28	74	102
2	62	89	151
3	65	48	113
4	102	32	134
5	104	17	121
6	88	13	101
7	77	7	84
8	33	3	36
9	14	0	14
10	15	1	16
11	1	0	1
12	1	0	1
14	1	0	1
Total	602	298	900

Tables 6.33 and 6.34 clearly indicate that there is a negative correlation between illiteracy and a greater number of children among the sample. Moreover, by giving two values of (0) for illiterate and (1) for literate women, a statistically negative correlation of -0.45 between the level of education and the number of children is shown in table 6.35.

Table 6.35. Correlations between the educational level of women and the number of children

	Number of children	Educational level of women
Number of children	1	-0.451*
Educational level	-0.451	1

* Correlation is significant at the 0.01 level (1-tailed).

Grouping literate women into five categories and comparing them with illiterate women gave the correlation in table 6.36. The mean number of children decreases in each group against the increase in the level of education.

Table 6.36. Mean number of children according to educational group of mother

Educational level	Mean	Number
Illiterate	4.8	602
Basic reading skills	3.1	58
Primary education	2.7	184
Under Diploma	1.9	44
Diploma and more	1.5	12
Total	4.1	900

Information Based on Interviews

Now I examine the distribution of children among the women who were interviewed in the second stage in terms of their literacy. As stated in chapter 5, the sample of interviewed women was composed of 74 married, 19 widowed, 29 single, and 3 divorced women, and 1 who was deserted. The sample was divided into five groups: illiterate, literate with primary level of education or less (this includes 20 women with basic reading skill plus 19 with primary education), literate with secondary or higher level of schooling, literate with national diploma or more, and women who were studying during the interview.

Table 6.37. Marital status of interviewees at the time of interview (n=126)

MS	S.	M.	W.	D.	Deserted	Total
Numbers	29	74	19	3	1	126
%	*23*	*59*	*15*	2	*1*	*100*

Before examining the relationship between women's educational level and the numbers of children each had, this is a note about five single unmarried women still in education. Of these five, two were studying at secondary level, two at high-school level, and one was a university student at Tabriz University. Their ages were between 16 and 20 and all had high ambitions for their future. Except one, who was from a relatively well off family, the other four girls were from poor families. Two of the girls (who were also sisters) had lost their father a couple of years before the interview and their education was threatened by their sheer poverty, but they had managed to continue studies despite all their difficulties.

Table 6.38. Marital status of interviewed women who were still in education

MS at the time of migration	Number	%
SWPs.	3	*60*
SFM.	2	*40*
Total	5	*10*

At this stage I had also been made aware of the stepchildren—as well as deceased children—of the interviewed women and have included these into the following discussions[39]. Table 6.39 looks at the number of existing children among women.

Table 6.39. Number of existing children among 97 women

Number of children	Number of women	%
0	8	*8.2*
1	9	*9.3*
2	18	*18.6*
3	12	*12.4*
4	14	*14.4*
5	8	*8.2*
6	12	*12.4*
7	6	*6.2*
8	6	*6.2*
9	3	*3.1*
10	1	*1.0*
Total	97	*100*

Note: Twenty-nine single interviewees are excluded from this table.

The total number of children among these women was 376.

Table 6.40. Number of deceased children among women who reported loss of a child (n=26)

Number of deceased children	Number of women	%
1	8	*31*
2	8	*31*
3	3	*12*
4	3	*12*
5	1	*4*
6	2	*8*
7	1	*4*
Total	26	*100*

Note: Altogether 26 women lost 69 children due to preventable illnesses.

Table 6.41. Number of stepchildren among interviewees (marital status of interviewee given at time of interview)

	MS			
Number of step children	**M.**	**W.**	**Total**	**%**
1	3	1	4	*40*
2	0	1	1	*10*
3	1	0	1	*10*
4	0	1	1	*10*
6	1	0	1	*10*
7	1	1	2	*20*
Total	6	4	10	*100*

Note: Thirty-tree stepchildren in the sample. Of the ten women all, except one were illiterate; one, with *Nehzat* education, had six stepchildren.

Tables 6.42 to 6.52 separately examine the age and marital status of interviewed women in each educational level at the time of migration, as well as their current marital status and number of children including existing, deceased and stepchildren. (The tables exclude the unmarried single women).

Number of children among illiterate women

There were 52 illiterate women who provided information for tables 6.42–6.45, 1 of whom was single and excluded from the calculations.

Table 6.42. Marital status at the time of migration for 51 illiterate women

MS	Number	%
SWPs.	7	13.7
SFM.	4	7.8
M.	36	70.6
W.	4	7.8
Total	51	100

Illiterate women represented 41 percent of interviewees. Among them the number of children varied widely, from 0 to 10 (257 children or 71 percent of the total).

Table 6.43. Marital status of 51 illiterate mothers at time of interview and the number of their children

	MS				
No. of children	**M.**	**W.**	**D.**	**Total**	**%**
0	0	1	1	2	*3.9*
1	2	1	0	3	*5.9*
2	4	1	0	5	*9.8*
3	2	4	0	6	*11.8*
4	4	1	0	5	*9.8*
5	3	2	0	5	*9.8*
6	6	2	1	9	*17.6*
7	3	3	0	6	*11.8*
8	6	0	0	6	*11.8*
9	3	0	0	3	*5.9*
10	1	0	0	1	*2.0*
Total	34	17	2	51	*100*

Table 6.44. Marital status of 51 illiterate interviewees and the number of deceased children

	MS			
Number of deceased children	**M.**	**W.**	**Total**	**%**
1	4	3	7	*30.4*
2	3	3	6	*26.1*
3	3	0	3	*13.0*
4	2	1	3	*13.0*
5	0	1	1	*4.3*
6	1	1	2	*8.7*
7	0	1	1	*4.3*
Total	13	10	23	*100*

Comparing this table with table 6.40 in which in total 26 women stated that they had lost between 1 and 7 of their children, it can be seen that 23 of them are illiterate. The 64 deceased children reported represented 93 percent of all deceased children among this set of interviewees. About 10 women, most of whom were illiterate were not asked this question.

Table 6.45. Marital status of illiterate women who had stepchildren

	MS			
Number of stepchildren	**M.**	**W.**	**Total**	**%**
1	3	1	4	*45*
2	0	1	1	*11*
3	1	0	1	*11*
4	0	1	1	*11*
7	1	1	2	*22*
Total	5	4	9	*100*

Again, comparing this table with table 6.41, it is clear that illiterate women are often less privileged in status and a number of them have experienced marriage to older men already with children, either due to death of first wives or divorces that were often initiated by men. Ninety percent of women in this study who had stepchildren were illiterate women.

Comparison of tables 6.39 and 6.43 indicates that 30 women out of 97 (almost one-third) who had 5 or more children were illiterate. According to this data, the average number of children per woman is 5.04. There were 64 deceased children, which if added to the total raise the average number of children to which these women had given birth to 6.29 children each. Moreover, 9 of these women had between 1 to 7 stepchildren (27 altogether or 82 percent of all stepchildren in the sample).

Two illiterate interviewees had no children; one was a 30 year-old divorcee and the other was a 55 year-old widow, who had seven stepchildren. She was very destitute when I interviewed her in her neighbor's house; her situation was desperate and she was suffering from prolonged hiccups. She had looked after her husband's seven children. When I wanted to take out my pen and notebook to write down the interviews, she thought I was giving something to her neighbor, who was also very very poor. She started begging terribly for me to give her something also. I told her I was not giving anything to anybody and then she begged me to treat her illness. Although there was a state clinic in their neighborhood, which did not charge very much, she perhaps needed an operation that she could not afford. She said that none of her stepchildren visited her, most of whom, however, were living in Tehran. For her living, she was selling secondhand clothes and was supported by the government with two thousand *Tomans* per month, which was a meager support[40]. Although the divorced woman was living with her brother and was working on carpets to look after herself, at her relatively young age there was a possibility of her getting married to an older man with children. Women, particularly divorced women with no children, may prefer to get married than to be dependent on their families. Often, for these women engagement in income-generating activities and their help around the house are not appreciated by the family and they may be considered a burden. One of the women whose husband was murdered in Kurdistan during Kurdish insurgencies in the early 1980s said:

> It was in the early months of the revolution, when my husband was killed by the Kurdish rebels. We had about 100 sheep and my husband with about 6 or 7 other shepherds had taken the herd to grazing in Kurdistan. That day about 56 people were killed, 2 of them from our village including my husband. Those who had survived had told them that they were Sunnis, but my husband refused to say so. They had managed to bring back some of our sheep. We had also an apple orchard. After the death of my husband we sold both the orchard and the remaining sheep. I moved to my mother's house with my two young children, and started working at their land and at home. My sisters used to come to the village for a visit. They sat, talked, and enjoyed their visit, but I had to work like a slave in my mother's house for eight years, without receiving a payment. The only thing that we received was our food and clothes. I suffered a lot at my own mother's hand after the death of my husband[41].

Three women had one child each. Two of them were married, aged 25 and 26 years old, and one was a 60 year-old widow with a severely disabled child in his late 20s. I did not ask her if she had any other children that had died in childhood. Six women had two children each; one was a 45 year-old widow, and the other five were still married. Three of them were between 24 and 29 years old; one was 40 years old, and one was a 56 year old woman. Six illiterate women had three children each; two were still married, aged 30 and 35 years old; four were widows, two of whom were 32 and 39 years old, the two being 65 and 71 years old. Five women had four children each; one was a 34 year-old widow, and the remaining three were aged between 36 and 57. Five women had five children each. Three were married, aged between 30 and 43 years old, and the other two were widows, one 47 years old and the other 100 years old. Nine women had six children each. Three of them were widowed aged between 40 and 55 years old; the rest were married, aged 38 to 58. Of the six illiterate women who had seven children each, three were married and aged between 47 and 50, and the remaining three were widows between 58 to 70 years old. Six women had eight children each. All still had their husband, and were aged between 44 and 57. The three illiterate women who had nine children each were still married and aged 35 to 54. One woman had ten children; she was 40 years old.

The ages given by women in both stages of the study do not seem to be very reliable, especially those given by older as well as illiterate women. Some of the women in response to my question simply said: "I am illiterate and don't know my age." In rural areas, and among illiterate and older migrants and even urban native illiterate women, date of birth is rarely used. Sometimes during the interviews, the age given by the women was corrected by their literate daughters or daughters-in-law. In many cases by using their married age and their oldest child's age, I found a big gap between the calculated ages and the ages that they claimed to have. This was repeated for the older, mostly illiterate women. In order to estimate the duration of their residency in the city, they either made it known by their own family calendar (such as how many children they had when they migrated, the age of the oldest child born in the city and the current age of that child, their married age in the case of migration for marriage), or they gave a hint by major national events such as the revolution, before or after the arrival of the Ayatollah Khomeini to Iran, departure of the Shah from Iran the early or the closing years of the war between Iran and Iraq).

Number of children among women with primary level of schooling

There were 39 women educated at primary level or who had attended the *Nehzat* classes, representing 31 percent of the interviewees. Eight were single aged between 14 and 39, excluded from the tables of 6.46 and 6.47, which examine the situation of 31 women.

Table 6.46. Marital status of 31 interviewed women with primary level of schooling or less, at their time of migration

MS	*Nehzat*	Primary	Total	%
SWPs.	6	9	15	*48*
SFM.	1	4	5	*16*
SFW/E.	0	2	2	*7*
M.	6	3	9	*29*
Total	13	18	31	*100*

The number of children the women in this category had was 95; each had between 0 to 6 children (25 percent of the children).

Table 6.47. Marital status of interviewed women with primary level of schooling or less, and the number of their children

	MS				
No. of children	**M.**	**W.**	**Deserted**	**Total**	**%**
0	1	0	1	2	*6*
1	2	0	0	2	*6*
2	9	1	0	10	*32*
3	4	0	0	4	*13*
4	7	0	0	7	*23*
5	2	1	0	3	*10*
6	2	1	0	3	*10*
Total	27	3	1	31	*100*

Only one woman in this category had stepchildren (6) and three women had lost one or two of their children during their childhood. They had 5 deceased children between them. According to this data, the average number of children per each woman was 3.1, without counting deceased children and excluding single women. If deceased children are added on this raises the average number of children to 3.3 which women in this category had given birth to.

There was a childless married woman of 24 years old, and a 35 year old woman whose husband left her not long after their marriage and married another woman, but she preferred to stay married officially and hide from most of her relatives and friends due to the stigma attached to being deserted, which is much greater than the stigma towards divorced women. Two married woman with one child each were young, aged 22 and 23.

Ten women had two children, one of them a 45 year-old widow, and the remainder were aged between 23 and 36. Three women with three children each were aged between 30 and 56. Seven women, all married and aged between 29 and 44 had four children each. Three women, two married and aged between 50 and 55, and another 44 year-old widow had five children each. Three women had six children each; two of the women were married and one was widowed. One married 40 year-old woman had six children.

Number of children among women with secondary level of schooling

Twelve women were educated at the secondary level, representing 10 percent of the interviewees. All of these were single during migration and had accompanied their parents. Four, aged between 19-21 were single during the study and are excluded from the following table.

Table 6.48. Marital status of interviewed women with secondary level of schooling and the number of their children (n= 8)

	MS		
No. of children	**M.**	**Total**	**%**
0	2	2	*25*
$1	2	2	*25*
2	1	1	*12.5*
3	2	2	*25*
4	1	1	*12.5*
Total	8	8	*100*

The eight married women had between 0 to 4 children each (14 children altogether or 4 percent of the children). None of them had any deceased or stepchildren. The average number of children in this category was 1.75. The married women were aged between 22 and 48 and those without any children were aged 22 and 27.

Number of children among women with national diploma or higher degree
Eighteen women who held a national diploma or higher level of education represented 14 percent of the sample. All of them had either migrated to the city with their parents or had made an autonomous migration. Of the 18 women in this category, 11 were single aged between 18 and 30, who are excluded from the following table.

Of the remaining seven women, six aged between 24 and 49 were married with 0 to 4 children each, and one was a 27 years old divorced woman with one child. None of them had any deceased or stepchildren. These women had 10 children among them, the average being 1.4 children.

Table 6.49. Marital status of interviewed women who held Diploma degree or higher (n= 7)

MS at the time of migration	Number	%
SWPs.	2	*29*
SFW/E.	5	*71*
Total	7	*100*

Table 6.50. Marital status of interviewed women who held Diploma and the number of their children (n= 7)

	MS			
No. of children	**M.**	**D.**	**Total**	**%**
0	2	0	2	*29*
1	1	1	2	*29*
2	2	0	2	*29*
4	1	0	1	*14*
Total	6	1	7	*100*

In total, women who had participated in interviews had 376 children. Counting the deceased children raised the number to 445. I divided the interviewees into illiterate and literate women. Two hundred and fifty seven existing children (68 percent) and 64 deceased children (93 percent) belonged to the illiterate women. If the totals are added together, the number of children that the illiterate women had given birth to would be 321 (72 percent), while the illiterate women constituted 41 percent of the sample. The number of stepchildren among these women was also high. Table 6.51 shows the total and average number of children for illiterate and literate women.

Table 6.51. Total and average number of children in each category of illiterate and literate women*

Level of literacy	No. of women	Live children	Average	Live and deceased children	Average all
Illiterate	51	257	5.04	321	6.29
Literate	46	119	2.59	124	2.70
Total	97	376	3.88	445	4.59

* The table excludes single unmarried women.

Grouping the interviewees into two categories of illiterate and literate women also indicates a negative correlation between illiteracy and high number of children. The tables above show that the mean number of children in each group decreases with an increase in the level of women's education. Compared to illiterate women, the literate ones were more aware of sexual and reproductive health and available services in terms of contraceptive methods. They were also concerned with the responsibilities towards bringing their children up well, and the costs of raising children in terms of financial and other support.

Table 6.52. Cross tabulation count of the number of children among illiterate and literate mothers (n= 97)

	Literacy		
Number of children	Illiterate women	Literate women	Total of women
0	2	6	8
1	3	6	9
2	5	13	18
3	6	6	12
4	5	9	14
5	5	3	8
6	9	3	12
7	6	0	6
8	6	0	6
9	3	0	3
10	1	0	1
Total	51	46	97

Figure 6.18. Cross tabulation count of the number of children among illiterate and literate mothers

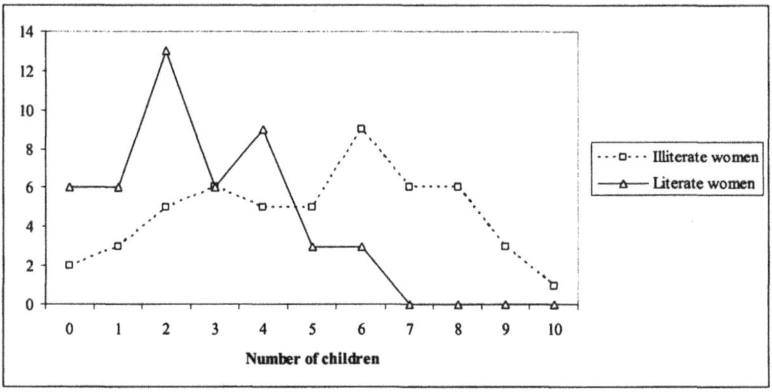

As discussed in detail above, the older illiterate women have many children compared to younger literate ones. The main reason for this, especially for the older women who mainly gave birth to their children in the villages, was lack of health services in rural areas. Children simply died and women carried on with reproduction. One woman said that:

> I've lost five of my children when they were infants. In those times there were no doctors, vaccinations, nothing. Epidemic diseases such as whooping cough and measles easily destroyed the life of young children. Thirty-four years ago vaccines came to our village. My daughter was vaccinated against those diseases and she didn't catch them.

Another woman who was 71 years old, with only three children who survived death and disease, said that:

> Five of my children have died. Four of them were 17, 15, 10, and 7 years old when they died, and one was a baby. When I talk about their deaths, I become very sad. In the village unexpected death happened more often. Children and adults became ill very suddenly. They were told they had caught a cold, but soon they passed away. In our village, there was no health centre, no doctor, no car, nothing. Sometimes we could not find a horse or donkey to take the ill ones to the city. One of my children who died at the age of 15 perished from measles. All of my deceased children died in the village. The three children whom I brought to the city are all alive. Whenever they became ill I took them to the doctor. My sister has given birth to nine children, seven of whom died. At nighttime they became ill and by the following morning they were dead. In the village we were fighting with death. God bless the doctors, they have found the cure for most of the diseases which easily killed people, particularly the young children (Kh.).

A 64 year-old woman put it in this way:

> I've got three (live) children. Six of my children died in their childhood. In the old days, there was no doctor, medicine nor remedy. When a disease came, many perished at once. In those days we had no other alternative except bringing up more children.

Another woman who had seven surviving children and seven deceased ones, said that:

> Seven of my children (four boys and three girls) all died in their childhood. In the village there was no doctor and we did not have money to bring the ill children to the city.

Nowadays family planning offers Iranian women free access to contraceptive methods such as the pill, condoms or sterilization by obstruction of the reproductive organs. Illiterate women, however, were reluctant to use sterilization and thought that they would lose one of their important womanly functions. They prefer to use other contraceptive methods, if they take the idea seriously. The duration of migration did not have a very strong impact on old, illiterate and poor women's reproductive habits. A proportion of them were unaware of the health resources available to them and some did not take an active responsibility towards obtaining contraceptives. Some of these women had severe living conditions and were the poorest of the poor. The family income was barely sufficient for subsistence and the only example of mass media that could be found in some of these houses was radio. The women in these households were isolated and not assimilated into urban life. S. was one of them. She had two children, one of whom was very ill and they were not able to treat him due to their indigence. When I told her that there is no point having more children and not being able to feed or cure them when they are ill, and it would therefore be better for her to use birth-control methods, which are completely free of charge, she would not believe me. During the interview process, I also informed deprived and married women of family planning programs and encouraged them to use birth-control methods. The condition of these women shows how much adult literacy programs can be an important element in delivering useful information to women have no social contact with the outside world. M.D., one of the poorest and illiterate women interviewed, had 10 children. Her youngest child was five years old, but due to malnutrition looked to be only two years old. I asked her why she had many children despite their absolute poverty and having access to the health services in the city. She responded that:

> I don't know! We suffer great misfortune. Once somebody told me that I should limit the number of my children. I didn't listen, for I thought the cost of their food and clothing wouldn't impose that much economic burden on us. But now, I realize how expensive it is to have many children, especially girls for whom you have to provide dowry (M.D).

She seemed unaware of a child's educational and other needs.

A.Gh. had a large family of seven children with a disabled son. In response to my question about family planning, she said that:

> My husband was the only child of his parents to be alive. All his siblings died in childhood. When my children were born, I was told that this one is his sister, this one is his brother, this one is his son, this one is his daughter and so on, until I bore eight children, one of whom died when he was a baby.

Some of the women had better economic conditions and most of their children were born in the city. When I asked them why they did not take advantage of family planning programs, most of them mentioned the low cost of living in the past and the current inflation, which put economic and social pressure on them and their children. Some of them simply said that:

> In those times, the cost of living was low, and we were unwise. Inflation was not this high so, we thought we would be able to manage having many children.

Another woman put it in this way:

> In the old times, the children's expectation from the parents was little. The cost of living was reasonable and we could meet their little expectations. But nowadays, both the expectation of the children and the living cost has increased. When we are not able to meet their expectations, they start to criticize us for having many children.

All the above-mentioned reasons, plus the privileging of male children, resulted in bigger families. One woman put it in this way:

> In the old days, people wanted to have more male children, and there wasn't this much inflation. So we did not care much about birth control.

Surprisingly, a mother of seven children (six boys and one girl), in response to my question about birth control, said that:

> I've given birth to my last three children, for I wanted to have a sister for my daughter. But all were boys and I gave up.

The younger migrant women who are to some extent educated, who migrated in their childhood, are more likely to practice family planning and have fewer children. Unlike the older women, they are more aware of children's diverse needs and desires and feel more responsibility towards their welfare and are very concerned about how to raise their children and meet their needs. In terms of the quality of upbringing of her son, one of the younger women told me that:

> I am very concerned about my child's progress. He is going to kindergarten, but if I don't spend more time with him from now on, I won't be able to bring him up well and his talents won't flourish.

In his study of the relation between fertility and female education in Iran during between 1987-1992, Salehi-Isfahani (2001: 311-37) found a close association between women's education and their fertility behavior at national level, which leads women to substitute quality for the quantity of children and become more productive in terms of raising the human capital of their children. Salehi-Isfahani's study also supports the findings of my study in terms of the impact of education in increasing the age of first marriage age among educated women. As the first marriage age increases, the chance of becoming a widow at a young age, and any other problems related to early marriage decreases. Many women who married early suffered from marital abuses, not only from their husband, often much older than them, but also from their in-laws. Mehrangiz Kar, one of the female activists in the field of Women's Rights, in her study of Violence Against Women argues that: "financial dependency and the fear of losing their children and the stigmatization of divorce in Iranian society, makes women tolerate hard and sometimes abusive marital conditions, which affects women's mental health (Kar, 2000). This situation is even harder for the illiterate migrant women, whose lives are ruled by traditional beliefs and practices and who find the city a strange place. Many women mentioned how they lost their family support after their marriage and migration to the city.

One of the main differences between older, illiterate and poor women and the younger ones is their perception of children. The older women perceive them, particularly male children, as assets, while children are perceived by the younger women as cost which need more care in order to become assets. For many younger the sex of a child did not matter. What was important for them was to have healthy children. A.P. was a young mother with primary education. She and her husband have two daughters and were in favor of having a small family. She took family planning seriously and used the contraceptive methods available in health centers. She and her husband did not privilege male children. She said that:

> Rural and old people privilege males. Whenever we go to the village to visit our family, my in-laws insist on me bringing a son. They are very serious about it. I have tried to convince my mother in-law that nowadays there is no difference between boys and girls. A girl can bring her parents pride and make them honored by being educated and getting involved in social life. I gave her an example of my uncle, whose daughters are educated and employed and bring him honor like a male child can do. Last time when we were in the village, they tried to manipulate my husband. But he told them that we wouldn't go to the village any more, for they interfere in our personal life. I hope his threats work..

Conclusion

The study revealed that there is a considerable difference between the older and younger generations of migrant women or those who migrated to the city with their parents, in terms of access to education. As a result of limited educational opportunities due to social inequalities, and poverty and ideological issues in both villages and urban settings, the only alternative for the older women was marriage at an early age. This had an important effect on their fertility behavior, leading them to have a high number of children. Migration and better access to education has brought social changes to migrant families. Younger women, unlike their older counterparts enjoy the emancipatory potentials of education. Marriage, therefore, does not become the only alternative for both young women and their families. This supports Salehi-Isfahani's findings that education delays women's age of first marriage (Salehi-Isfahani, 2001). The rise in marriage age has a profound impact on women's physical and psychological health and welfare. They tend to have more self-confidence and are better able to promote their own interests in the marital relationship. As level of education increases, the age disparity between them and their husbands often decreases and they may experience more egalitarian relationships with their partners. For instance, some illiterate women in this study were the second wife of their husbands, either because of divorce or the death of their co-wives, whereas none of the women with some level of education had this sort of marriage. Although the increased economic burdens of marriage on both sides have also made it difficult for poor families to marry off their daughters at an early age, it does not necessarily mean that they will enjoy egalitarian relationships.

Younger women's fertility behavior is also different from that of older women as they have a desire for smaller families with fewer children. They have more aspirations for their children's welfare in terms of better education, better health, and better conditions for their upbringing. The illiterate women, who mainly had a higher fertility rate, were either unaware of free and accessible contraceptive methods in hospitals and clinics, or were more concerned about the net cost of children. This was mostly irrespective of the duration of their stay in the city. As is clear from the fertility behavior of women, the effectiveness of the family planning program depends on women's awareness of its existence and also their willingness to practice it. These factors are more related to women's education and their awareness of children's needs.

In the next two chapters, I will concentrate on migrant women's involvement in income generation activities and how women's age, education, and marital status play an important role in determining the different sectors of the economy in which my informants were engaged.

Notes

1. Some *ulama* admitted the backwardness of Iranian society, but were adamant that any innovation and imitation of ideas imported from the West was un-Islamic and through a return to true Islam, they could regain the glories of the past. The majority of the Iranians belonging to lower social classes were faithful to the *ulama*, whose ideas therefore, received mass support. Other conservative forces including social, political, and economic elites who perceived any reform as a threat to their interest and status, also resorted to the *ulama's* arguments to keep their power intact. See The Qajar Period in Menashri, *Education and the Making of Modern Iran*. Ithaca and London: Cornell University Press, 1992.

2. Educated Iranian intellectuals promoted educational reform and gave importance to elementary education based on new and Western methods, as a prerequisite for social and economic advancement of the country and achieving equality and justice. They even obliged the government to provide compulsory nationwide uniform education, outside clerical control and free of charge for the poorest sections of the population. The logic behind this demand was to bridge social gaps between different classes, gaps between urban and rural areas, and between the capital and provinces. These demands were optimistic and beyond the capacity of the educational system to deliver. To receive popular support for development of the country as a whole, some even promoted the accommodation of western ideas with Islam. Others, critical of traditional religious schooling, criticized the *ulama* and other elite groups who opposed the "new education," for deliberately keeping people illiterate, ignorant, and thus dependent on them. See Menashri, 1992: 27-45 and 77-79.

3. Modern elementary and secondary schools were opened privately in the 1870s, and public schools from the 1890s onwards. They all had different curricula and educational approaches, but differed from traditional schools called *maktab* and *madrase*.

4. For detailed information on Reza Shah's background and how it took him to power, see: Donald N. Wilber, *Riza Shah Pahlavi: the Resurrection and Reconstruction of Iran*. New York: Exposition, 1975. Almost all studies dealing with contemporary Iran refer to Reza Shah and the establishment of the Pahlavi dynasty and his anti-clerical attitudes and policies.

5. The main opposition by clerics to modern education was towards elementary level rather than to dispatch students to Europe or other higher education initiatives which attracted a limited number of adults mostly from elite groups. Through the spread of elementary schools, they were bound to lose both control over education and their main source of income. See Menashri, 1992: 60-65.

6. Although many laws were passed and declarations made to attract children from lower classes to educational systems, in practice little was done towards this. Education in rural and tribal areas, where 65 percent of Iranians lived, was as restricted as before, partially due to lack of facilities and partially to opposition from elite groups and *ulama* to mass education, because of perceived threats to their social status and/or danger to faith and religion. In 1962, only 24 percent of children in rural areas were attending school, compared to 74 percent in urban ones. In the same year only 14 percent of villages had schools. In remote areas, both urban and rural, these proportions were even lower. See "Education under Reza Shah" and "Education under Mohammad Reza Shah" in Menashri, 1992.

7. Literacy Corps (*Sepah-e Danesh*, literally meaning "the Army of Knowledge") were military conscripts of high school graduates who were required to serve a two-year compulsory military service in rural areas as teacher-soldiers. However, the scheme was generally unsuccessful due to many factors including inadequate teaching qualifications, lack of continuity or stability in the teaching process, frequent replacement of conscripts by new and inexperienced ones, lack of motivation and enthusiasm due to linguistic difficulties in remote areas, the responsibility in teaching both in public education and adult literacy, and inadequacy of the budget allocated to educational service. See: Godazgar, *The Impact of Religious Factors on Educational Change in Iran: Islam in Policy and Islam in Practice*. New York, Ontario, Lampeter: The Edwin Mellen Press, 2008: 95-96.

8. In 1968, to encourage village girls' access to education, Parliament passed a law for Women's Social Services that aimed to send female teachers to rural areas for a period of eighteen months. The first group of women went out in 1969 (Menashri, 1992: 178-79).

9. Failure of Pahlavi's educational program for rural women has been attributed to the modernization program. Sullivan (1998) interviewed the former head of the Literacy Campaign, who was responsible for the education of village girls and the promotion of women's rights during the program. She explained how the organization's lack of understanding of village psychology led to reactionary violence and anger on behalf of male villagers against rural women. As part of facilitating rural women's participation in society, some village girls were selected to be trained as "agents of development," outside their villages in educational centers like English boarding schools (very different from their own environment). The project of social development, and progressive rights of rural women, however, took place in the form of reconstruction of identity, loss of sense of community, and even the use of repression and violence by educational authorities. See: Sullivan, "Eluding the feminist, overthrowing the modern? Transformation in twentieth-century Iran." In L. Abu-Lughod (ed.) *Remaking Women: Feminism and Modernity in the Middle East*. Princeton, New Jersey: Princeton University, 1998: 223-27.

10. The High Council of Education listed the basic goals of education in this order: religious and spiritual goals, scientific, cultural, social, political, and economic goals. See: Higgins and Shoar-Ghaffari, "Women's Education in the Islamic Republic of Iran" (1994: 19-27).

11. For detailed information on closure of universities and institutional changes in both higher and general education, and changes in the educational curriculum, see Godazgar, 2008: 101-155).

12. Known as *Nehzat,* these classes are organized in local mosques and schools. At the beginning, these classes were delivered in two phases, elementary and supplementary. Since 1991, however, two more phases have been added. To prevent the growth of illiteracy, since 1986 the organization has also covered school-age children in both rural and urban areas. These children, called "indispensable to teach" (*Savadamouz-e lazem-ottaleam*), aged between 7 and 18, and out of school either due to inaccessibility of formal education or its incompatibility with their daily lives, are taught at the primary level in a formal education program. From 1986, the Iran Statistical Yearbook and National Census of Population and Housing have allocated some tables for the indispensable to teach children.

13. The female proportion of literates is defined as the percentage of female literates among the literate population aged six years and older.

14. Information from table 2.3 in page 25 in Higgins, Patricia J. and Shoar-Ghaffari, Pirouz (1994). "Women's Education in the Islamic Republic of Iran". In M. Afkhami and E. Friedl (eds.) *In the Eye of the Storm: Women in Post-revolutionary Iran*. London and New York: I.B.Tauris.

15. Female literacy rate is defined as the percentage of female literate among the female population six years and older, regardless of their educational status of literate or illiterate.

16. See chapter 1.

17. A small town in the proximity of their village

18. When I was teaching in Iran during 1989-1993, in the cities of Khoy (a city in West Azarbijan province) and Tabriz, both in high-schools and Teacher Training colleges, some students from rural areas commuted daily by mini-bus for not more than an hour each side, and some were resident in the city.

19. A city in northwest Iran located in West Azarbaijan Province, with a predominately Kurdish population.

20. According to the Ministry of Science, Research, and Technology, there was an increase in the percentage of women enrolled in public universities from 27.3 percent in 1990 to 66 percent in 2003. This steady increase raised alarm among conservative religious authorities. They were in favor of an equal ratio for male and female students to reduce the number of female students in the universities.

21. For the educational level of the respondents, see table 5.11.

22. Some families still have a fear that education will open girls' eyes, or the possibility that they will bring shame to the family, or that they will reject early or arranged marriage. Ideologies around practices to control girls' sexuality or protect their chastity directly lead to women's marginalization, poverty, lack of confidence, lack of participation in social, economic and political life and are important parts of gender-based violence.

23. Polygamy remained legal in Iran under the monarchy, and even under the Family Protection Act of 1975 which reduced the legal impact of Islamic law and significantly increased women's rights in marriage. A man could have up to four wives simultaneously, but taking more than one was conditional on consent being granted by the first wife, and all wives were required to be treated equally. However, polygamy lacked and still lacks a popular support, and socially it is not accepted. Economic pressures often make it unrealistic for a man to marry more than one wife, particularly in cities. After the Islamic revolution, Islamic law was applied strongly to the Family Protection Law and severely reduced the civil rights Iranian women gained in 1975, in areas of marriage, child custody, and divorce. Although men require the first wife's permission before taking another, they often acquire a second wife and then seek permission, or more accurately, the approval of the first wife. Such announcements cause problems in the family and eventually the first wife has no choice but to accept her husband's second marriage. Sometimes if a man is sufficiently well off to keep his wives in separate accommodation, it may take years for the first wife to be aware of her husband's remarriage. In 2008, Ahmadinajad's government sent a controversial "Family Support Bill" to parliament, that, if passed, would have removed consent of the first wife for the second marriage, but the bill

was removed from the parliament agenda. Grand Ayatollah Saneii stated that any remarriage without the permission of the first wife is sin/*haram* (not permissible in Islam). In an interview with German Radio he said: "If the first wife does not provide consent, and the marriage to the second wife has already taken place, the second marriage is to be considered illegal [according to Islamic law]." See: http://www.we-change.org/english/spip.php?article283.

In 2009 again, the government drafted a new family law that includes laws on divorce, fixed-term marriage contracts for men, child custody, and legislation that would allow a man to take a second wife without the permission of the first in certain circumstances. The abolition of the polygamy from Iranian Family Law is one of the demands of Iranian rights activists in their "One Million Signature Demanding Changes to Discriminatory Laws" launched officially in 2006.

24. I noticed during the interviews that many older and poorer women had often married men much older than themselves. Frequently they had unequal relations with their husbands, were widowed, or had to care for old or invalid husbands at a relatively young age.

25. Unlike many cases in which mother-in-law and daughter-in-law do not get on well with each other, the support of this mother-in-law was due to the guilt that she felt towards the young woman. She was a distant relative of her daughter-in-law and had arranged the marriage for her son, knowing that he was irresponsible, but hoping he would change as a result of marriage and marital responsibilities. In such cases, the married woman is expected to be patient, particularly if she is from a poor background. Irresponsibility in the man might not be approved of by the family and surroundings, but is hardly condemned. These unequal expectations are the main roots of gender-based violence and discrimination for many women like M.L. who come to the city to start an unknown married life, but end up in unequal relationships without no way out.

26. Sometimes, to encourage children and raise motivation, and especially in the early stages of primary level, parents buy presents, of stationery, books, or educational materials and ask the teacher to present them in front of their classmates, pretending to their children that they are unaware of it. This often motivates the children and raises their self-esteem among their classmates.

27. Fasting month for Muslims.

28. *Kanareh* is a kind of carpet that is woven by the poorer women. See chapter 7.

29. The Iranian educational system puts emphasis on specialization in high school. Pupils choose an optional field of study from one of four categories: Social Science; Experimental Science; Mathematics-Physics; and Technical-Vocational, to obtain their diploma in one of those areas.

30. Children may lose their mother through divorce or death. However, loss of a father is often due to death rather than divorce, leading to female-headed households. In the case of divorce, often the children's custody is given to the father. In the case of a husband's death, if the woman remarries, she loses custody to the children's grandfather or uncles from the father's side of the family, unless they are very poor or not alive.

31. In her study of Muslim migrants in West Yorkshire, Afshar (1989d) also discusses immigrants' willingness to accept social change and to believe in the educa-

tional system as a means of upward social mobility, regardless of their own educational achievement (Afshar, 1989b; and 1989d).

32. Now most Quranic teachers for girls are female. After the revolution, some women entered into the realm of religion and received training to meet the religious needs of women and conduct religious services and congregations, including recitations of Quran at special religious events or memorial ceremonies for deceased family members at home. During my interviews and trips to Iran, I met some of these women with religious education, who were well-organized and have taken over male clerics' places in many women's congregations.

33. Dress code is a set of clothes, called *man'to-shalvar*, invented by female students during the revolution as an alternative to *hejab-e Islami* (Islamic veiling). After the revolution this was adopted by the Islamic state as an alternative to the *chador*, the traditional Iranian covering, which covers women from head to toe. *Man'to-shalvar* comprises: *Manto* (a long coat) and *Shalvar* (trousers); and *Maghnaeh* (a large scarf covering the head, hair and shoulders), came into fashion after the revolution and particularly after the adoption of a compulsory dress code in 1981. Modern, educated and employed women as well as the younger generation of traditional families, usually wear *Man'to-shalvar* instead of *chador*.

34. One of the changes to the high school program took place in 1992-1993 academic year as a pilot project to change the four-year one to a three-year program with two major divisions: General Education (divided into the Academic and Technical-Vocational branches) and Professional Education (with an emphasis on teaching specific work-related skills). The graduates of both divisions receive a Diploma certificate on successful completion of their course. Graduates of Academic divisions then enter a one-year pre-university program administered by the Ministry of Education in cooperation with the Ministry of Culture and Higher Education, called "*pish daneshgahi,*" which literally means "pre-university course." The aim was to tackle the high unemployment rate among high-school graduates and the mismatch between schooling and the job market (Mehran 1992: 10).

35. In most cases, male migrants or the younger generation of migrants find wives in their neighborhood and marry girls who are more likely to be migrants, either from different villages or the same as their own. Yet sometimes they marry girls still in the village. It seems that those who find their wives from their own villages usually marry their own close relatives. Those who marry girls from other villages are usually socially and economically very deprived and the women they choose have almost the same or worse socio-economic condition. Although we cannot generalize this pattern, the story of 10 women who migrated for marriage, as well as some interviewees' comments about their own children's marriage, to some extent supports the above argument.

The change in pattern of selecting future spouses among male migrants was also stated by Zahra Shojaie, the advisor to president in "Women's Affairs" who referred to an increase in the number of unmarried rural women because of increased male migration to the cities. She added that "the statistics indicate that in the year 1380 (2001) the percentage of unmarried rural women was 41% against 21% in the previous year 1379 (2000)" (Shojaie, 2001). However, she did not mention the minimum age of marriage by which the number of unmarried rural women was identified.

36. Iran's Fertility Survey 1989 cited in Aghajanian, 1994: 48.

37. This was very interesting. Most illiterate women do not often do anything without their husband's knowledge, as they have been brought up traditionally to require their husband's consent when they want to go out or do anything important. But younger educated women, even religious ones such as L.Y., do not easily accept traditional beliefs about gender relations, particularly those related to wife and husband. They question them and use their own wisdom to get away from such beliefs.

38. *Jahaz* is different from *mehr* (dowry). The latter is one of the financial obligations of a man towards the bride upon marriage, which becomes a woman's exclusive property that she can claim at any time. According to the *Sharia*, it should be paid before marriage consummation and is a price for women's sexual and reproductive services. However, in Iran women use it as economic security and only in the case of divorce claim their *mehr*. *Jahaz* indicates household items that bride's parents give to their daughter to take to her husband's house. The value of *Jahaz* and its quantity and quality varies with the social class of the bride's family, the number of female children and how much they can afford. In some parts of the country, the groom's family often makes a payment to the bride's family, which is called *Shir-bah* (the price of milk) in order to compensate the costs of *Jahaz* that the bride's family undertake. For detailed information on *mehr*, see Mir-Hosseini, Z. (1993: 72-83): "Legal Anatomy of Divorce: the Iranian Case". In Z. Mir-Hosseini. *Marriage on Trial: the Study of Islamic Family Law: Iran and Morocco Compared*, Second Edition. London, New York: I.B. Tauris 1993.

In Tabriz to my knowledge *Shir-baha* is not a common practice, but in the city the bride's *Jahaz* is a more important contribution to the newly established nuclear family than in the rural areas, where often a bride lives with the groom's family for many years. Some of my informants or their daughters had a very small amount of *Jahaz*, or none at all among the very poor and those who became their husband's second wives. However, among the migrant families, the pressure to provide a good amount of *Jahaz* is becoming problematic, particularly for poorer families with many daughters to marry off.

39. In the first couple of days of interviews, I did not ask if the women had lost any of their children. Later on during the conversation, I noticed that some of the women had lost one or more of their children in childhood, due to preventable illness. After that I asked my informants if any of their children were deceased.

40. *Rial* is the Iranian monetary unit. One *Toman* is equivalent to ten *Rials*. During the period of fieldwork, £1 was approximately equivalent to 1,300 *Tomans*. To show the purchasing power of Iranian currency, in the following chapters, I quote statements from the women interviewed.

41. Immediately after the Islamic Republic of Iran was established in 1979, the Kurdish Democratic Party of Iran (KDPI) waged a guerrilla war against the Islamic Republic with the aim of achieving Kurdish autonomy. They took advantage of the Iran-Iraq war which began in September 1980 and intensified their insurgent activities in northwestern Iran. The Kurdish revolt has since dispersed from Iranian territory into Iraqi territory.

Chapter 7

Migrant Women in the Domestic Carpet Industry

Iranian state policies played an important role in determining women's socio-economic position in society in both pre- and post-revolutionary eras. State gender policies have had different and sometimes very contradictory outcomes for women from different social backgrounds. Until the twentieth century, women of all social classes were generally deprived of social rights. There was a prevalent negative attitude towards their participation in the labor force, particularly among the urban upper and middle-classes (Touba, 1980; Tabari and Yeganeh, 1982:143). From a political point of view, the constitutional movement of 1906-11 generated a significant interest in ideological discourses on women's questions and their places in a modern society. However, any major political and ideological discourse in Iran, including the "Women's Question," has been fought in an uneasy triangle of Islam, Westernization, and Nationalism (Tohidi 1994: 112). Due to the secular nature of early twentieth century Iranian nationalism, an interest in women's liberation brought some slow changes to traditional values with respect to women's socio-economic status in society.

The consequences of socio-economic change on women's lives, particularly during the Pahlavi era, have been viewed differently by scholars. Although women's participation in social, economic, and educational terms was expanded during this time, there was a continuation of social inequalities between rural and urban women as well as urban women from different social classes (Tabari, 1980; Touba, 1980; Tabari and Yeganeh, 1982; Afshar, 1989a, 1997; Najmabadi, 1991: 48-50; Moghadam, 1993; Hoodfar, 1993; Moghissi, 1994; Tohidi, 1994; Mir-Hosseini, 1995, 1996; Paidar, 1996). Elite women whose male relatives had social, economic, and political power benefitted most from the social changes and educational opportunities of the state-building project of Reza Shah (Najmabadi, 1991: 54). However, they still faced many structural restrictions from patriarchal and cultural traditions in terms of employment (Tabari and Yeganeh, 1982: 148). A woman in paid employment was seen as a negative indicator of a family's position. Society's definition of appropriate types of economic activities for women, the availability of training (mostly in certain sex segregated traditional occupations), and the marginality of the market economy were other important factors contributing to their limited access to a wide range of economic activities (Najmabadi, 1991). Therefore, until the 1950s, despite the development of industry and services, women from elite and upper-class families were largely absorbed into education and medicine (Touba, 1980: 69). Since the 1960s, due to a rapidly growing economy and the penetration of capitalist relationships offering women some opportunities, many women from the middle and upper classes forced their ways into other professional positions, contributing positively to society. However, despite modernization policies of the state to utilize potential or actual labor of women by providing regulations for their benefit, such as insurance, maternity leave, provision of nurseries and day-care centers for children of employed mothers, social relations were still dominated by traditional values of patriarchal/conservative ideologies. The policies were hardly put into practice; facilities were not widespread enough to attract many women, and unequal wages for the majority of them made economic independence almost impossible for most educated women (Etemad Moghadam, 1994: 88-93). They were rarely promoted to higher managerial and decision making positions (Kar, 2005). Educated women from traditional families, who for the first time benefited from educational opportunities, were exposed to different sets of values and found themselves in between contradictory role models of womanhood[1].

Lower working class families, on the other hand, have always been subject to the joint income of men, women and children. National economic development or development of capitalism in Iran has local effects on women's traditional status in rural areas as well as on the village economy. Some women in working households provide essential economic support for their families, though they remain mostly invisible due to the nature of their work. Some have worked as servants, cooks, nannies, and washerwomen, mostly for wealthy families, often on an irregular basis. Others worked in occupations such as spinning, weaving or needlework, at home or in small workshops (Touba, 1980; Afshar, 1989a, 1985b; Razavi, 1992, 1993; Ghavamshahidi, 1996; ShadiTalab, 1996). The majority, however, has not been counted among the labor force and is not eligible for any entitlements provided by state employment regulations. The majority of these women preferred, and some still prefer, to work in sex segregated environments. Studying urban low-income families in the 1920s and 1930s in Hamadan, Hoodfar (1993) argues that by working in small workshops or other community networks, women's work gave them freedom of mobility to pursue their legitimate social relations. However, the modernization policies of Reza Shah and its gender ideology, particularly the introduction of forceful unveiling in 1936 in the name of women's emancipation, had negative consequences on their economic activities and social status. Since veiling was the only socially acceptable way of dressing for the majority of women and had a fundamental value concerning honor and shame (Touba, 1980: 67), many independent women were driven into voluntary seclusion to avoid embarrassing violations (Hoodfar, 1993; Tohidi, 1994: 125) and became dependent on men for carrying out daily public tasks. If their male relatives had migrated to the larger cities they suffered more as their veils would have been pulled off and torn by the police. As a result, some skilled women set up private carpet frames through the putting-out system, but they were exploited to a greater extent and were paid even lower wages by carpet traders who provided raw materials and knew that women had no other choices. Women lost control over their wages and became subject to more control by their families through cultural, patriarchal and religious norms (Hoodfar, 1993: 9-11).

Although the unveiling law was relaxed during the second Pahlavi State, in practice there was discrimination against veiled women in the labor market, particularly in state occupations. As a result, women from traditional, conservative and lower classes hardly benefitted from educational and employment opportunities of modernization policies. In 1972, only 20 percent of officially recognized working women had insurance, let alone female workers in small workshops, or private houses absent from official statistics. In 1976, the female share of the total labor force was 20 percent, which included cottage industries particularly carpet-weaving workshops or traditional industries where production methods are labor-intensive and tasks are usually accomplished with the use of hands and application of customary traditional techniques. The female share of manufacturing was 38.4 percent in 1976, where women, due to their socio-economic conditions, were confined to traditionally segregated female labor sectors of industry doing so-called "unskilled," repetitive, and monotonous jobs (Moghadam, 1995: 180-83). In the service sector, women were also at the bottom (Afshar, 1989a: 43-44). We have to bear in mind that by this time the percentage of migrant women had increased to above 50 percent of the total, most of them illiterate and from the poorest sections of the peasantry. Workers who were not insured had no rights after an accident, had to pay for medical treatment, medicine, and worked without sickness, maternity or retirement benefits. In state textile and food factories where female workers were dominant, they not only earned less than their male co-workers, but even less than the minimum wage set by the state (Tabari and Yeganeh, 1982: 147-51).

Despite the growth of commerce and modern techniques in industry, the attitude of employers towards women's employment remained traditional. A 1976 report by the Plan and Budget Organization of Iran in collaboration with UNDP/ILO indicated that for the majority of employers, women's employment and training were considered a waste of time and resources[2]. Thus, despite the existence of economic opportunities, many women, particularly married ones who were more affected by religion and patriarchal culture were forced out of paid jobs (Tabari and Yeganeh, 1982: 149). Conservative attitudes towards women's participation in paid jobs were also observed by Fisher, where he states that "on the local level attitudes and practices lag behind the government push" (1978: 192). Thus a small proportion of married women were reported to be economically active (Touba, 1980: 93). The proportion of economically active divorced and widowed women has been always greater than that of working married women in urban areas, as they usually obtain less economic support from their families, and have to fend for themselves and their children through earning an income.

The Islamic ideology of the post-revolution era, by regulating gender relations, putting emphasis on dress code, and reinforcing patriarchal ideology has also affected many women's lives. The introduction of the compulsory veil/*hejab* by the Islamic state and its long-standing national policy of retaining women within the household through the ideology of domesticity, had various and sometimes very contradictory outcomes for women from different classes, but they did not lead women into seclusion (Tabari 1980; Tabari and Yeganeh 1982; Mahdavi 1983; Afshar 1989a, 1989c, 1994, 1997, 1999; Najmabadi 1991; Hoodfar 1993, 1996; Tohidi, 1991, 1994; Mir-Hosseini 1995, 1996; Moghissi 1993, 1994; Paidar 1996; Poya, 1999; Bahramitash, 2004). Rather, the Islamic state's policies, by reintroducing and enforcing the ideology of sex segregation generated employment opportunities for women to deal with female clients. For instance, there are an adequate number of female physicians[3]: in Qum (one of Iran's most religious cities and the largest centre for *Shi'a* scholarship in the world) there is a Female Medical School and hospital run entirely run by women (Bahramitash, 2004: 517). Since among religious scholars women's participation in the social, political and economic arena is open to interpretation, it was difficult for the Islamic state to prevent women from working (Etemad Moghadam, 1994: 92-93).

From the beginning, many modern educated middle-class women found themselves in a confrontation with Islamic ideology and left their jobs voluntarily or were made redundant due to their disagreement with or resistance towards compulsory *hejab*, and some even chose to leave the country due to incompatibility with political Islam and Islamist rulers. The introduction of segregation ideologies, on the other hand, became an empowering tool for many young women who had been discriminated against in the past due to their observation of traditional and religious values. Many women from conservative middle or lower middle-classes who were less privileged and had been discriminated against by the gender policy of the Pahlavi state used Islamic ideology, particularly the *hejab*, as an empowering tool of emancipation. For them and their families, who formed a much larger segment of Iranian society, the practice of veiling and its moral code changed the definition of public and work outside the home, and paved the way for women's public presence and economic engagement (Tabari 1980: 20; Hoodfar, 1993: 12; Omid, 1994: 189; Mir-Hosseini, 1996: 149-156; Velayati, 1998)[4]. The poorest women, however, some of whom were the principal providers in their families, had to carry the double burdens of poverty and state policies and ideologies which gave priority to male employment after the establishment of the Islamic Republic (Afshar, 1989a; Etemad Moghadam, 1994; Ghavamshahidi, 1996).

In terms of official employment statistics, the censuses of 1966, 1976, 1986 and 1996 demonstrate a slow upward trend for the first two decades and a rapid fall and women's labor marginalization in the post-Revolutionary era.[5] The female share of the total labor force and manufacturing sector fell markedly to 9 and 14 percent respectively in 1986 (Moghadam, 1993).[6] Between 1976 and 1986, the number of employed women dropped from 1.2 million to about 1 million[7]. It is worth noting that the imposition of Islamic ideologies on women was not the only reason for the decline of the female labor force in industrial employment in the 1980s. The weakness of this sector, due to the generally depressed state of the national economy, adversely affected both men and women (Moghadam, 1993). Increasing pauperization, however, along with the general emphasis on domesticity had a more dramatic influence on poor, unsupported women than men. The 1996 census revealed an increase: almost 1.8 million or a 12.12 percent of female share of the total labor force and 33 percent female employment of the total in the industrial sector. But by 1996 the total female population was well over 29 million as against some 16 million in 1976 (Afshar, 1997). In the 2006 National Census, women constituted less than 20 percent[8] of the paid labor force in the formal sector, with entitlement to paid holidays, maternity leave, pensions, and other provisions of labor law[9].

It can be argued that the ideological commitment of state policy was successful in limiting participation of women in the formal labor market, particularly in higher levels of management. However, there has been an increase in the number of women working in the informal sector both at the high-end and low-end (Etemad Moghadam, 1994; Afshar 1997; Poya, 1999; Moghadam, 2009).

Chapter 6 examined, in great detail, women's access to education in rural and urban areas in both pre- and post-revolutionary eras and the correlation between women's level of education and other aspects of their lives. In the remainder of this chapter, and the next, I concentrate mainly on economic aspects of women's lives, their engagement in economic activities in or outside the home, and their contribution to household incomes in Tabriz, particularly among migrant families. These two chapters also examine how migrant women in my sample are affected by class, age structure, marital status, education, and access to the means of production. Although the majority of migrant women are involved in informal sectors of the economy, the analysis will show that the above mentioned factors play an important role in determining sub-sectors of the informal or even formal economy, within which women can fit better. In terms of economic activities, my informants can be categorized into two groups: unpaid family laborers, and wage earners. The first group is formed of mainly unpaid family laborers who are involved in producing market goods in their own compounds in slum areas, for national and international markets, but at the same time remain invisible to the public at large. They constitute not only the bulk of my informants, but also the wider migrant communities in Tabriz and other industries in different parts of Iran. However, there is no statistical information about their exact number and different degrees of work[10]. The second group are scattered in different sectors of the formal and informal economy: some have home-based jobs and are home-workers, who earn their wage on piece-rate; others are self-employed and have their own business. The unpaid family laborers are the focus of this chapter and in the next chapter I will concentrate on wage-earners.

First, I will briefly describe the carpet industry and the range of weaving activities, and then examine women's work and their contribution to the household economy.

The Carpet Industry

The carpet industry in Iran has been an important traditional home industry for centuries. Persian carpets/*farsh*are traditionally known for their tremendous variety in designs, colors, sizes, and weaves[11]. They are used for floor covering and wall decoration in homes, offices, palaces, and shrines. The particular pattern of Persian carpets, palettes, and weaves are uniquely linked with indigenous cultures, and weaving techniques are specific to an identifiable geographic area or nomadic tribe. They include floral designs, natural scenery, historical and mythological characteristics, and calligraphic and religious symbols[12]. Before Iran's industrial development, particularly through the oil industry, hand-woven carpets were an important export and a major source of foreign currency for the economy. The peak of the Persian carpet's prosperity was the Safavid era, particularly during the reign of Shah Abbas[13].

In the 13th century, Tabriz was an important weaving centre and by the 16th century, the city became one of the leading producers of carpets in the east and the first carpet making area to provide carpets for the Western market[14]. The carpet industry, in addition to its commercial role in generating considerable revenues and job opportunities for many people, the majority of whom are women, plays an important role in preserving Iran's cultural heritage and art over many centuries, and is an essential part of the living environment for Iranians.

In the Qajar era (1794-1925) the incompetence of Qajar kings and the foundation of foreign manufacturing carpet companies such as Ziegler Co. at the end of the 19th century in central Iran, particularly Arak, led to simplification of designs, repetitive patterns, and even to complete disappearance of a unique carpet type of Iran, called "*Sarroug*" (Sour-Esraphil, 1993: 40-43)[15]. In the early decades of the 20th century and during the Constitutional Revolution of 1906-1911, when Iran was occupied and divided between the imperial powers of Great Britain and Russia, the articulation of Iranian national sovereignty and awareness of past Iranian cultural and national heritage led to the establishment of art schools for reviving and protecting art, including the design of carpets, miniatures, and calligraphy. 1911-1941 was a period of blossoming for Iranian carpets in terms of design, color, and the number of famous designers. However, World War II adversely affected the Iranian carpet tradition again (Sour-Esraphil, 1993: 43). After the war, the carpet production was seen as a traditional cottage industry, rather than a modern one. Therefore no effort was made to promote the industry to its full potential during the reign of the second Pahlavi Shah (1941-1979). Lack of attention to the carpet industry led to decline in demand for Persian carpets in international markets, and increasing imitation of Persian designs by Pakistani, Indian, and Chinese carpet weavers who exported them as world-famous Iranian carpets. This resulted in some 40 percent loss of Iran's share in the global hand-woven carpet market.

After the revolution of 1979, promoting indigenous industries and skills was viewed as a strategy for economic development and reducing dependency on oil revenues. For instance *Jahad-e Sazandegi,* as part of its rural development programs, provided training courses in rural areas of some provinces where the industry had become less valuable or completely redundant. The aim was to revive the industry, create occupational opportunities, train new learners, and improve skills of home-based women not only in weaving and spinning, but also the other essentials, particularly coloring, design, setting and finishing the entire work[16]. Since the late 1990s, the government[17] and higher education institutions made substantial efforts to revive the art by training students who have mastered making Persian carpets professionally[18].

According to the Chief of Iran's National Carpet Centre, in 2005 two million people were engaged in producing handwoven carpets, contributing 470 million U.S. dollars to the national economy and 41 percent of the global carpet trade[19].

Today, in slum areas of Tabriz and surrounding villages, carpet production and related activities are the largest domestic industry, producing 35 percent of all Iranian carpets. Tabriz carpets have been prized for their intricate designs and for being finely woven with many more knots per inch than most Persian carpets.[20]

The Range of Weaving and Related Activities

Carpet producers make different kinds of pile carpets in different sizes including *kenareh* (side carpets), and Tableau (mainly for hanging from the wall); and pile-less carpets such as *kilim*[21] and *varny*. In areas where women participate less in agriculture, including most regions of East Azarbaijan, their active and continued participation in the carpet industry is an important source of additional income for the family (Afshar, 1985b; Ghavamshahidi, 1996). Materials used in a carpet and their quality, the pile of warp (cotton threads running the length) and weft (cotton threads running the width), a knot density (the number of knots per each square inch), different kinds of knots, the size and design of the carpet, the quality of processed wool, all determine the quality and price of carpets. My informants normally talked about carpets by subdividing them into two main categories of "normal" and "finely woven," each with different subdivisions, sizes and designs. The materials used in normal carpets are woolen yarn on a cotton base, and their value depends on the coarseness or delicacy of the yarn. The coarseness of the carpet does not necessarily mean a low quality of carpet. Rather, in most parts of Azarbaijan, where the cold seasons are longer, coarse carpets with thick and long pile are useful for insulation and people prefer this kind of carpet for their day-to-day usage. Lesser quality carpets are made of thicker yarns dyed with chemical colors, have fewer knots per square inch, with simple designs, repetitive patterns, and limited coloration. The lowest quality carpet is natively called a village carpet (*kat farshi*). Normal carpets are usually in room size or larger size which varies from 6 feet 5 inches squared to 14ft by 12ft. The number of knots in good quality normal carpet is 200 to 300 per square inch. According to my informants, the completion of any normal carpet, in room size, usually takes six to eight months.

Fine-textured carpets (also referred to as *ghali*) have thinner yarns compared to the normal carpets. The thinner the yarn, the more luxurious, desirable and expensive the carpet is. They have a dense structure and are strongly beaten so that the wefts are almost invisible on the back, which means the details of the design can clearly be seen on the reverse. This kind of carpet is used by richer people. Finishing work might not be done necessarily by those who are involved in weaving: shearing, polishing, and trimming the pile needs specific skills and some artisans are mainly involved in these types of work.

During the period of this study, depending on the quality and size of carpets, selling prices for the weavers varied between 300,000 to 400,000 *Tomans*[22] for normal carpets, and from 700,000 to 4-5 million *Tomans* for finally woven ones depending on size, design and delicacy of the carpet. In international markets, prices for Tabriz carpets are very high.

Kenareh is one kind of normal *farsh*/carpet; its length is usually three times greater than its width. It takes between two and three months weaving and the materials used for it are not normally of good quality. During my field work, each *Kenareh* was not normally sold for more than 100,000 *Tomans*.

Finely woven *farsh*[23] is the most luxurious version of this type of carpet and its luxuriousness is increased by deeper pile and the beauty and variety of yarn colors and elaborate designs and patterns. Production of fine-textured carpets requires the highest skills, dexterity, and finest materials. The material used in this carpet is a mixture of thin multi-colored woolen and silk yarns, or even only silk yarns which are thinner than knitting thread. The number of knots in each square inch is variable, between 400 and 500 or even 500 to 600. In other words, they vary between 50 and 80 *Raj* (a *raj* indicates density) depending on their elegance. One woman involved talked about the time spent weaving fine *farsh* in this way:

> Finely woven *farsh* are high quality products with various nice natural colors, but it take longer time and greater efforts to be finished. If two people together weave for eight hours a day, they have woven only eight rows. If they weave every day continuously, it takes a year and three or four months to finish this type of carpet.

For this reason, finely woven carpets usually are in smaller sizes compared to the normal *farsh* (often known as *Zar-nim*). The value of finely woven carpets motivates relatively better off families and skilled artisans to work on these types, even though they might get a loan or borrow money from money-lenders, particularly carpet-dealers. Only a small portion of women interviewed or their families in my sample were solely involved in this as it demands high quality skills, the investment of extra capital, and completion of the work takes more time. Although finely woven carpets are very expensive, there is no guarantee of high returns due to the ups and downs of the market. When the market falls, the weavers lose heavily.

Tableau, a woven portrait used for wall decoration, is another kind of finely woven carpet. These take between one and three months depending on the size, complexity, and the number of people working on them.

At the time of this study, the price of finely woven carpets had dramatically fallen. One of the informants mentioned that:

> Despite our huge investment financially and arduous effort into our last *farsh* 8 years ago, we fared badly. We invested 200 thousand *Tomans*: 90 thousand *Tomans* just for the design of the carpet. In those days, that kind of carpet could easily be sold for 800 to 900 thousand *Tomans*, whereas we sold it only for 315 thousand *Tomans*. The design of the carpet was very difficult, and by the time we finished it, the market had fallen badly and we were forced to sell it cheap. We carpet weavers are not able to keep the carpet until the market rises, as we need the money. Since then, we quitted weaving such carpets.

Another informant said:

> Last year, the prices of each of these carpets were 4 million *Tomans*, but this year it has fallen to 1.5 million *Tomans*.

These two quotations and similar comments that I heard from interviewees show the fluctuation of the market for carpets, and the lack of regulation or support from the government and the vulnerability of carpet weavers even from wealthier backgrounds. Most of the women did not know how the market worked, as, unlike the weaving which is mainly a female craft, the sale of the carpets is entirely in the hands of men; women are not involved in marketing their products at all[24]. This division of labor creates a gender disparity in households, where women do not enjoy the fruits of their labor, and remain mostly unpaid laborers whose skills are under-valued, even by women themselves. A son of one of the respondents, who was present at the interview, explained it in this way:

> Finely woven carpets are traded on the basis of the value of the dollar and gold. If their prices fall, the price of this kind of carpet will also fall and vice versa.

Varny is the most basic and primitive variety of carpet woven among my informants. It is similar to *kilim,* but much thinner, simpler, and smaller for which a carpet-knifeis hardly used during weaving, the knots mostly being tied by the weaver's fingers[25]. It is simple to weave and requires neither complicated designs, nor large capital investment, particularly for those who are also involved in other sorts of weaving. The production of *varny* is mostly done by the settled nomads of Azarbaijan, and women who were involved in weaving this type of *kilim* were mainly from nomadic parts of East Azarbaijan. The designs are simple and inspired by nature, often with simplified pictures of domesticated or wild animals. According to the weavers *varnys* are mainly exported to Turkey and do not have national or local market. When I talked about *varny* to friends and families in Tabriz, they did not know what this was and asked about its features. One of the interviewees involved in *varny*-weaving said that:

> *Varny* does not cost us dear; we use the left-over yarns from our other carpets.

But another woman who had to buy the yarn said that:

> With 16 thousand *Tomans*, you can easily start a *varny*. Tradesmen buy it from us at about 35 thousand *Tomans*. They make a good profit from our work by selling each *varney* for between 70 to 100 thousand *Tomans*.

In addition to gender disparity between women and their male relatives in terms of controlling income from carpets, there is another unequal relationship between carpet producers and dealers and traders who have access to national and international markets. Due to the lack of protective state policies and unions of carpet producers, the industry has unfortunately become an exploitative one, in which carpet-dealers, middlemen, and traders often took advantage of the plight of producers, most of who remain in poverty and are exposed to many health hazards[26].

Migrant Women in Unpaid Sectors of the Carpet Industry

In migrant families, particularly laboring households, women's subsistence production is essential for the survival of the family. There are degrees of poverty among the migrant households, and the poorest are the most disadvantaged and marginalized group. In poor households, as other empirical studies in the field of women and development indicate, women often tend to devote more time to working in income-generating activities. In the city, the range of occupational options available to migrant women is extremely restricted and their traditional skills such as bread-making, animal husbandry, dairying, and agricultural tasks are not useful anymore. Most illiterate women are well aware of not having marketable skills in the city, and realize that this will force them into lower status jobs in the informal sector, if they want to seek a job outside the home. In the first stage of the study, women gave nine different reasons for their low response to work in the labor market. Their main reasons were: illiteracy; lack of husband's permission for either working or going outside the home; illness; having many children and the burden of housework; lack of skill; not having somebody to guide them; lack of interest; and other specific reasons for some respondents such as not being in need; being unfamiliar with the city; being in education; and preparing for university entrance exams[27]. One of my widowed informants, 34 years old and involved in the carpet industry, desperate and depending greatly on her poor family, in response to my question as to why she did not search for a job in the labor market, said that:

> I am illiterate. The only job that I might be offered in the city is laboring. I don't mind doing those kinds of jobs to fend myself and my four children, but

> my father and brothers would not allow me to do those sorts of low status jobs so that people perceive me negatively. They say I would not earn more than what I could earn from weaving carpet at my own home, in which I am my own boss (S.B.).

As Hoodfar argues, women's low response is "more often the result of rational economic assessment of the opportunity-cost ratio than the consequence of purely cultural factors" (Hoodfar 1997:138), though the latter play an important role in female response to work in the labor market. In general, most migrant women with fewer educational credentials have limited access to non-domestic spheres due to both practical and ideological factors. Many women in migrant families do not work outside the home unless they are too needy, or have higher educational credentials and/or better social networks. The next chapter explores the nature and diversity of work that wage-earners are involved in and how they deal with domestic responsibilities and patriarchal norms and practices which disapprove of women's engagement outside the home, particularly in low status jobs.

Based on the traditional model of sexual division of labor, the majority of poor women often become involved in predominantly home-based female occupations of the carpet industry. The ideological consequence of women's work in this industry is the reinforcement of patriarchal and sexist norms and institutions, particularly when they blend with male-structured religious doctrines about gender relations within the household in the name of Islam. Within patriarchal ideologies men are considered as breadwinners and women as housewives and dependents on the income of their husbands (Mies, 1982). This ideology leads to women's unequal access to, and control over, resources which have been partially produced by their labor (Afshar, 1985b; Goldschmidt-Clermont 1982, 1987; Whitehead, 1984).

Most migrant households that I visited were more or less involved in the exchange-value enterprise of carpet industry in which unpaid labor of women contributed to the well-being of their family and the national economy. The industry is a supplementary or even essential part of the income in many migrant households. It employs mostly women and children, particularly in poor households, as the income of male breadwinners does not cover families' reproductive costs. In most migrant families to guarantee the survival of the family, the combination of men's income, mainly from wage labor, and women and children's income, mainly from market-oriented production of carpet, is essential. The skills and knowledge of people involved in the industry are mostly home-based.

In poorer households, men are often engaged in low paid, irregular jobs such as porters, hawking, and casual laboring on construction sites and women are mainly involved in spinning or low quality weaving activities. Although rapid construction in the domestic sector of Tabriz creates a demand for unskilled and semi-skilled male laborers, the over-supply of labor makes it still more competitive for the laborers. Many women in laboring families stated that their husbands are unemployed at times and that their subsistence work is part of the survival strategy adopted to improve their families' lives. About 70 percent of the interviewees in this study were/have been involved in one or both of the weaving and spinning activities. However, they do not appear in the statistics, precisely because their work is done within the confines of their homes and is unpaid.

Spinners

A few women interviewed for this study were only involved in spinning. By using simple tools such as hand-spinning tools including a spindle and a whorl, and/or a wooden spinning wheel, they convert the woolen fibers into yarn. They were often unable to weave carpets. The spinners in my sample were the oldest, poorest and most disadvantaged of all the women engaged in the industry. They either did not have the opportunity to learn the skill of weaving, or had shifted from weaving to spinning, as they needed to earn a living, but were unable to weave anymore due to poor health. The extreme poverty that prevented the poorest families having access to the means of production, in combination with cultural practices that often limited women's freedom to work in workshops, were the main reasons for some women not having learnt the skill. Spinning is closely linked with poverty, and the proportion of women's income from spinning was the lowest in the carpet industry. In general, spinners' wages are "below the value of their labor power" (Beechey, 1977), mainly because of the low status of the work and the secondary nature generally of women's work and earning power.

With the expansion and prosperity of the carpet industry, processing of fibers into yarn has also been largely transformed from a domestic industry into industrial spinning, which has had an impact on poor women's jobs and incomes. Although the work has declined as a result of labor-saving techniques and mechanization, there are still some disadvantaged women who are involved in spinning. One of these women stated that:

> T years ago when we first came to the city, many women used to do spinning. The dealers used to come to the streets, provide wool to women and then come back to collect the finished work later. But now, their number has decreased. Most of them get the job done on machine, rather than giving it to us. We are/were given work in terms of *batman*[28]. The price of finished work depends on the quality of yarn and wool.

One of my informants was extremely poor and destitute and had eight children, some married and some not married yet. She had worked for decades on carpet and *varney*, but was unable to weave anymore. However, after so many years of hard work, she still had to work to help the family with her meager income from spinning. About this she said:

> From a very young age, I was always involved in weaving carpets, normal ones, *kanareh*, and *varney,* except fine carpets, which we could not afford to do. Despite this, we have lots of financial problems. So far, I have not worn a new skirt, or shirt, or even a new pair of socks. My children are most important; I alter most of my clothes. Now that I cannot weave carpets, I do spinning to manage our life. It takes three days to finish two and half kilograms of wool, for which I receive 350 to 400 *Tomans*. Our main food is bread with some cheese, if we can afford it.

A couple of days before our interview, her daughter and husband had visited them, and she had to buy a chicken (cost approximately £1 at the time) to prepare a dinner, but since she did not have enough money, she had to spin for a couple of days to pay back the cost of the chicken.[29] F.M. was a 64 year-old woman, according to her daughter-in-law[30], living in an extended family of five, including her 32 year-old daughter who had not married yet, and her son and daughter-in-law who had married 8 months earlier. I interviewed her not long after the death of her husband. She and her daughter were also involved in spinning. Regarding their involvement in income generating activities, and how and on what they spend their money, she said:

> Since we came to the city, sixteen to seventeen years ago, we have been spinning. I used to spin one *batman* (five kilograms) of wool in four to five days. But after the death of my husband, I am not able to do as much as I used to do. We don't get much from spinning, and the money we are paid goes straight to the necessities of life, particularly food (F.M).

The number of spinners was relatively low and they were predominantly older and poorer migrant women. Most of them had experienced strict gender relationships and subordination to the male heads or members of even their extended families. Some of these women when talking about their husbands used the word of *sahab* or *sahabim.*[31] In the traditional extended families, however, the older women often have control over younger ones, particularly their daughters-in-law, a practice that leads to a double burden for younger women who have to be subordinate to their husbands and the senior women in the household, particularly mothers-in-law. Many older women had experienced this double burden and were expecting the same respect from younger women in the family[32]. Only one of my informants said that:

> We left the village, mainly because my mother-in-law was bad-tempered and cruel to me. My husband's family was well off in the village, had land and good living, but his mother's viciousness drove us from the village. I am his second wife. His first wife who was his mother's own blood-relative was forced to divorce.

Some of these women have a strong belief in the superiority of their husband even from a religious point of view. This belief and women's consciousness of subordination pave the way for domestic violence in many households, which came out in interviews, sometimes openly or was sometimes easily elicited. It was notable that some might not consider mistreatment by their husband as violence, blamed themselves and were very careful of their actions so as not to be provocative. Relating to this one of the relatively old women said:

> I always obey him. So far, I have not left the house in showing my objection, even when I was beaten by him or his brother, when we used to live together. I have also advised my daughter and daughters-in-law not to do so. He is a very stubborn man. It is almost ten years since I have been deprived of going to my son's house and he and his family are deprived from coming to our house. He disobeyed his father by going to Tehran. Whatever I do I can't convince him. Recently, my daughter-in-law went to one of our relatives' house and I went to see her without him knowing that I would see my son's wife.

Another woman said:

> I have not done anything without my husband's permission. When my daughter was engaged, he told me that she is not allowed to cross the road. I didn't let her go out with her fiancé, even when my husband was not in Tabriz for more than twenty days.

The following statements were offered by some women, for instance when I asked their permission to take some pictures while they were doing their work.

> I don't have permission from my husband.
>
> No my husband will be annoyed. He says that the secrets of the house should not leak to outside.
>
> We don't do anything without our husbands' permission. Otherwise what answer would we have in the judgment-day?

Widowed women were subordinate to their own brothers or their late husband's extended family, and even their own young sons. For instance, one relatively young widow (34 years old, who was widowed from the age of 30), had an 11 year-old son. In response to my question, will she consider remarrying, she said:

> In our family it is not a custom for a woman to remarry. God bless me a good health to be able to look after my four children. It is not also fair to leave my children and get married. My mother says: if you son has *gharat,* he will take care of you when he gets older. My only worry is that he would not look after

> me when I get older. But my brothers say, we will look after you, if your son wouldn't.

These beliefs and practices are institutionalized among many families, provoking women to be involuntarily subordinate to male relatives for survival and becoming dependent on them their entire lives. On the other hand, they make male members of the family (as young as 11 years old) feel superior toward the female ones including their own mothers, or feel pressure of responsibility from a young age.

Below are some quotations about this subordination of widows:

> If *sahabim* was alive, I would not mind you to record my voice. But his cousins talk a lot of nonsense. If they hear, they will ridicule me by saying our cousin died and his wife has recorded her voice (64 year-old widow).

This women's face was full of wrinkles and looked much older than her age. Her daughter, in affirming a sister-in-law's statement that "their lives are being controlled by others: uncles, cousins, and . . . ", said:

> Even if my aunt's (father's sister) husband hears that my mother had talked to you, he will make a big fuss.

Most of these women had married very young, some even at the age of nine or ten, most without being consulted. Some became second wives and some had stepchildren to look after, even when they themselves were very young; some had lived with their in-laws in the village, while their husbands worked in the city and visited them infrequently. Life for younger women who lived for many years in the villages while their husbands went to the city for wage labor was even harder. Such a woman was no longer part of her father's family, had the least access to resources, and yet was considered costly; she had the least freedom of movement and was confined to the home without any economically productive tasks. With no husband around they were most vulnerable in terms of issues around morality, as they are viewed with suspicion and any unapproved socialization would bring about scandal and allegations of misbehavior; and there was little sympathy from migrated men towards young wives, so that things often ended in violence and even divorce, as some of my informants discussed from their own or their mother's experiences.

Two different points can be made from these women's reasoning for not doing anything without permission from their husbands, or members of their husbands' extended families. One is to avoid any violent behavior from men, and the other is religious teaching which demands a woman's absolute subordination to her husband, and threatens them with eternal punishment in Hell for not fulfilling their marital obligations (Nashat, 1983: 8-10). One of the older women had strong traditional and religious ideas about the roles of men and women and believed that a man (husband) is a woman's second God[33]. Such patriarchal structures and ideologies, particularly when partially internalized by women themselves, lead to their social and economic subordination in terms of the social relations of production which regulate women's work within the confines of their homes (Mies, 1982; Mackintosh, 1984; Bennholdt-Thomsen, 1984). Although these patriarchal ideologies were shared by many illiterate old women in the weaving sector, it seems that they were more prevalent among the most disadvantaged women, particularly spinners. Most of them believed that a woman had to tolerate her husband's and his family's misbehavior in the hope of a better life one day. Many of the older women related their husband's violence towards them to their ignorance and being influenced by their family. One woman told of her experience in this way:

> He was young and ignorant and was so influenced by his mother. I stayed in the village living with his family (his parents, four sisters, and two brothers). Once every two to three months he came to the village. Those times we women did not have any rights: I ate after my in-laws finished, slept after they went to bed, and in the morning I woke up when the birds started singing; I only visited my parents if my in-laws allowed me or took me with them. If I talked to village girls, they would tell my husband and he would beat me. Now the situation has got even worse; men in those days were only beating their wives, now they even divorce them. This is worse than beating.

Although the spinners are aware of the exchange-value of their labor within the home and their contribution to the wellbeing of their poverty stricken families, they do not appreciate their skill, and are not happy with their earnings and working conditions. When I asked permission from two women to take a photo while they were spinning, they were reluctant to have their picture taken with their spinning devices. One of them gave permission after her children convinced her, and in the other case I was given permission on condition that I took another picture of her with her grandson.

Carpet weaving through the putting-out system or family business

The weaving sector employs the largest number of women in slum areas of Tabriz, who mainly carry out the work at home, along with their reproductive functions in the domestic unit, like their sisters in the spinning sector. The poorest families rarely own the means of production and cannot afford to buy raw materials. In such cases, merchants usually step in and take advantage of women and their poverty through the putting-out system, supplying equipment and raw materials. Raw materials are usually distributed among the individual home-workers by middlemen, and finished work is paid for at very low rates. The contract is often agreed between the dealers and the men in the households. However, women are responsible for the maintenance and management of the production process until delivery of the completed work.

Poorer women's work, either in spinning or the putting-out system, is a fundamental part of capital accumulation and advantage for the dominant economic class in the society. As Mies (1982) argues in detail about the lace-makers of Narsapur in India, the putting-out system creates class polarization between female producers and non-producing male dealers. In this system, women are the most exploitable labor force in the carpet industry, completely dependent on the traders and bound to weaving out of economic necessity. They work hard, often in hazardous situations, but are not protected by any labor legislation, and receive no benefits or social services from the government, and no proper wages from their employers. I interviewed a 25 year-old woman who was involved in carpet weaving through the putting-out system. Her husband was a casual laborer, most of the time unemployed. They were very poor and living with the extended family of her husband in a very small self-built house of mud bricks. Ten people lived there. They were given the worst part of the house which was a small dark room with no window, where she had also set up her carpet loom. They had two young children one of whom was suffering from a lung illness; they did not have enough money for his medication, and the child looked much younger than his age. Many women complained of lung illnesses, due to the dust of the threads they were using in the carpet. (For spinners the problem was even worse.) I asked her about work and wages and why her family was involved in the putting-out system, rather than working for themselves. She said:

> We are very poor, do not have the loom and cannot afford to buy the raw materials; I am weaving for carpet-dealers. I am used to this sort of work, because we have always been very poor. When I was in our village, my father used to take the raw material from carpet-dealers and we wove the carpet. The carpet which I am working on now, it is not a big carpet (two meters by two and half meters) which usually takes seven to eight months to finish, but it is eight months since I started and I haven't finished it yet. Our deal was 33,000 *Tomans* for the whole work. I have taken the money bit by bit in advance to take my son to the doctor and not much of it remains. My son is suffering from a lung disease, but the doctor's fee is eight hundred *Tomans* and the medicine costs three to four thousand *Tomans*. The doctor urged us to hospitalize him, but we couldn't, because we didn't have the money. (S.B.)

By the figures that S.B. provided about her income from weaving the carpet and the cost of medicine and the doctor's fees, it becomes clear just how vulnerable these poor women and their families are. Their vulnerability is not only in the case of illness, but also normal life, especially when the husband does not have regular earnings[34]. Moreover, because of their involvement in the informal and invisible sector of carpet-weaving and related industries, they do not have access to subsidized health services, insurance or credit. If one calculates S.B.'s income for the eight months of working on a carpet, we find that she would earn 4,125 *Tomans* per month which is equivalent to one medical prescription; or 137.5 *Tomans* per day, which is almost one-sixth of a fee for visiting a doctor. This means that her meager income is extremely low, for work only, and not for the reproduction of labor power, as Marxist theorists and feminists argue. The income from one month working on a carpet through the putting-out system rarely covers the cost of basic necessary expenditure, let alone the costs of a doctor's fee and prescribed medicine.

However, most of the families involved in the carpet industry own the means of production, usually the loom. Those who were not able to buy good quality raw materials often became involved in weaving ordinary carpets or coarse weaving work such as *farsh*, *kanareh* or *varny*. Compared to good quality carpets, the initial investment is cheaper and the time required to finish these sorts of carpets is relatively shorter. As a result, they can exchange their products for cash with less difficulty. In these families, women, the majority of whom are skilled weavers, are responsible for directing and carrying out the whole production from beginning to end without any supervision and do the largest portion of work. I visited a skilled weaver as young as 12 years old, who had started carpet weaving from the age of 6 during summer holidays in a neighborhood workshop. At the age of 12, since she was being harassed by the sons of her employer, her parents decided she would weave the carpets at home through the putting-out system.

Better off families

Economically better off families are more involved in weaving high quality carpets. These families own the means of production, mainly looms and carpet-designs as their own capital; have the financial means to buy good quality raw materials or have access to credit; and are not desperate for the immediate income from the carpets. In most of the good-quality carpet weaving households, men are partially or entirely involved in carpet weaving activities. When the men's main job is weaving, they are more responsible for carrying out the job as well as pre- and after-weaving preparation and polishing tasks which are essential for a good quality finished product. In most cases, skilled women sit at the loom to share the weaving task with men or work at their own carpets. Some unskilled women do only preparation or lateral tasks which do not need specific skill. They do not see themselves as part of the labor force involved in the production process, but view their contribution as part of their household tasks. P.T. was a 23 year-old woman and her husband was a professional carpet weaver involved in finely woven *farsh*, and she helped him with preparation and side work. She said:

> My husband is a carpet weaver and he has a business partner. For doing casual labor, he could only earn 15 hundred *Tomans* per day. Earning from this kind of carpets is much better, but nowadays the price of our carpets has fallen badly. I don't know how to weave a carpet, as I was the only daughter of my parents and I used to do the easiest tasks at home. He does the weaving and I help him with winding hanks of wool or silk into balls, washing the yarns and doing the other tasks of carpet production. When we start a new carpet, normally in each day I wind 10 hanks into balls, each of which usually takes 20 to 25 minutes.

Most master-weavers of finely woven carpets are men who have more access to training opportunities as well as credit facilities. Some young women are also professionals in the weaving of these carpets. They learn the initial skills from their mother or female relatives and the complementary skills from their brothers or husbands. F.G., a 21 year-old unmarried girl, worked with her brother on finely woven carpets, and said that:

> My brother and I are weaving together. It takes us more than a year to finish this carpet. We work between 8 and 9 hours each day. Everyday we work from 7.30 in the morning until 6 o'clock in the afternoon, except Fridays. Everyday, we have to weave 8 lines.

F.G's mother, however, was working on her own carpet. Relating to this, she said:

> I cannot work on delicate carpets. I work through the putting-out system and the carpet which I weave is a coarsely woven one. When I finish it, they will pay me 80 thousand *Tomans*. If I work well, it takes me three to four months to finish. I also do some spinning, which enables me to earn some extra money, before receiving the carpet money (A.G.).

Z.T. was a 23 year-old married woman working on a very delicate carpet with her husband. Most of the yarns were silk, but he had been jailed for burglary for about six months and she had to work alone on a big carpet while looking after her three-year-old son and seeking financial support from the charitable organization of Imam Khomeini's Relief Committee (*Komiteye- emdad-e Imam Khomeini)*[35] and the organization that provides support to prisoners' families. She said:

> Our situation has worsened since my husband was jailed. He was the main provider for our extended family of 9 people. I had not gone out of the house to buy even a loaf of bread. But now in the past 5- 6 months I am going everywhere, meeting many people to get some support, but without any success. He works in the prison's bakery and receives 300 *Tomans* per day, but that is not enough for his cigarettes, food and other things. We have to take him money each week when we visit him.

Another woman, who worked with her husband for years, said that:

> Since I got married, I started to weave carpets with my husband over about 10 years. However, he didn't work full time on the carpets. When we were in the village, we used to have two or three apprentices and I used to work with them from morning until 4 o'clock in the afternoon. But, after we moved to the city and I had my children, my working hours became flexible. We always used to weave delicate carpets, 70 and 80 *raj* carpets. The yarns that we used were very fine, and most of them silk. There was a lot of drudgery involved in weaving that sort of carpet, but at the end, we could sell them for a good price. However, there wasn't a guarantee for the price of the carpets. Although my husband and I were working together, if you kept a record of the time I spent on each carpet, it would show that I was doing most of the work. He was going to evening classes to get his diploma, and, in the afternoons, I was working alone. I did all the work by myself. When he was unable to help me in the weaving, we set up a small carpet of one meter by one and a half meters in order to finish it faster. I usually worked six, seven hours per day, with the exception of Fridays (A.P.).

Many women stated that they do the largest portion of the weaving, and their husbands or children helped them when they had spare time. For instance, one of them said:

> We used to finish a normal carpet every four months. Carpet weaving was my main job, and my husband and the children were helping me in their spare time. In those days, our carpets could be sold for 200 thousand *Tomans*, while my husband's wage was not more than 20 thousand *Tomans* per month. The money we earned from the carpet was spent on household expenditures and children.

Another woman said that:

> Although my children and I were doing the job, my share was the largest, since I was working when they were in school or doing their homework.

Most women were aware of the value of their work, but often considered it as a cooperative, which operated in the interest of their family. A.P. stated that:

> For several months, my husband found a job in the Tractor Factory and earned 18 to 19 thousand *Tomans* per month, but when we counted my contribution to the production of carpet, it was almost one and a half times as much as he earned, despite the fact that I was also doing housework: cooking, washing and looking after two young kids.

Despite women's active participation in the production process, they are excluded from money relations. Buying and selling of the raw materials and carpets is exclusively a man's job, even in female-headed households. I interviewed a widow involved in weaving good quality carpets. In response to my question of who sells her carpets and who buys the raw materials for her work, she said:

> I weave *Zar-nim,* a small size quality carpet. When I finish my work, I send it to my sister in the village and her husband sells it for us. In our village, the buying and selling of carpets is very common.

The gender-specific ideological barriers, which traditionally prohibit the participation of female producers in any transactions in the market (Afshar, 1985), create gender inequalities between men and women as well as exploitation of women's labor in most carpet producing families. This inequality, which Mies (1982) calls "gender polarization" restricts women's access to capital and excludes them from the cash economy. Concerning the sale of the carpets, one of the informants said that:

> When the carpet is finished, men take it to the *bazaar*. They usually take a portion of the money from the *farsh* to buy raw materials to start another work, take some money for themselves, and give the remainder to women. We usually spend the money on household and children's school expenditures such as uniform, books, and stationery (M.M.).

In most of the households the income from the sale of a carpet, into which women put the largest portion of labor, is not considered a joint income of wife and husband, even by some women. A 47 year-old woman who enjoys an egalitarian relationship with her husband said that:

> The main reason we have this house is me. I don't mean that I worked and bought this house. NO!! But, we only have this house because of my management. I saved my husband's earnings and salaries and managed the budgeting of the household and we were able to buy the house (K.M.).

She had already stated that apart from her other subsistence activities, she was working on carpets at home, but she could not consciously recognize that part of her unpaid labor had also contributed to the purchasing power of their family and the purchase of their house. Regarding her work, she said that:

> Until last year, I was weaving carpet and my husband was also involved in weaving after returning from work. Once I fell down from the loom and my foot was fractured; I was nine months pregnant then. I did not even tell this to my mother; instead I told her that I had fallen down outside the house. I have been unable to work for almost a year now. We have kept our agricultural land at the village and until three years ago we cultivated that as well. Whenever my husband went to the village, I went too in order to help him. So as not to pay for the fertilizer, I collected the droppings of the animals. We had a truck; if my husband lifted one sack, I would have lifted another. He became an-

> noyed and told me not to lift the heavy sacks, but I did not listen to him (K.M.).

Almost all of the women in my sample stated that they spent the money on food, household and children. However, within the gender relations between the couples, men hold the greatest power and women are subject to the economic control of men over the fruits of their labor. This control is very tight in the poorer and very traditional households where patriarchy is strongly practiced and women are almost secluded from the outside world and confined to the sphere of domesticity, working in the pre-capitalist mode of production. M. M. was involved in and responsible for producing a big ordinary carpet and a small delicate *Tableau* simultaneously, but she remained outside the money economy and experienced the social construction of gender and the ideological superiority of her husband. She explained that:

> When my husband sells the *farsh*, he gives the money to our eldest daughter. She is our treasurer; whenever we need money, we ask her. My husband did not trust me and used to ask me too much about how I spent the money: what I spent it on and why, despite the fact that I rarely spent it on my own needs. He was getting on my nerves very much and I couldn't take it, so I told him to give the money to her. She is good at keeping the statement of expenses in her notebook in order to keep her father happy.

Another woman also mentioned that her husband gives the money to their eldest daughter, who was 21 years old, despite the fact that they had an older son of 24, whose main job was weaving delicate carpets at home with his sister.

In extended families, it is not only the husband who exercises his power over money relations, but also his extended family, particularly his father. G.K. stated that:

> I started to weave carpet after my marriage and my father-in-law used to take the carpet money saying that he had paid for our marriage. In the end, after many years of working on carpets, we were dismissed empty-handed from his house.

Yet, despite the autocratic control of men in some older and poorer families, there have been changes in the attitudes and practices of the younger generation compared with that of the older ones. Many young women, particularly in nuclear families, said that their husbands were gentle and that there was a great deal of loyalty between them. They stated that their husbands trust them over how and on what they spend the household's money. A.P., who for almost ten years wove delicate carpets, in response to my question about her relationship with her husband in terms of money-related issues, stated that:

> All the money is in my hands. Whatever my husband has, is for all of the household members. When we used to sell the carpets, he brought the money to me, and when he gets his wage, it is the same. He trusts me fully; he knows how I spend the money. . . . when we have money, I manage and spend it very carefully. He has never complained about how and on what, and why I spend the money.

Another young woman laughed when I asked her whether she receives any wage from her husband for her labor. She said:

> No!!! All his efforts are for my comfort. When we sell the carpet, we buy household items, clothes and jewellery for me.

As I already mentioned, some women work on more than one carpet: one main carpet and one small carpet; or they combine weaving and spinning activities. Having additional work enables them to have "their own money" and to spend it or save it in terms of their own priorities. A.G. stated that:

> I spend my money according to my own priorities. I buy clothes for myself or for my children. I buy gifts and presents when I am invited to a wedding, or if there is childbirth in the family or neighborhood. My husband is not aware of this spending. I also buy dowry[36] for my daughter or save some money.

Another woman also said that:

> For many years I did spinning, but Allah is aware that I did not spend a *Rial* of it in the house. With whatever I earned, I bought gold for myself. One of my sons was unemployed with a wife and a child. I could not bear his suffering, and me having lots of jewellery. Last year, I gave all of my gold to him to sell it and use the money as a deposit to buy a car to work with and feed his family. He sold them for a million and 200 thousand *Tomans*, and bought a car, but one of his friends convinced him that, instead of boarding passengers in the city, which is not very profitable, the two of them could smuggle goods through one of the borders in Kurdistan and thereby make more profit. Now I regret doing so. He doesn't listen to me, and I am sure that one day he will be arrested.

Although in the end, both of the women spent their money for the welfare of the family, they considered it as their "own money," not the family's money.

Retirement from weaving

After many years of weaving, women engaged in the market-oriented industry of carpets are no longer able to work long hours and are forced into retirement due to either old age or health problems. One of the poor and old women said that:

> It is almost 30 years since we came to the city. In the village, we didn't have any land to cultivate and we were *gara*[37]. I used to do spinning until two or three years ago when my arms went numb. I went to the doctor and I was told that if I don't stop spinning, I will be paralyzed.

F.J. was about 42 years old. She had stopped carpet-weaving almost a year before the interview, because of her health problems. She said:

> From the age of six to sixteen, I was weaving carpet in my father's house. After I got married, I continued the work at my husband's home. For eight years, I was unable to get pregnant. In those years the only thing I did was weaving carpet and *Kanareh*. Since last year, I have been unable to weave anymore, as it was getting on my nerves; I was having bad headaches and my eyes were hurting. Now my eyesight is very weak; I cannot see the design properly. So I decided to stop weaving. The last work I did was weaving a *Kanareh,* which took me eight months to finish while I was looking after my ill child. Before, when I was younger and I had good nerves, I used to weave a similar *Kanareh* in 20 days.

I asked her how many hours she would normally work when she was younger and could weave a *Kanareh* in twenty days. She replied that:

> I was working constantly. I didn't have any children for eight years and there wasn't any amusement for me. I could not go to a neighbor's house or visit my family, or go to a park in order to say that, I was working that many hours, and so had that much leisure time. I was always weaving carpet. I worked from the morning until late afternoon. The only time I left the loom was the time I spent on the cooking and housework.

One of the informants, aged 12 said that:

> It is almost two years since I last went to the workshop. Since then, I had two operations for my tonsillitis. At the moment, I have a gland on the back of my ear. It is small, but hurting. The doctor says that if it gets bigger, it should be operated on. Some nights I can't sleep for the pain and I have bad headaches at times. I am too weak to weave a carpet. Since I had my operations, I have become anemic and sometimes I feel dizzy.

But for some, stopping the activity does not mean that they will get some rest after many years of weaving. Their poverty often obliges them to devote themselves to working in a low paid job, i.e., spinning, to earn a little money to meet the necessities of their lives. Z.N. was a poor old woman whose main job was weaving low quality carpets and *Kanareh* (side carpet), and had ended up with spinning. She said that:

> I used to weave carpet and *Kanareh* at home until recently, as we were not

> able to manage the maintenance of a family of 10 by my husband's laboring income. Now I am not able to weave any more. But I do spinning, because we need the money. Within three days, I manage to spin two and half a kilo of wool and earn about 400 *Tomans*.

In many cases, however, the economic upward movement of the family results in the discontinuation of women's work or the reduction of their work load. As soon as the families become sufficiently well-off to live on the men's income, women give up carpet weaving completely or lessen their work. One of the women who had reduced her work load, said:

> At the moment I don't have anything in the loom. A couple of months ago, I finished a *Zar-nim*. We don't need my work on the carpet and I do not spend much time on it, particularly now that the price of these sorts of carpets has fallen. The only reason I weave is to overcome boredom.

One of the informants said:

> Now I am only a housewife[38] and don't weave carpet anymore.

Sometimes the whole family stops their engagement in the carpet industry, if their earnings from other economic activities are substantial. K.B. said that:

> We have stopped carpet-weaving. My husband has two jobs now and his earnings cover our expenses. My oldest son, who is studying electrical engineering in the Open University, earns enough money to cover his own costs; the second one has a scholarship from his university. Not only do they not pose any difficulties for us with their studies, but also they help us when we need their help. We are building a house, and the boys are helping financially and with their skills. For instance, one of them will do all the wiring for the building, which otherwise would have cost us a lot.

Learning skills

Carpet-weaving skills are usually obtained from informal training on the job, in homes or in neighborhood workshops, for which no cash payment is made. Some women have small looms beside their full-sized ones and their children, particularly the girls, help them in weaving as part of the skill learning process. In laboring families, because of economic pressure, girls from as early an age as four or five start to get involved in carpet related activities, learning from their mothers or other female relatives within extended families. Among the poor, particularly in the past, education for girls has not been considered productive in the short term. The most accessible skill for many poor girls has been carpet weaving. They are often trained in the skill which can maximize the family's income. A mother stated that:

> For girls in poor families like us, craft and skill learning, particularly carpet making, is much better than education.

During the interviews, the eight year-old daughter of one of the interviewees came home from school and said with joy that:

> I finished my exams and from now on I will help you to finish the carpet sooner.

One of the interviewees was working on a carpet in her basement, and her two daughters were helping her in their spare time. Concerning the work, she said:

> For us, the big *farsh* usually takes six to seven months to be woven, but *tableau* takes one month, and I work on them simultaneously. Every day, three of us manage to weave 10 rows of the big *farsh* and the rest of the kids, whoever has the spare time, helps me by working on *farsh* or *tableau*.

M.T. was 64 and worked with her two daughters aged 16 and 14, on their three looms. She said that:

> We work every day from 8 o'clock in the morning until 5 in the afternoon. My eldest daughter does most of the housework and cooking. We take a break from the weaving only to cook food, have dinner or to prepare materials for weaving.

In poor migrant families, if women are not involved in carpet weaving, their children, boys and girls as young as 7 or 8 and sometimes even younger, are usually sent to neighboring workshops on a sub-contract basis as draw-boys or girls. P. P., a widow almost 50 years old, did not remember when she moved to the city. She had been involved in carpet activities since she moved there until a year before the interview. She said:

> My eldest brother motivated the family to migrate, but my father did not like the city and returned back to the village. We stayed in the city with our mother. I was very young, not more than six or seven years old. In those times there were carpet factories in the neighborhood and my mother sent all of us to the factory, where we learnt the carpet. Our job was to tie knots. My mother used to collect our wage and spend it for household consumption.

E.B. was a young girl of 12 who dropped out of school because of poverty. Despite her young age, it seems that she left tender years behind a long time ago. She seemed to be tempered by the difficulties of life and was talking like a grown up adult about her daily life and problems. About her work, she said:

> I started to learn to weave *Varny* at the age of 4. We used to live with my grandmother who used to do spinning work and my aunt was weaving *Varny* and carpet. I learnt my skills from them. At the age of 6, I started to work in a workshop during the summer holiday. When school started, I worked part-time while I was going to school. In the beginning, I was slow and my boss was only paying me between 250 to 350 *Tomans* per day, which my mother used to collect. When I was able to work faster, I was paid 600 *Tomans* daily.

M.N. and her family were living in poverty too. She did not have weaving skills, but her children learnt by working in neighborhood factories, while she was involved in spinning work at home. She stated that:

> I have been spinning *Jahra* [the spinning device] since we've moved to the city. I don't know how to weave a carpet, but my three daughters do. One of them married at the age of 12; now she is weaving carpet at her home and her opium addict husband buys cigarettes and drugs with the money of her labor. My 17-year-old daughter has recently married, but her husband is unemployed, and thrown out of his parents' house. Since he had no job and no capital, we gave him a guarantee payment and borrowed some money for him to start a carpet. Now, the couples are weaving together at home. My third daughter is 14 years old and is weaving carpet in a neighbor's workshop. She is paid five hundred *Tomans* per day, which I spend on our food[39].

Girls' work in workshops, however, is held back when they grow up or reach puberty and in most cases they continue the work at home. One of them said:

> The main reason for not going to the workshop was my boss's sons. My boss has grown up sons. When I worked for him, I had to work until late afternoon, and I didn't like it. At first I didn't realize, but then I didn't feel comfortable working there. Now I am able enough to do a whole carpet by myself and I prefer to bring the work to home and to do it without any boss. Last year, my boss provided me the loom and yarns to weave the carpet at home, but because I became ill and had household responsibilities[40], I was unable to finish it and they took it incomplete. I want to weave a *varny,* but my mother says that "weaving *varny* doesn't pay off".

P.P. also said:

> I stopped going to the factory, when I got engaged. After the marriage, I started to weave carpet at home until last year when my sons stopped me from weaving.

Women's contribution to family income

The value of women's contribution towards the family budget and how well the family esteems it mostly depends on the social and economic well-being of the family. In the carpet industry, as is clear from most of the interviews, the majority of women are unpaid family laborers and are not involved in the trading part of the industry. As a result, they do not have any control over their income from the carpets. The exclusion of women from the market and their ability to weave carpets "enslaves them in an unpaid relation of production which is kept separate from the money economy" (Afshar, 1985b: 76-77). However, the structure of female authority in maintaining some degree of familial control (Afshar, 1989a) exists in most migrant families and as Kandiyoti argues: "through patriarchal bargaining, women gain old-age protection and security in exchange for their submissiveness and propriety" (Kandiyoti, 1988: 285). Moreover, due to the cyclical nature of women's power in Muslim, particularly extended, families senior women usually inherit authority and control over the younger ones, particularly their daughters-in-law. Although younger women, due to culture and socialization, are expected to be subordinate to men as well as the old women of the family, particularly mothers-in-law, in nuclear, young and better-off families, women enjoy a greater degree of self-esteem and a more egalitarian relationship than older ones in poorer households.

Many young women stated that they are actively involved in making key decisions in their households regarding children's education, management of the household budget, and assigning priorities. They stated that, although they do not get a wage for their labor, men bring the money home and they decide together how to spend it.

Women's contribution towards the family budget through engagement in weaving or spinning often goes towards the household's daily and basic expenditure mainly on consumption and the reproduction of labor power. The use of every conceivable source of material for the benefit of the family is a woman's primary job. The tasks of providing food, clothes and the general living conditions for the family combined with the task of supplementing the income with their work, all indicates the sheer physical burden which the women bear in their domestic life, particularly in the poorer households. In these women rarely spend money on their own clothing or health. One of the informants said:

> I don't know how to buy clothes. My husband buys them, even for me. Some times it takes a year for us to buy a new garment. One of my uncle's wives is from a well off family. She gives us the old clothes of her relatives. We provide most of our attire in this way. Their [referring to her son and daughter] clothes all come from her family.

One of the women stated that:

> We have lots of financial problems. My husband is a casual laborer in a factory and his income has never been enough to cover our expenditure, particularly since he has lost one of his kidneys and has been unable to work full-

> time. I have never worn a new garment, even though I have worked most of my life on weaving carpet or spinning. My eight children come first.

Recreation is also something that is almost non-existent for poor women. Through the combination of productive and reproductive activities, women have shorter resting hours and a greater intensity of multiple, simultaneous occupations. Apart from socializing with neighbors or visiting immediate family and relatives, the only diversion I witnessed among my interviewees was participation in the mourning ceremonies of Imam Hossain,[41] which was held at some homes, often in afternoons.

Food is an area in which the majority of women's earnings are concentrated. Many poor women found food expenditure costly in the city when they compared it to the village. One of the poorest women said that:

> In the village, food was cheaper. We provided our yogurt, cheese and bread, but here we pay 200 *Tomans* for a small piece of cheese, which children grab from each other and yet are not filled up.

This is almost half the daily income of her daughter, who earns 500 *Tomans* for a full day's work in the carpet industry in the neighborhood; what is earned is spent on inadequate amounts of food. This mother has a young son aged 5, who was badly malnourished and looked as if he was 2 years old. Sometimes, women's incomes are diverted even beyond their basic needs. One of the women said that:

> I am weaving to pay off my husband's debts, as he is underemployed and the creditors keep asking for their money.

Some women mentioned that money from their work was used in the purchasing of building materials for their house. One of them said:

> At first, we badly needed money. We had a small and very old house. It was such a ruinous place and was almost collapsing. We had to tear it down and build it over again. My husband was a laborer in a firm and I was weaving carpet at home. The money from the sale of the carpet was going toward the building. We bought doors, windows and these sorts of materials for the house with the money from the sale of the carpet.

Another single woman and her parental family of six were living in the basement of her grandfather's badly self-built house of mud-bricks. On the first floor of the house, the grandparents, her uncle and his family lived in two rooms. I was guided through crooked steps and a dark passageway to the yard, not to the room. She described their place in this way:

> The small room is our living room, bedroom, kitchen, and workshop. We have land to build a house, but we don't have the money. We [she, her mother and

> sisters] are working hard to save some money either to rent a place to move out or to build on our land if we can. If it were up to my father, he would make us work until two o'clock in the morning. But we resist him and ask him if we are not humans!

However, despite the crucial contribution of women, men are the owners of the property and women's contributions are valued differently in better-off and poorer families. In better-off families women often gain respect as well as old-age protection and security in exchange for their contribution to the welfare of the family, whereas the social status of poor women is as bad as their economic plight. The old-age security of poor women is sometimes undermined by the socio-economic conditions and social transformations. Their contribution to the family's survival — it cannot be called well-being — is ignored by family members. F.M. was a 60 year-old widow, who had contributed to the household economy and to the purchase of part of their small house with money she had earned from spinning. However, after the death of her husband, his sons demanded their small inheritance share from their "father's house." She said:

> I have worked hard in this house and suffered a lot. For 15 years we were almost alone in this place which used to be a valley. I had managed to buy half of this house's land with my money from spinning. For 6 years, we were living in the basement, which is now wet all over and soaked in water. Then we had to level the courtyard with filling and make two rooms, as it was impossible to live in the basement. When we were building these rooms, we hired a bricklayer and my husband and I did all the laboring jobs. It is not a strong house. If an earthquake comes, all of us will be buried under the debris. I was carrying heavy stones and bricks, and doing other relevant tasks. Before my husband died, he called some of the neighbors and bequeathed the house to me, but one of my sons insisted that his will does not have any credit as it has not been registered in the notary office and I don't have any document to indicate that I gave some money to my husband to buy half of the land.

Most of the poor old women have spent a large portion of their life in income generating activities such as wool spinning and/or carpet weaving, but some gain less security for their old age. Old widows, particularly those who did not have children, or any support of an adult male, were the most deprived among my informants. This is because, traditionally, sons are expected to look after their old parents.

S.N. was an ill, helpless and anxious widow, who was suffering badly from long-term hiccups as well as loneliness. She was 55 years old and had migrated to the city 22 years ago, as the second wife of her husband with 7 children, whose mother had died. She did not have any children of her own, and none of her stepchildren took care of her. To explain her social as well as economic plight, she said:

> We were very poor and I used to do spinning. Everyday I could make two or three spindles and earned 200 *Tomans* which was spent on food, but now I am ill and unable to spin. I have no child of my own and nobody to support me. The *Emdad Commitee* is giving me 2 thousand *Tomans* per month, but I cannot manage to live on that money; I hardly manage to pay for electricity and water bills. I am selling second-hand clothes to get some food. I need an operation, but I have no money for it.

Work alone, even based on skills and producing surplus, does not in itself bring a woman a higher status, particularly the childless widow. Even if the widows have children, in some cases the disappearance of patrilocally extended families and earlier separation of male children from the parental household as a result of socio-economic transformation, break up the normative orders. Since men are the owners of property, after the death of a husband/father, the children usually ask for their inheritance. Having a house, for most of my informants and particularly the older women, in most cases which they had even contributed to building, is the only valuable thing that they had managed to gain in their lives. Children's requests for their heritage is one of the major issues that, in many cases, exacerbates the older women's anxiety and insecurity, practically or psychologically. The large proportion of these women's daily activities have been unpaid, both for the maintenance and the reproduction of the domestic unit, and for the production of items that entered into the market and made a significant contribution to the economic function of the household as well as the national economy. Thus, poor widows find not only that the contribution of their labor to household income is ignored or unvalued by their children, but also that they face an insecure future.

Changes in material conditions seriously undermine the normative order and affect the bounds of obligations between family members. This is particularly noticeable in the case of sons' fulfillment of their normative obligations towards their mother. Therefore, the widows became the head of their households, struggling to make their living while their options are extremely limited either because of age or of the segregated and strict nature of the labor market. The uncertainties to which they are exposed serve to deepen the condition of their poverty and this transformation represents a personal tragedy, for they lack any empowering alternatives in the event of losing normative forms of protection (Kandiyoti, 1988). One of the widows, who had six children, two of them unmarried girls, said:

> My sons are waiting for the girls to get married, and then they will sell the house. God knows what my share will be or where I will live. One of my sons was urged by his in-laws to get his parental inheritance, but I resisted and told him that, if we sell the house, he won't get that much money and besides that, from my work and that of these two girls, we will not be able to buy a small one-room house to live in. I told him, do you want your mother and sisters to

> keep moving from one rental room to another one all the time? When your sisters get married, I won't have any objection and you are allowed to do what you wish.

However, such experiences for the widows have motivated some men as well as women to think about women's security in old age. Men, who are the owners of the property, sometimes make a registered will insisting that the property not to be sold while their wife is alive. It is even sometimes the case that older married women ask their husband to make the will.

Attitude change towards carpet weaving among younger women

Although the carpet industry is the most common income generating activity in most migrant households, young, unmarried, educated girls are not keen on learning weaving and do not have positive attitudes towards it. Working in the carpet industry is devalued, and, in their view, very arduous and with little remuneration, though they might have more opportunity than older, illiterate women to learn the professional skills of the industry, which would be profitable for them or their families. In many cases, young unmarried women show resistance towards learning professional skills of traditional carpet weaving and express interest in working outside the home or obtaining a better education, state employment or other fashionable skills such as those of tailoring, beauty therapy, and computing.

I interviewed two single girls who had come to the city for education at secondary and higher-school levels. The family was involved in a circular migration and they were living in a house that their father had bought in one of the slums of the city. They had divided the domestic work between themselves, and in the evenings when they had finished their homework, they wove *Varny* in order to maintain themselves. Although their brothers were professional carpet-weavers, they only knew the basic skills of carpet weaving and had resisted learning more professional ones. They said that:

> Our parents have agricultural land in the village and send us our food supplies. Sometimes my father sends us some money, but we still need to weave *Varney*, to be more independent in order to stand on our feet and manage our needs. For us, each *Varney* usually takes three months to be woven. We have woven carpet since we were in year one, and later on we learnt *Varney* weaving. Although our brothers are professional carpet weavers, we deliberately chose not to learn carpet design. All we know about the carpet is how to tie knots; none of us learned *Nagsheh* [the design skill]. We did not want carpet weaving to be imposed on us by the family. We would like to be employed by the state after we finish our study. We prefer the city and believe that migration is good for the young people, as they can easily decide for their future. The only thing which is hard for us here is the workload. Our friends, when they go home, find everything ready for them, but we have to start cooking,

> cleaning, washing, and, after doing our homework, we have to do some weaving.

This attitude is echoed in Cho's study (1989) of female divers in Cheju Island in South Korea, where women are traditionally associated with productivity. She argues that the economic transition and increased access of village families to cash income in the 1970s enabled them to send their daughters to high schools in the urban areas. Exposure to education and city lifestyles, and access to modern alternatives in the city, changed the concept of femininity and masculinity to the village girls for whom diving was now regarded as "primitive" and "hard labor" (Cho, 1989: 163-172).

M.G. was a 19 year-old single girl educated with up to ten years of schooling. She knows how to weave carpet and helps her mother and sister, but has not learnt the skill properly. She stated that:

> One of my sisters knows everything about carpet-weaving. She can do all pre-weaving preparation tasks, work on difficult designs, and do polishing and all other relevant tasks. She has learned them from my mother. But I did not want to learn the skill fully; I knew my work would be a lot and my responsibility would increase. I do help my mother in weaving, because we do need money desperately. But that's it, nothing more. She is responsible for carrying out of the *Nagsheh* [design] and other tasks. I like and prefer tailoring. Carpet gets on your nerves. Besides, my mother is a professional weaver, but what has she achieved from her skills that I can achieve? Nothing, except work, work and work without respect and any reward.

Ram (1989: 141-45) has shown that in Munkkuvar society,[42] the younger generation of female fish-traders reject their mothers as role models. M.G. and many other unmarried, educated girls in Iran do the same. This, as will be discussed in the next chapter, is the result of increased access of girls to education and the availability of other alternatives in the city, which gives them freedom of choice, small as it might be. In carpet weaving families, as the interviews indicate in most cases, women had no input into how their work is arranged, nor in the allocation of money gained by their labor. Their skills in carpet weaving give them no authority or power in domestic or public spheres. They are often unable to perform trade: a women's place is the domestic sphere, not the marketplace. Any transaction should be delegated to a man. Money from carpets is managed and converted to family assets by husbands.

Other skills, as I will discuss in the next chapter, might bring a woman informal social recognition via her knowledge and wisdom, but often in low status jobs, her work is considered either as proof of her neglect by her husband or his insufficiency to provide for his family.

Conclusion

This chapter illustrates how women's unpaid labor is crucial from dawn till night for the survival of migrant households. In many cases it is wrong to call their income supplementary, as the total amount of the use- and exchange-value work women do every day well exceeds that of male members of the family. But the lack of spatial separation of home and workplace means that the nature of their work, due to the combination of productive and reproductive activities in households (production unit), under the ideology of housewifezation, makes this economically active population invisible.

The analysis also illustrates that, due to patriarchal ideologies in which men are the breadwinners of the family, there is a use-value-orientated attitude towards women's labor when they are the main producers of carpets. In general, it is assumed that women are working in their spare time and that their main responsibility is bringing up the children and fulfilling their domestic duties. Many women stated that they do not work and are housewives, mainly because their labor is not remunerated. Some women even mentioned that the carpet industry is good for women as they can do the work while doing their housework and looking after their offspring. By contrast, when men are the main producers in the family, there is an exchange-value-orientated attitude towards production (Bennholdt-Thomsen, 1984) and what they do is considered as proper work. These attitudes can also be extrapolated from the level of investment and the household's engagement in production of different qualities of carpets. According to my own observations, in almost all good-quality carpet-producing households, men were partially or entirely involved in the process of production. But in lower quality or simple weaving and spinning activities, men were not involved at all, even when they were un- or underemployed.

Assumptions and attitudes about and towards unpaid women workers have significant implications for their status in their households and in wider society. It is clear from the interviews that the traditional patriarchal structures of gender and social relations, such as the authority of men, subordination of women and their dependency on men, are deeply embedded in the poorest and most deprived migrant families, regardless of women's economic contribution to the household income. However, despite the deprivation and hardship women have experienced throughout their lives, they, and particularly the older ones in poorer households, are often part of the internalization process of patriarchal structures and their own subordination.

Notes

1. One model was reinforced by religious standards of womanhood recommending marriage, motherhood, and domestic responsibilities, which were regarded by young educated women as old-fashioned; another by the state and its Western imported ideas, which was seen as cultural imperialism, not emancipation for the majority of Iranian women in general, and educated women from traditional segments of middle class in particular. For more detail on how young women sought an alternative role model of womanhood in the late 1970s and their massive participation in the anti-Shah movement of 1978-79, which led to the establishment of the Islamic republic in Iran, see Tohidi (1991: 255-260; and 1994: 120-132).

2. Unreliability in attendance, absence during maternity, reluctance to do shiftwork, religious objections, traditional attitudes towards women's work, the inconvenience and expensiveness of social legislation regarding female workers, social problems arising from women working with men in the workplace, and the fact that women left to follow their husbands if they moved, were all given as reasons for not providing training for women or putting them in skilled occupations (Lindsey, 1977: 94 cited in Touba, 1980: 94). In another study from 25 factories in the Province of Mazandaran, employers from 14 factories raised similar reasons for not preferring female workers in their factories. Although employers in the remaining 11 factories gave reasons for preferring female workers, even there women occupied lowest ladders of jobs and received lower wages compared to male workers (Kar, 2005:126-29). The following chapter discusses different attitudes of male employers towards employing female workers in Tabriz.

3. Although sex segregation has created significant opportunities for women to become physicians, to some extent this has affected medical education and deprived male medical students from being gynecologists or receiving training in obstetrics.

4. For the Islamic regime as well as the Western world, veiled women in the streets of Iran were seen as a moral and cultural transformation of society.

5. Mehrangiz Kar, however, believes that the low female share of the total labor force in the official statistics of 1956-1976 does not reflect the reality of women's labor participation for many reasons. She argues that, not only there were no great upward changes in the female share of the labor force, but also there was a decrease in the percentage of working women in urban areas. Population growth in both rural and urban areas during these three decades and a decline in many economic arenas have not been reflected in the censuses. One of the reasons she mentions is that since Iranian women's involvement in income generating activities occurs in traditional ways, unorganized, often as unpaid family laborers, their work has not been recognized by society in general and the women themselves. Sometimes, women deliberately or unintentionally do not report activities that generate income for the family, mostly due to fear of paying extra tax. Often many families do not trust data collectors and perceive them as government agents collecting information for tax purposes. Moreover, since most data collectors for the National Censuses were young men, affected by social and cultural attitudes towards women's work, they did not take women's work seriously, despite strong recommendations from high rank officials responsible for the censuses (Kar, 2005: 110-112).

6. Moghadam (1995) attributes this decrease to methodological differences, as the cottage industry was not adequately counted in 1986, and also to the emergence of

Islamic discourse on the role and place of women in society and the importance of women's reproductive roles and responsibilities, rather than their productive work (Moghadam, 1995: 180).

7. The statistics, however, have not recorded voluntary unpaid work of women particularly during the Iran-Iraq war period (about eight years), which can be seen as one of the major steps towards engagement of women from traditional and religious backgrounds in the public sphere. See also Hoodfar's paper on voluntary work of women in the community health service in low-income neighbourhoods in Tehran. The initiative was launched in 1991 as a pilot project training 200 women, and by mid-1996, the project covered between 25,000 to 37,000 women throughout Tehran and all major cities (Hoodfar, 1998).

8. According to the World Bank, the employment rate for Iranian women in 1999 was approximately 23 percent, in line with a generally high unemployment rate for women in the Middle East. However, the low employment rate of women in oil-centered Middle Eastern countries of should not be generalized to all Muslim countries. For instance, according to UNDP 2000, the female employment rate in Indonesia, with political Islam in power, was 40 percent. The comparison of female employment rates in different Muslim countries, regardless of the secular or Islamic nature of states, shows that "the female employment rates are more closely tied to regional factors than to religious factors" (Bahramitash, 2004: 513).

9. According to the 1385/2006 Iranian census, only 3.5 million Iranian women are salaried workers, compared with 23.5 million men. Moghadam in her 2009 article: "Where are Iran's Working Women?" argues that: "Given high unemployment and inflation in Iran, it is likely that the vast majority of non-employed women engage in an array of high-end and low-end home-based economic activities. Thirty years after the Iranian revolution, we have yet to see a systematic study of the informal sector in Iran, or a series of services performed by women from their homes" (Moghadam, 2009: 54).

10. According to Hossein Yavari (1996), the Technical and Research Programme Manager of the Institution of Iranian Handicrafts in 1993, between 65 to 70 percent of the people involved in handicrafts were women and 90 percent of them were working from their homes or nomadic tents.

11. *Farsh* or *ghali* are Persian names for carpet or rug and I will use these terms interchangeably.

12. For a detailed study see: Elton L. Daniel and Ali Akbar Mahdi (2006): "The History of Persian Carpet Weaving in Iran." In *Culture and Customs of Iran*. See also The Department of Heriz Carpet's website: http://www.hcacademi.blogfa.com/cat-26.aspx (the English site).

13. Under Shah Abbas I (1587-1629), carpet weaving evolved from a nomadic and peasant craft to a well-made handicraft for international trade. The industry reached its peak in elegance during this time inspired by the art of miniature painting, and received particular support from the royal court. The Shah promoted Persian culture and art to Europe through the production and trade of Persian carpets and silks. The trade was advanced by building and safeguarding roads, which brought Iran commercial benefits as well as political alliance against the common enemy, the Ottomans. (The Encyclopedia Britannica).

14. The Silk Road, an extensive interconnected network of trade routes extending from southern Europe through Arabia, Somalia, Egypt, northern Iran, India and China, was revived in the 16th century by order of Shah Abbas who supported direct trade with Europe, particularly with England and The Netherlands. Tabriz, due to its strategic position on the Silk Road, became the center of this industry and international trade.

15. The capital city of the Markazi Province of Iran and one of the industrialized cities in Iran.

16. Although the training course enabled many rural women to learn a new skill and make a good profit from the sale of carpets, some problems limited their ability to better exercise their learning. According to a three-part report in a women's journal, *Zan-e Rouz* (1995) some problems were: restrictions of membership to cooperatives, access to loans, lack of suitable places for setting up looms, and the elementary level of training, all of which adversely affected women's work or the quality of their work. Information on this scheme and recommendations to improve it in general, and improve the conditions of female carpet weavers in particular, were detailed in *Zannan-e Ghlibaf dar Karghahhaye Amouzeshi-e Jahad-e Sazandeghi-e Ostan-e Kermanshah* (Female Carpet Weavers in Training Centres of *Jahad-e Sazandegi* in Kemanshah Province. *Zan-e Rouz,* 1995).

17. In recent years, Iran set up carpet research and marketing groups to promote the international sales of Persian carpets. *Iran Daily*, Domestic Economy. 1 October 2005, page 3.

18. For the first time in Tabriz, University of Islamic Art of Tabriz (*Daneshghah-e Honar-e Eslami-e Tabriz*) was established in 1999 to offer accredited undergraduate and graduate programs in different areas of Islamic art. The Department of Heriz Carpet (*Daneshkade*-e *Farsh-e Heriz*) is one department of this institution with the aim of students mastering at professional levels the art of Persian carpets. The department website is: http://www.hcacademi.blogfa.com/.

19. *Iran Daily,* Domestic Economy. 1 October 2005, page 3.

20. To see prices and designs of Persian and Tabriz carpets go to the following websites:
http://www.art-arena.com/tabrizc.htm;
http://www.oldcarpet.com/;
http://search.ebay.com/search/search.dll?query=Tabriz+Rug&newu=1;
http://www.hcacademi.blogfa.com/cat-7.aspx;
http://iranpazirik.com/htmls/carpet&kilim.htm.

21. *Kilim* is a flat type of carpet without pile; therefore, they are less durable and much cheaper than the other types of carpets and rugs in which weft and warp are protected by pile. *Kilims* are mostly used in rural areas. They have secondary status and even the poorer urban people prefer to use machine carpets to *kilim.* Hardly any urban people display this kind of carpet in the most used places of their dwellings, such as living rooms. The lesser durability of these might be an additional reason for not preferring to use *kilim* on a regular basis.

22. *Rial* is the Iranian monetary unit. One *Tomans* is equivalent to ten *Rials* and during the period of the fieldwork, £1 was approximately equivalent to 1,300 *Tomans*. *Toman* is widely used, rather than *Rial.* To illustrate the purchasing power of Iranian currency, I will later give statements from interviewed women.

23. A kind of carpet natively called "*Jins farsh*" or "*Zar-nim*."

24. Bazaars are traditionally male-oriented places, where the trade in carpets and distribution of raw materials takes place. Although women shop in less traditional bazaars, they are almost completely excluded from wholesale trades such as the carpet trade. All Iranian cities have bazaar(s), traditionally the pillar of public institutions. Architecturally, a bazaar is a long narrow roofed web, with a central emporium surrounded by several shopping arcades, specialised retailers, guilds, professions, and special services; centres of wholesale business deals and distributions; mosques; and caravansaries on both sides. Tabriz, due to its strategic position on the ancient Silk Road, has several old bazaars with magnificent architecture and high arched roofs.

25. A carpet-knife is a scalpel-like tool with a hook fixed to the end. The hooked part is used to make knots and the knife part is used for cutting the excess thread.

26. Shirin Sour-Esraphil has made some recommendations in *Zan-e Rouz* (1993) to promote the importance of the industry, improve marketing and innovate designs in accordance with cultural and geographical backgrounds, and most importantly develop a humanistic attitude towards the producers, and find ways of reducing health hazards for women, the main producers of carpets. Shirin Sour-Esraphil (1993). "Female Carpet Weaver: the Symbol of Effort". *Zan-e Rouz*.

27. For detailed statistical analysis of reasons for not looking for an urban job or not being successful in obtaining one, see the section on economic activities of respondents, chapter 5.

28. One *batman* is equivalent to five kilograms and is the common yardstick for spinners and dealers. Spinners usually take one or half a *batman* of wool from the dealers.

29. In Iranian tradition, respect for a son-in-law is very important. Due to the patriarchal culture, usually a woman's parents show great respect to a son-in-law to try to avoid any possible violence towards their daughter due to their behaviour. Despite being aware of their parents' financial situations, some daughters expect such actions from their parents. Many poor families end up borrowing money to hospitalize their sons-in-law, but it is rarely heard of that someone borrows money to treat a daughter-in-law appropriately, regardless of her social status and upbringing. It is possible for a man from a poor background to marry a woman from a better off or wealthy background, but the reverse is almost impossible.

30. During the interviews, most old women did not know their ages. They either guessed and were often corrected by their daughters/daughters-in-law, or if they did not have any idea, asked their children to bring their birth certificate. One of the women even said: "I don't know my age. In olden times, when a child died, parents kept her or his birth certificate for the new born children. I also inherited my birth certificate in this way." Another practice in rural areas was to get boys, birth certificates younger than their real age to delay their conscription, and to get girls' birth certificate older than their real age to get them married earlier. However, this was not a widespread practice.

31. *Sahab* (in Turkish language) or *saheb* (in Persian) literally means owner or master and *sahabim* means "my owner."

32. In most cases women talked about mistreatment from their mothers-in-law. Part of this mistreatment was due to traditional patriarchal values and beliefs in which a husband's family have privilege over the wife and her family. In many cases,

however, poverty exacerbated the plight of young illiterate women, who were totally dependent financially on their husband or his family, and whose own parents were often poor and unable to support their daughter in cases of family violence, by taking them back home. In extreme cases, they blamed their own daughters for provoking any quarrel, or they encourage their daughters to be patient and tolerant. However, among the literate women there was intolerance towards unquestionable superiority of mothers-in-law and that was one of the social changes for older women who suffered in youth and now, in old age, found their superiority was being challenged.

33. There is a *hadith* (narration) attributed to the Prophet of Islam, which says that: "if I was allowed to order women to prostrate themselves in front of someone other than Allah, I would have ordered them to prostrate themselves in front of their Husband." This discredits the main message of Islam that there is no God but Allah. However, it has credibility among illiterate traditionally minded people.

34. In the case of S.B., even though her husband was unemployed most of the time, he was not even prepared to help her weaving, as the kind of carpet she worked on was not seen as suitable work for a man.

35. Imam Khomeini's Relief Committee is a charity organization funded by Ayatollah Khomeini in March 1979, soon after the revolution to provide financial support for poor families. The foundation received funds from the government, Islamic taxes, and the charity boxes installed all over the country to collect public donations.

36. See note 38 in chapter 6.

37. In Turkish language, *gara* literally means "black" and in the rural community, the people who have no land are called *gara* indicating their lowest social stratum.

38. In fact all of the women involved in the carpet industry are categorised as housewives by themselves, their family, statistics, and policy makers. But this informant's emphasis on "only a housewife" indicates her separation from the production unit.

39. As is clear from the interviews, there is no standard payment for the work of the girls, and it is not surprising they do not get equal pay with boys for the same work in carpet workshops. See the next chapter for daily wages in other informal sectors outside the home.

40. Her mother was working as a domestic servant and the daughter took on her responsibilities at home.

41. Imam Hossain is the third Imam of *shi'a* sect, to which almost 90 percent of the population of Iran belongs. Iranian people sustain the memory of the martyrdom of Imam Hossain and his followers in Karbala over 1400 years ago by participating in *Aza'adari* (mourning) ceremonies, which are held in mosques or homes for almost two months. I conducted most of my interviews during this time, after the end of the ceremony, often with groups of women who stayed on and took part in the research.

42. A fishing community in South India.

Chapter 8

Migrant Women in Different Sectors of the Economy: Women in Wage-Earning Occupations

In the previous chapter I reviewed the laboring activities of unpaid home-based workers involved in the carpet industry, their economic experience and marginalization. I concentrated on the concepts of housewifization, patriarchy and subsistence labor, which were relevant to the analysis of women's work in the household carpet industry. In this chapter I concentrate on women who were involved in wage-earning activities. In terms of the sphere of their employment, some of them were active in home-based jobs as home-workers and/or self-employed, and some worked outside the home. In this sample most of the home-workers were young and often educated to some degree. The women who worked outside the home were located in different sectors of the informal or formal economy in terms of age, education and marital status, as well as economic needs. Most middle-aged, illiterate, married or widowed destitute women who worked outside the home were involved in low-paid laboring activities, predominantly in informal sectors of the urban economy. They were mainly employed in "cleaning" occupations in hospitals, schools, university dormitories and kitchens, or in private houses as domestic laborers. Younger, unmarried and educated women in the sample were more visible in factories, small-scale units of production, or even in state employment, depending on their educational achievement. Reviewing women wage-earners in different sectors of the economy shows how women take advantage of changing socio-economic conditions for their own benefit.

Women's Involvement in Home-Based Activities

Women involved in different types of home-based activities can be categorized into two groups: self-employed and home-workers. Both groups earn their wages as piece rates. Self-employed women work in their own homes and run their own small business. They are often involved in activities such as tailoring, hairdressing, handicrafts and embroidery. Some women work in their own small shops, which are part of their house, and sell vegetables, dairy products, and other household supplies that meet the needs of their community. In fact, they are often helping their husbands, when the latter are not around. Some women are involved in home-working activities for factories, or do cleaning and cutting vegetables and legumes for greengrocery shops or private customers.

Self-employment and skill learning

To receive a professional vocational training a basic education of at least secondary level is needed. Given the removal of illiteracy, one of the main obstacles, younger women are keener on learning new and modern skills, giving them opportunities for lucrative activities and better returns on their investments. Tailoring was a favored skill among my informants. This not only minimizes household expenses but also enables some women to set up their own small enterprise and earn from their skill and investment. Most women value this skill highly, as it stimulates the growth of their small business whilst they stay at home and assume reproductive responsibilities, particularly when they have younger children to look after. One of the informants said that:

> I am planning to go to a sewing training course this summer. My husband has also agreed with my decision. If I learn how to sew professionally, I will do our sewing as well as others. After all, it will bring in money.

Many women in the carpet industry stated that because of their illiteracy, they were unable to learn any professional skills such as tailoring, machine knitting, hairdressing or beauty-therapy. However, the majority, due to irregular and low income, do most or all dress-altering tasks for their family, to reduce costs and meet immediate needs. Despite literate women's ability to learn a professional skill, for the poor, skill acquisition is costly and needs initial capital investment in training fees and in purchasing learning tools, equipment and raw materials. In the case of tailoring or knitting, raw materials such as fabric as well as the necessary equipment, mainly sewing or knitting machines, are quite expensive. The state provides craft and skill training courses through youth clubs for lower prices than private trainers, but other lateral expenses are still very high. Thus, the poor face substantial difficulties when they are exposed to such opportunities. They are either not able to commence the training at all or are obliged to give it up during their course. One of the informants said:

> One of my daughters went to a tailoring course, but its high cost compelled her to stop it in the middle of the training. She was learning the skill from her father's relatives, for which we did not pay any fee, but her trainer was living very far from our house and she needed daily transport[1]. More importantly, she didn't have a sewing machine to practice what she was taught. Thus, she gave it up. (Z.P.)

One of the widow informants also had sent her daughter to a tailoring course, but she failed to complete it due to poverty. She said:

> My sons were against my daughters going outside the home, because they assumed that: if they [girls] go out, they will be harassed or followed by young men. Then, we won't be able to stay in this area any longer. Despite this objection, I managed to send one of them to a tailoring course, but because we had very little money, we could not manage its expenses, and she had to give it up halfway through. (F.M.)

However, some girls had managed to complete their vocational training. They work and earn money running their own businesses. R.T. was a single young woman in her mid-twenties, a professional tailor living in one of the slums of Tabriz. Regarding her training and work, she said:

> I conducted my tailoring and embroidery training in *Kanoun*[2] during the summer holidays, before I finished my school. For almost a month I have had this room of the house as my own workplace. I have applied for a business license; as soon as I get my license, I will be able to change this room to an independent workshop and get apprentice(s). I have already got some customers. My father has invested in my business. I've got two sewing machines: one is for doing ordinary sewing tasks and the other operates more finishing tasks, such as making button-holes, the finishing parts of clothes or embroidery jobs.

A business license increases the small business holder's commercial and economic viability. It enables them to have access to small loans from banks, publicize their occupation by fixing a business board on the wall of their house to alert the public, have a fixed rate for their work, and get customers outside their own small network. They sometimes turn one of the rooms or the garage into a workplace that they often call a "workshop", which attracts more customers. Those who do not have enough space in their home to have their own allocated workplace often do not get many customers, apart from their own relatives or acquaintances who do not pay an appropriate fee for the services they receive. Instead they assume they do a favor for the new learners, providing them with an opportunity to practice their training.

Another informant also said that her daughter participated in a vocational course and had already managed to recoup the training expenses:

> During the last summer holiday, one of my daughters took a handicraft and doll-making course, and taught it to her younger sister too. Now, both of them follow TV's handicraft programs and make dolls and other handicrafts and sell them to neighbors or relatives. They have managed to earn what we had paid for the training and have found some customers.

Some of the younger girls even embark on more modern training. One of the widows' daughters from a carpet-weaving family had finished a film-making course and was working for her instructor. She said:

> My youngest daughter wanted to work and earn money. I paid five hundred *Tomans* to register her in the Labor department (*sazeman'e kar* — job centre). She was given a night-shift job, but after only one shift, she was unhappy with the conditions. My sons did not let her continue with that job, as they told her that if she wants to work only on night-shifts, she would fall sick. I sent her to an intensive film-making course. The fee for the course was eighty thousand *Tomans*, but we paid fifty thousand *Tomans*, as her trainer is one of our acquaintances. She learned the skill in ten days. Whenever there is a wedding, she is called to take a film of the women's section. For each session, she is paid 3 thousand *Tomans*. They send a taxi for her to and from the wedding. She has not yet gained back the course-fee, as she has only recently learnt the skill, and now because of *Moharram* and *Safar*[3], there are no weddings.

Unlike single unmarried women, their young married counterparts have less opportunity to attend skill training courses. This is sometimes because of the family's poor financial situation, which means they cannot afford the investment costs involved in any professional training. One married woman said that:

> In the early years of my married life, I loved to learn professional tailoring. But, we were unable to pay the necessary expenditures, my husband was a casual laborer and we were hard pressed for a living.

Sometimes this is because of having to look after young children, or other domestic responsibilities which do not leave spare time for women to attend training courses and practice their skills. Sometimes married women encounter their husbands' or in-laws' disapproval for getting engaged in anything outside the home. One of the informants in response to my question regarding skill learning, said:

> I got married at a young age and since then my husband has not liked me going out. He even hardly allows me to go to my parents' house. How could I be able to learn any skill?

R.M. was a newly-wed young woman, who had married about eight months before the interview, and was living within her husband's family including his widowed mother and unmarried sister. The income of her husband was very low to support the extended family of four. She had migrated to Tabriz due to the marriage, and did not have any marketable skill other than carpet-weaving, but had been prohibited from this by an ophthalmologist due to her poor eyesight. She wanted to learn a skill to enable her to work and earn money to help support her husband, but her mother-in-law was strongly against her wishes. She described her frustration and idleness in this manner:

> I feel upset and I am bored most of the time. Whoever does not work has too much spare time, sleeps too much, and becomes bored and impatient, especially when you don't have anywhere to go and anything to do. I would like to learn some skills such as hairdressing or sewing, which would enable me to work and supplement my husband's income and not spend my time uselessly. But my mother-in-law strictly disagrees with my desire and is convinced that if I, as a newly wedded woman, go out of the house very often, people will create rumors that the in-laws are unable to take care of the bride. Either way I try, I cannot gain my husband or my mother-in-law's consent.

Young unmarried girls usually win over the opposition of a family member such as father or brother with less difficulty and enjoy more mobility, particularly when they have the support of their mother. But for married women, particularly if they are newly wed and living with in-laws, this battle is much more difficult. Not only do they not enjoy the same support as unmarried girls, but can suffer inappropriate interference from in-laws, mainly mothers-in-law. One informant said that:

> My daughter has got a national diploma and a hairdressing certificate. She works at home and her business is good, though she has not opened a workshop. Recently, she has got engaged and her fiancé is against her working.

Different reasons can be given for why a husband has the right to prevent his wife from working or engaging outside the home. Some can be explained in terms of the Islamic ideological framework and perception of women and their marital duties. Firstly, according to the Islamic legal system, women's sexuality is sold in marriage, and since it is an integral part of a woman, a married woman is partially owned by her husband, who is entitled to a degree of control over his wife: such as the right not to give permission for her to work outside the home (Etemad Moghadam, 1994; 2001: 348). Secondly, it has been argued that since in Islamic law a woman is entitled to *mahryyeh*[4], *nafaqeh*[5], and *ojrat-ol mesl*[6], her employment outside the home should be approved by her husband. Thirdly, family law recognizes the productivity of female labor at home, and introduces a man's right to give permission for his wife's paid employment, particularly outside the home (Etemad Moghadam, 1994; 2001: 348). However, there is no agreement between religious leaders on this issue, and some argue that: "the law requiring the husband's permission is an incorrect interpretation of the Islamic jurisprudence" (Ayatollah Bojnurdi, 1993 cited in Etemad Moghadam, 2001: 351). Although before the revolution, when the state was secular women's personal and legal status was defined within Islamic law, post-revolutionary changes in family law reinforced patriarchal structures.

The fourth reason, which is more cultural, is that since men are traditionally considered to be breadwinners in the family, women's direct involvement in cash-generating activities, particularly outside the home, undermines this important masculine responsibility. Men's frustration and humiliation in being unable to fulfill their breadwinning role has been mentioned in Hoodfar's and Poya's studies (Hoodfar, 1997; Poya, 1999). This attitude is more widespread in more traditional and less educated households. A man's or his family's[7] resistance towards women's paid work or direct involvement in income-generating activities is in fact to protect his gender identity and his breadwinning role. None of my informants in the carpet industry mentioned their husband's resistance towards their involvement in the spinning or weaving activities[8]. In many cases, however, a man's legal, religious and traditional right to deny his wife's right to work or to leave the house is not exercised strongly, particularly if a woman is determined in her legitimate demands. It is socially and traditionally supposed that a woman asks for her husband's permission and he is supposed to agree (Hoodfar, 1997: 255). As interviews show, many women faced initial disagreement when they decided to work or to take training, but they later managed to obtain their husband's consent. However, as a woman's income and her contribution to family economy is treated differently from that of man's, the attitude serves "to maintain the general characteristics of the sexual division of labor under capitalism" (Whitehead, 1984: 113), within both the labor market and the home.

The problems of self-employed women

Despite young women's enthusiastic efforts in obtaining and using commercial skills, many factors cause the reaping of these fruits to be meager. These factors are directly or indirectly related to poverty. A poor neighborhood is one, where poor families do not see the services of skilled women as major commodities, and offer modest money for services that they occasionally have to use. R.T. was complaining about her poor neighborhood and its effect on her earnings as well as the kind of jobs she gets. She said that:

> I charge my customers two thousand *Tomans* for each costume I make, while in the city[9], the same work is done for six to seven thousand *Tomans*. The people here are poor; they only manage to get new clothes for the New Year or if there is a wedding. The busy season of my work is before the New Year and after *Safar*, during the period when most marriages take place. Most of my

> customers are young women. Sometimes I am annoyed by the customers, who bring low quality materials and expect a smart dress, or they bring a small quantity of fabrics when more is needed. I have to struggle to use every bit of the cloth very economically, which takes more time and doesn't look as good. I tolerate these difficulties in my job, because I like it and it brings in money. (R.T.)

A successful woman very skilled in tailoring, hand-embroidering and decorative arts such as needlework with pearls, sequins, lace, silk threads, and metal stripes, had moved to a slum area after her marriage and experienced a serious fall in earnings due to high financial and time costs of her work with falling returns, failing to make the best use of her investment. She soon noticed that her skills were not profitable in the slum and changed her activity to piece-rate work for a firm making industrial gloves for factories. Most self-employed women including those in the carpet industry, as their capital was small, needed to sell their products and have immediate returns to buy raw materials to continue their businesses. Otherwise the lack of a substantial amount of money leads to loss of capital. For instance, for this woman, for every one thousand *Tomans* that she invested in making goods, she made at least two thousand *Tomans* profit from the finished products. She explained her situation in this way:

> In my parents' area, more people appreciated my work and were interested in my artwork than here. Here nobody notices the significance of my work, and fewer people are willing to pay for it. Two years ago, I was making embroidered portraits, which cost me one thousand *Tomans* and I managed to sell each for five thousand *Tomans*. There I saved money and put most of the money I had earned before my marriage as a deposit to buy this house. But in this area, it took me a couple of months to get my portraits to be sold, so I couldn't receive the money immediately. As I waited for my goods to be sold and the money to come in, the costs of the raw materials were increasing due to inflation. After putting my capital as a deposit for this house, I didn't have enough capital to produce more portraits one after another. The same portrait that cost one thousand *Tomans* two to three years ago, now costs five thousand *Tomans*, and in order to make a profit, I have to sell it for fifteen thousand *Tomans*. After moving here, I was also doing tailoring, but because the people are very poor in this area, they haggled over my fee. They either gave me the money bit by bit, or sometimes I pitied my poorer customers and made their clothes free of charge. These factors not only decreased my profits, but also made me lose my capital. Therefore, I decided to work on piece-rate. In this way, at least I earn my money daily. (F.B)

It was interesting that the wage-earning women were good in terms of calculating their incomes, profits, and losses. Kh.B. was a hairdresser in one of the most deprived slums of Tabriz, where she and her husband could afford to buy a house and set up a nuclear family. Before moving to this area, she was living with her in-laws and had rented a shop for her business, which was doing well. However, her work was affected by changing the location. She explained it in this way:

> First, when I wanted to learn the skill, my husband was against my wish, but I begged him and finally I got his permission. Before coming to this area, I had rented a shop and I was getting a sound return from my business, but here I do not have many customers to justify a separate workshop. I work at home and the customers come in once every two to three months to get their eyebrows and facial hair plucked, and have their hair cut, for which I charge them 250 *Tomans* (half of what I was charging in the other area). Here, rarely women dye or perm their hair. During *Moharram* and *Safar*, I almost get no customers. This has affected my business very badly. (Kh.B.)

I interviewed another hairdresser in another slum, a relatively better off area. Regarding her job and earnings, she said:

> It is almost five years, since I've learned hairdressing and beauty-therapy. As soon as I got my certificate, we immediately changed our garage into a workshop, so I would not forget the skill. For one year, I studied at school to get my diploma and simultaneously worked at my business. If I work well, I earn between 40 to 50 thousand *Tomans*, every two to three weeks. In these two months of *Moharram* and *Safar,* I don't get many customers: mostly state employees come these days to get their eyebrows and faces cleaned. I have different sorts of customers: some just come for simple services, I charge them one thousand *Tomans;* and some come for beauty treatment, I charge them higher prices. Married women usually dye their hair, and single girls prefer curling, though in our area this is not very common for single girls. I also dress up brides in the wedding seasons for which I receive very good money; for one day's work, I receive more than a normal week's earning. In general, I am very satisfied with my job. (M.M.)

A comparison of these two statements about jobs in hairdressing and earnings makes it clear how the location of the worker-owned enterprises affects success, not only financially, but also in terms of the diversity of services provided. For instance, for the same work, Kh.B. was charging her customers one quarter of what M.M. was charging her customers. Or Kh.B was confined to the basic services of haircutting and facial cleansing, whereas M.M. had more diverse, enjoyable, fun, and challenging tasks each day that contributed to job satisfaction, self-confidence, and earning the respect and trust of her customers. The same applied to F.B., the professional woman in tailoring, embroidering and decorative arts whose job was drastically affected by the change of location.

One of the informants talked about the satisfactions of her sister who lived in a relatively better off area and often ran training classes to teach 'city native' women carpet weaving and knitting skills. She said:

> My sister has learnt her skills from *Kanoun*, and runs training classes at home.

> For the carpet training, she sets up weaving loom(s) at home and trains those who want to learn the skill. Her carpets are usually portraits of a half-meter square. There is no exchange of money between them, but at the end, she gets the final products woven by her trainees, so that she sells them in the market. In this way she earns good money. For knitting training, she has fixed rates for different types of knitting courses.

Apart from the poor neighborhood, and small and overcrowded houses, unpaid services to close relatives affect young women's occupational success and earning ability. Some young women complained that unpaid sewing for family and relatives deprives them of the opportunity to work for money. M.G. and another young single girl were unhappy with what they earned from their skills. One said that:

> Since I have learned sewing skills, I do all the costumes of my family and relatives, including making new dresses or repairing and altering old ones. This does not leave me enough time to sew for money. Sometimes, I think I would probably be better off with carpet weaving. This week I've made four dresses: one for my aunt, who gave me one thousand *Tomans* (almost one third of what she had to pay for a tailor); one for my cousin, for whom I didn't accept money, as we are close friends. For the other two dresses, which I made, I don't know if they would pay or not. I don't ask for money; if they offer it, I will take it, if not, I won't ask.

And the other:

> Last year my mother sent me to a tailoring course. Since then I have become the tailor of the whole family, including my mother's family. I make my aunts' dresses, as well as the neighbors. I also have to help my mother with the carpet; I don't get enough time to work for money. Most of my service is unpaid. (S.B.'s daughter)

Another informant, whose daughter failed to complete her sewing training course, as they could not afford the initial investment in fees and purchasing fabrics and machinery, stated that:

> Even if she had learnt it, there is no space for her to work. We only have one room for all of us six people.

Therefore, women in poor families who want to learn new and lucrative skills face many practical obstacles, and there is no guarantee they will reap the fruits of their skills and investments. However, these women have more self-confidence and are able to try different alternatives and not get stuck with only one option.

Shopkeepers

Some women in slum areas were involved in family shops[10], which are either set up to supplement the household's cash income, or are a proper business for some. Many young unmarried girls, however, were paid shop-assistants in shopping centres, *pasaj(s)*[11], often selling women's clothes and underwear, toiletries and hosiery. I only managed to interview a few women in this sector. My request to interview some of the female shopkeepers in their own shops or in their homes was simply refused under the pretext of not having time for the interview, even when they had no customers around. In fact, they were afraid that I might be a state agent, who had been sent to collect tax or information that would lead to paying more tax. When a family owns a shop in their own home, women are often involved in management and running of the shop, but purchasing goods and material from wholesale markets, *bazaar*, or administrative tasks with the city council regarding tax, license, or operating rules are mainly men's responsibility. These women were often middle-aged or even older and illiterate. In my sample only one woman was young and unmarried. In her early thirties, she held a national diploma and had set up her own haberdashery and hosiery enterprise in one of the relatively better off slums with many migrant residents. She herself denied being a migrant. Younger successful migrants often do not wish to be disregarded and disrespected for having a rural origin[12]. My request to interview some of the shop-assistants in *pasajs* was refused as they mostly denied being migrants. Similarly this young woman also denied being a migrant, despite her good knowledge about migrants' geographical location in Tabriz, one of the slums of the city and the origin of its residents, their reasons for migration, condition in their place of origin in terms of the lack of educational and health facilities, agricultural conditions, rural employment and many other issues. She explained in detail rural women's daily problems such as lack of access to clean water, carrying heavy washed dishes and clothes on their heads from the spring to their homes, and their fights over public water taps, and how their quarrels transferred to men, and so on. About her work, she stated that:

> My family has provided the initial capital for my business and to rent this shop. I deal with the management of the shop, in terms of accounts, buying, selling and other issues. I open the shop every morning at 9.30 am and close it at 9 pm, with a one-hour break to eat my dinner and have some rest. I often arrive home at 10 o'clock at night. We people in business do not have enough resting time and would be very happy if the government set some regulations about the start and finishing times, in order to give us some time to meet our other needs. To survive in the business, you have to compete with the competitors and in my case with men, who do not have any domestic responsibilities. I cannot close my shop earlier than them; otherwise, I would lose my customers and they would go to other shops. I am an unmarried woman and do not have family responsibilities, so I can stay longer in the shop. But I have other needs to meet too. I struggle to find a trusty person to take my place,

> when I have to go to the doctor or to a party or to buy items for the shop. (F.B.)

Although F.B.'s shop was in a better off migrant area and was full of goods and commodities, and customers kept calling in, she tried to not talk about her income. Instead she tried to imply that without her parents' financial assistance, she could not manage to survive and preferred to talk about migration and the migrants' lives in their places of origin and destination. About her income from the shop, she said:

> My income from the business is not enough. Because I am single and do not have to pay much for the costs of living, I have stayed in this business. If I was a man and had to maintain a family, I would be compelled to try different activities. Most of the young people in business move their capital from one activity to another in order to find the most profitable activity, and each time they endure much loss.

Other small groceries, particularly in poorer areas, are not very competitive and not prosperous. Due to lack of initial capital to purchase fresh vegetables and fruit constantly for their shops, some of them cannot attract or keep customers. One of the poorer women, whose house had been partly changed into a shop, stated that:

> We did not have enough capital to run the shop and were forced to close it. Though we have a refrigerator in the shop to preserve dairy products, we cannot afford to buy food supplies and sell them in the shop. One of my sons is doing his military service and for almost 15 months my husband is doing animal husbandry in one of the villages and sends us his meager earnings to feed ourselves. I cannot even rent the shop to other people to run it, as I have young daughters and people will think that I do this to attract young men around my house. (M.N.)

Poverty and being under moral pressures from the community in terms of unmarried girls' honor often worsens their economic plight. M.N.'s older unmarried daughter was fourteen years old at the time of interview and was working in a carpet factory in the neighborhood. But the family decided to avoid breaking any unspoken rules in the community in order to prevent any action that might jeopardize their daughter's prospective marriage.

Home-working based on piece rate

Some women in my sample worked for clothing factories at their homes. Younger literate women had more freedom of mobility and faced fewer restrictions from their families towards their work and engagement outside the home. Their network was also wider than their sisters in the carpet industry.

Greater freedom, social mobility, and wider social networks gave them more chance to explore their environment to discover occupational opportunities through which to contribute to the household economy, or be flexible and work from home whilst carrying out domestic and other gender-based responsibilities. They could easily shift from one activity to another according to changes in their conditions. Some illiterate informants in the carpet industry knew that some factories gave part of their work to be done at home, but because of restricted mobility and social networks (mainly due to low self-esteem), they did not know how to find out about these, how the system worked, and the requirements. Some of them hardly left their homes, unless there were urgent or necessary reasons, such as visiting doctors, or doing daily household shopping. Some younger, newly migrated or wedded women were even accompanied by senior female relatives when they had to go out.

However, apart from the advantages of piece work for young women, for the employers, like everywhere else, young unmarried women are considered to be a convenient pool of cheap labor. In terms of exploitation in home-working activities, one of the informants who used to get work from a towel factory stated that:

> I used to bring sacks of towels to sew their borders. If I brought a very big sack, which normally took me a week or more to do the finished products, I would have been paid 10 thousand *Tomans*. However, at the end, in fact what I gained was about 4 thousand *Tomans*, which was very little for all of the time and effort that I put in the work. I had an apprentice for whom I had to pay from the same money; I had to pay for the sewing-thread and strip, which should be sewn into the edges of the towels. The factory only provided a sewing machine for its workers. I gave it up after a while, as the money was not good. Now I am a domestic laborer working in private houses.

F.B., the professional woman whose handicraft work was affected by the poor neighborhood as a result of which she worked for a factory at home, said that:

> The firm that I am working for provides laboring gloves for manufacturers. The cutting job is done in the firm and then glove-pieces are distributed among the women, who have been trained in the firm to do the stitching tasks with the provided sewing machines at their homes. I see other women, who work for the firm, when I deliver the finished work, or when I was getting my training. One of them has been working for ten years and another single woman for seven years. For each pair of gloves, we are paid thirty *Tomans* and we have to do at least fifty pairs per a day, to earn 1500 *Tomans*.

Although F.B's earnings have been dramatically reduced, her skills helped her to shift to alternative work when the other option became unviable in the poor neighborhood.

When I was doing my fieldwork, a new type of home-working activity was becoming popular in Tabriz and attracted some women, mostly literate, who had a positive attitude towards this type of work. Some slums or squatter areas of Tabriz are scattered around the relatively good areas of the city, where professional employed women, mainly from the formal sector or economically well-off families, can afford to pay for some domestic tasks to be done outside the home. Some greengroceries detected a demand for providing extra services for customers who could afford or were willing to pay. Herbs such as spinach, coriander, parsley, mint, tarragon, dill, leek[13] and many others, and vegetables such as carrots, green and broad beans, and cabbages are common and important ingredients in Iranian cuisine and diet. Many stews, soups, and salads use large amounts of herbs and vegetables. Hitherto, and still in most places, greengroceries only provide unprocessed herbs and vegetables, but cleaning and chopping them, and mixing different types according to the dish is women's work and a time-consuming activity. However, in recent years in some parts of the city, cleaned and ready-chopped herbs and vegetables for sale was an innovation that become more widespread and more visible. The idea was soon commercialized and within two or three years integrated into service jobs in the informal sector, creating employment opportunities for some women, and liberating others who could afford to buy such services.

Some women who work for this sector get different kinds of vegetables and herbs from the greengroceries, do all the cleaning and chopping, and get their wages in terms of the weight of the end product. In the poor and isolated slums this practice does not exist and more marginalized and poor women are not even aware of this activity. Or, if some might have heard of it, they live very far from these shops or their home is too small and crowded to let them to get involved in this activity.

One of these shops, which had attracted many customers by this service, was a small shop located between one of the slums and a busy area of the city. The shop was a family business mainly run by a man and his two young sons. Sometimes when the shop was busy or when the men were not around, the wife helped them in the running of the shop and the serving of customers. I asked her: who does the cleaning and chopping jobs for the shop? Herself and some other women, was her reply. Relating to this, she said:

> I started to offer this service informally to some of our female customers, as I knew how busy they were, and soon more women asked me to do their herbs and vegetables. I find myself not coping with the orders and refusing some of them. I sought help from my network and got one assistant. As the orders increased, we saw a need to offer the service openly to all of our customers. So apart from receiving orders from particular customers, we put some ready-to-use herbs and vegetables for sale and surprisingly we noticed they sold well. So we got more people to help us and offer more services. Now this has be-

come an integral part of our service and every day at least four to five work for us at their own homes and prepare different kinds of combinations for sale.

I asked for permission to interview her and the other women who worked for the shop. One afternoon I went to interview them. There were four women working together in a big courtyard; two of them were sisters-in-law (their husbands were brothers) and sharing a house; one was their neighbor; and the other one was the shopkeeper's wife who would only help out in the shop when needed. All of them were educated, two of them had up to ten years of schooling, and two held a national diploma. They were preparing all sorts of vegetables. For instance, they peeled and trimmed carrots and chopped them into three shapes for different uses: very small dice (using a knife), to be put in soup, and two different sizes using a hand grater. However, there was more demand for small dice and since chopping takes more time and effort, they were paid one hundred *Tomans* per kilo of finished work. For the shredded carrots, they were paid eighty *Tomans*, later reduced to fifty *Tomans*, as the shopkeeper could not make much profit from it. Some vegetables such as artichokes, legumes like broad beans, green beans and peas have their own seasons, during which the women became very busy preparing them. One of them stated that:

> We also do different green vegetables in terms of their usage, which should be in different sizes, and combinations, all of which are chopped by hand and we are paid 100 *Tomans* per kilo of finished work. Apart from working for the shop, we also have some private customers, who are employed now, and have not much time and are satisfied with our service. They give us different sorts of work. For instance, one day, a woman brought me 4 kilos of onion with some oil and asked us to chop and fry them for her. One day a woman, who had a big party, brought us grape leaves and stuffing to make her "*dolma*." [14] Another time, a woman, who brought me 5 kilos of aborigine, asked me to take out its inside. [15] We have decided to distil the water and essence of plants and herbs such as musk-willow, mint, rose, and other plants. In the pickle season, we will also make pickles; women like us make all the different pickles you find in the shops, why shouldn't we do it.

Their work hours differ in terms of workload. One of them said:

> Some days, we are given 3 big sacks of carrots or sacks of green vegetables with different orders. In this case, it is clear that we will have a very busy day. My neighbor and I do the peeling and cutting with a knife, which takes more time. For instance, today we started our work in the early morning and had managed to do 20 kilos of chopped carrots. At most, we manage to chop 25 kilos per day. With the green vegetables we can even do more. Since working together, the speed of our hands has almost become the same as each other.

Another woman described the way she found her job in this manner:

> I had heard about this sort of job in *Valiasr* (one of the wealthiest areas of Tabriz). Within the last year, it has become widespread in our area too. It is three months since I started this job. One of my relatives was very needy and was looking for a job. She said she could even take vegetable cleaning and chopping jobs for the shops or private customers. I didn't like her idea, but when I saw she was very desperate, I took her to the greengrocery in our neighborhood. The shop-keeper gave her work, and because her house was very far away and it was very difficult for her to carry the large amounts of vegetables to and from work, he also agreed to deliver the vegetables to her house. He even asked me if I wanted to do the same job, but I did not accept it. They talked about payment and when everything was agreed between them, she was given a special grater. When I saw the grater, I noticed that I have a similar one at home, which I had kept unused to put in my daughter's trousseau. When I talked to my mother, she blamed me for not taking the job. Her reproaches were effective and I started the job. (H.M.)

At the beginning, she felt disgraced for doing this kind of job and tried to avoid people finding out about her involvement, but she could not hide it from her sister-in-law with whom she was sharing a house, or the neighbors, who came to their home regularly[16]. In the early days, she pretended that all the herbs and vegetables were for their own consumption, and knew that those with whom she had close contact did not believe her. However, earning a daily income and the encouragement of some women whom she respected, such as school teachers and employed women, changed her attitude towards her job though her teenage daughter was still unhappy about it. She talked about her feelings in this way:

> Now I see my job as a service job and think that this is my contribution to society and the people who need this service. The educated women, as well as my mother, encouraged me a lot. In less than three months, since I've started it, I have earned seventy thousand *Tomans*. I have a diploma and always wanted to work. I worked in a food factory as a secretary, for about three months, but many things were happening to the kids at home. My husband is also a biased man, he used to take me to work and bring me back home, when I worked. He was against my work and used the kids as an excuse and opposed the continuation of my work. After a while, I found another job and it was the same story. But now he cannot disagree with this because it is a home-based job and I can look after the kids and do my own housework at the same time. I love working. I accustomed everybody in my family to turn over part of their job for me to do. For instance, I was doing my brother's bank-related jobs. A few days ago, he asked for my help, but I told him: I am sorry, now I am busier than you, if I leave my work for one day, there are others who will take it. But my daughter is still very unhappy about my current job. Since I have started this job she uses another route to her school so she does not see the shopkeeper for whom I am working. Once, when I told her about my conversation with one of her teachers in the shop, when I was delivering the finished vegetables, she became very angry and didn't talk to me for a few days.

Her involvement in this has encouraged other women to commence similar jobs and enjoy earning money. She also managed to play an intermediate role between these women and the shopkeeper as well as private customers and enjoys some power relations. She said that:

> One day I had to clean and chop twenty kilos of artichoke[17]. I told my sister-in-law that if she cleaned half of it for me, I would pay her. She accepted and later on, my neighbor's daughter showed an interest. They asked me to bring them work and even suggested that I get a portion of their wages for myself for acting as intermediary for bringing them work. I did not accept this, but instead I asked them to do the carrot-peeling task for me. Now, the responsibility of getting orders, delivery and paying the wages is with me. They do not deal with either the shopkeeper or the customers. I ask the customers about their views on how they want their vegetables to be prepared. A few days ago, I received orders for chips from the Tabriz University's kitchen. I provided them some samples, in terms of their preference. We have to keep the customers happy; otherwise they will go to others. Apart from the three of us, three other women are also working for the same greengrocery.

Another woman, who joined us during the interview and had worked at home as self-employed, for many years, also talked about her experience. She said:

> I have worked for many years: tailoring, knitting, and hairdressing were the most important jobs. My husband was unemployed for three years. I even learnt how to give injections from my brother's wife who was a nurse[18], and practiced it for many years. On top of all this, I was the only woman in my husband's extended family of six. Later on I became ill and gradually I reduced my workload.

All these women appreciated their work, which gave them opportunity to earn money. None of them handed over their income to their husbands: they either saved their money, or spent part of it on their children or household. One of the women said: "Women's money is spent on the household" but she immediately was corrected by another women that: "both men and women's money is spent on the household." However, they stated that a woman's money gives her more power in the household in terms of self-recognition and more economic independence, as she can spend her money on children's well-being and things that a husband could or would not spend on. One of the women said:

> The money that we are earning from our work is as pure as mother's milk. We can invest our money in children's education and health. We don't even need to ask our husbands for money.

Women's Work Outside the Home

Women's work outside the home differs in terms of their education, age and marital status. In this sample, the middle-aged illiterate women, who were often widows, were involved in domestic services in private households or low-paid cleaning jobs in the public sector (hospitals, schools and university dormitories and kitchens) to keep themselves and their children after the death of their husbands, or to enhance the family's income. Younger women, however, were more visible in production lines in factories or small tailoring workshops and in state employment. I will start with more disadvantaged women in low-status jobs and move on to the younger and educated women.

Women in cleaning jobs in the public sector or in private households

The majority of the widows, or impoverished married women whose husbands are un- or under-employed due to physical problems or old age worked as cleaners. Their employment in this sector is out of dire necessity, for this work ranks amongst the lowest in prestige. Women often avoid taking these low status jobs unless they are desperate to work to sustain themselves and their families. I first describe the conditions of paid domestic workers in the private households, then those of women who are doing the lowest status jobs in the public sector.

Domestic workers

In this sample, some domestic workers are full-time, whose employers either work themselves or are too old to look after themselves; in such cases they do almost everything in their employer's household. Some are part-time workers employed by housewives to work one or more days a week; or just to do some specific tasks such as window cleaning, ironing, preparing and freezing vegetables for winter use, New Year cleaning, or to work on special occasions such as weddings, funerals, and parties. The use of part-time domestic labor reduces the conflict of interest between middle-class women and their husbands over the gendered division of labor in reproductive work, mainly in nuclear families (Anderson, 2000: 1).

Domestic workers are often introduced to other people, if the quality of their service as well as their honesty is proven. Thus, access to paid domestic work in private households for a beginner is not an easy task. The domestic workers whom I interviewed, and other women in professional jobs or housewives who had a part-time domestic worker, stated that they find the jobs or the workers through their social networks.

N.B. was a widow with five daughters. When her husband died, her oldest and youngest daughters were aged eight and one respectively. For five years, her father and father-in-law supported her, but life was getting difficult as the children got older, and the father-in-law died. She said:

> I didn't have any skill and didn't know what to do and how to support the girls and myself. One day I heard that somebody was looking for a domestic worker. I met the person, and explained my situation and my willingness to work. I started my work in her house and extended my customers through her network and worked in other people's houses too. In the last five years, my main employer set up a restaurant near their house and I became a full-time worker for them to work in the house and the restaurant. It is almost 10 years since I began working.

Z.P. was another poor widow with six children whose husband died suddenly fourteen years prior to the interview, soon after her youngest child was born. The only thing that her husband had left for the family was their unfinished house, in which her in-laws had an interest. Regarding her struggle to survive with her six children, one of whom was diagnosed with hemophilia, she said:

> We were very poor and without any support and income when my husband died. In addition to our poverty, one of my sons was suffering from hemophilia. One day, a man, who had heard about our plight and struggle, came to our house on behalf of a religious mission (*Heyat-e Azadary*), and issued an income for us. Initially it was four thousand *Tomans* per month, and later on it was increased to twelve thousand *Tomans*. However, it was insufficient and I had to work. Three years ago that income was cut off, because the children have grown up. They used to give us New Year gifts, school accessories and uniforms at the start of the school year. I worked for some teachers of the nearby school, and I did anything I could do at home, so I wouldn't have to leave my children alone in the house. They were satisfied with my work, and recommended me to other people. Sometimes, they asked me to serve tea at their parties and special occasions. When my children got older and were able to look after themselves, I started to work in private households, which embarrassed my children, particularly the girls. For the last two years, I was a nanny for two young children of employed parents.

F.Z. was a 58 year-old widow whose husband had died a year and a half before I interviewed her. Her husband had been a porter whose income was too small to support his family of seven children. In the last three years of his life, he was bedridden, which made the situation even more difficult for F.Z. who had to work to earn money to look after her ill husband and manage their lives. She expressed her working history in this way:

> Since I moved to Tabriz, I have worked. I was doing spinning, when I was younger. Then I started to work in people's houses doing everything from morning until evening. Some of my employers were housewives and some were state employees. One asked me to go and clean her house, while the other wanted me to wash and make their bedding[19], and one wanted me to do

> other household tasks. Some pleased me by paying a fair wage, while others were stingy with their money. When I was younger, I could work better and earn more money, but as I was getting older, I could not work at the same speed as I used to and started to lose my customers. Then I started to do other jobs. For two years, I was cleaning broad beans for a factory. Sometimes I did the work with my daughter and sometimes with my daughter-in-law. I had to work, otherwise we could not survive. For three years, my husband was in bed; not only he was unable to work, but he was also unable to speak. Sometimes, when his condition got worse, I preferred to stay with him, but he gestured to me by his hands to go to work. Now I can't work. I have heart and stomach problems, and my only income comes from renting one of the rooms in the house.

H.B. was a 30 year-old woman with three children and a deaf and dumb husband. She was from a very poor family and had started work as a maid at six years old. She worked in the carpet industry after marriage, and then moved to other home-working jobs and ended up as a domestic worker:

> I have always worked since I was a child. In my first job, I was sent to Tehran to live with a family. I stayed with them for six years, during which, they never let me come to visit my family in Tabriz. I just saw my father a few times when he came to collect my wages. After six years, I returned to my family and never saw the family in Tehran again. Then I was sent to another house in Tabriz, where once every two months I was allowed to come home. We were very poor and since I remember, my mother was, and still is, working in people's houses. That's why she married me off to my deaf and dumb husband. She was very concerned about our honor and wanted to remove responsibility for her daughters from her shoulder. She married all of us almost to the first suitor. After my marriage, I learnt spinning from my mother-in-law, but one day my husband broke the spinning device, as the wool dust irritated his chest. Then I tried other jobs, either outside or at my home, but in each I faced different difficulties and ended up with domestic labor again. I tried very much to find a permanent cleaning job in a hospital, but wherever I went I was told that they prefer to give the job to women who had at least five years of schooling.

S.Z. was a 22 year-old childless married woman whom I interviewed in prison. In the last year of her three years of married life, her husband lost his job, as his employer closed down the business since it was not making any profit. His unemployment forced her to work as a domestic worker for an old couple, doing everything for only one thousand *Tomans* per day, which was paid monthly, while their house rent was twelve thousand *Tomans,* almost half of her earnings. She had objected about her wage twice, for which the answer was that if she was not satisfied with the wage, she could leave after paying off her debts, money that she had borrowed from her employer. Later on, her 74 year-old employer became interested in her and started to harass her and treat her as his property. The employer, who sometimes asked her to stay overnight, ignored her dignity and sense of humanity. Regarding her work and how she was harassed by her employer and ended up in prison, she said:

> He, who is even older than my grandfather, started to harass me, but I could not leave, because we did not have any income to live and to pay off our debts to him. For the New Year, he bought me a ring as a gift (*Eidi*), but reduced my wage, which was equivalent to 5 to 6 days of my work. Many times, I told him that it is true that I am poor, and I have lots of financial needs and problems, but if I wanted to commit wrong deeds, I could have earned much more money, and I wouldn't work in this house six days a week from morning until evening for only 1,000 *Tomans* per day. One day, when I was hovering, he took my hand and threw me on the bed, but I resisted and pushed him aside, and left the house immediately. I went home; my husband realized that something was wrong. I first denied it, but then I told him what had happened to me. He told me to take a tape, and record him, so I would have proof[20]. But I decided to go and kill him first and then myself. The next day, I went to work; he asked me if I would stay that night. I said "no"!! He told me that basically I didn't deserve anything except my poor, lazy, unemployed husband. I told him that he was taking advantage of my social and economic situation and taunting me. He left the house and I took some medicine, trying to commit suicide. When I wanted to leave the house, I saw my employer's wife (who was disabled, and unable to protect herself and talk), and that time I thought I might as well steal her jewellery, while I was leaving. I took her earrings, and her necklace, but in order to show that I had not been the one who had stolen these, I injured my hand with a knife, and rang her son, and told him that there had been burglars, who broke into the house. They didn't believe me, and took me to the police station and complained against me. There I told the police about my employer's abuses and harassment, but I saw him pay 10 thousand *Tomans* bribe to the police to not record what I had said. My case was referred to the court for stealing, and there I didn't talk about my employer's sexual abuse and harassment, as I thought that I won't win the case and I admitted my crime.

Due to class differences, employing a paid domestic worker for a middle-class employer seems to be more a matter of buying the worker's personhood, rather than buying her labor (Anderson, 2000: 2). However, the experience of harassment and abuse by the employer was only mentioned by S.Z., for it is most usual that female employers deal with the workers. Moreover, the majority of the domestic workers are often middle-aged women with many children. Only one of the workers mentioned that she was a maid when she was young and unmarried. Although women's work in private households is a rational response to survival and economic motivations, they are aware of gender identities, sexual codes and cultural and ideological constraints. They often challenge these constraints and carefully consider and practice the cultural expectations and norms (Kabeer, 1994). Most of the workers or their families are concerned about the possibility of harassment and abuse by male members of the family, and are conscious about choosing safe homes to work in. About this N.B. said:

> At the beginning, my brothers-in-law were opposing my work by saying that I was too young to work in private houses. I told them I would be happy not to work if they, as three brothers, take part of our expenses and provide our food, clothes and other needs. I told them I can re-marry and leave the kids[21] with them, but I want to stand on my own two feet to bring up my children, and nobody or nothing will stop me. I've heard too many things spoken behind my back, but I try to ignore them and get on with my life. I've had a very difficult life. When my children were younger, I had to leave them alone at home. At the beginning, my oldest daughter looked after the kids and later on, they got older and were able to take care of themselves and help me with the housework.

Women often use mixed strategies to confront constraints that deny their access to limited material resources. In my sample, they were rarely rebellious against the patriarchal and ideological constraints; rather, most of the time, they bargained with patriarchy conforming to most of its rules to secure access to economic resources (Kandioti, 1988; Poya, 1999: 148-154). For some poor older women, the low status of the work is another constraint that puts women in a dilemma between choosing to work or to guard the poor family's dignity. One informant stated that:

> We first moved from our village to Marand (a city close to Tabriz) where most of our relatives were settled. Even though we were very poor, I didn't go to work, because of our relatives. Since we have moved to Tabriz, I started to work in people's houses; nobody knows me here. In the early years, I was working a lot, particularly doing mattresses, each for 500 *Tomans*, as well as other domestic work. Now I have reduced the amount of my work; firstly because of my health, due to overworking with water, and secondly, whenever I go to work, the children became embarrassed in front of the neighbors and quarreled with me. But whenever I am offered a job, I don't say no. Now one of the neighbors has land and has planted tomatoes and chilies, and I go for weeding and get paid 1,000 *Tomans*.

Most of the women who were working in the lowest status jobs, especially those who were domestic servants, mentioned their children's, particularly their daughters' dissatisfaction with their work, though they were well aware of the material reality of their lives and the importance of their mother's domestic services in private houses as a survival strategy. In one of the interviews with a domestic worker, her young teenaged daughter could not help herself from crying and left the room in the middle of the interview becoming more embarrassed as her mother explained her work experience and the frustration with her employer. One of the domestic workers who was also widowed said that:

> I tell my daughters to study well to be able to find a better job, so if their husbands die, they will not be compelled to do the demeaning jobs.

A mother-in-law who had been a midwife for many years working at private houses, said:

> I have three daughters-in-law: the oldest and youngest ones insisted that I train them my skill, but I didn't accept. They were quite young. How could I take young women to strangers' houses? It was a very hard and stressful job, sometimes being involved in complicated births. Many many nights I had to stay awake, sometimes I fell asleep on the shoulder of women who were giving birth.

She complained about the low status of her job and that was another reason that she did not want to train her daughters-in-law. Relating to this, she said:

> I told them, did my husband and my sons appreciate my work, no. There was almost no difference between me and those women who did not work. I was not even paid adequate money. I told my daughters-in-law, you will not be appreciated either by your family or by your employers.

Wage and work hours of domestic workers

Domestic laborers normally work from 8am to 5pm; some even work longer hours, depending on the needs of their employers. As Anderson (2000) argues, a domestic worker at the same time as being treated as a worker, may be treated as part of the family, when there is a matter of hours and flexibility. Due to the informal nature of the work, there are no controls over this sector at all, no minimum wage, no insurance, and no protection in cases of harassment. Better wages and good treatment often depend on the sense of humanity of the employers. The part-time workers, who work for many employers, are paid daily but those working for one family are often paid monthly. Most of the workers were unhappy with their wages. Only one woman was paid adequate and reasonable remuneration of 3,000 *Tomans* per day for her service, but she was part-time and said that for the last two months, she had not been called for work. Between 1,200 and 1,500 *Tomans* per day was common, but barely adequate for a family's subsistence, particularly if the family relied only on this income, which was often the case for the domestic workers. One of the retired domestic workers said:

> When I started my work at people's houses, I was paid 500 *Tomans*, lately it was 1,200 *Tomans*. In those days, you could manage with 500 *Tomans*, but nowadays because of inflation, it is difficult to manage life with 2 to 3 thousand *Tomans* per day. Otherwise, you have to stay in hunger, in order to pay off your bills. (F.Z.)

Sometimes they were paid on a piece rate. Many women, whose main job was making mattresses, said that they were paid 500 *Tomans* per mattress, which includes washing and beating the wool, and the re-making of the mattress. They hardly could make more than two a day, if they were very fast and skilled.

These women, particularly widows, often had to struggle in different ways. Apart from their limited access to material resources and low wages for low status jobs, they were facing interference from their in-laws, who perceived themselves as the guardians of these women and their children due to Islamic and traditional ideologies. Z.P. described her problems in this manner:

> For two years I worked as a baby-sitter. I started my work from 6 o'clock in the morning until 5 o'clock in the afternoon, and got paid 20 thousand *Tomans* per month; less than 700 *Tomans* per day. I stopped working since the New Year, because they hadn't increased my wage over 2 years, and the money wasn't even enough to pay for the bills, let alone to cover our other costs. I am looking for work, I have two unmarried daughters for whom I have to prepare *jahaz.* I don't receive any support from either my own family, as they are very poor, nor from my in-laws financially or emotionally. Not only they do not support me, but they also get upset whenever I work. They don't like us to stand on our own feet, and want us to be in need of them to survive. They think that their son has left me lots of treasures, but they don't recognize the difficulties that I face, bringing up the children. When my husband was alive, he abused me and was violent towards me, but now that he is dead, his family and poverty infuriate me.

Some employers are, however, more generous or helpful in terms of providing their workers assistance in kind, or giving them useful information about other alternative jobs that might be regular and more secure in terms of continuation of the work and other labor benefits. For instance, one of the workers said:

> One of my employers gave me a sack of 10 kilos of rice and another one gave me 5 kilos of cooking oil at the beginning of the *Ramadan*. They also give their old and too outgrown clothes and I occasionally bought clothes for the kids or myself.

Or another woman whom I interviewed in the university dormitory stated that:

> I was doing domestic work in private houses. One of my employers encouraged me to do the same job in public places, such as hospitals, schools, or university dormitories. She told me I would secure my earnings, and besides that I could benefit from insurance and other lateral benefits, which I could not get from private employers.

N. B. who has been working as a domestic worker for ten years, the last five years of which she has worked for one employer, both in the house and the family business, has a different experience:

> I start my work every weekday, sometimes even Fridays, from 8am to 3-4pm. It is now five years that I have worked in the restaurant every day and done everything, including the cooking, serving food, washing the dishes and cleaning and chopping the vegetables, but my employer doesn't insure me. He has recently increased my wage to 2,500 *Tomans* per day. For the other workers in the restaurant he pays 1,200 *Tomans*. My extra wage is for working as a supervisor in the restaurant, and at his house as a domestic laborer. I am paid daily and get dinner too. He pays the same for ordinary days, holidays, *Eid*, and overtime. A few days ago, I started from the morning and stayed till 11 o'clock at night, as they had a party, but still he paid me the same wage. I came home and got mad, as I had worked from morning till mid-night without any overtime pay. I have told him several times that I will not forgive him for what he pays me. However, his wife is more generous, and when I do her house cleaning for the New Year, I receive 10 thousand *Tomans Eidi* (New Year gift).

When she was explaining this, she was full of anger and saying that if she did not have so many children, she would not be obliged to work until midnight. But immediately, she said that she should not be ungrateful as her daughters were very good, and it was not their fault that she had produced so many children. However, her work and earning was valued by herself, as it had given her independence and enabled her to meet her children's needs. By doing domestic work, she moved from her first survival goal, to secure the socio-economic conditions of her family and the future of her children. Her work was also valued by her children, which made the hard work bearable. Her only grievance was about not being insured by her employer, which would have given her an old-age security. She was the most successful woman among my many domestic work informants. About her motivation to work, she explained that:

> Women like me are working because of their children. I believe that I have to work and meet my children's needs and desires. I have managed to send all of my daughters to school, and the one with the least education has nine years of schooling. Without my work and earnings, this would have been impossible. My oldest daughter has told her husband, many times, that what I have provided for my children, her husband is unable to provide, and this is everything to me and encourages me to work harder. I am happy that I can keep my children satisfied.

Most of the women working outside the home mentioned that their employment was valued by their families as their job was not only essential for the improvement of the family's economic situation, but also for their survival, particularly when women were the sole breadwinners of the family. Some mentioned that when they go home, their children hug them and show their love and affection towards them and directly or indirectly thank them. Some, particularly those who have grown up daughters, mentioned that their daughters did most of the housework. There were, however, always exceptions or sometimes women's expectation of their family was more than the family's actual ability. F.Z. for instance, complained much about her children's disrespect towards her. She said they should look after her for three years, as she had done for her husband (their father). At the same time, she was aware of their problems as unemployed youth, with emotional and sexual demands and the need to form their own families, but coping with economic deprivation and unemployment as well. Her daughter, who had a teenage boy, blamed the mother and believed that she was teasing them and had too many demands. Regarding her children's behavior towards her, F.Z. said that:

> My husband was neither good tempered, nor bad tempered, he was a normal man. I could get on with him; we were both working to raise the children. Now they have grown up and this is my fate; they break my heart. I cannot tolerate their bad behavior. Now when I look back, I notice that my husband, being a porter and carrying loads on his back all the time, did not transfer his pressures of work on to me as much as my sons do.

Low status jobs in public sector

For low status jobs in the public sector, I interviewed women working in kitchens and dormitories of Tabriz University, a woman in the medical school's dissection department, and some female prisoners in the city prison. Most of the women had found their jobs through their relatives and friends who had already worked at the university. Some years earlier, the Medical School with its affiliated teaching hospitals had become independent from Tabriz University, but until that time cleaning staff at the university and the hospitals were moved from one place to another. Some of the women interviewed were employed by the university and were permanent, insured, paid during national holidays, had one month paid holiday and worked eight hour shifts. Others were employed by private firms, and insured only during the time they worked; for instance during summer holidays when the students were on vocation, they did not work and were not paid or insured. If they were needed during this time, they were called in to work for several days and paid a daily rate.

Privatization of some parts of state sectors was among changes that had happened in recent years. Cleaning and catering sectors of the university were given over to whichever private firm offered to run them at the lowest cost. One-year contracts were made by the university and the firms, which were then renewed or terminated the next year. Lack of or inadequate control by the university over those sectors had made the workers more vulnerable and exploitable. All of the women employed by private firms were unhappy about their work conditions and believed that they were better off when they were working under the university.

Work in the catering sector was done in different sections. Men were mostly involved in cooking, and chefs and kitchen assistants all were men. There were three main dining areas in the university, one for the university's academic and administrative staff, one for male students, and another for female students. Serving food was also a male responsibility, even in female dining areas. Both men and women did washing up and cleaning the eating areas. Some women worked near the rice store and their main responsibility was cleaning rice and sometimes grains. There were seven women in the rice-cleaning area; only one was permanent, and five were migrants. Of these seven women two were middle-aged widows with some children; one was a deserted and childless woman, who was also responsible for her mother's maintenance; and four were married. One married woman's husband was in prison, and another woman's husband was unemployed. Most of these women had worked in the hospital and the university's dormitories.

The workers in the dormitories whom I interviewed were four women who were employed by a private firm, of whom two had already worked in the university's affiliated hospital: one had been a domestic worker, and one was a newly migrated woman who had found her job through her sister-in-law already working there. Only one of these women was unmarried: a 41 year-old woman whose unpaid contribution to family agricultural land in her village was too valuable for her father to marry her off. (This practice was also observed by Afshar (1985a) in another Iranian village among the carpet weavers, despite the lowering of the marriage age of girls by the Islamic state.) After the death of her father, Gh.V. came to visit her sister and her family in Tabriz, when she was told by her brother-in-law about the availability of a job in the hospital. She stayed in the city and never went back to the village except to visit her immediate family, who migrated to Tabriz soon after. She supported her two younger brothers for many years. Then when her sister's husband was building a house, she helped them financially, and in return she received free accommodation from her sister. The moral economy of kin (Afshar, 1989b) is very strong among the migrants, and they support each other by providing useful information, emotional support, free services, and many other things. The other three women interviewed in the dormitories were married with children and their economic contribution made a big difference to their families. Only one of them faced disagreement from her husband towards her job, but she secured it first, and then told her husband that in any case she had to start work the following day and his written permission would not really matter, as it was only a bureaucratic issue. In this way, she managed to get his permission.

To compare and illustrate the situation of the permanent workers employed by the university with those employed by private firms, I use quotations from the two groups. During the interview, one of the permanent workers, who had worked as a rice-cleaner, cleaner in the hospital, and many other jobs in the university, joined us and talked about her work experience. She was a deserted woman, who explained her working conditions in this way:

> I have been working for twenty-two years. I started my job in the hospital, then after many years I was moved to the dormitory; I worked there for many years. Now I am working here making four to five *dami*[22] everyday and helping these women. I am also responsible for sewing the covers of ballot-boxes, and money-bags. I am employed permanently, and have insurance and one month paid holiday per year. If I don't use my holiday, I will save fifteen days for the next year and so on. Once I fell over and my hand was broken. The doctor issued me with a six-month sickness leave, and I asked for two more months of my previous unused holiday allowances. Then the doctor said that I can carry on with my work, but wrote a letter to the university and asked them to change my work and they moved me here. I should have been considered as disabled (*as kar oftadeh)*, and given early retirement, but the university didn't consider me as disabled.

A.A. was a fifty-five year-old woman, who had married at the age of fifteen, and started to work as a cleaner when she was seventeen, as her first husband was a drug addict. She was about to retire and was working as a caretaker in one of the university's departments. She said:

> A lot of people from my area are working in the University. My husband was a drug addict and couldn't support the family. One day our neighbour told me that there was a need for a window cleaner at the university. I started my work as a window cleaner and was given different jobs during my 38 years of service. I have worked in the kitchen as a rice-cleaner, but my longest service was in the University's hospitals, where I worked for 18 years. When I was in the hospital, the nurses trained some of us to inject and for about 20 to 22 years I have injected patients outside the hospital, including my colleagues, which gives me extra income.

M.T. was a 56 year-old married woman, who had worked for more than 20 years at the Medical School and her main responsibility was to dissect female corpses for anatomy examinations. She migrated to the city when she was almost 13 years old, after the sudden death of her young brother, a day before his wedding. The incident gave the family a great shock: the father threw himself in a oven, and the mother lost her speech from horror and became completely dumb. As the oldest child of the family, M.T. brought her mother to the city with the help of close relatives, but she was never cured from her illness, and died 3 months before the interview. All these years, she had lived with M.T. and helped her with childcare and domestic work, while M.T. was working outside the home in different factories and workplaces. She found her jobs through the network of relatives. About her paid work and being the main provider for the household, she said:

> I have been working since I moved to the city in different places and then I ended up at the dissection sector of the Medical School. I married a man who didn't want me to continue with my work, but I insisted on working to support my mother, who had moved to live with us, and who also looked after the children and did the housework. After a while, my husband became ill, so I had to support the whole family, including four children. It was almost 25 years ago that he died. My second marriage also became a disaster, and I remained the main provider of the family. He was working as a taxi driver for his employer. Since I had access to credit, I bought a coach for him to be self-employed. He started to carry passengers between Tabriz and Tehran. Before we had paid even half of our debts, he had an accident and two people were killed and I became responsible for the blood money, as I was the owner of the coach. I sold the coach, and paid for a part of the blood money, but we ran into big debts. I was about to be jailed, so my husband drew cheques to pay off my debts, in order to be jailed instead of me. In more than 10 years, we managed to pay off his debts and it is almost 7 months since he was released from jail. In all these years, the burden of all the responsibilities has been on my shoulders. All of my children are educated up to 6 years of schooling, but they gave up their education, as they didn't want to put more pressure on me, and they started to work to earn an income.

To supplement their income to pay off debts and meet the family's needs, she used other survival strategies mainly through developing her social network. In her case this meant having free access to some public services as well as in-kind support of the hospital's professional personnel, such as free treatment and free medicine. One of the doctors in the hospital bought her a house when she became widow with four young children. In her spare time, she worked in the private households of the doctors. She also worked every day, from 12pm to 2pm in the university's self-service cafe helping the staff with the washing-up in return for free food. During that time her two male colleagues[23] covered her shift and she was very grateful of them. She said that:

> For years I have provided most of my family's food in this way. I am not paid for my work, but I receive free food. It was, in fact, my colleagues' idea to explain my situation to the authorities in the university, so I could take food for my family, but in my conscience, I wanted to make the food lawful (*halal*) by doing some unpaid work. We also cut some of our expenses by using my workplace facilities. For instance, till last year, all of the family was using the showers at the dissection sector of the hospital, because we didn't have a bath of our own. I brought my mother and children on weekends, and if one of the

> authorities noticed, and became angry, my colleagues tried to hide it from me, so I wouldn't get upset; or denied it when they were asked directly.

Other workers, who were employed by private firms had bitter experiences, particularly under their current employer. This company undertook the management of the catering sector a year before my research. I interviewed some workers whose main job was cleaning rice, whose numbers had been reduced to cut costs by removing male workers. Before, women sat and cleaned the rice in big trays, and men emptied it into big sacks, took them out of the room and passed more rice to the women. The firm removed the men and when women objected their removal, the manager told them that they had to choose between having men in that area, or having a reduction of 5,000 *Tomans* of each of the women's wages by keeping the men. Women did not have to have a wage cut, which is why they accepted the removal of men and taking on the men's work. But the employer both removed the men and reduced the women's wages, leading to an even greater increase in their workload, so in addition to rice-cleaning, they also had to move heavy rice trays around, empty them into big sacks and remove them from the room. The rice came in 50 kilo bags, but cleaned bags were between 65 and 70 kilos. Women were doing these tasks in shifts and every three days, two of them did the standing tasks, and the rest did the cleaning tasks. They were angry about their work conditions, wage, and their exploitation by the firm:

> We are paid 38 thousand *Tomans* per month, 5,000 less than last year, which is not even paid on time; sometimes it is paid once every 45 days or even every two months. Our *Eidi* (30,000 *Tomans*) was also less than last year. One of the women protested against the *Eidi* as well as the wage reduction. The manager sacked her and said that she doesn't need money and she is a troublemaker. Then all of us mediated with the manager, as her husband was in prison and she did not have any source of income. When we were under the university's authority, married workers with children were paid 4,900 *Tomans* per month as *Hagg-e olad* (child allowance), in addition to their wages. The firm has cut that off too, in addition to the uniform, tea and sugar for our consumption at work. Now we only get dinner, and that is because it is the University's dinner; if it was the firm's, we couldn't get that either. We work from 7.30 in the morning till 3.30 in the afternoon, sometimes even till 5 or 6. It is not our responsibility to clean and wash chickens, but they sometimes take us to the kitchen to work with men, to clean chickens and pay only 200 *Tomans* per hour, which is the price of a packet of crisps. Even then, they put too much pressure on us to finish an hour or so quicker, so they would pay even less. They exploit us and whenever we want to protest against it, they say two of us are too many. Nobody is on our side, and when we complain to the university authorities, they say it's not in the realm of their authority.

At the same university, under another firm, women who worked in dormitories were paid 42,500 *Tomans* per month for 8 hour shifts and were more satisfied with their conditions, though they also believed that the work of four people had been given to three people.

K.M. was a 33 year-old married woman with two children, who had been working for more than 7 years. Her husband was a bakery laborer and his income was not sufficient to meet their needs. Regarding the factors which affected her decision to work and the different kinds of work she had done, she said:

> When my oldest son was seven months old, my husband was taken for military service for two and a half years, during the war. He could only manage to cover our expenses for four months. After that we had to borrow money from relatives. When my husband finished his conscription, he was not able to pay off the debts by his income. One day, I talked to my son's headmaster and informed him of my interest in working in the girls' school as a cleaner. He introduced me to a male Teacher Training College, and my job was cleaning the lecture rooms and serving tea. Since it was my first job outside the home and I was among men, I was not comfortable and was suffering. If it was now, I think I would be more comfortable, it was not that a hard job at all. One day, I told about my feelings to my employer and asked him to introduce me to another place. He introduced me to a hospital, where I became porter for one year, and then I was sent to the operation section to help the nurses. There I was more involved with dead bodies. I had two night shifts and some nights I was asked to move the dead body to the morgue, which was so scary and distressful, and I couldn't continue any more. I told them either to send me to another job or to clear my account and let me go. Now for five years I have worked in the dormitories. Here my workload is more than when I was in the hospital, but here I am happier. I am among women and because there are no men around we are much freer in terms of dress code.

Although the status of the jobs these women were doing, in either the public sector or private households, was low they and their children were much better off compared with the other poor women, who were concerned with cultural and ideological constraints and regarded women's work outside the home as disgraceful to family honor. Working women were more concerned about their children's education, particularly their daughters, and encouraged them by any means to do their schooling or vocational training so as not to follow their mother's path. The fertility rate was lower among these women, except for widows, who worked in public only after the death of their husbands. The working women had more access to social capital and their social network was much wider, which in many cases enabled them to get more work in their spare time and earn additional income as required. They had also more access to social welfare such as insurance, credit and pensions for their old age security, particularly the permanent employees. These social changes activate women's gender consciousness and they become more aware of gender equalities, and some questioned the existence of both gender and class inequalities in the society and culture. S.Z., a domestic worker who was jailed for stealing from her employer, talked bitterly about the position of women and the poor in society and the importance of having female lawyers and judges to defend female offenders, as they would understand women's situations better and fight for their rights. She said:

> Here (in prison) there is nobody to inspect jailed women's problems and the reasons why they end up in prison. I was sentenced for only six months, but I was told that it was two years. Last week when I went to court, the same judge told me that my sentence is six months; I asked him why last week he said it was two years. In response, he said that if I talk too much, it would be changed to one year. I told him there is no Ali's justice[24] (*Adl-e Ali*) in this society; if there was, I would have been inspected separately and asked the reasons that provoked me to steal. This talk offended him, and he issued me with twenty lashes. I didn't see the reign of *taghout,*[25] but I have heard and read that women were treated as commodity (*kala*), but now it is claimed that under the Islamic state women are given more privileges and are treated as human beings. But, in practice women are worthless and nobody serves their rights, and I think being a *kala* in the Shah's time would be better than this. A woman doesn't know what to do; if she wants to commit suicide from the pressures of life, the people will say: "see what she had done, that she wanted to hide it by committing suicide"; if she gets aggressive and fights, people will say: "she is insane"; if she doesn't say or do anything about her problems, people will condemn her for her insularity. Now in our society, there is much talk about humanity, but in practice, there is no humanity and spirituality. Now, money is the solution to all problems. If my father or husband had money, I wouldn't end up in prison or even have to work at all or in such circumstances. When I come out of prison, the people will behave differently towards me. I haven't committed a sin; I have made a mistake, and I am being punished for it.

Young women in factories

The Anata Chocolate Factory is one of the export-oriented factories in Tabriz, producing confectionery products which sell in national and international markets. The factory's products are exported to neighboring countries, particularly those in the Persian Gulf as well as some African and East European ones. During the study, more than 60 percent of the factory's employees (250 out of 400) were young unmarried educated women. All of them hold national Diploma certificates. All of the five supervisors, however, were men.

According to the factory's manager, who was responsible for the recruitment of staff and present during the interview, 80 percent of the girls were "villagers." By this, he meant that they were originally from rural areas, directly or indirectly. I interviewed four of the workers: two had migrated to the city because of the factory work from a small town and a village in the proximity of Tabriz; one had migrant parents; and another one had migrated to the city in her childhood. Most of the girls in this factory had found their jobs through relatives or friends who were already working there.

I interviewed four women whose main motivation for migration was lack of employment in their villages, plus the example of their peers (friends and relatives) who already worked in the city. In their own turn they became active agents encouraging sisters or friends to migrate. They mostly lived in pairs in those parts of the city that were either cheaper or close to relatives and co-villagers.

Their work shift was 12 hours, starting at 7am and finishing at 7pm with a one hour break. Part of this shift was overtime work for which they got a reasonable overtime wage. According to employment law, the minimum monthly salary was 50 thousand *Tomans*. Most of the girls, however, earned about 90 thousand *Tomans* with overtime and incremental increases. The factory had some mini-buses, which collected the staff in the mornings and gave them a lift to their homes in the afternoons. The factory also organized some recreational day-off trips to which the workers contributed.

All employees were subject to insurance and were entitled to a one month holiday per year, but most worked in their holiday time to get overtime wages. The rate for overtime was 100 percent of the minimum wage, whereas according to the manager, in other factories, it was 40 percent. Equal pay legislation operated in this factory and women's earnings, in comparison to other factories were quite high. However, the manager thought that equal pay was a discriminatory law against the male workers, who accordingly were doing the heavy jobs and were also the main providers for their families. In his opposition to the equal pay, the manager said:

> The 50-kilogram sugar sacks, 17 kilogram bags of flour or any other heavy items are moved around by men. The girls sometimes move around the 10 kilogram sacks. They mainly sit behind machines and whenever the machines go wrong, they call men to fix them.[26] Moreover, the former employment codes used to differentiate between single and married workers, but now they are treated the same by the law. We, the managers, told the owner of the factory that these laws will cause discontent among male workers. He told us that the allowances and other benefits are in our own hands, and we can manage them in a way that they benefit male workers more than female workers.

However, the major discriminatory act against female workers in this factory was the women's redundancy from work as soon as they got engaged. This affected female workers' attitude towards marriage, as they would have lost their job and economic independence by getting married.[27] They knew the consequence would be dependency on their husbands or to get another job, the income of which would not be comparable and much lower. One of the workers had been working in the factory for nine years and because she did not want to lose her job, had chosen to remain unmarried. In response to my question about marriage, they preferred not to think about it. M.A. was 20 years old and told me that:

> It is very early to think about marriage. I think work outside the home gives me more freedom. I have worked in the factory almost a year and half. I wouldn't be able to stay at home from morning till night. I passed the entrance exam to study at the Open University, but my parents couldn't afford to pay the tuition fee. I wanted to do a job outside the home in a textile workshop or to be a shop assistant, but the work-conditions were not suitable. I applied for this factory and after a month I was given the job.

R.A. was 23 years old and told me that:

> Whenever I think about marriage, I become upset. I refuse my suitors. I don't want to lose my job and seek another job, but living alone in the city and being far from the family has got security and safety problems.

I asked the manager why they sack the girls when they get engaged, even before starting their married life. He responded that:

> For us, the moral behavior of female workers is very important. We don't like to recruit, or keep, married women to come and disturb the work environment by their misbehaving, such as talking about their private relationships with single female workers. The families of these girls have trusted our safe environment and sent their daughters to our factory.

I asked him: "Are you more anxious about the morality of your single female workers or about the production of the factory? Don't you take into account, the married female workers' marital responsibilities, which will affect their productivity in the workplace? Anyway, there are moral codes in the society, as well as the factory, that they will be obliged to follow even after their marriage." He responded:

> We consider both factors: their potential impact on single girls' behavior as well as on the factory's productivity.

With the exception of this discriminatory act against married women, in this factory the workers enjoyed more benefits.

In some other factories they either do not recruit women or their working conditions were not satisfactory for women or their families. One of the widows, who was a domestic worker, was uneasy about sending her unmarried daughters to work in a factory:

> My neighbors tell me to send the girls to work in the factories, but I can't trust the factories, and I'm frightened that they might be deceived because they're young and inexperienced. Work in the factories starts from early morning till late afternoon, and the supervisors are all men. They get along with women

> who are easy going, but not with dignified women. My oldest daughter worked in a factory for seven months, but she didn't want to go any longer.

Many other informants also said they refused giving permission to their young daughters to work in factories due to long shifts or the lack of an allegedly safe environment in factories because of male supervisors and their sometimes inappropriate attitudes and behavior towards young unmarried women.

In one of the food factories close to the Anata Chocolate Factory, the management had a negative attitude towards the presence of female workers on the factory floor in that they would decrease efficiency of the work due to their supposedly seductive behavior. "The work of men and women in one environment is not suitable" was the rationale behind this when I asked why the factory did not employ women. It was interesting that they did not even let me into the factory, and we had a short conversation over the door. I challenged the guard and told him that in other factories women work side by side with men and that does not make any disruption in the factory, but his answer was shutting the door in my face.

However, in a small-tailoring workshop that produced trousers for men, the male employer talked about his preference for female workers in this way:

> I have worked with both male and female workers. Each has got pros and cons. Before this, my employees were all men, as I wanted to work with male employees. However, most of them were rural migrants from deprived backgrounds and on my absences they used to do lots of illicit things. So I made all of them redundant and recruited female workers. I am very satisfied with all four of them, of their honesty and truthfulness. In my absence, they never act illicitly.

There were several issues with this employer's satisfaction with his female employees. The primary reason was that almost all female employees, particularly those from rural backgrounds and unaware of employment rules and regulations, are subordinate to their male employers due to the patriarchal structure of the society: male employers in the workplace replace male members of the family. Secondly, female employees are not considered as the main providers of the family and their wages can be paid late or less than the agreed amount. However, male employees resist late or lesser payments; they might even steal from their employers. Thirdly, male employees, if single and unmarried might conduct morally unsuitable acts that bring disgrace to honorable and respected employers in the *bazaar*. However, female workers are more cautious of gender codes and behaviors.

The workers' contribution to the household income

Three of the four workers interviewed mentioned that they contributed regularly to family income; one was the main contributor to her family's income in the village and supported her younger siblings in continuing their education. One of them was supporting her family financially, particularly the education of her youngest brother, who instead would have had to work and support the family from a young age. The good income gave the women greater autonomy to make important decisions about themselves regarding marriage, earning and disposal of their income, and about whether to save their money or help their family with their income. Here are some of the girls' comments about their earnings and the way it was spent:

> I give my wage to my parents, who either spend or save it. Whenever I need money, I ask my parents for it. My mother gets me trousers for my married life.

> My family back home belong to the laboring group. They were struggling of the lack of work in the village and the low income we were getting from working in agricultural lands as laborers. My mother had become depressed due to our poverty and prayed to God that I would be able to find a job, as I was educated and had a national Diploma. My cousin, who works in the factory too, had encouraged me to come and work here. My parents are very happy now that I am working and my sister also wants to come and work here. Two months of my income is more than my father's annual earnings from agriculture.

Only one of the four workers interviewed said that she spends her money for her own expenses. She said:

> My cousins and I have rented a flat and we pay 30 thousand *Tomans* per month. One of them got married and moved on. I spend my money as I wish. I buy jewellery, clothes and whatever else is needed for the house. On Fridays and other public holidays, I go to see my parents and I sometimes buy them small gifts. Whenever they come to visit me, they bring me dairy products and sometimes meat; they spend more on me than I spend on them.

In rural areas, the family usually opposes young, single women working outside the home. However, when the girls gain education, they also gain negotiating power and actively get involved in cultural negotiations for their own benefit. In this case, one of the girls said:

> Because I had been educated, my family was aware that I would finally get a job. One of my cousins used to work in this factory and I had asked her to inform me of any job opportunities in the factory. At first, when I got the job, both my parents were against my decision, as I was the only daughter of the family and we were among the wealthiest in the village, but I finally convinced them. Now I have been working in this factory three and a half years.

Single unmarried women faced difficulties in the city such as living alone and being away from their family, and in some cases loneliness made them vulnerable and gave some safety and security concerns. Work outside home and earning a good income had increased the social status of the girls within the family. For them marriage was not the only alternative to gain social prestige. One of them remarked that:

> I have been working since 1999. My status in the family has risen remarkably, by at least 80 percent. Before I worked, my parents did not discuss any family issues with me, but now they ask for my advice and now three of us make decisions together, and this gives me satisfaction and the feeling that I am important. In the area where we live, the slum area of Tabriz, there are not many girls who work outside. Most of them weave carpets or do sewing.

Young single women's work on other production lines

In Tabriz, garment production lines are small-scale units and the number of their workers is often between three and nine[28]. They are often owned privately[29] and do not observe the country's employment laws and legislation. During the interview period, the work hours were usually from 9am to 5.30 pm or even 7am to 4.30 pm. In most of the small-scale workshops the wages of employees were not fixed, and they varied in terms of the volume of production and the sales of the workshop, as well as the experience of the workers and their involvement in different stages of production. In most of the workshops there was a division of labor between the workers. Machine operators, finishers and ironers were young, often unmarried women and cutting was often done by the male owners, a task also monopolized by men in other countries (Custers, 1997: 109). The machine operators usually get higher wages than unskilled workers, who start working as apprentices and are trained as they go along. These young women also found their jobs through social networks of family and friends, and learnt new skills, including cutting. However, most of them mentioned that they would not be able to work in the workshop after marriage, because of the hours of work and demands of housework and child-rearing. They often saved their money to buy a sewing machine and work at home. One of the informants was an ironer three years before I interviewed her. About the conditions of her work, she said:

> I worked in a garment workshop for a year, as an ironer, with my cousin. I didn't face any opposition from my family towards my work and learning a new skill. We were seven single women: two machine operators, an overcast stitcher and four ironers. Our employer was the owner of the workshop, who was doing all the cutting jobs and passed them onto the machine operators. The ironers were paid six thousand *Tomans* per month, while the machine op-

> erators were paid three times as much. The only benefit of working there was that we sometimes made clothes of our own material, without having to pay for it. After a year, my dad didn't let me go to work because I was getting too tired by working long hours for a very low wage (a nineteen year old girl).

One of the informants, who was working in another clothes workshop, said:

> My stepmother wouldn't let my father pay the fees of a tailoring training course, so I worked in a workshop as an apprentice to earn money and to learn the skill. My father didn't object about my decision, but my brother was seriously opposed, as he felt sorry for me and wanted to pay for my training fees, but I didn't accept it. We are three single women in this workshop, and every day we make sixty to seventy bras. I take orders from my relatives and friends, and do all the jobs myself. I write all my own work in a booklet and my employer deducts three hundred *Tomans*, per each item, but I charge my customers eight hundred *Tomans*. My training took two to three months, and now my wage is higher than before. I have been trained to do cutting and I can cut ten at once, but not sixty or seventy. My monthly wage is between twenty and twenty two thousand *Tomans*, but including my own work, my earnings are between thirty and thirty five thousand *Tomans*.

Since women's earnings are "not lucrative enough to pull most women out of poverty, and not sufficiently different in their content or context to seriously challenge existing ideological constructs" (Afshar and Agarwal, 1989: 14), the majority of women have a framed concept of "femininity" and "masculinity." Almost all of my informants believed that providing for the family's welfare is the men's responsibility, and many girls in paid employment stated that they will quit when they marry. R.T., a nineteen year old unmarried woman said:

> I will not work after I marry, I like my husband to work and bring money for me. I might buy a sewing machine and work at home and set up my own business.

Part of this idea that they will quit after marriage is due to the labor market conditions, such as lack of flexibility for married women in terms of working hours so as to manage domestic and working responsibilities. Lack of child-care facilities is another major obstacle for women, particularly in nuclear families. The women whose mother or mother-in-law looked after their children while they were working had fewer problems with child-care responsibilities. Cultural norms and practices such as men's responsibility for doing outside jobs and women doing housework and looking after children is a normal and acceptable practice in the majority of households. I asked a twenty-three year-old single woman, who was earning very well from her business and was satisfied with her job as well as earnings, what would she do, if her married partner did not agree with her work. She replied:

> If he is my desired partner, who has a permanent job and a good salary, I will accept not to work and focus on my life.

State employment

I mainly interviewed one head teacher and three teachers in two primary schools, all migrants. Two of them had made a secondary migration from smaller towns. All were permanent employees with health insurance and pensions. All the women, with the exception of one, had nuclear families. Two of them did not have any children, one of them had three and another one had four children. All played important roles in family decisions. Unlike most of the migrants who came to Tabriz for a better life, one of these teachers had to leave a relatively privileged life and big house in Ahar for her children's education. In the city, they bought a small flat, but in a good area to enable their children to benefit from further education facilities and opportunities available in Tabriz such as extra school programs and English classes. She said:

> In Tabriz living expenses are high, but facilities are also greater for children. For instance, the privately run English or private courses help students to get higher marks in *konkour.* We mainly came because of my older daughter who was doing well in her studies and I wanted to give her better education. Now all my children are enjoying better education in Tabriz.

All of them talked about their good relationship with their husbands and how they make joint decisions for any aspect of their life, such as children's education, or important household purchases. All of them married after securing their job and played important roles in their marriages. One of these women said about her marriage:

> When I was 17 years old, I wanted to get married, but my mum did not allow me. She insisted I should give priority on my education to be economically independent before I married. I see how important it is. I tried lots of fertility treatment that with one salary would have been almost impossible. I do not have children and my sisters blame me for not saving my money for old age. But I am not that concerned. With my pension, I could buy services for my old age or stay in an old people's home.

All of the women spent their earnings on the house, and gave the priority to their children's education regardless of gender, unlike the poorer women in low-status jobs who gave priority to their female children to get adequate educations or skills, except religious families who gave more priority to boys' education. One of the daughters of these women was a very successful university student in Tabriz University, doing a Chemistry Engineering course, who wanted to do an MA course in Tehran University and planned to continue overseas. Her mother spent quality time with her daughter and gave her good advice. In terms of their support for the daughter's education, she said:

> Once my daughter said, mum I need a computer for my course. I talked with my husband, prioritized our expenses, and bought her a computer. Now we see how important it is having a computer at home, that my other children also use it.

In response to my question whether they asked for their husband's permission to get their jobs, one of them said:

> I started my job after marriage. My husband did not oppose it. He wanted to have an employed wife, not because of money, rather because an employed woman is more social, more aware, and better at raising a good and healthy family. Beside, an employed woman's salary brings in cash to home which is used for children's progress.

All of these women were very highly motivated and had good self-esteem. Although the number was too small to generalize their experiences to all other educated and employed women, having an active social life makes them aware of their rights. They were not forced to stay in unhealthy relationships and were aware that they are economically independent.

Conclusion

This chapter illustrates the diversity of economic activities among migrant women and their contribution to the total earning power of their families. It also illustrated the four factors of age, education, marital status and economic situation of the family that are important elements in determining sectors and sub-sectors of the economy into which women fit better. By earning money directly women's contribution is more visible and valuable for the family, and they have more control over their labor and means of production, particularly in the case of self-employed women, in spite of their individualized and atomized existence. In the case of married women, men's resistance towards their paid activities is more a matter of power management on the part of husbands, to sustain their traditional role as the unquestioned heads of households. Most of the time, as the informants mentioned, as well as from my own observations, there was no violent disagreement between husbands and wives. Some married women first find and secure their job, then ask for their husband's permission.

As the interviews revealed education plays an important role in empowering young, particularly unmarried, women to move out of the carpet industry, the most common, and invisible sector of the economy among migrant families. Although their incomes in some sectors are less than their sister's economic contribution to the family in the carpet industry, they enjoy greater self-esteem and have greater gender consciousness, and see their outside engagement as a positive change.

Notes

1. Although public transport is cheap and available in even very poor and remote areas of the city, some still find it costly, particularly when they use it often.
2. The full name for "*Kanoun*" is *Kanoun-e parvaresh-e fekri-e kudakan va nojavanan*, which literally means: the Society for Contemplative Training for Children and Young Adults.
3. *Moharram* and *Safar* are two consecutive Arabic lunar months in which, because of the martyrdom of Imam Hossain, the third Imam of Shiites, weddings and other kinds of parties and celebrations do not usually take place.
4. A financial obligation of a husband towards his wife, which has been agreed during the marriage contract, *aqd*, and is due when the marriage is consummated. However, in practice, women demand it at divorce and use it as a financial security.
5. The full financial support of a husband for daily living costs of a wife such as food, clothes, accommodation, and health services.
6. In 1992, parliament amended the divorce section of the Family Protection Law. According to the new reform, called *ojrat-ol mesl*, if a man wants to divorce his wife unilaterally, he should pay his wife a wage equivalent to the household labor performed during the marriage. The household labor of women is not covered by *nafaqeh* and *mahryyeh*. For detailed information regarding *ojrat-ol mesl*, see Mir-Hossaini, 1995.
7. Younger women, mainly in extended families face the disapproval of their in-laws towards paid work outside the home. In some cases, however, living within the extended family gives working women the advantage of transferring some domestic responsibilities, child-rearing particularly, to their mothers-in-law.
8. Hoodfar (1997) writing anthropologically about household economy and women's role in three low-income neighborhoods in Cairo, questioned men's views about women and work. She writes that: "traditional and older men said a woman should go out to work only if her husband fails to feed her and her children but she should participate if there is a family business and her husband needs her help" (Hoodfar, 1997: 138).
9. The non-migrant areas of Tabriz are usually called "the city" by the slum dwellers.

10. Different items are sold in these shops; some of them mainly provide essential food items and other household supplies in the neighborhood; some sell small household non-electrical domestic appliances and kitchen utensils, often cooking and serving appliances, such as cutlery, plates, mugs, pots and pans; others sell clothes and costumes, decorative accessories and haberdashery; or hosiery products including socks, scarves, and women's underwear. In the poorer areas, however, most of the shops are mainly groceries, selling daily necessities.

11. *Pasaj* is a modern shopping centre for economic activities, with shops called boutiques. Women are more visible in *pasajs*, both as customers and traders. This is one of the important differences between *Pasaj* and traditional *bazaar*.

12. In response to my question "do you consider yourself an urban person (*shaharli*) or an individual with rural background," unlike older women who mostly considered themselves as a villager (*katdi*), most young women stated that they are *shaharli,* even though they were aware of the differences.

13. The Iranian type of leek, which is something between leek and chive.

14. A kind of Mediterranean food, the stuffing is mostly minced meat, rice, savory and aromatic herbs.

15. This is used for making a different type of *dolma*. Removing the inside of the aubergine by hand without using a knife is very skillful.

16. For most housewives, socializing happens informally in each other's houses in the neighborhood when men are at work and not around. This is one of the most common ways of recreation, gossiping, building social networks, and helping and supporting each other. Whenever and wherever possible they take part of their daily tasks such as knitting, or cleaning and chopping herbs and vegetables to each other's houses. It was this cultural custom that opened my way to many houses of my informants in which interviews took place in a more relaxed and informal way.

17. Artichoke in Iran is a kind of leafy wild vegetable, which is covered with sharp prickles. After removing the prickles it is used for stew. The plant comes to the market for a short period of time and women usually buy it in large quantities, remove the prickles, then chop and freeze it the later use.

18. Some of the women in my sample mentioned that they had learnt the practice of injection from professional nurses and had practiced it for many years. In Iran self-medication, and self-prescription and purchase of even prescription-only drugs such as antibiotics over the counter are widespread. Apart from the health hazards of over- and misuse of antibiotics, Hatam *et al.*'s study indicates the economic burden of inappropriate usage of them — about 98 percent of all cases in their cross-sectional study of antibiotic usage in the surgical wards of 6 teaching hospitals affiliated to Medical University of Shiraz. Apart from self-medication, in poor communities and among illiterate or less educated people it is also common to use non-professional people to inject antibiotics, as they charge less than professional nurses in health clinics. For detailed information see Zargarzadeh *et al.* (2008) and Hatam *et al.* (2008).

19. In Azarbaijan, due to the cold climate and long summers, bedding such as mattresses, duvets and pillows are made from wool. Mattress and pillows are unsewn at least twice a year: once at the end of winter as part of the New Year cleansing, and once at the end of summer. The wool is washed and beaten with thin, long rods and sticks. When the wool is finely dried and beaten up, the washed mattresses are filled

up with wool and sewn up with special needles and thread. Duvets are also made at home and they need a special skill of quilting. Washing and making the bedding are hard labor and often if the family can afford to pay for the service, they may employ a worker to do these jobs. Most of the part-time domestic workers whom I interviewed mentioned their involvement in this activity.

20. This was very surprising for me when I heard it, as I was expecting to hear about her husband's anger and frustration towards the man; or embarrassment as he could not function in his religious and cultural breadwinning duty. Unlike other men, who are often concerned about the family honor, her husband, instead of preventing her from going to work, where there was a great threat to the family honor, suggested his wife take a tape with her to record the man's sexual harassment.

21. When a widow re-marries, her in-laws usually take the custody of the children, but if she does not re-marry, she would be in charge of her own children. One of the widowed informants mentioned something stranger in this regard. She said that: "Three days after the death of my husband, I saw that my in-laws are dividing my children between themselves and telling me that I could be free to re-marry. I told them that I won't marry, and will take care of my children. I have already married once and if it was my fate, he would have stayed alive."

22. *Dami* is a kitchen utensil which is used for the steaming of rice, and is made of lots of fabric and a cane basket. The basket is covered by the fabric and sewn by hand, then it is again covered by another layer of fabric and sewn, and this continues until a very thick, firm and hard *dami* is made.

23. One of her colleagues was originally from Tabriz, and the other one was a migrant from a rural area, and she was blessing both of them.

24. Ali is the first *Shi'a* Imam. For *Shiites*, he is a good example of justice and fairness even to his enemies.

25. *Taghout* literally means Satan, who prevents humans from being on the right path; or any idol. After the revolution, the period of the Pahlavi dynasty became known as "*doran-e taghout*" (*Taghout's* reign).

26. The girls were also responsible for cleaning the machines at the end of each day.

27. This attitude was different from what their single sisters in other sectors had. For them marriage with a reasonably well-paid man can free them from working for meager wages.

28. According to the 1996 census, 93 percent of the manufacturing workshops in East Azarbaijan employed between one and five workers and 4 percent of them employed six to nine workers.

29. According to the 1996 census, 99 percent of the manufacturing workshops in East Azarbaijan were categorized as "privately owned workshops." All or at least 50 percent of invested capital in privately owned workshops belongs to individuals, often the owners.

Chapter 9

Conclusion

In this book, I have tried to bridge a gap relating to the invisibility of migrant woman. This exists both in migration literatures in Iran and in Western literature on Iranian women's issues. In the former the invisibility is mainly due to general assumptions and perceptions of gender roles in migrant families. According to these, women are mainly assumed to accompany their economically active male relatives in migration. In the latter, the main focus of most studies is at the macro level, analyzing political discourse and legal changes, particularly Islamic state policies, gender ideologies and doctrines, that construct or affect the living conditions and life experiences of Iranian women in general. Few studies, however, concentrate on the micro level, analyzing the economic role of working class women; in those that do, migrant women are largely ignored. Thus, the central concern of this study was to examine the role of women in rural-urban migration in Iran and the impact of this on migrant women's socio-economic status within the family and society. This was done by revealing individual voices and women's motivations and experiences based on their own accounts, bearing in mind that they may be motivated to migrate by factors different to those affecting men.

This book has extended our understanding of rural-urban female migration in East Azarbaijan and the nature of women's work in Tabriz through an analytical focus on the subjective experiences of migrant women. Before the empirical study, I assumed that migrant women in Tabriz were more or less a homogenous group who benefited from migration and changes in social and economic conditions; and who, like their counterparts in different parts of the world, played an active role in migration-related decisions. My data indicated that the majority of the respondents were willing to leave their villages, and in general they mostly chose economic pull and push factors as their first and second priorities for migration. Social factors such as the lack of health and educational services and facilities were important factors after economic ones, mostly as second, third, or fourth priorities. These findings are strongly supported by Iranian literature that discusses rural-urban migration in Iran in general as a result of industrialization and modernization processes in urban areas as well as the land reform project in rural areas (Afshar, 1985a; Ajami, 1976; Akhavi, 1986; Bayat, 1997; Hoodfar, 1993; Keddie, 1972; Pesaran, 1985; Razavi, 1992; for Tabriz see Hossein-Zadeh-e Dalir, 1982; Jamali, 1985).

Looking at women's marital status and their age groups at the time of migration, however, my data indicates various prioritie among different categories of women. Almost one-third of my respondents were bound to the familial residence as children and the majority of them were less than ten years old at the time of migration. For 75 percent of this category, accompanying their family was the only reason behind their migration and they did not play a role in the decision-making process, though generally the net gain from migration was positive for them. For a group of women who migrated to the city to start married life, marriage was the main reason for their migration and for those who experienced unhappy marital relationships, the net effect of migration was negative due to the loss of family network and support. For a few single women who had migrated independently, access to better employment and educational opportunities were the main reasons underlying rational decisions. For married women, economic inducements were the important reason for migration of families, economic units responding to rural-urban inequalities. However, age-group subdivisions indicated that migration for a high percentage of the younger ones was a response to positive socio-economic characteristics of urban life; for the older respondents, it was a response to negative circumstances in their place of origin. The "human capital investment model" and economic and non-economic costs and returns of migration in terms of longer or shorter periods of net benefits can explain the diversity in response of different age groups to pull and push factors, both in general and in this case study.

Economic migrants were often the male relatives of my respondents, mainly due to the sexual division of labor and ideological beliefs and practices that consider men as the main providers of family income. For some married women, however, migration was considered an opportunity which could free them from the rural workload, though most of them ended up working in the cottage industry of carpet weaving, almost with the same socio-cultural restrictions and practices. More than two-thirds of migrant women in this study undertook family-related migration, mainly due to marriage. It is almost impossible for married women in rural areas of East Azarbaijan to migrate independently, due to gender ideologies and the sexual division of labor that defines married women's places in the home. This situation differs from that in many parts of China, South-East Asia, North Africa, and Latin America where married women at times leave their children in their villages in the custody of female relatives or even their husbands, and migrate independently to the city in search of employment (Brydon, 1989; Campani, 1995; Chant, 1989; Davin, 1998 and 1999).

The lack of primary health care services in the villages, which affected families economically and emotionally at events such as sudden death of family members, especially children, and also animals, was another important factor mentioned by married women both in poorer and better off households. Lack of educational opportunities in the villages was only mentioned by women whose families could afford better educational services for their children in the city.

The value of interviews with migrant women from different generations was great, as they revealed issues in terms of their life and work that have received relatively little attention in Iran. One of the most important and interesting aspects of the interviews was that they illustrated the variety of living standards and the status of women in migrant families, who are often seen as an undifferentiated social group. Although the main concern was to examine migrant women's socio-economic conditions within a social and cultural context with a specific focus on their income generation activities, during the study I noticed considerable differences between different generations, mainly in terms of literacy levels. Relationships between different members of the family, particularly between a wife and her husband, a married woman and her in-laws, a mother-in-law and her daughters and daughters-in-law were widely covered during the interviews. Whilst processing the data, I focused on three specific areas, namely education, employment, and family relationships to assess migrant women's socio-economic status.

Until the late 1960s, rural women were almost excluded from education and according to UNESCO, 92 percent of rural women in Iran were illiterate (Touba, 1980; Moghissi, 1996). There was a consensus among my older informants in stating that there were no schools in their villages. Apart from lack of access to educational services, ideological norms have also played a role in female illiteracy in both rural and urban areas. In urban ones inequalities between different social classes, as well as ideological factors, resulted in a high female illiteracy rate in migrant families. Despite the establishment of a national system in 1918, and promotion of female education by the state during the era of Reza Shah's nation building and modernization, clergy and traditional families strongly criticized the educational policy of the Pahlavi State. This struck a chord with many working class as well as traditional and religious families. The ideological criticisms often exacerbated gender inequalities in traditional families, particularly in terms of female children's access to limited educational opportunities. Ideological factors, particularly those related to honor, seemed to affect girls in migrant families more than their counterparts in traditional and religious urban families. Most often, the migrants do not integrate into mainstream society and thus do not trust it easily and are afraid for the vulnerability of their female members, particularly that of their daughters (Bauer, 1984 and 1985). In most of the migrant families whom I interviewed, the older female children had usually been prevented from receiving education by their families. Some of the informants mentioned the influence of the clergy on their parents' decision, particularly in relation to their fathers. However, many younger sisters of these women who had had their education interrupted were studying at higher levels of schooling without too much parental anxiety concerning loss of honor as a result of education.

By comparing the women who had interrupted education with their younger sisters in migrant families, it can be argued that as duration of residence in the city increases, fear or lack of trust towards the city environment declines. This may partially signify the importance of socio-psychological empowerment achieved by overcoming initial experiences of marginality and insecurity. It can also be argued that the de-secularization of the educational system, regulating female contact with the outside world in terms of the accepted traditional gender ideologies of veil and sex segregation, as a result of the gender policies of the Islamic state, might have had a positive impact on many young girls in migrant working class families. In terms of young women's access to educational opportunities, it seems that the current gender policies have ironically freed and facilitated their attendance at primary and secondary school by creating a sense of security for parents who are concerned about their daughter's morality and modesty. This study clearly indicates that there are working class or religiously orientated people who do not have a problem with modernity and modern education and the social mobility of their daughters, as long as moral issues have been acceptably taken into account. Rather, as Tohidi (1994: 113) stated, the way modernity and modernization policies were introduced during the Pahlavi era and implemented in Iranian society played a significant role in restricting women's access to important necessities of modern life. If earlier traditional and ideological values and beliefs had a stronger preventive role in female literacy in most migrant families, nowadays it is the poverty of the families and their material circumstances that restrict not only young females, but also young males in access to education.

Earlier, almost all female migration in this part of Iran occurred in the family context. Now there is a change in the pattern of female migration, particularly among younger women in their mid-teens or early twenties. They come to the city with a purpose, independently from their families, to be educated, acquire different skills, and take skilled jobs, as a result of which they even postpone marriage. The migration of young single women either to continue education or to seek employment also illustrates an improvement in female education in rural areas. For these young women, education plays an important role in expanding their human capacities as well as their freedom of mobility. Still single, they are being helped by their parents who feel that their daughters' morality is not under threat in an allegedly Islamic context. There is a change of attitude towards independent female migration as level of education increases. However, this change is slow, due to the perception of single women's vulnerability in dealing with the wider and unfamiliar world.

The study also indicated that female literacy has a profound impact on women's age of marriage, their fertility behavior, their relationships with their husbands and in-laws, particularly mothers-in-law, as well as their engagement in different income generating activities. For the majority of illiterate women involvement in the production of goods at home for exchange values or in the informal economy formed part of the survival strategies that many migrant households adopt to cope with the commercialized style of urban life. This involvement, however, does not detract from the role of ideological factors, mainly gender and traditional ideologies such as the sexual division of labor, sex-segregation and the domestication of women, which undermine the valuable contribution women make to the family income. The great burden of the struggle to survive in laboring migrant families falls not only upon male migrants, who have been the focal point of interest in almost all Iranian migratory literature, but also on women. Informal and traditionally segregated sectors of the economy in Tabriz in which female workers have traditionally been concentrated, such as the carpet industry, cleaning jobs, and the domestic sector, absorbed a large proportion of the impoverished female migrants. In most laboring families, women are obliged to work to supplement insufficient male incomes, as the majority of men do not work the entire year and are unemployed at times. The poorer the family, the more crucial the contribution of a woman's earnings to the total income of the family, often through an invisible burden of work. As the analysis showed, older women, particularly the first generation of migrants, were mostly confined to the locality, weaving carpets or spinning wool according to the economic well-being or poverty of the family. Some of these women have participated in literacy classes, but because of the nature of their work and the lack of an immediate use for literacy, the classes had little impact, except in offering an opportunity to socialize with other women.

Impact of the household production system on the living conditions of the women indicate similar problems to those faced by their poor and impoverished counterparts in lace-making industry in Mies's study (1982). In both cases, there is a basic patriarchal structure responsible for the exploitation of women's labor and the invisibility of their work. As unpaid family members, they are not considered to be workers; rather they are seen as housewives who work in their spare time. They do not have access to the market and their exploitation in the family is strong, mainly in terms of money relations, particularly in poorer households. They are less self-confident, and more dependent on male relatives, even their own male offspring, and their work and income remains invisible, both at household and national levels. At the policy level, women's involvement in household industries such as carpet making is not defined as "work" and women are not defined as "workers"; therefore, they are totally deprived of access to social and economic resources, particularly in terms of health insurance, loans, and credit. This lack of access, particularly in the poorer households, exacerbates the plight of women and their children and makes them more vulnerable to external exploitation from those who are engaged in the carpet business, who obtain considerable benefits from women's cheap labor in this industry.

The low rate of female participation in the labor market in oil-centered Muslim countries, including Middle Eastern Arab countries and Iran may be explained by the widespread belief that Islamic ideology is hostile towards working women. But although Iran is an Islamic country in terms of governance, it seems that it is not the Islamic ideology that is the main obstacle for women's involvement in work outside the home. Out of 126 women whom I interviewed, only two illiterate and old women talked about Islam and sin, but their comments were made in the context of women's obedience towards their husbands. No others mentioned anything about Islam prohibiting women's work outside the home. Instead, they mainly talked about traditional ideologies and values that prevented them from having access to paid employment. In response to my question as to whether they searched for a paid job outside the home after migration, many women said "no" and the reason for that was: "it was *ayeb* (dishonorable) for us to work outside the home." Although some women were in favor of a single-sex work environment, their preference was more social than religious.

Apart from traditional ideologies as well as patriarchal practices that sometimes prevent male employers from employing female workers, the supply factor, i.e., women's unwillingness to work outside the home, seems to be another important reason for their low participation rate in the labor force. Most women are not inclined to undertake low status jobs in the labor market, due to their illiteracy or lack of skill, or their womanhood/motherhood responsibilities in the domestic sphere. Some middle aged migrant women, most of whom had very little education, managed to work outside the home in the lowest sectors of the informal economy, but did so out of necessity, as they were from very poor families, and were often widows who had to fend for themselves and their children. Although they found a space outside the home to work, they also experienced great exploitation as well as class and gender polarization in their workplace, often perpetuated by their male employers. However, since these women earn money and engage with the outside world, they do receive some benefits from their low status jobs, have more self-confidence and play a greater role in household decisions. Their work is more visible and more valued by their families, as it brings in cash. These women strongly encourage their daughters to study so that they can work in improved conditions and not experience their mother's circumstances.

It seems that the state's gender policies emphasizing family values and gender relations within the society have been more beneficial to younger women. Although women's work outside the home still carries a social stigma among the majority of migrant families, there is a change of attitude towards women's education and their work in the labor market. As a result of the gender policies of the Islamic state, which has re-articulated gender codes and definitions in terms of women's behavior and appearance compatible with the traditional culture of many working class families, women's involvement outside the home is not considered as something that would necessarily lead to disgrace or dishonor. These policies have removed some obstacles in terms of social values and brought changes in the attitudes of families towards the role of women in society, particularly that of young and educated women. Otherwise they would have faced the disapproval of their families in their interaction with the wider society and opposite sex.

Greater access to higher levels of schooling increases women's chances of getting employment outside the home, or running their own business. As the level of women's education increases, women become more aware of their social rights and become active participants in the process of social change. This is obvious from the cross-generational comparison of migrant women in this study. Education clearly increases younger women's aspirations, and they bypass the early stages of unfamiliarity with the city which their mothers experienced, and assimilate easily into urban living conditions. In terms of marriage they marry men with less age difference, play an important role in choosing their partner, often prefer to have a nuclear family, are better able to manage family relationships to their own benefit, and are less subordinate to the senior women of their families compared with their illiterate sisters.

Younger literate women mostly resisted learning the professional skill of carpet weaving and showed interest in learning modern and new skills, which would give them greater freedom of mobility, self-esteem and control over their labor and income. The service sector and the demands of the modern economic sector along with access to educational opportunities, have increased women's employment opportunities. Some of these young women who are single and do not have family responsibilities work for many years in the paid labor market. They save money either to set up their own small business after marriage or to some extent finance the setting up of their married life, while in rural areas or among those who do not work, this is the sole responsibility of the parents. The investment ability of young women gives them negotiating power as well as prestige in the family.

The social changes seem to have accelerated female migration too. This is particularly so for young women whose independent migration is facilitated by social networks in the city based on kinship ties. Their successful migration encourages their peers, younger sisters and relatives to join them. Single women's success working in the Anata Chocolate Factory, or those who came to the city to be educated, are good examples of the new developments in female independent migration for employment and education. They emphasized that their independent migration promoted their autonomy and their central role in the decision-making processes in their own and their families' lives, which in the past were rarely shared with them. They were proud of their jobs or education and postponed their marriage for that reason, though the number of these women was limited in my study. Unlike their counterparts in many rapidly developing countries (particularly East and Southeast Asia) for whom there is a strong demand for labor, particularly in the export-oriented manufacturing sector, there is little such demand for female labor in the city of Tabriz that could encourage the development of female independent migration from rural areas.

On the part of women, these changes, particularly the opportunity to gain paid employment, raises their gender consciousness and their experiences are important in bringing about social change and encouraging other women with whom they have close connections. They might earn less in paid employment than they could contribute to the family income in the carpet industry, but paid work is very important as they have choice and exercise more control over their own resources and enjoy more freedom of mobility. They often use different strategies to challenge traditional gender roles and family authority and negotiate with their families, most of the time through their conformity to some gender ideologies, for their own benefit; Poya (1999) also refers to such conformity on the part of young women. Some gender ideologies applicable to older women become less pronounced for young single women. There are even changes in some younger women's dress pattern in some migrant families, from *chador,* the traditional form of women's dress, to *manto-shalvar,* the officially accepted middle class women's clothing since 1981.

Migration and the urbanization process in Tabriz have benefited younger women and the second generation of migrants more than the older women. Yet new forms of inequalities are created for them in the wider society, particularly in the labor market. While younger women have better mobility, vision and desires, they face some major problems with labor market participation or self-employment as gender relations have been regulated on a patriarchal framework that demands women's subordination to men not only within the family, but also within wider society. They are affected by demand factors, such as limited employment options for women and also a limited market for women's labor; by job conditions, such as low wages and the lack of long term security, as employment is often based on temporary contracts; and the inflexibility of employment for married women, particularly in the informal sector of the economy, such as the lack of part-time jobs as well as the unwillingness of employers to employ married women. Although state employment and the formal sector offer some employment benefits to female employees, the privatization process in some sectors of the economy and also lack of sufficient qualifications or skills prevents many women from gaining access to better paid jobs in middle-level positions with good conditions.

Although the patriarchal structure is responsible for the exploitation of women's labor, it is consolidated by Islamic ideology and practices.

The discriminatory and gendered practices towards women's paid employment, particularly in the informal sector, give women no choice but to leave employment after marriage, which makes them economically dependent on their husbands. However, most of them do not wish to be totally dependent on the financial support of their husbands, and try to save their earnings to buy essential machinery or equipment to run their own small business after marriage. Many younger women stated that they would leave their job as soon as they got married, as their work outside the home would not be compatible with the requirements of married life. They face low rewards in their jobs, and do not see themselves as the main breadwinner of the family, due to their tacit approval of the gendered ideological definitions of women as wives and mothers, and men as breadwinners, but now desire the context of a more egalitarian relationship.

To sum up, the findings of this study indicate that rural-urban migration has had different impacts on migrant women in Tabriz in terms of their age, marital status, education, the duration of the migration and other socio-economic factors. Migration has been more beneficial for younger women as well as the second generation of older women. The life experiences of different categories of migrant women suggest that migration and urbanization can only be beneficial to women if they facilitate and increase their upward socio-economic mobility. For many older poor women, due to class and gender inequalities as well as traditional gender ideologies, migration did not improve their economic and social situation. They remained the poorest of the poor, particularly those who did not benefit from the support of a male member of the family. However, socio-political transformation has brought some sense of security and potential opportunities for younger women, who are resourceful in responding to socio-economic as well as socio-political changes within the social and cultural context. As active agents, they adjust to the available opportunities and negotiate and challenge the cultural constraints to promote their interests in the family and society. Although there is a long way to go for many young migrant women, they have started their journey towards liberation.

Appendix 1

Questionnaire

No:

Location (*Mahalleh*):

Area:

Respondent's name:

A. Background Questions

Please circle the right answer.

1. How old are you?

    a) Less than 20 years old   b) 20-34
    c) 35-50   d) 51-65   e) More than 65

2. What is your marital status now?

    a) Single   b) Married
    c) Divorced   d) Widowed   e) Deserted

3. How many children have you got?

    Boys ------   Girls -----

4. Please specify the gender, age, educational level, and occupation of all the members of the household, including their relation to you.

No.	Relationship to Respondent	Sex	Age	Education	Occupation

5. How old were you when you moved to Tabriz?

a) Less than 10 years old b) 10-19 c) 20-29
d) 30-39 e) 40-49 f) More than 50

6. When you moved to Tabriz were you:

a) Single b) Married
c) Divorced d) Widowed e) Deserted

7. What is your current educational level?

a) Illiterate b) Primary Education
c) Secondary Education d) More than Secondary Education
e) Informal Education

8. Where were you educated?

a) In the village at my school age
b) In the village in my adulthood
c) In the city at my school age
d) In the city in my adulthood

B. Household Information

9. Is your home:

a) Owned b) Rented
c) Other --------------- (please specify)

10. Is your home a:

a) House b) Flat
How many rooms do you have? ------

11. What amenities are available in your home?

a) Kitchen b) Bath c) Gas main
d) Electricity e) Telephone line f) Piped water
g) Sewage

12. Is the location of your home .... *(Please tick)*

a) Close to shops Yes ----- No -----
b) Close to my workplace Yes ----- No -----
c) Near to bus stop Yes ----- No -----

13. Please rank the level of your satisfaction in terms of access to the following services:

Access/ Proximity to	**Level of satisfaction of respondents**				
	Very Low	Low	Fair	High	Very High
Schools					
Workplace					
Health centre					
Doctor					
Pharmacy					
Transport					
Main road					
Mosque					
Shopping Centre					

14. What electronic household appliances and other luxury items do you own in your home:

a) Gas cooker	b) Fridge	c) Freezer
d) Fan	e) Sofa	f) Rug
g) Television	h) Radio	i) Computer
j) Sewing machine	k) Knitting machine	l) Satellite TV
m) Vacuum cleaner	n) Video-recorder	
o) Washing machine	p) Heater (*Bokhari)*	

C. Questions on Migration and Related Issues

15. Which village did you come from? (The name of the village and the region)

16. With whom did you come to the city?

a) With my parents b) With my husband
c) With my children d) Alone
e) Other --------------- (Please specify)

17. Did you come straight to Tabriz?

a)Yes b) No

If your answer is no, please specify the right answer.

a) First to another village, then to Tabriz.
b) First to another city, then to Tabriz
c) Other --------------- (Please specify)

18. Who in your family first came to the city?

a) My father b) My Mother c) My brother
d) My husband e) My son f) My daughter
g) Myself h) Others --------------- (specify)

19. Did you want to leave your village?

a) Yes (Please give a reason)

b) No (Please give a reason)

20. Why did you decide to leave your village? (*Rank them according to their importance to you: Rank the most important one 1, and the next 2 and so forth*).

Because my family was leaving the village --------
Insufficient or poor land to cultivate --------
Lack of agricultural land and facilities to work on land --------
Unfavorable land for agriculture in the village --------
Marriage --------
Loss of family breadwinner --------
Access to better employment and higher income in the city --------
Lack of educational services for children in the village --------
Lack of health service in the village --------
Lack of rural employment for women --------
Escape from family authority and rural hegemony --------
Other -------------- (Please specify)

21. Who helped you in the process of your migration?

a) Family b) Friends c) Future employer
d) People from my village e) Potential employer
f) Nobody

22. Why did you choose this part of the city? (*Please rank*)

Because of cheap housing/land to build on --------
Proximity to my migrated relatives --------
Proximity to friend and fellow countrymen --------
Proximity to my village --------
Other ------------- (Please specify)

23. Did you initially decide to migrate to Tabriz permanently or temporarily?

a) Permanently b) Temporarily c) Did not know

D. Questions on Economic Activities after Migration

24. How long did it take for you to find an urban job?

a) Immediately after migration
b) Between 1-2 years
c) Between 3-4 years
d) Did not find any job

25. Specify the type of your first job in Tabriz after your migration.

a) Unpaid work at home in a family business
b) Paid home-based work
c) Working outside the home as a self employed
d) Working outside the home as domestic worker
e) Working outside the home in a factory
f) Working outside the home
g) Other places

26. What is your current job?

27. Who does/did look after your children while you were/are at work?

28. Who is contributing to the family income in your household?

Contributors	Type of work	Income	Does it meet your basic needs

29. What types of problems do you face in Tabriz?

30. Would you include any other questions which you think we should have included?

31. Would you like to be interviewed?

a) Yes b) No

If you would like to be interviewed, what time of the day will be convenient for you?

a) In the morning, when I am alone b) Afternoon, after work
c) Anytime of the day

Thank you very much for your co-operation.

Appendix 2

Interview Questions

No:

Date:

Time:

Respondent's name:

Address:

1. From where did you receive your education?

   a) Through Literacy Corps (*Sepah-e-Danesh)*
   b) Formal Education
   c) Literacy Campaign (*Nehzat-e savad amouzi)*
   d*)* Others -------------- (Please specify)

2. Is/was your mother literate?

   a) Yes b) No

3. How old were you when you got married?

   a) Less than 12 years old b) Between 12 and 15
   c) Between 16 and 18 d) 19 or above

4. How many children do you have and how many of them were born in the village?

5. Did they go to school in the village?

a) Yes (Specify the kind of school) -------------

b) No (Specify the reason) -------------

6. Did/do they go to school in the city?

a) Yes (Specify the kind of school) -------------

b) No (Specify the reason) -------------

7. How were your living conditions in the village?

8. What did your family possess as a means of production?

9. What was your husband's job in the village and what was his first job in the city?

10. What was your father's job in the village and his first job in the city?

11. What was your mother's job in the village and her first job in the city?

12. What was your role in the decision making process of migration?

13. Did you think you would get a job in the city?

14. Apart from housework, what sort of work did you do in the village?

15. Were you paid for your work? *(If yes, how?)*

a) Yes, in cash b) Yes, in kind
c) No ------------- (Give a reason)

16. Did you have a means of paid work before marriage, after marriage, or both?

17. Were you paid directly by your employer or would your wage be received by someone else? If so, who received it?

18. Why did you choose this part of the city?

19. Were living expenses more expensive in the village or in the city?

20. Do you prefer to live in the city or in the village?

21. How often do you visit your village, and for what purposes?

22. Would you like to return back to your village and live there permanently? Why?

23. Are you satisfied with your migration?

24. What did you do following your migration to Tabriz?

25. Were you happy with your job?

26. Was there anything about work which you did not like?

27. What made you quit working at your first job in the city, if you are now working in a different place to your first job in the city?

28. What are you doing currently?

29. Why did you choose your current job?

30. How did you get information about it?

31. Were/are your husband or your male relatives against your working in income generating activities?

32. For those who do not have a job, can you please state why you did not get a job after you moved to the city?

33. Whom do you consider as the head of your family?

34. Who is responsible for your maintenance?

35. Would you like to work for money? *(Give your reason)*

36. What are your responsibilities at home?

37. Apart from housework, what do you do usually?

38. How do you spend your spare time?

39. Is it common for women to have paid work in your location?

40. What sort of jobs usually involve paid work?

41. What are your main problems as a woman?

42. Would you include any additional questions which you think we should have included in this questionnaire?

Thank you for your time and your responses.

Glossary

Abero	Honor, credit
Aib/Ayeb	Shameful, immodest
Amou-zesh yaran	Teachers in adult literacy
Aqd	Contract. Most commonly a marriage contract
As kar oftadeh	Disabled
Azza'dari	Mourning
Batman	A unit equivalent to five kilograms
Belaava	Living in parents' or in-laws' house without paying any rent
Bisavad	Illiterate
Boneh	Traditional group farming system
Bonyad-e Shahid	Martyr Foundation
Chador	Traditional Iranian veiling covering from head to toe
Dabirestan	High school
Dami	A kitchen utensil
Danesh- ghah-e Azad-e Eslami	Open Islamic University
Defa-e moghaddas	Holy Defence
Ebtedaei	Primary level of schooling
Eid	New Year day or any special religious celebrating days
Eidi	New Year gift, or gift given on any special religious days
Faaliyyatha-ye Egtesadi	Economic activities
Farsh	Carpet
Gara	Black
Ghirat	Honor

Hadith	Narration attributed to the Prophet and his successors
Haram	Sin
Hejab	Veiling
Hejab-e Islami	Islamic veiling
Irandokht	Daughter of Iran
Jahad	The holy struggle
Jahad-e Sazandegi	The holy struggle for construction
Jahaz	Dowry, trousers that a bride takes to her marital household
Jahra	Wooden spinning wheel
Jang-e tahmili	Imposed War
Jins farsh	Finely woven carpet
Kadkhoda	Headman in a village
Kala	Commodity
Kanareh	Side carpet
Kanoun	Society/club
Kanoun-e parvareshi-e kudakan va nojavanan	Society for contemplative training of children and youth
Katdi	A villager
Kat-farshi	Village carpet. Referred to as low quality carpet
Khane-dar	Housewife
Khanoum	Lady
Khwushneshin	Landless peasant
Komiteye-emddad	Relief and aid committee
Konkour	University entrance exam
Madrase	Traditional and religious schools
Mag'na'eh	Scarf sewn to keep shut under the chin, which covers hair and the chest
Mahryyeh	A financial obligation of a husband to his wife, which has been agreed during the marriage contract, and is due when the marriage is consummated
Mahryyeh/mehr	Bride price
Majles	Parliament
Maktab	Traditional and religious schools
Man'to	Long loose dress down to the knees or ankles
Man'to –shalvar	An alternative veiling to *chador*, adopted by the Islamic state after the revolution
Moghaddamati	Elementary

Moharram and *Safar*	Two consecutive Arabic lunar months
Mullah	Clergy
Nafaqeh	The full financial support of a Muslim man towards his wife's living and other relevant costs
Namous	Honor
Nehzat	Campaign
Nehzat-e savad-amouzi	Literacy Campaign
Ojrat-ol mesl	A wage equivalent to the household labor performed by a married woman during her married life, which is not covered by *nafaqeh* and *mahryyeh*.
Ostan	Province
Payam-e Hajar	Hajar's message
Pish daneshgahi	Pre-university course
Purdah	A practice of preventing women from being seen by men or excluding from society
Rahnamaei	Secondary level of education
Rahni	Lease
Raj	The number of knots tied in each inch
Ramadan	Fasting month for Muslims
Rial	Iranian monetary unit
Sahab	Owner or master
Sahabim	My owner or my master
Savad amouzan	Pupils, often referred to as adult learners
Savad-amouz-e lazem-ottaleam	Indispensable to teach
Savad-e khandan va neveshtan	Basic reading skills
Shahrestan	Smaller administrative division of a province
Shalvar	Trouser
Sharaf	Honor
Sharia	Islamic law
Shi'a	A sect among Muslims
Shogl	Paid employment undertaken outside the home
Tableau	Portrait
Taghout	Satan
Takmili	Supplementary
Toman(s)	one *Toman* is equivalent with 10 *Rials*
Ulama	Religious scholars
Varny	A very simple type of *kilim*

Zan	Woman
Zanan	Women
Zar-nim	Finely woven carpet in smaller size

Bibliography

Abdel Taher, Nadia. 1987. Social Identity and Class in a Cairo Neighborhood. *Cairo Papers in Social Science* 9, vol. 4 (winter).

Abu-Lughod, Lila. 1988. Fieldwork of a Dutiful Daughter. In *Arab Women in the Field: Studying your own Society*. Edited by S. Altorki and C. El-Solh. New York: Syracuse University.

——. 1993. *Writing Women's Worlds: Bedouin Stories*. Berkeley, Los Angeles and Oxford: University of California.

Afkhami, Mahnaz. 1994. Women in Post-Revolutionary Iran: A Feminist Perspective. In *In the Eye of the Storm: Women in Post-Revolutionary Iran*. Edited by M. Afkhami and E. Friedl. London and New York: I. B. Tauris.

Afshar, Haleh. 1982. Khomeini's Teachings and their Implication for Women. In *In the Shadow of Islam: The Women's Movement in Iran*. Edited by A. Tabari and N. Yeganeh. London: Zed. And *Feminist Review* 12, vol. 3: 59-73.

——. 1985a. An Assessment of Agricultural Development Policies in Iran. In *Iran: A Revolution in Turmoil*. Edited by H. Afshar. London: Macmillan.

——. 1985b. The Position of Women in an Iranian Village. In *Women, Work, and Ideology in the Third World*. Edited by H. Afshar. London and New York: Tavistock.

——. 1987. Women, Marriage and the State in Iran. In *Women, State and Ideology: Studies from Africa and Asia*. Edited by H. Afshar. London: Macmillan.

——. and Agarwal, B. 1989. Introduction. In *Women, Poverty and Ideology in Asia*. Edited by H. Afshar and B. Agarwal. London: Macmillan.

——. 1989a. Women in the Work and Poverty Trap in Iran. In *Women, Poverty and Ideology in Asia*. Edited by H. Afshar and B. Agarwal. London: Macmillan.

——. 1989b. Gender Roles and the "Moral Economy of Kin" among Pakistani Women in West Yorkshire. *New Community* 15, vol. 2: 211-225.

——. 1989c. Women and Reproduction in Iran. In *Women, Nation, State*. Edited by N. Yuval-Davis and F. Anthias. London: Macmillan.

——. 1989d. Education: Hopes, Expectations and Achievements of Muslim Women in West Yorkshire. *Gender and Education* 1, vol. 3: 261-272.

—— and Dennis. 1992. Introduction. In *Women and Adjustment Policies*. Edited by Afshar and C. Dennis. London: Macmillan.

——. 1994. Why Fundamentalism? Iranian Women and Their Support for Islam. The University of York: *York Working Papers in Politics*, no. 2.

——. 1997. Women and Work in Iran. *Political Studies* 45, vol. 4: 755-767.

——. 1999. *Islam and Feminism*. London: Macmillan.

Afsar, R. 2003. Dynamics of poverty, development and population mobility: The Bangladesh case. *Economic and Social Commission for Asia and The Pacific*. Expert Group Meeting on Migration and Development. 27-29 August 2003. Bangkok

Agarwal, Bina. 1989. Women, Land and Ideology in India. In *Women, Poverty and Ideology in Asia*. Edited by H. Afshar and B. Agarwal. London: Macmillan.

Aghajanian, Akbar. 1994. The Status of Women and Female Children in Iran: An Update from the 1986 Census. In *In the Eye of the Storm: Women in Post-revolutionary Iran*. Edited by M. Afkhami and E. Friedl. London and New York: I.B.Tauris.

Ajami, Amir Ismail. 1976. Land Reform and Modernization of the Farming Structure in Iran. In *The Social Sciences and Problems of Development*. Edited by K. Farmanfarmaian. New Jersey: Princeton.

——. 1995. The *Boneh* System In Iran's Rural Society. *Iran Nameh* 13, vol. 4: Special Issues on Civil Society in Iran. Published by the Foundation for Iranian Studies.

——. 2005. From Peasant to Farmer: A Study of Agrarian Transformation in an Iranian Village, 1967-2002. *International Journal of Middle East Studies* 37: 327-349.

Akhavi, Shahrough. 1986. State Formation and Consolidation in Twentieth-Century Iran: The Reza Shah Period and the Islamic Republic. In *The State, Religion, and Ethnic Policies: Afghanistan, Iran and Pakistan*. Edited by A. Banuazizi and M. Weiner. New York: Syracuse University.

Al-Khayyat, Sana. 1990. *Honour and Shame: Women in Modern Iraq*. London: Saqi Books.

Altorki, Soraya. 1988. At Home in the Field. In *Arab Women in the Field: Studying your own Society*. Edited by S. Altorki and C. El-Solh. New York: Syracuse University.

——. and El-Solh, C. F. 1988. Introduction. In *Arab Women in the Field: Studying your own Society*. Edited by S. Altorki and C. El-Solh. New York: Syracuse University.

Amin, Sajeda. 1997. The Poverty-Purdah Trap in Rural Bangladesh. *Development and Change* 28, vol. 2: 213-233.

Amirahmadi, Hooshang and Kiafar, Ali. 1993. The Transformation of Tehran from a Garrison Town to a Primate City: A Tale of Rapid Growth and Uneven Development. In *Urban Development in the Muslim World*. Edited by H. Amirahmadi and A. Kiafar. New Brunswick: Centre for Urban Policy Research.

Amuzegar, Jahangir, and Fekrat, M. A. 1971. *Iran: Economic Development under Dualistic Conditions*. Chicago: The University of Chicago.

Amuzgar, Jahangir. 2004. Iran's Unemployment Crises. *Middle East Economic Survey* XXVII, vol. 41. Available on: http://www.mees.com/postedarticles/oped/a47n41d01.htm.

Anderson, Bridget. 2000. *Doing the Dirty Work?: The Global Politics of Domestic Labor*. London and New York: Zed.

Bacha, E. L. 1995. Industrialization and Agricultural Development. In *Leading Issues in Economic Development*. Edited by G. M. Meier. 6th ed. New York and Oxford: Oxford University.

Bahramitash, Roksana. 2004. Myths and Realities of the Impact of Political Islam on Women: Female Employment in Iran and Indonesia. *Development in Practice*, Vol. 14. No 4.

Bakker, Isabella. 1988. Women's Employment in Comparative Perspective. In *Feminization of the Labor Force: Paradoxes and Promises.* Edited by J. Jenson, E. Hagen and C. Reddy. Cambridge: Polity.
——. (ed.) 1994. *The Strategic Silence: Gender and Economic Policy.* London: Zed.
Banerjee, A.V., and Newman, A. F. 1998. Information, the Dual Economy, and Development. *Review of Economic Studies* 65, vol. 3: 631-653.
Bauer, Janet. 1984. New Models and Traditional Networks: Migrant Women in Tehran. In *Women in the Cities of Asia: Migration and Urban Adaptation.* Edited by J. T. Fawcett, S. E. Khoo and P. C. Smith. Boulder and Colorado: Westview.
——. 1985. Demographic Change, Women and the Family in a Migrant Neighborhood of Tehran. In *Women and the Family in Iran.* Edited by A. Fathi. Leiden (Netherlands): E.J. Brill.
Bayat, Asef. 1997. *Street Politics: Poor People's Movements in Iran.* New York: Columbia University.
Beck, Lois. 1978. Women among Qashqa'i Nomadic Pastoralists in Iran. In *Women in the Muslim World.* Edited by L. Beck and N. R. Keddie. Cambridge, Massachusetts and London: Harvard University Press.
Beechey, Veronica. 1977. Some Notes on Female Wage Labor in Capitalist Production. *Capital and Class* 1, vol. 3: 44-66.
Bennholdt-Thomsen, Veronika. 1984. Subsistence Production and Extended Reproduction. In *Of Marriage and the Market: Women's Subordination Internationally and its Lessons.* Edited by K. Yong, C. Wolkowitz and R. McCullagh. 2nd ed. London and Boston: Routledge and Kegan Paul.
Bienen, Henry S. 1984. Urbanization and Third World Industry. *World Development* 12, vol. 7: 661-691.
——. 1985. *Political Conflict and Economic Change in Nigeria.* London: Frank Cass.
Black, Richard. 2004. *Migration and pro-poor policy in West Africa.* Sussex Centre for Migration. Research, University of Sussex, Brighton.
Blumberg, Rae Lesser. 1995. Introduction: Engendering Wealth and Well-Being in an Era of Economic Transformation. In *Engendering Wealth and Well-Being: Empowerment for Global Change.* Edited by R. L. Blumberg and *et al.* Boulder and Colorado: Westview.
Boserup, Ester. 1970. *Women's Role in Economic Development.* London: Aberdeen University Press.
Brigg, Pamela H. 1971. Migration to Urban Areas. International Bank for Reconstruction and Development Association: *Economic Staff Working Papers*, no.107.
Bromley, Ray, and Gerry, Chris. 1979. Who Are the Casual Poor. In *Casual Work and Poverty in Third World Cities.* Edited by R. Bromley and C. Gerry. New York: John Wiley and Sons.
Brouwer, Lenie, and Priester, Marijke. 1983. Living in Between: Turkish Women in Their Homeland and in the Netherlands. In *One Way Ticket: Migration and Female Labor.* Edited by A. Phizacklea. London, Boston and Melbourne: Routledge & Kegan Paul.
Bryceson, D. F. 1985. Women's Proletarianization and the Family Wage in Tanzania. In *Women, Work, and Ideology in the Third World.* Edited by H. Afshar. London and New York: Tavistock.
Brydon, Lynne. 1989. Gender and Migration. In *Women in the Third World: Gender issues in Rural and Urban Areas.* Edited by L. Brydon and S. Chant. Aldershot:

Edward Elgar.
——. 1982. Summery of Educatio. Occupations and Migration from Avatime,Ghana: 1880-1980. In W.T.S Gould, Education and Internal Migration: A Review and a Report. *International Journal of Educational Development* 1(3):103-27
——. 1985. The Avatime Family and Migration, 1900-1977. In M. Prothero and M. Chapman (eds) *Circulation in Third World Countries*. London: Routledge & Kegan Paul.
Buijs, Gina. 1993. Introduction. In *Migrant Women: Crossing Boundaries*. Edited by G. Buijs. Oxford: BERG.
Byerlee, Derek. 1974. Rural-Urban Migration in Africa: Theory, Policy and Research Implication. *International Migration Review* 8, vol. 4: 543-566.
Campani, G. 1995. Women Migrants: From Marginal Subjects to Social Actors. In *The Cambridge Survey of World Migration*. Edited by R. Cohen. Cambridge: Cambridge University.
Changizi, Mehrangiz. 1993. *Barraasi-e Tahavvolat-e Eshteghal-e Zanan dar Do Bakhsh-e San'at va Khadamat bar Asas-e Dadehaye Sarshomari-e 1355-1365* (The Analysis of Changes in Women's Occupation in Two Sectors of Industry and Service According to Data from 1976 and 1986 Censes). In *Majmoueye Maghalat: Siminar –e "Barrasi-e Masael-e Jamieyati-e Iran"* (A Collection of Papers Presented in the Seminar of "The Analysis of Demographic Issues in Iran"). Shiraz: Markaz-e Jamieyat-shenasi-e Shiraz (Shiraz Centre for Demegraphic Studies).
——. 1996. *Mosh-kelat-e Eshteg hal-e Zanan dar Iran va Taj-zieh-e Ta-avoni-e Zanan-e Chini dar Afarinesh-e Eshtegal*. (The problems of women's employment in Iran and the analysis of Chinese women's cooperative in creating employment). In *Ta-avon, Zan, Eshte-qal: Maj-mouaye Maqalat ve Amal-kard* (Cooperative, Women, Employment: A Collection of Papers and Function).
Chant, Sylvia. 1989. Gender and Urban Households. In *Women in the Third World: Gender Issues in Rural and Urban Areas*. Edited by L. Brydon and S. Chant. Aldershot: Edward Elgar.
——, and Radcliffe, S. 1992. Migration and Development: The Importance of Gender. In *Gender and Migration in Developing Countries*. Edited by S. Chant. London and N.Y.: Bellview.
——. 1997. *Women-Headed Households: Diversity and Dynamics in the Developing World*. London: Macmillan.
Cho, Hae-Joang. 1989. Internal Colonization and the Fate of Female Divers in Cheju Island, South Korea. In *Women, Poverty and Ideology in Asia*. Edited by H. Afshar and B. Agarwal. London: Macmillan.
Clark, M. H. 1983. Variations on Themes of Male and Female: Reflections on Gender Bias in Fieldwork in Rural Greece. In N. Scheper-Hughes (ed.) *Confronting problems of bias in feminist anthropology. Women's Studies* series 10(1): 116-33 (special issue).
Cohen, Robin. 1996. Introduction. In *Theories of Migration: The International Library of Studies on Migration*. Edited by R. Cohen. Cheltenham: Edward Elgar: 14-24.
Craig, Daniel. 1978. The Impact of Land Reform on an Iranian Village. *The Middle East Journal* 32 (Spring): 141-155.
Custers, Peter. 1997. *Capital Accumulation and Women's Labor in Asian Economies*. London and New York: Zed.
Danesh, Abol Hassan. 1987. *Rural Exodus and Squatter Settlements in the Third*

World: Case of Iran. Lanham, New York, and London: University Press of America.

Daniel, Elton L., and Mahdi, Ali Akbar. 2006. "The History of Persian Carpet Weaving in Iran." In *Culture and Customs of Iran*. Edited by Elton L. Daniel and Ali Akbar Mahdi. Dublin, Ohio: Greenwood Publishing Group: 137-148.

Davin, Delia. 1996. Chinese Women and the Politics of Reform. In *Women and Politics in the Third World*. Edited by H. Afshar. London and New York: Routledge.

——. 1998. Gender and Rural-Urban Migration in China. In *Women and Empowerment: Illustrations from the Third World*. Edited by H. Afshar. London: Macmillan.

——. 1999. *Internal Migration in Contemporary China*. New York: Palgrave Macmillan.

De Groot, Joanna, and Maynard, Mary. 1993. Doing Things Differently?: A Context for Women's Studies in the Next Decade." In *Women's Studies in the 1990s: Doing Things Differently?* Edited by J. De Groot and M. Maynard. London: Macmillan.

Denzin, Norman K. 1978. *The Research Act: A Theoretical Introduction to Sociological Methods*. 2nd ed. New York: McGraw-Hill.

Dixon, Ruth B. 1978. *Rural Women at Work: Strategies for Development in South Asia*. Baltimore and London: The Johns Hopkins University.

Dixon-Mueller, Ruth. 1991. Women in Agriculture: Counting the Labor Force in Developing Countries. In *Beyond Methodology: Feminist Scholarship as Lived Research*. Edited by Mary Margaret Fonow and Judith A. Cook. Bloomington: Indiana University Press.

Ecevit, Yildiz. 1991. Shop Floor Control: The Ideological Construction of Turkish Women Factory Workers. In *Working Women: International Perspectives on Labor and Gender Ideology*. Edited by N. Redclift and M. T. Sinclair. London and New York: Routledge.

El Guindi, Fadwa. 1981. Veiling *Infitiah* with Muslim Ethic: Egypt's Contemporary Islamic Movement. *Social Problems* 28, vol. 4: 465-486.

Elmhirst, Rebecca. 1998a. Daughters and Displacement: Migration Dynamics in an Indonesian Transmigration Area. *Poverty Research Unit*. University of Sussex: Workshop on "Migration and Sustainable Livelihoods": 5-6 June.

——. 1998b. Gender, Culture and Space: Political Geography of Factory Labor in Indonesia. *Euroseas*. Hamburg: Conference on "Changing Labor Relations in Southeast Asia": 3-6 September.

Elshtain, Jean Bethke. 1981. Feminism's Search for Politics. In *Public Man, Private Woman: Women in Social and Political Thought*. Edited by J. B. Elshtain. Oxford: Martin Robertson.

El-Solh, Camillia Fawzi. 1988. Gender, Class, and Origin: Aspects of Role during Fieldwork in Arab Society. In *Arab Women in the Field: Studying your own Society*. Edited by S. Altorki and C. El-Solh. New York: Syracuse University.

Elson, D. 1991. *Male Bias in the Development Process*. Manchester: Manchester University.

Etemad Moghadam, Fatemeh. 1994. Commoditization of Sexuality and Female Labor Participation in Islam: Implications for Iran, 1960-90. In *In the Eye of the Storm: Women in Post-Revolutionary Iran*. Edited by M. Afkhami and E. Friedl. London and New York: I. B. Tauris.

——. 2001. Iran's New Islamic Home Economics: An Exploratory Attempt to Conceptualize Women's Work in the Islamic Republic. In *The Economics of Women's Work in the Middle East and North Africa: Research in Middle East Economics*.

Edited by E. M. Cinar. Vol. 4. Amsterdam: Elsevier Science B.V.

Farsakh, Leila. 1999. North African Labor Flows and the Euro-Med Partnership. Paris: Conference on "Europe and the South in the 21st Century: Challenges for Renewed Co-operation."

Fawcett, James T., Khoo, Siew-Ean and Smith, Peter C. 1984. Urbanization, Migration and the Status of Women. In *Women in the Cities of Asia: Migration and Urban Adaptation.* Edited by J. T. Fawcett, S. E. Khoo and P. C. Smith. Boulder and Colorado: Westview.

Feldman, Shelley. 1983. *Purdah* and Changing Pattern of Social Control among Rural Women in Bangladesh. *Journal of Marriage and the Family* 45, vol. 4: 949-60.

Fisher, Michael M.J. 1978. On Changing the Concept and Position of Persian Women. In *Women in the Muslim World.* Edited by L. Beck and N. R. Keddie. Cambridge, Massachusetts, and London: Harvard University Press.

Frankfort-Nachmias, Chava and Nachmias, David. 1996. *Research Methods in Social Sciences*. 5th ed. London: Arnold.

Franks, Myfanwy Carmel. 2001. *Women and Revivalism in the West: Choosing "Fundamentalism" in a Liberal Democracy.* Basingstoke: Palgrave.

Friedl, Erika. 1981. Women and the Division of Labor in an Iranian Village. *Merip Reports: Middle East Research and Information Projects*, no. 95 (March-April): 12-18.

Gallup, John Luke. 1997. Theories of Migration. Harvard Institution for International Development: *Harvard Development Discussion Papers*, no. 569.

Ghavamshahidi, Zohreh. 1996. *Bibi Khanum*: Carpet Weavers and Gender Ideology in Iran. In *Homeworkers in Global Perspective: Invisible No More.* Edited by E. Boris and E. Prugl. New York and London: Routledge.

Glucksmann, Miriam. 1994. The Work of Knowledge and the Knowledge of Women's Work. In *Researching Women's Lives from a Feminist Perspective.* Edited by M. Maynard and J. Purvis. London: Taylor and Francis.

Godazgar, Hossein. 2008. *The Impact of Religious Factors on Educational Change in Iran: Islam in Policy and Islam in Practice.* New York, Ontario, Lampeter: The Edwin Mellen Press.

Goldschmidt-Clermont, Luisella. 1982. *Unpaid Work in the Household: A Review of Economic Evaluation Methods.* Geneva, I.L.O.: Women, Work and Development Series, no.1.

——. 1987. *Economic evaluation of unpaid household work: Africa, Asia, Latin America and Oceania.* Geneva, I.L.O.: Women, Work and Development Series, no.1.

Graham, Hilary. 1983. Do Her Answers Fit His Questions? Women and the Survey Method. In *The Public and the Private.* Edited by E. Gamarnikow and *et al.* Aldershot: Gower.

GRCTU (*Markaz-e Pa-suouhesh-hi-ae Gog-raphi-ae Danesh-gah-eh Tabriz*) [Geographical Research Centre of Tabriz University]. 1374/1995. *Bar-rasi va Shenakht-eh Asarat-eh Tose-eh bar Mohit-eh Zist-eh Shahrestan-hi-ae Tabriz va Shabestar* (the Investigation and Acknowledgment of Development Impacts on Ecological Environment of Tabriz and Shabestar *Shahrestans*). Tabriz: Tabriz University Press.

Haghayeghi, Mehrdad. 1990. Agrarian Reform Problems in Post-revolutionary Iran. *Middle Eastern Studies* 26, vol. 1: 35-51.

Hakimian, Hassan. 1990. *Labor Transfer and Economic Development: Theoretical*

Perspectives and Case Studies from Iran. Hertfordshire: Harvester Wheatsheaf.

Hancock, Mary. 1983. Transitional Production and Women Workers. In *One Way Ticket: Migration and Female Labor*. Edited by A. Phizacklea. London, Boston and Melbourne: Routledge & Kegan Paul.

Harding, Sandra. 1983. Why Has the Sex/Gender System Become Visible Only Now. In *Discovering Reality: Feminist Perspectives on Epistemology, Metaphysics, Methodology, and Philosophy of Science*. Edited by S. Harding and M. B. Hintikka. Boston and London: D. Reidel.

——. 1986. From the Women Question in Science to the Science Question in Feminism. In *The Science Question in Feminism*. Edited by S. Harding. Milton Keynes: Open University.

——. 1987a. Introduction: Is There a Feminist Method? In *Feminism and Methodology: Social Science Issues*. Edited by S. Harding. Milton Keynes: Open University.

——. 1987b. Conclusion: Epistemological Questions. In *Feminism and Methodology: Social Science Issues*. Edited by S. Harding. Milton Keynes: Open University.

Harris, John R. and Todaro, Michael P. 1970. Migration, Unemployment and Development: A Two-Sector Analysis. *American Economic Review* 60, vol. 1: 126-142.

Harris, Nigel. 1999. Should Europe End Immigration Controls? Paris: 9th General Conference on "Europe and the South in the 21st Century: Challenges for Renewed Co-operation": 22-25 Sept.

Hatam, Nahid, Askarian, Mehrdad, Moravveji, Alireza, and Assadian, Ojan. 2008. Economic burden of inappropriate antibiotic use for prophylactic purpose in Shiraz, Iran . Paper presented in the 7th European Conference on Health Economics. July 23-26. Rome, Italy.

Heidary, Aligholi. 2003. Country Paper: Islamic Republic Of Iran. Paper presented in Seminar on Rural Life Improvement for Community Development, held by Asian Productivity Organization in Japan, 22-26 April 2002. Report of the APO Seminar was edited by Dr. D.A. Cruz. Tokyo: Asian Productivity Organization, 2003: 176-182.

Hein, Catherine. 1986. The Feminization of Industrial Employment in Mauritius. In *Sex Inequalities in Urban Unemployment in the Third World*. Edited by R. Anker and C. Hein. London: Macmillan.

Hemmasi, Mohammad. 1974. *Migration in Iran: A Quantitative Approach on the Occasion of the World Population Year*. Shiraz: Pahlavi University.

——. 1976. Migration and Problems of Development: The Case of Iran. In *The Social Sciences and Problems of Development*. Edited by K. Farmanfarmaian. New Jersey: Princeton.

Higgins, Patricia J. and Shoar-Ghaffari, Pirouz. 1994. Women's Education in the Islamic Republic of Iran. In *In the Eye of the Storm: Women in Post-revolutionary Iran*. Edited by M. Afkhami and E. Friedl. London and New York: I.B. Tauris.

Hirschman, Albert O. 1981. *Essays in Trespassing: Economics to Politics and Beyond*. Cambridge: Cambridge University Press.

Hoodfar, Homa. 1993. The Veil in Their Minds and on Our Heads: The Persistence of Colonial Images of Muslim Women. *Resources for Feminist Research: Colonialism, Imperialism and Gender* 22, vol. 3/4: 5-18.

——.1996. Bargaining with Fundamentalism: Women and the Politics of Population Control in Iran. *Reproductive Health Markets* 8, vol. 4: 30-40.

——. 1997. *Between Marriage and the Market: Intimate Politics and Survival in*

Cairo. Comparative Studies on Muslim Societies, 24. Berkeley, Los Angeles, and London: University of California.

Hossein Zadeh-e Dalir, Karim. 1361/1982. *Tarheh e-Tahqiqi e-Hashieh Neshinan-e-Tabriz* (The Research Project of the Slum Dwellers of Tabriz). 2nd ed. Tabriz: Tabriz University Press.

Hunt, D. 1989. *Economic Theories of Development: An Analysis of Competing Paradigms*. Hemel, Hempstead, Hertfordshire: Harvester Wheatsheaf.

International Labor Organization (ILO). Economic and Social Development: Gender and Development.
http://www.ilo.org/global/Themes/Ecosocdev/Genderanddevelopment/lang--en/index.htm.

International Organization for Migration (IOM). Reports on Labor Migration. http://www.iom.or.id/reports.jsp?lang=eng.

Iranian Civil Law. 1370/1991. *Dar Hogug va Takalif-e Zojain Nesbat be Yek-di-har* (Right and Duties of Couples Towards Each Other). *Book 8*. Tehran: Amirkabir.

Jahad-e Sazandegi Report. 1995. *Zanna-e Ghlibaf dar Karghahhaye Amouzeshi-e Jahad-e Sazandeghi-e Ostan-e Kermanshah* (Female Carpet Weavers in Training Centres of *Jahad-e Sazandegi* in Kemanshah Province. *Zan-e Rouz*.

Jamali Zanjeerabad, Firooz. 1985. Inter-Provincial Migration in Iran with Specific Reference to East-Azarbaijan Province. Unpublished Ph.D. Thesis, University of Durham.

Jayaratne, Toby Epstein and Stewart, Abigail J. 1991. Quantitative and Qualitative Methods in the Social Sciences: Current Feminist Issues and Practical Strategies. In *Beyond Methodology: Feminist Scholarship as Lived Research*. Edited by M. M. Fonow and J. A. Cook. USA: Indiana University.

Jeffery, Patricia and Jeffery, Roger. 1996. *Don't Marry Me to a Plowman! Women's Everyday Lives in Rural North India*. Boulder: Westview.

Kabeer, Naila. 1994. Women's Labor in the Bangladesh Garment Industry: Choice and Constraints. In *Muslim Women's Choices: Religious Belief and Social Reality*. Edited by C. Fawzi El-Solh and J. Mabro. Oxford: Berg.

Kandiyoti, Deniz. 1988. Bargaining with Patriarchy. *Gender and Society* 2 (Sept.): 274-290.

Kar, Mehrangiz. 1379/2000. *Pasuoheshi dar Bareye Khoshounat Alayhe Zanan dar Iran* (A Study on Violence Against Women in Iran). Tehran: Roshangaran and Women's Studies Publishing.

——. 2001. Women's Strategies in Iran from the 1979 Revolution to 1999. In *Globalization, Gender, and Religion: The Politics of Women's Rights in Catholic and Muslim Contexts*. Edited by Jane. H. Bayes and Nayereh Tohidi. New York: Palgrave.

——. 1384/2005. *Zanan dar Bazar-e Car-e Iran, be Enzemam-e Theorihaye Nabarabari Jensi* (Women in the Iranian Labor Market, Including Theories of Gender Inequalities). Translated by Parvin Raiesi Fard. 3rd ed. Iran: Roshangaran and Women's Studies Publishing.

Karbalai Saleh, Mariam. 1375/1996. *Taavon, Zan va Eshteqhal* (Cooperation, Women and Employment). In *Taavon, Zan, Eshteqal: Majmouaye Maqalat ve Amalkardha* (Cooperation, Women, and Employment: Collection of Papers and Approaches). Tehran: *Vezarat-e Taavon* (The Ministry of Cooperation).

Katouzian, Homa, M. A. 1981. *The Political Economy of Modern Iran: Despotism and Pseudo-Modernism, 1926-1979*. London: Macmillan.

Keddie, Nikki R. 1972. Stratification, Social Control, and Capitalism in Iranian Villages: Before and After Land Reform. In *Rural Policies and Social Change in the Middle East*. Edited by R. Antoun and I. Harik. Bloomington and London: Indiana University.

——. 1981. *Roots of Revolution: An Interpretive History of Modern Iran*. New Heaven and London: Yale University Press.

——. 1995. Postscript: Revolt, Resistance, and Gender in the Muslim World. In *Iran and the Muslim World: Resistance and Revolution*. Edited by N. R. Keddie.

——. 2006. *Modern Iran: Roots and Results of Revolution*. New Haven and London: Yale University Press.

Kelly, L. 1988. *Surviving Sexual Violence*. Cambridge: Polity Press.

Kelly, Lis, Burton, Sheila and Regan, Linda. 1994. Researching Women's Lives or Studying Women's Oppression: Reflections on What Constitutes Feminist Research. In *Researching Women's Lives from a Feminist Perspective*. Edited by M. Maynard and J. Purvis. London: Taylor and Francis.

Lambton, A. K. S. 1953. *Landlord and Peasant in Persia: A Study of Land Tenure and Land Revenue Administration*. London, New York.: Oxford University Press.

Lee, Everett S. 1966. A Theory of Migration. *Demography* 3, vol. 1: 47-57. And in *Theories of Migration: The International Library of Studies on Migration*. Edited by R. Cohen. Cheltenham: Edward Elgar, 1996: 14-24.

Lee, Wendy. 1991. Prostitution and Tourism in South-East Asia. In *Working Women: International Perspectives on Labor and Gender Ideology*. Edited by N. Redclift and M. T. Sinclair. London and New York: Routledge.

Leeds, A. and Leeds, E. 1976. Accounting for Behavioral Differences: Three Political Systems and the Responses of Squatters in Brazil, Peru and Chile. In *The City in Comparative Perspective*. Edited by J. Walton and L. Magotti. London and New York: John Wiley.

Leiva, F. I., Petras, J. and Veltmeyer, H. 1994. *Democracy and Poverty in Chile: The Limits to Electoral Politics*. Boulder: Westview.

Lessinger, Johanna. 1990. Work and Modesty: The Dilemma of Women Market Traders in Madras. In *Structures and Strategies: Women, Work and Family*. Edited by L. Dube and R. Palriwala. New Delhi and London: Sage.

Lewis, W. A. 1954. Economic Development with Unlimited Supplies of Labor. *The Manchester School of Economic and Social Studies* 22, vol. 2: 139-191.

Lloyd, Rodwin. 1979. *Planning Urban Growth and Regional Development: The Experience of the Guyana Program of Venezuela*. Cambridge, Mass.

Mabogunje, Akin L. 1970. Systems Approach to a Theory of Rural-Urban Migration. *Geographical Analysis*, vol. 2: 1-18. And in *Theories of Migration: The International Library of Studies on Migration*. Edited by R. Cohen. Cheltenham: Edward Elgar, 1996: 43-61.

MacEwen, Scott. 1994. *Divisions and Solidarities: Gender, Class and Employment in Latin America*. London and New York: Routledge.

Mackintosh, Maureen. 1984. Gender and Economies: The Sexual Division of Labor and the Subordination of Women. In *Of Marriage and the Market: Women's Subordination Internationally and its Lessons*. Edited by K. Yong, C. Wolkowitz and R. McCullagh. 2nd. London & Boston: Routledge and Kegan Paul.

Makower, H., Marschak, J. and Robinson, H. W. 1938. Studies in Mobility of Labor: A Tentative Statistical Measure. *Oxford Economic Papers* 1 (Oct.): 83-123.

——. 1939. Studies in Mobility of Labor: Analysis for Great Britain, Part I. *Oxford*

Economic Papers 2 (May): 70-97.
——. 1940. Studies in Mobility of Labor: Analysis for Great Britain, Part II. *Oxford Economic Papers* 4 (Sep): 39-62.
Maynard, Mary. 1994. Methods, Practice and Epistemology: The Debate about Feminism and Research. In *Researching Women's Lives from a Feminist Perspective*. Edited by M. Maynard and J. Purvis. London: Taylor and Francis.
Meier, Gerald M. 1995. What is Economic Development? Note and Lewis's Dual-Sector Model-Note. In *Leading Issues in Economic Development*. Edited by G. M. Meier. 6th ed. New York and Oxford: Oxford University.
Memon, Rashid. 2005. Pakistan: Internal Migration and Poverty Reduction, in *Migration, Development and Poverty reduction in Asia*. Regional Conference on Migration and Development in Asia, Lanzhou, China, sponsored by the UK Department for International Development, IOM, Geneva.
Mehran, Golnar. 1991. The Creation of a New Muslim Woman: Female Education in the Islamic Republic of Iran. *Convergence* 24: 42-52.
——. 1992. Cultural Revolution and Educational Transformation in the Islamic Republic of Iran. *WENR – World Education News and Reviews*.
——. 2003. Gender and Education in Iran. Commissioned for the *Education for All Global Monitoring Report 2003/4, Gender and Education for All: The Leap to Equality*. UNESCO.
Menashri, David. 1992. *Education and the Making of Modern Iran*. Ithaca and London: Cornell University Press.
Mernissi, Fatima. 1984. *Doing Daily Battle: Interview with Moroccan Women*. London: The Women's Press.
——. 1985. *Beyond the Veil: Male-female Dynamics in Modern Muslim Society*. London: Al Szaqi.
Mies, Maria. 1982. *The Lace Makers of Narsapur: Indian Housewives Produce for the World Market*. London: Zed.
Millman, Marcia and Kanter, Rosabeth Moss. 1987. Introduction to Another Voice: Feminist Perspectives on Social Life and Social Science. In *Feminism and Methodology: Social Science Issues*. Edited by S. Harding. Milton Keynes: Open University.
Mirani, Kaveh. 1983. Social and Economic Change in the Role of Women, 1956-1978. In *Women and Revolution in Iran*. Edited by G. Nashat. Boulder: Westview.
Mir-Hosseini, Ziba. 1993. Legal Anatomy of Divorce: The Iranian Case. In *Marriage on Trail: The Study of Islamic Family Law: Iran and Morocco Compared*. Edited by Z. Mir-Hosseini. 2nd ed. London, New York: I.B. Tauris.
——. 1994. Strategies of Selection: Different Notions of Marriage in Iran and Morocco. In *Muslim Women's Choices: Religious Belief and Social Reality*. Edited by C. Fawzi El-Solh and J. Mabro. Oxford: Berg.
——. 1995. Stretching the Limits: A Feminist Reading of the *Shari'a* in Iran Today. In *Feminism and Islam*. Edited by M. Yamani. London: Ithaca.
——. 1996. Women and Politics in Post-Khomeini Iran: Divorce, Ceiling and Emerging Feminist Voices. In *Women and Politics in the Third World*. Edited by H. Afshar. London and New York: Routledge.
Moghadam, Valentine M. 1993. *Modernizing Women: Gender and Social Change in the Middle East*. Boulder and London: Lynne Rienner.
——. 1995. Women's Employment Issues in Contemporary Iran: Problems and Prospects in the 1990s. *Iranian Studies* 28, vol. 3/4 (Summer–Autumn): 175-202.

——. 1998. *Women, Work, and Economic Reform in the Middle East and North Africa.* Boulder and London: Lynne Rienner.

——. 2009. Where Are Iran's Working Women? In *Viewpoints Special Edition: The Iranian Revolution at 30.* Washington DC: The Middle East Institute: 52-54. Also available on: www.mideasti.org.

Moghissi, Haideh. 1993. Women in the Resistance Movement in Iran. In *Women in the Middle East.* Edited by H. Afshar. London: Macmillan.

——. 1994. Women and Fundamentalism in Iran. In *Gender and Catastrophe.* Edited by R. Lentin. London and New York: Zed.

——. 1996. *Populism and Feminism in Iran.* 2nd ed. London: Macmillan.

Mohtadi, Hamid. 1986. Rural Stratification, Rural to Urban Migration and Urban Inequality: Case of Iran. *World Development* 14: 713-725.

——. 1987. Industrialization and Urban Inequality in LDCs: A Theoretical Analysis with Evidence from Pre-Revolutionary Iran. *Journal of Developing Areas* (Oct.): 41-58.

——. 1990. Rural Inequality as Determinant of Push vs. Pull Migration in Iran: 1956-1976. *World Development,* 18: 837-44.

Moosavi Ghahderijani, Seyed Mohammad. 2003. Country Paper: Islamic Republic Of Iran (1). Presented in Seminar on Rural Life Improvement for Community Development, held by Asian Productivity Organization in Japan, 22-26 April 2002. Report of the APO Seminar was edited by Dr. D.A. Cruz. Tokyo: Asian Productivity Organization, 2003: 99-102.

Nafisi, Rasool. 1992. Education and the Culture of Politics in the Islamic Republic of Iran. In *Iran: Political Culture in the Islamic Republic.* Edited by S. K. Farsoun and M. Mashayekhi. London and New York: Routledge.

Nahi, Tytti. 2002. Unemployment in Iran: An Emerging Social Crisis? *IranMania-Business and Economy.* July 2002. Available on
http://www.iranmania.com/news/economy/features/unemployment/default.asp.

Najmabadi, Afsaneh. 1991. Hazards of Modernity and Morality: Women, State and Ideology in Contemporary Iran. In *Women, Islam and the State.* Edited by D. Kandiyoti. London: Macmillan.

——. 1998. Crafting and Educated Housewife in Iran. In *Remaking Women: Feminism and Modernity in the Middle East.* Edited by L. Abu-Lughod. Princeton and New Jersey: Princeton University.

Nakanishi, Hisae. 1998. Power, Ideology, and Women's Consciousness in Post-Revolutionary Iran. In *Women in Muslim Societies: Diversity within Unity.* Edited by L. Bodman and N. Tohidi. London: Lynne Rienner Publishers.

Nashat, Guity. 1983. Women in Pre-revolutionary Iran: A Historical Overview. In *Women and Revolution in Iran.* Edited by G. Nashat. Boulder: Westview.

Oakley, Ann. 1974. *The Sociology of Housework.* London: Robertson.

——. 1981. Interviewing Women: A Contradiction in Terms. In *Doing Feminist Research.* Edited by H. Roberts. London, Boston and Henley: Routledge and Kegan Paul.

Oishi, Nana (2002) *Gender and Migration: An Integrative Approach.* Working Paper, The Center for Comparative Immigration Studies, University of San Diego, California, USA.

Olson, Roger T. 1981. Persian Gulf Trade and the Agricultural Economy of Southern Iran in the Nineteenth Century. In *Modern Iran: The Dialectics of Continuity and Change.* Edited by M. Bonine and N. R. Keddie. New York: State University of

New York Press: 173-189.

Omid, Homa. 1994. *Islam and the Post-Revolutionary State in Iran*. London: Macmillan.

Pahl, J. 1980. Patterns of Money Management in Marriage. *Journal of Social Policy* 9, vol. 3: 313-35.

Paidar, Parvin. 1996. Feminism and Islam in Iran. In *Gendering the Middle East: Emerging Perspectives*. Edited by D. Kandiyoti. London and New York: I. B. Tauris.

——. 1997. *Women and Political Process in Twentieth-century Iran*. Cambridge: Cambridge Middle East Library.

Papps, Ivy. 1993. Attitudes to Female Employment in Four Middle Eastern Countries. In *Women in the Middle East: Perceptions, Realities and Struggles for Liberation*. Edited by H. Afshar. London: Macmillan.

Pesaran, M. H. 1985. Economic Development and Revolutionary Upheavals in Iran. In *Iran: Revolution in Turmoil*. Edited by H. Afshar. London: Macmillan.

Pearson, Ruth. 1998. Nimble Finger's Revisited: Reflections on Women and Third World Industrialization in the Late Twentieth Century. In *Feminist Vision of Development: Gender Analysis and Policy*. Edited by C. Jackson and R. Pearson. London and New York: Routledge.

Pelto, P. and Pelto, G. 1973. Ethnography: The Fieldwork Enterprise. In *Handbook of Social and Cultural Anthropology*. Edited by J. L. Honigmann. Chicago: Rand McNally.

Planning and Budget Organization of East Azarbaijan. 1986. Quantitative Comparisons of 1976 and 1986 censes. Tehran: PBO.

Planning and Budget Organization. Islamic Republic of Iran and the United Nations. 1999. *Human Development Report of the Islamic Republic of Iran, 1999*. Tehran: PBO and UN.

Poya, Maryam. 1999. *Women, Work and Islamism: Ideology and Resistance in Iran*. London and New York: Zed.

Ram, Kalpana. 1989. The Ideology of Femininity and Women's Work in a Fishing Community of South India. In *Women, Poverty and Ideology in Asia*. Edited by H. Afshar and B. Agarwal. London: Macmillan.

Ramazanoglu, Caroline and Holland, Janet. 2002. Can Feminists Tell the Truth? In *Feminist Methodology: Challenges and Choices*. Edited by C. Ramazanoglu and J. Holland. London, Thousand Oaks and New Delhi: Sage.

Ramin, Taghi. 1988. A Regression Analysis of Migration to Urban Areas of a Less-Developed Country: The Case of Iran. *American Economist* 32, vol. 2 (Fall): 26-34.

Ranis, G. and Fei, John. 1961. A Theory of Economic Development. *American Economic Review* 4, vol. 4: 533-565.

Ravenstein, E. G. 1885. The Laws of Migration. *Journal of Royal Statistical Society* XLVIII.

Ravenstein, E. G. 1885. The Laws of Migration. *Journal of Royal Statistical Society* LII.

Razavi, Shahrashoub. 1992. Agrarian Change and Gender Power: A Comparative Study in Southeastern Iran. Unpublished Ph.D. Thesis, Oxford University.

——. 1993. Women, Work and Power in the Rafsanjan Basin of Iran. In *Women in the Middle East: Perceptions, Realities and Struggles for Liberation*. Edited by H. Afshar. London: Macmillan.

Redford, Arthur. 1964. *Labor Migration in England 1800-1850*. 2nd ed. Manchester:

Manchester University.
Rostow, W.W. 1960. *The Stages of Economic Growth*. Cambridge: Cambridge University.
Rothenberg, Jerome. 1977. On the Microeconomics of Internal Migration. In *International Migration: A Comparison Perspective*. Edited by A. A. Brown and E. Neuberger. New York: Academic Press.
Rowbotham, Sheila. 1973. *Hidden from History: 300 Years of Women's Oppression and the Fight against It*. London: Pluto.
Rudnick, Anja. 2000. Bengali Migrant Women in Malaysian Industry: The Impact of a Contemporary Adventure on Women's Lives. University of York: Women and Development Study Group's Seminar: 27 May.
Safa, Helen I. 1986. Runaway Shops and Female Employment, the Search for Cheap Labor. In *Women's Work*. Edited by E. Leacock *et al.* Massachusetts: Bergin and Garvey.
——. 1995. The Dominican Republic: Export Manufacturing and the Economic Crisis. In *The Myth of the Male Breadwinner: Women and Industrialization in the Caribbean*. Edited by H. I. Safa. Oxford: Westview.
Salehi-Isfahani, Djavad. 2001. Fertility, Education, and Household Resources in Iran, 1987– 1992. In *The Economics of Women and Work in the Middle East and North Africa: Research in Middle East Economics*. Edited by M. E. Cinar. Vol. 4. Amsterdam, London and New York: JAI.
Sanasarian, Eliz. 1982. *The Women's Rights Movement in Iran: Mutiny, Appeasement and Repression from 1900 to Khomeini*. New York: Praeger.
Schirazi, Asghar. 1993. *Islamic Development Policy: The Agrarian Question in Iran*. Translated by P. J. Ziess-Lawrence. Boulder & London: Lynne Reinner Publishers.
Schuetz, A. 1944. The Stranger: An Essay in Social Psychology. *American Journal of Sociology* 49: 499-507.
Schwartz, M. and Schwartz, C. 1955. Problems in Participant Observation. *American Journal of Sociology* 60: 343-53.
Shaaban, Bouthaina. 1988. *Both Right and Left Handed: Arab Women Talk About Their Lives*. London: The Women's Press.
ShadiTalab, Jaleh. 1375/1996. *Eshteqal-e-Zanan dar Farayand-e-Toseah* (Women's Employment in the Process of Development). In *Taavon, Zan, Eshte-qal: Majmouaye Maqalat ve Amal-kardha* (Cooperation, Women and Employment: Collection of Papers and Approaches). Tehran: *Vezarat-e- Taavon* (The Ministry of Cooperation).
Shaheed, Farida. 1989. *Purdah* and Poverty in Pakistan. In *Women, Poverty and Ideology in Asia*. Edited by H. Afshar and B. Agarwal. London: Macmillan.
Shahshahani, Soheila. 1368/1987. *Chahr Fasl-e Aftab: Zendegi-e Ruzmarreh-e Zanan-e Escan Yafteh Ashayer Mamasani* (Four Seasons of Sun: Daily Lives of Women among Settled Nomads of Mamasani). Tehran: Tous Publishers.
Shakori, Ali. 1998. Rural Reform Policy in the Post-Revolutionary Iran. Unpublished Ph.D. Thesis, University of York.
Shojaie, Zahra. 1380/2001. *Dokhtaran-e Rousti-e Ezdevaj Nakardeh Ham Ziyad Shode-and!* (The Number of Unmarried Rural Women has also Increased!). *Ettela'at International*, 20 September (*29 Shahrivar*), p. 4.
Skeldon, Ronald. 1997. *Migration and Development: A Global Perspective*. Essex: Longman.
Smith, Dorothy. 1979. A Sociology for Women. In *The Prism of Sex: Essays in the*

Sociology of Knowledge. Edited by J. A. Sherman and E. T. Beck. Madison: University of Wisconsin.

——. 1987. Women's Perspective as a Radical Critique of Sociology. In *Feminism and Methodology: Social Science Issues*. Edited by S. Harding. Milton Keynes: Open University. And *Sociological Inquiry* 44, vol. 1 (1974): 7-13.

Smith, Peter C., Khoo, Siew-Ean and Go, Stella P. 1984. The Migration of Women to Cities: A Comparative Perspective. In *Women in the Cities of Asia: Migration and Urban Adaptation*. Edited by J. T. Fawcett, S. E. Khoo and P. C. Smith. Boulder and Colorado: Westview.

Soto, Hernando de. 1989. *The Other Path: The Invisible Revolution in the Third World*. London: I. B. Tauris.

Sour-Esraphil, Shirin. 1993. Female Carpet Weaver: The Symbol of Effort. *Zan-e Rouz*.

Stanley, Liz., and Wise, Sue. 1990. Method, Methodology and Epistemology in Feminist Research Processes. In *Feminist Praxis: Research, Theory and Epistemology in Feminist Sociology*. Edited by L. Stanley. London and New York: Routledge.

——, and Wise, S. 1993. *Breaking Out Again: Feminist Ontology and Epistemology*. London and New York: Routledge.

Statistical Centre of Iran (*Markaz-e Amar-e Iran*). 1345/1966. *Sarshomari-e Omumi-e Nofus va Maskan, 1345: Natayej-e Tafzhili-e Koll-e Keshvar* (National Census of Population and Housing 1966: Comprehensive Findings of the Whole Country). Tehran: Planning and Budget Organization.

——. 1355/1976. *Sarshomari-e Omumi-e Nofus va Maskan, 1355: Natayej-e Tafzhili-e Koll-e Keshvar* (National Census of Population and Housing 1976: Comprehensive Findings of the Whole Country). Tehran: Planning and Budget Organization.

——. 1375/1996. *Sarshomari-e Omumi-e Nofus va Maskan, 1375: Natayej-e Tafzhili-e Ostan Azarbijan Sharghi, Shahrestan-e Tabriz, 3-4* (National Census of Population and Housing 1996: Comprehensive Findings of East Azarbaijan Province, Tabriz District, 3-4). Tehran: Planning and Budget Organization.

——. 1375/1996. *Sarshomari-e Omumi-e Nofus va Maskan, 1375: Natayej-e Tafzhili-e Koll-e Keshvar* (National Census of Population and Housing 1996: Comprehensive Findings of the Whole Country). Tehran: Planning and Budget Organization.

——. 1362/1983. *Salnameh-e Amari-e Keshwar, 1362* (Country's Statistical Yearbook of 1983). Tehran: Planning and Budget Organization.

——. 1374/1995. *Salnameh-e Amari-e Keshwar, 1374* (Country's Statistical Yearbook of 1995). Tehran: Planning and Budget Organization.

Stiefel, Matthias and Wolfe, Marshall. 1994. *A Voice for the Excluded: Popular Participation in Development: Utopia or Necessity?* London: Zed.

Stouffer, Samuel A. 1940. Intervening Opportunities: A Theory Relating Mobility and Distance. *American Sociological Review* 5, vol. 6: 845-867.

Strauch, Judith. 1984. Women in Rural-Urban Circulation Networks: Implications for Social Structural Change. In *Women in the Cities of Asia: Migration and Urban Adaptation*. Edited by J. T. Fawcett, S. E. Khoo and P. C. Smith. Boulder and Colorado: Westview.

Sullivan, Zohreh T. 1998. Eluding the Feminist, Overthrowing the Modern? Transformation in Twentieth-Century Iran. In *Remaking Women: Feminism and Moder-*

nity in the Middle East. Edited by L. Abu-Lughod. Princeton, New Jersey: Princeton University.

Swaisland, Cecillie. 1993. Female Migration and Social Mobility: British Female Domestic Servants to South Africa, 1860-1914. In *Migrant Women: Crossing Boundaries and Changing Identities*. Edited by G. Buijs. Oxford: Berg.

Tabari, Azar. 1980. The Enigma of Veiled Iranian Women. *Feminist Review* 5: 19-31.

——. 1982. Islam and Struggle for Emancipation of Iranian Women. In *In the Shadow of Islam: The Women's Movement in Iran*. Edited by A. Tabari and N. Yeganeh. London: Zed.

——., and Yeganeh, Nahid. 1982. *In the Shadow of Islam: The Women's Movement in Iran*. London: Zed.

Tabriz University Report. 1995. *Report on Migration to Tabriz: Findings from the Slum Areas*. Tabriz: Tabriz University Press.

Thadani, Veena N. and Todaro, Michael P. 1984. Female Migration: A Conceptual Framework. In *Women in the Cities of Asia: Migration and Urban Adaptation*. Edited by J. T. Fawcett, S. E. Khoo and P. C. Smith. Boulder and Colorado: Westview.

The Hutchinson Softback Encyclopeadia. 1996. The Softback Preview, 3rd ed. Middlesex: Helicon.

Todaro, Michael P. 1969. A Model of Labor Migration and Urban Unemployment in Less Developed Countries. *American Economic Review* 59, vol. 1: 138-148.

——. 1976. *Internal Migration in Developing Countries: A Review of Theory, Evidence, Methodology and Research Priorities*. Geneva: International Labor Office.

——. 1994a. Urbanization and Rural-Urban Migration: Theory and Policy. In *Economic Development*. 5th ed. Edited by M. P. Todaro. New York and London: Longman.

——. 1994b. Education and Economic Development. In *Economic Development*. 5th ed. Edited by M. P. Todaro. New York and London: Longman.

Tohidi, Nayereh. 1991. Gender and Islamic Fundamentalism: Feminist Politics. In *Third World Women and the Politics of Feminism*. Edited by Chandra Talpade Mohanty, Ann Russo, and Lourdes Torres. Bloomington: Indiana University Press.

——. 1994. Modernity, Islamization and Women in Iran. In *Gender and National Identity: Women and Politics in Muslim Societies*. Edited by V. M. Moghadam. London: Zed.

——., and Bayes, Jane H. 2001. Women Redefining Modernity and Religion in the Globalised Context. In *Globalization, Gender, and Religion: The Politics of Women's Rights in Catholic and Muslim Contexts*. Edited by J. H. Bayes and N. Tohidi. New York: Palgrave.

Touba, Jacquiline Rudolph. 1980. Sex Segregation and Women's Roles in the Economic System: The Case of Iran. In *Research in the Interweave of Social Roles: Women and Men*. Edited by H. Z. Lopata. Vol. 1. Greenwich: JAI.

United Nations. 1970. *Methods of Measuring Internal Migration: Manuals on Methods of Estimating Population*. Department of Economic and Social Affairs, Population Studies. New York: United Nations.

UNESCO. 2002. *Education for All: Is the World on Track?* Paris: UNESCO.

UN-HABITAT. 2007. *Twenty First Session of the Governing Council*, 16-20 April. Nairobi, Kenya.

UN World Survey. 1999. 1999 World Survey on the Role of Women in Develop-

ment: Globalization, Gender and Work. Avaiable online:
http://www.ucl.ac.uk/dpuprojects/drivers_urb_change/urb_society/pdf_gender/UN_1999_World_Survey_Women_in_Development.pdf.

Velayati, Masoumeh. 1998. *Does Hejab Serve Iranian Women's Interests?* Unpublished MA Thesis, University of Warwick.

Whitehead, Ann. 1984. I'm Hungry, Mum: The Politics of Domestic Budgeting. In *Of Marriage and the Market: Women's Subordination Internationally and its Lessons*. Edited by K. Yong, C. Wolkowitz and R. McCullagh. 2nd ed. London and Boston: Routledge & Kegan Paul.

World Development Report. 1990. Box 5.2: Education and Economic Growth. In *World Development Report (1990): Poverty*. Oxford: Oxford University.

——. 1991. Figure 2.5: Female Educational Attainment and Decline in Infant Mortality in Selected Economies, 1960-87. In *World Development Report (1991): The Challenge of Development*. Oxford: Oxford University.

Wright, Caroline. 1995. Gender Awareness in Migration Theory: Synthesizing Actor and Structure in Southern Africa. *Development and Change* 26, vol. 4: 771-791.

Yavari, Hossein. 1996. *Bist Sal Talash: Shahkarhaye Farsh Irani* (Twenty Years of Effort: Masterpieces of Iranian Carpets). *Ettelaat-e Syassi-Iqtisadi* 9-10.

Yap, Lorene Y.L. 1975. *Internal Migration in Less Developed Countries: A Survey of the Literature*. World Bank Staff Working Papers, no. 215.

Yeganeh, Nahid. 1993. Women, Nationalism and Islam in Contemporary Political Discourse in Iran. *Feminist Review* 44, vol. 2: 3-19.

Yu, Xion and Lincoln H. Day. 1994. Demographic Characteristics of the Migrants. In *Migration and Urbanization in China: Studies in Chinese Environment and Development*. Edited by L. H. Day and M. Xia. New York: An East Gate Book.

Zahedi, M.J. and Kazeroni, M.R. and Darvishi, K. 1367/1988. *Mohajerat Rustaie va Ravan-e Yek Sad Saleh-ye Akhir on dar Iran* (Rural Migration and its a Century Process in Iran). *Ettelaat-e Syassi-Iqtisadi* 11: 31-43.

Zargarzadeh, Amir H., Minaeiyan, Mohsen., Torabi, Amir. 2008. Prescription and Non-prescription Drug Use in Isfahan, Iran: An Observational, Cross-Sectional Study. *Current therapeutic research* 69, vol. 1: 76-87.

Zhang, Heather Xiaoquan. 1999. Female Migration and Urban Labor Markets in Tianjin. *Development and Change* 30, vol. 1: 21-41.

Index

Notes are indexed as 123n4, ie. note 4 on page 123

About the Author

Masoumeh Velayati has obtained a multi-disciplinary educational background and knowledge in the fields of International Development through her MA and PhD courses at Warwick and York universities. Her PhD in politics explored the relationship between development, migration, and gender in Iran. She mainly concentrated on migrants' involvements in incomegenerating activities in the formal and informal sectors of the economy; their survival strategies; their spatial movement; the socio-economic liberation of some peasants and degrees of deprivation among others; and the international political economy that immensely affected the process of internal migration in Iran. She paid particular attention to the feminization of labor market and feminist debates on the role of state gender policies and their impact on social changes in terms of women's access to socio-economic and political resources. This book is the final result of the research.

Masoumeh is currently working as funding development co-ordinator, for International Service—an International Development organization based in York, UK.

www.ingramcontent.com/pod-product-compliance
Ingram Content Group UK Ltd.
Pitfield, Milton Keynes, MK11 3LW, UK
UKHW012035150926
475560UK00001B/20

9 780739 114520